MY LIFE WITH THE TALIBAN

ABDUL SALAM ZAEEF

My Life with the Taliban

Edited by

Alex Strick van Linschoten and Felix Kuehn

Columbia University Press
New York

Columbia University Press
Publishers Since 1893
New York   Chichester, West Sussex
Copyright © Abdul Salam Zaeef 2010
Editors' introduction and translation Copyright
© Alex Strick van Linschoten and Felix Kuehn, 2010
Foreword Copyright © Barnett R. Rubin, 2010
All rights reserved

Library of Congress Cataloging-in-Publication Data

Za'if, 'Abd al-Salam, 1967 or 8–
  My life with the Taliban / Abdul Salam Zaeef.
    p. cm.
  Includes bibliographical references and index.
  ISBN 978-0-231-70148-8 (alk. paper)
  1. Za'if, 'Abd al-Salam, 1967 or 8– 2. Taliban—Biography. 3. Afghan War,
2001—Biography. 4. Prisoners of war—Afghanistan—Biography.
5. Prisoners of war—United States—Biography. 6. Guantánamo Bay
Detention Camp—Biography. I. Title.

  DS371.33.Z34A3 2010
  958.104'7—dc22
  [B]

                                2009040865

∞

Columbia University Press books are printed on permanent and durable
acid-free paper. This book is printed on paper with recycled content.
Printed in USA

c 10 9 8 7 6 5 4 3 2 1

References to Internet Web sites (URLs) were accurate at the time of writing.
Neither the author nor Columbia University Press is responsible for URLs
that may have expired or changed since the manuscript was prepared.

CONTENTS

CONTENTS

This "freedom" put a proud people in chains
And turned free men into slaves
"Independence" made us weak
And slaughtered us
In the name of kindness
This is democracy by the whip
And the fear of chains
With a whirlwind at its core

Mullah Abdul Salam Zaeef
(written in Guantánamo*)

* Special thanks and credit to Jean MacKenzie and Abaceen Nasimi for working on this poem.

KANDAHAR

PORTRAIT OF A CITY

Alex Strick van Linschoten and Felix Kuehn

You could tell it was a big bomb from the numbers of corpse-laden pickup trucks that passed us on our way to the river. There were so many bodies that in death they were shown disrespect, tossed into the back of cars and trucks for the journey back to town.

As we approached the scene we could see a gathering crowd of police cars and onlookers. Policemen and local villagers stood among what remained: overturned thermos flasks of green tea; vendors' plastic baskets with nuts, biscuits and matches; a bright green, red and orange woven mat—all stained with bright red blood.

Young police officers mill around, manifesting a faint attempt at standing guard, as if they could somehow bring him back; three 4 × 4 cars, the fronts gnarled as if chewed by some subterranean monster; and everywhere the shoes that people had taken off before stepping onto the mats.

In front of the cars, the mat is ripped and mixed with a twisted mess of skull-caps, woollen blankets, shreds of clothes, half of someone's brain, a trail of intestines. In the midst of all this lay a pair of primitive, rusted metal crutches. Trampled oranges, mixed with splatters of blood—now starting to darken as they soaked into the ground.

These were the meagre traces of the people who stood here before the explosion, watching, laughing, talking. Witnesses at the hospital told of scores of severed feet being collected together, all detached from their bodies and a surprisingly common injury on that day.

It was 17 February 2008 in Kandahar, a clear-blue day with thin wisps of clouds in the sky. Abdul Hakim Jan, a well-known local military commander and tribal strongman, was dead. The suicide-bomber also took the lives of at least a hundred[1] others with him in Afghanistan's deadliest attack ever. Abdul Hakim Jan had driven to the banks of the almost-dry river to watch a dog fight. The commander was well-known for his unique style and appearance: he only ever wore blue, and used to wear three pairs of the Afghan traditional clothes, one on top of the other. His death was traumatic for his Alikozai tribe—already decapitated by the loss of Kandahar's pre-eminent *mujahedeen* commander, *Mullah* Naqib—and an irreversible loss for the city.

As milestones go, this was an important one. Abdul Hakim Jan was one of the last of his generation of *mujahedeen* commanders still alive, and the only remaining guarantor of security in his native Arghandab district. It showed just how bad things had become in the south.

* * *

Two years later, Kandahar is even more dangerous. The average Kandahari faces daily NATO bombings throughout the region, occasional suicide attacks within the city, pervasive and unabashed corruption, rising food and fuel prices, and an increasingly brutal campaign of assassinations.

Kandahar never had what could be described as a bustling night-life, but now the streets are deserted after dark. Even eighteen months ago there were many more people out and about in the evenings. Almost every week residents in the centre of the town are woken in the middle of the night by the crackle of a heavy machine gun or the boom of a rocket detonating, a sign that government installations are under attack.

Corruption is the norm in the Afghan government, and accompanies the majority of interactions between Kandaharis and officials at all levels. Bribes are needed for even the simplest operations, such as paying bills. Contractors frequently wage wars over foreign donor money, while tribal and personal disagreements are on the rise.

Drug-related corruption is endemic, particularly during the poppy harvest, or when the authorities make their half-hearted attempts at eradication. This links into the government security apparatus, which is often seamlessly attached to the drug traffickers and traders who seek to limit the power of the Afghan state. Particularly in southern Afghanistan, these links are common knowledge and are the cause of confusion and disappointment among the local population.

Few areas in Kandahar province can be termed safe, particularly when you remember that feeling safe and being safe are not the same thing. City-dwellers are largely restricted to the urban areas, and travelling from Kandahar to other parts of the country is a perilous undertaking. The main highway west from Kandahar to Herat is plagued by *Taliban* patrols and attacks, sporadic banditry and police corruption. The road passes through many notorious trouble-spots of Kandahar, Helmand and Farah provinces. Insecurity on the road has made it increasingly difficult to find drivers willing to transport goods the 136 kilometres to Lashkar Gah. One construction company owner said that shifting material from Kandahar City to Lashkar Gah costs him several times more than getting the same material from Lahore to Kandahar.

When you travel east of Kandahar City towards Kabul, the road passes through Zabul province as well as through dangerous areas of Ghazni and Wardak. *Taliban* fighters regularly attack convoys on this road, snipers have been known to target passing vehicles, and *Taliban* inspections and checkpoints are a standard feature. The road itself is heavily damaged, with many deep potholes from IEDs and other attacks scattered along the way. All bridges seem to have been destroyed. For foreigners, there is no longer any place where it is safe to spend an extended amount of time. The only option is to make trips into the districts almost at random, which severely hampers movement and makes planned or extended work nearly impossible, especially for international organisations. Indeed, almost no foreigners visit the districts on any occasion.

One of the most serious problems is the invisibility of the people who pose a threat to ordinary Kandaharis. This is the major difference between Kandahar in 2009 and early 1994: in 1994 you knew—at least to some extent—where the danger was coming from. In 2009, hazards can emerge and disappear out of nowhere without explanation. Assassinations, beheadings, suicide bombers, IED attacks, aerial bombing, large-scale infantry attacks, or just crime-with-a-gun remain actual and present threats to ordinary residents of Kandahar province. As one tribal elder put it: "I am not afraid of being killed by the *Taliban*. If the *Taliban* want to get you, they get you. There is nothing you can do. I am afraid of the suicide bombings, the random attacks, bandits and the fighting that can literally break out anywhere at any time".

Ordinary Kandaharis believe a bewildering array of conspiracy theories about foreign forces and NATO. Some of these are almost touchingly naive rumours; in February 2009, for instance, people sent each other frantic text messages not to answer any phones because NATO forces were testing out a new type of laser ray that would instantly kill them if they picked up. Very few calls were answered in the south that day.

Then there are the more insidious conspiracy theories that suggest the Americans (all foreigners are automatically "Americans" in southern Afghanistan) are themselves funding the *Taliban* and play a part in the arming of *Al Qaeda* members. Or the pervasive rumours that the two most recent assassinations of senior figures in Kandahari society by the *Taliban* were in fact carried out by "the Americans". People claim, for instance, to have seen helicopters in the air in the moments before the assassination of the well-known commander, Habibullah Jan. The real story is irrelevant.

You will have read about these things in newspapers or seen television news reports, and you know this part of the story all too well. But you may not know so much about the parts that came before.

* * *

All over the world, 1968 was a year of change, a year of revolution. It was the year of the Tet Offensive and the Mai Lai massacre. Martin Luther King was shot dead in Tennessee, and in May the French took to the streets. It was the year of the Baader-Meinhof cells in West Germany, the Red Brigades in Italy, and the rebirth of the IRA in Northern Ireland. In 1968, Saddam Hussein seized some power in Iraq as Deputy Chairman of the Baathist Revolutionary Command Council after a *coup d'état*, and it was the year of the Phoenix programme in Vietnam. It was the year of Czechoslovakia and the Prague Spring, the year John Steinbeck and Thomas Merton died, the year of Apollo 8 and the first time the whole planet was photographed from space; it was the year of Simon and Garfunkel's *Mrs Robinson*.

This is the world into which *Mullah* Zaeef was born.

The Afghanistan of 1968 is probably not the one you imagine. Not the anti-Soviet *jihad* of the eighties, nor the destructive civil war of the nineties; it was a time when you were just as likely to run into a young girl in a miniskirt at the university as to be confronted by an uneducated *mullah*. If we look back at that time, over forty years ago, it is easy to fall into a nostalgic lull.

Tourists flocked to all parts of the country, making journeys of self-discovery—one such tour departing from Europe was called the "Magic Bus". Groups of young people, male and female, would cross into Afghanistan from Iran, initially stopping in Herat but passing through the south in Kandahar. Others would arrive from Quetta or Peshawar. Kandahar was "the gentle oasis";[2] a guidebook from the 1970s even described it as "a thriving commercial and budding industrial centre".[3]

Hippies from Europe and America would congregate in Kandahar, Lashkar Gah and elsewhere in the villages. One traveller remembered the foreigners producing community journals: "grimy spiral notebooks or pieces of paper stuck between wide strips of leather where all the wanderers, adventurers, draft dodgers, drug runners and addicts, small-time wheeler-dealers—misfits who, because they were white, got away with more in the East—and seekers of Nirvana could write a tale. These were the logbooks of the new Eastern traveller—as if we were the first to go out there—and a guide for those on the way".

Locals to this day recall the music parties that were hosted in villages outside the city. Afghans and Europeans, locals and foreigners, all would congregate for several days to make music, discuss poetry, eat barbecued meat and fish together. It is difficult to imagine this now, over forty years later.

* * *

Zangiabad itself, the village of *Mullah* Zaeef's birth, is fairly typical of southern Afghanistan. The second-largest village in Panjwayi's grape-growing district, it is situated between branches of the main river in Kandahar province. As such, the area is fertile and agriculture is the main occupation. Exact population figures are hard to come by, but during the 1960s and 1970s we may assume that there were one or two hundred thousand people living in the district.[4]

The rhythms of daily life are determined by the needs of family and field. Most rise with the sun; electricity still has yet to penetrate the districts outside the main regional centres in Afghanistan. Younger male members of the household and the women busy themselves with tending livestock. Breakfast is usually green tea served with Afghan flat-bread. Poorer households like that of *Mullah* Zaeef are unlikely to have enjoyed such luxuries all the time, though.

Household chores take up a large part of the day in the villages, be it washing clothes or preparing food. Young boys and men growing up outside the cities would not necessarily be educated, but *Mullah* Zaeef was lucky to have parents who sent him to religious and secular government schools. When he wasn't busy studying or helping out around the house, there would have been few activities specifically to engage the children. As *Mullah* Zaeef narrates in the pages that follow, he made up games, playing soldier with his cousins in the alleys and vineyards surrounding his house.

Like any other local boy, he was exposed to the basic institutions of Pashtun social life. Weddings would often last three days, a chance for general celebration and a hiatus in the tedium of daily life. Families from among the village—most likely from the same tribe or extended family—would contribute food in the days leading up to the ceremony. Women would dye their hands with henna, and there might have been music depending on how fastidious the particular family was in their religious observance.

His father would have been the primary officiator at funerals, so it is likely that *Mullah* Zaeef saw his fair share of those. The dead would most often be laid into the ground on the day they died, and then the *fateha* or prayers from the *Qur'an* would be read in the village mosque. By the fourth day, unless the deceased was a well-known figure, the ceremony would be finished.

The Afghan institution of *jirga* or *shura* would have been known to *Mullah* Zaeef, although the role that religious families played in these tribal consultative bodies at the time was relatively small. The *mullah* of a village would often recite a few verses from the *Qur'an* at the start, but then would have very little input in the course of the discussion. Only occasionally would a very strong and charismatic religious figure be included in the discussions, probably because he had some tribal standing at the same time.

If *jirga* is the wellspring of Pashtun identity and culture, then the village mosque is the locus of religious belief. *Mullah* Zaeef's father was the key figure among those who would gather for the daily prayers, and as such would occasionally be called to mediate between conflicting parties. This was both an essential part of his role, and one of the main sources of his authority. The socialisation of the next generation of Pashtuns—into their culture, into their religion—would have been mostly a process of osmosis achieved by sitting in on such gatherings.

Zangiabad is far from the city, both in distance and in culture. Only a few hours away by car, much longer by foot, these rural communities existed in a separate space from the debates and political manoeuvrings of the city. Even further still was the capital city, Kabul. Provincial reforms in March 1964 created twenty-eight provinces (all of equal status) out of a previous system of seven major and seven minor provinces. It was intended to increase central government control over the distant provinces—a perennial problem in Afghanistan since its formation as a state—but in reality there were two separate cultures, urban and rural. The next twenty years would accentuate these differences.

***

Mullah Zaeef was eleven years old when Soviet troops entered Afghanistan. His family were living in Sanzari at the time, a medium-sized village to the west of Kandahar City. Small local guerrilla groups had already started fighting against the Communist government at the beginning of 1979, but when the 85,000–strong Soviet forces invaded Afghanistan in December the resistance swelled and huge numbers of the local population fled to Pakistan.

Communist ideological influence in Afghanistan had been manifested following King Zahir Shah's reforms of 1964. The political groups that would go on to define the Afghan Communist movement during the 1980s all began work in earnest at this time. The rise of Soviet influence over Afghanistan was, though, part of the wider context of international influence in the country.

America's ambitious agricultural infrastructure project in Helmand, for example, began in 1945, and US assistance soon took on the character of a game, with the Americans always trying to gain the upper hand over the Soviets. By 1979, though, President Daud had come down firmly on the side of the Russians: "Soviet military aid to Afghanistan had totalled $1.25 billion. Further, 3,725 Afghan personnel had received military training in the USSR, Russian was the technical language of the Afghan armed forces, and Afghanistan was heavily dependent upon Soviet sources for spare parts".[5]

As an ideology, Communism never had broad popular appeal. This was especially true in southern Afghanistan where, once the government implemented substantive land and social reforms that impinged on rural society, active resistance began on a small scale in early 1979.

These legal decrees sought to bring a profound change in the formal and informal organisation of Afghan life—infringing on local marriage customs, land ownership and the education of boys and, more crucially, girls—and, as such, were one step too far for the rural communities.

The reforms decreed by the Taraki regime in late 1978 became symbolic grievances for local rural communities, but people were more concerned with the aggressive suppression of local figures of authority. As most Kandaharis who remember that time will tell you, *Khan*s, *Malik*s, *Sayyed*s and *Mullah*s all started to disappear; in many cases these local leaders were imprisoned and executed. This policy was even more energetically implemented under Hafizullah Amin, Taraki's short-lived successor.

The imprisonment and execution of the local leadership was the first stage in the dismemberment of the old systems of influence—mainly tribal—that were previously so strong in Kandahar. There were some instances of popular opposition in mid-1979, however.

A Tajik teacher named Abdul Mohammad from Mushan, a small village in Panjwayi, was killed by a man called *Hajji* Akhtar Muhammad and some five hundred local villagers took white flags and went to the central district authority to complain. Witnesses present that day tell how a white MiG plan flew over and fired on the demonstrators. Tanks also were dispatched from inside and fired on the crowd. Some thirty people are said to have died.

The next day, government forces deployed in the area and arrested many people. Over one hundred villagers managed to escape that day to Pakistan, and twenty days later they started a guerrilla movement against the government, operating mainly from small bases in Registan, the desert area south of Kandahar City.

When the first Russian armoured convoy entered Kandahar City almost half a year later, everyone came out of their houses. The people were very scared, but children would wave at the Soviet soldiers atop their tanks. A curfew was later imposed with a shoot-to-kill policy against anyone caught on the streets after ten at night.

The years 1979 and 1980 saw massive numbers of Afghans flee into Pakistan. *Mullah* Zaeef and his extended family were part of this movement of people from the increasingly volatile atmosphere in southern Afghanistan to the camps of Baluchistan.

These events were the beginning of a ten-year struggle, initially spontaneous and local but later increasingly funded by outside players as part of their foreign policies and wider ambitions. The *jihad* had begun.

* * *

The importance of the 1980s war against the Soviets cannot be over-stated. This is true for domestic politics, tribal alliances, figures of power and authority and so on; all of these strands that are manifest today, fraying at the ends and tangled beyond easy comprehension, derive from that period. Similarly in the international sphere, the *jihad* was fundamentally important for the United States (and the Soviet Union) as well as for the idea of a "global *jihadi*".

From a purely local perspective, the war created strong friendships, alliances and enmities that exist to this day. Many of the *mujahedeen* who fought in the villages and along the roads are still alive, the younger generation now in their forties and the older participants in their sixties and seventies. All of these survivors were deeply affected by the experience, and the networks that helped them get through the conflict years still function and are active, a fact often overlooked by foreigners. Indeed, for *Mullah* Zaeef, the atmosphere and context of the 1980s *jihad* went on to influence his life in the 1990s and into the new millennium. If he hadn't returned to Kandahar to fight in 1983, choosing instead to study, he would probably never have been involved with the *Taliban* movement in such a significant way, and would never have been imprisoned in Guantánamo for years.

Unfortunately, there is a dearth of materials on the last three decades of the twentieth century available to the lay scholar of southern Afghanistan. Anyone hoping to learn more about the precise alliances, networks and *mujahedeen* figures that defined the 1980s will find that there are few English-language sources on the matter, let alone a big-volume history of the period which examines and analyses the developments in anything more than sweeping generalisations. Pashtu-language materials[6] are somewhat better given the total absence of anything aside from oral testimony, but there is still much work to be done. This poverty of understanding has necessarily negatively influenced the actions of outsiders, both in the 1990s and in the current war.

Most important for the purposes of this book is the knowledge of the presence of the *Taliban*—they were identified as such at the time—among the ranks of *mujahedeen* in the 1980s in southern Afghanistan.

Readers may be confused to learn of a pre-history to the movement that supposedly started (or was created by Pakistan) in 1994, but even a cursory knowledge of the history confirms it.

As you will witness in the pages of *Mullah* Zaeef's autobiography that follow, the *Taliban* groups were somewhat set apart from the other *mujahedeen*, in part because there were certain rules and habits they observed, which some other fighters—in the rollicking freedom of the times—considered too strenuous, or perhaps even ascetic. *Mujahedeen* affiliated with the comparatively liberal *Mahaz-e Milli* party of *Pir* Gailani, or with Rabbani's *Jamiat-e Islami*, say they viewed the *Taliban* units as naysayers and too strict by far.

The *Taliban*, the only legitimate authorities on the *shari'a*, were of course best known for the formal justice system and mediation services that they provided to all groups in the south. The first judge, *Mawlawi* Abdul Bari, was killed in the early 1980s and was then replaced by *Mawlawi* Pasanai *Saheb*, a name that continues to conjure respect and fear in present-day Kandahar. These courts would adjudicate on issues small and large, from petty theft to murder, and their authority was perhaps the apex of religious scholars' influence in southern Afghanistan prior to the time of the *Taliban* movement proper—except, of course, their absolute power over the war through their sanction of the conflict as a *jihad*.

The exact numbers and strengths of the various factions and *jihadi* fronts are still vigorously debated to this day, and, in the absence of better sources of information, it is difficult to come to more than a very vague assessment of the relative sizes of each particular contingent. Everyone still alive and with an opinion agrees, though, that the *Taliban* played a significant role in the greater Kandahar area, with a particularly important set of front lines and groups established in the fertile triangle in between the two branches of the River Arghandab in Panjwayi district.

In the end, though, *mujahedeen* groups worked together in a much more co-operative manner than others elsewhere in the country. The divisions between particular parties were fierce and contested in Pakistan (where the money and assets were distributed), but the southern fronts were more prepared to co-operate, and even now the party allegiance of certain *mujahedeen* from that time is difficult to trace for this reason.

One point that everyone can agree on, however, refers to the ferocity of the war in southern Afghanistan. The human, social and agricultural costs of the conflict were massive, and it is perhaps only the paucity of information and coverage that has prevented this point from being better emphasised. Scholars researching from outside Afghanistan are forced to rely on fragments in books and documentaries—Jere van Dyk's *In Afghanistan*, for example, Robert Kaplan's *Soldiers of God*, or Alexander Lindsay's wonderfully evocative documentary, *Jihad: Afghanistan's Holy War*.

Kaplan quotes: "The following year, 1987, the situation in Kandahar worsened still. A State Department publication noted, 'By the onset of summer, the capital of southern Afghanistan and its surrounding areas had become the scene of what has been probably the heaviest concentration of combat of the war'". The Soviets, who by this time were starting to tell their own people the truth about what was happening in Afghanistan, brought an *Izvestia* correspondent to Kandahar in September. He wrote that the city "is one big ruin. There is shooting all the time. Nobody would give a brass farthing for your life if you took it into your head, say, to walk down the street unarmed."

Above all it is the experience of the war—ten years of hard combat, the deprivations and humiliations of life as refugees in Pakistan, the cold calculations made to survive, but also the camaraderie of the trenches—that endures in the Kandahar of the twenty-first century. They were, in the words of one well-known *mujahedeen* commander from Arghandab, "happy *mujahedeen*" and those times are viewed with a mixture of horror and nostalgia. Or, as *Mullah* Zaeef puts it, "What a happy life we led!"

The withdrawal of the Soviet Army and the cooling of hostilities, as *mujahedeen* commanders began to accept payoffs from the Afghan government, was not the end of the story for the people of southern Afghanistan. A new phase was beginning.

* * *

After the last Soviet soldier had left the country, there was a general feeling of satisfaction and pride, and a brief hiatus in the onslaught of conflict, while forces made plans to gather together to defeat the Communist government, then lead by President Najibullah. In Kandahar, this interim period was taken as a chance to rest, to make some money, and above all to consolidate some of the gains that their respective groups had made.

In their final months, Soviets had provided for security forces and militias to take their place in southern Afghanistan. The two militias of Jabbar "Qahraman" and Abdur Rashid Dostum were unparalleled in their success against the *mujahedeen*. At the same time, the then-governor of Kandahar, Noor ul-Haq Ulumi, was also engaged in a programme to encourage the *mujahedeen* groups not to fight against the forces of the government, or at least to fake their attacks.

As had been the case for many of these peace initiatives throughout Afghan history, money was a strong motivating factor. In the words of one Afghan government official closely involved in the implementation of the plan to fund militias (and to fund the opposition to slow down their operations), "We wanted to find people to fill the gaps that the departure of 150,000 Soviet soldiers would leave". These strategies served their purpose: the Najibullah government remained effective for several years, much longer than many expected at the time.

The government, for example, established a base for paramilitary forces to keep Helmand and Herat supplied from Kandahar. These forces were commanded by Jabbar "Qahraman". The *mujahedeen* opposition, upon hearing of this base, decided to mount an attack, including the combined forces of: Aref Khan, *Hajji* Bashar, *Mullah* Naqib, Sarkateb and Habibullah Jan. This list reads almost like a who's who of the known big commanders of the time. One would think that they would have had no problem against a small militia in Maiwand district.

In actual fact, they were so confident of their success that the operation started haphazardly and without co-ordination. The one tank that they had deemed necessary to send with their forces took nine days to arrive in Maiwand, whereas the battle was over after just one day, with Jabbar "Qahraman" victorious and *mujahedeen* forces routed.

This period of massive funding given to the opposition *mujahedeen* commanders was effective in that it encouraged the habit of luxury. New clothes brought from Pakistan, or shoes from France, were the norm. In the end the commanders had so much money that they bought up major tracts of land and *kareezes*.

The Afghan government, too, started to lose its grip on the country in April 1992, and plans were made to hand over the city to the *mujahedeen* parties. The forces of the *Taliban* were excluded from these deals, and, as *Mullah* Zaeef narrates here, they completely missed the takeover of Kandahar city—more a chaotic rout than a handover—and were left only with some small assets outside the town.

The transfer of authority was meant to be a calmer event, but when news leaked that parts of town were being handed over to certain commanders, everyone else rushing in to grab whatever they fancied. Gul Agha Shirzai, the son of the famous commander *Hajji* Latif, seized the governorship, *Mullah* Naqib took the Army Corps base, Amir Lalai took another area, the textile mill and workshops, *Hajji* Ahmad took the airport, *Ustaz* Abdul Aleem took the police headquarters and the prison, *Hajji* Sarkateb took the Bagh-e Pul area and Silo, and so on.

From this point on, with the tribes and their commanders comfortably ensconced in positions throughout the city, no rules obtained. Anything was possible, from robbery to murder. Within the city, the commanders started to sell off the assets within their control: the tanks in the Army Corps went to Ahmad Shah Massoud further north, and copper cables, factories and airport assets found eager buyers as well. The great sell-off was general knowledge.

After roughly one month of making money and settling in, the euphoria began to wear off, and it was at this point that the first clash between commanders took place. None of them could tolerate their colleagues, and in this first burst of violence *Ustaz* Abdul Haleem was expelled from the police headquarters to his base to the west of the city near Sarpoza prison. By April 1993, these clashes were indiscriminately killing scores of civilians.

It was at that point, according to those living in the city at the time, that the people realised that the commanders were intent only on increasing their power. From that point on there was no more law, no more order, and, as the local saying goes, everyone was either a king or his subject. *Mullah* Zaeef and many of the *Taliban* commanders of the 1980s, meanwhile, had returned home or banded together to study and teach in the districts.

Witnesses to the excesses and abuses of the *mujahedeen* commanders in the city didn't take long to reach those in the districts, but it was only by the end of 1993 and 1994 that these stories started to have an effect. The villagers of the districts themselves were being harassed on the roads to the city by numerous checkpoints manned by the *topaki-yaan*, the men with the guns.

* * *

The movement that we now know as "the *Taliban*" didn't suddenly emerge from nowhere. As *Mullah* Zaeef reveals here, in the most detailed account of the early days of the group in their 1994 incarnation, there were months of meetings and consultations prior to deciding to take action.

This differs from the story frequently assumed and related in the academic literature. Scholarship on the *Taliban* in the 1990s, while voluminous, has been exceptionally varying in quality, and in fact there are only a limited number of accounts which give adequate detail on these early days. *Fundamentalism Reborn?*,[7] a volume edited by Professor William Maley, which was also the first English-language book about the *Taliban* phenomenon in Afghanistan, was one of the few that got it right.

The discussions were extremely local to begin with. Old commanders from the *jihad* were visited, and their opinions on how to fix the situation were taken into consideration. They eventually came to agree that some sort of force should be formed to restore order and justice in the area. The issue of leadership was the next to be raised, and head-hunting teams were dispatched around greater Kandahar, and eventually these groups settled on *Mullah* Mohammad Omar as the senior commander charged with running the day-to-day operations, while *Mawlawi* Abdul Samad was chosen as its *Amir* or head.

Initial actions were envisioned to clear the main highway from western Kandahar towards the city. Success built upon success, and the *Taliban* soon moved outside the provincial boundaries east and west into new territories. This is not the place for a revisionist account of those early days; *Mullah* Zaeef's account should give enough impetus to scholars of the period, and in any case the broad outlines of those times are already somewhat known.

The subsequent stages of *Mullah* Zaeef's life are more familiar: his work in an assortment of *Taliban* government positions, culminating in his appointment as Ambassador to Pakistan in 2000; his interactions with journalists after the 11 September attacks; his imprisonment in Guantánamo in 2002 and his release without charge in 2005.

* * *

An introduction to the life and times of *Mullah* Zaeef is as much a history of Kandahar as it is of a particular person. The span of his life, the past forty years, extends over many profound changes and an appreciation of the historical context is essential for an understanding of who he is now.

Indeed, as a man who grew up in Kandahar, he played a significant role in many of the events for which the province is known, and as the author of the first book from Kandahar to be published in English fully to scrutinize the history of these times, *Mullah* Zaeef must somehow be seen as an "everyman" for southern Afghanistan.

Notwithstanding the very different possible life choices and paths that Kandahar contains, he grew up in the districts as a child of the villages; he took refuge with his family in Pakistan following the Soviet invasion; he fought as a young *mujahed* on the front lines during the 1980s; he sought further education as a religious scholar following the departure of the Soviets; he served as an official within the movement that came to be known as "*Taliban*" during the 1990s; he was later imprisoned by American forces in an assortment of jails culminating in several years of incarceration in Guantánamo; he now lives in Kabul and plays roles as an occasional media commentator, go-between and author. In this way, *Mullah* Zaeef is representative of so much that has befallen Afghanistan.

At the same time as being an actor in these events, he has remained an observer, reluctant to take up the reins of power himself, each time retreating back to the districts, each time needing the distance of non-engagement. This book is a testament to that observation.

Attempts to remain disengaged are harder nowadays, in a time where polarisation and a Manichean expectancy on the part of foreigners dogs those with knowledge and experience. As *Mullah* Zaeef narrates in the final pages of this book, the representatives of his former captors continue to seek his help and co-operation in spite of clear requests to be left alone.

He now lives in Kabul, and watches the situation becoming bleaker in the provinces beyond the city limits. A new surge of American troops is set to arrive in Kandahar and the people brace themselves. A common saying these days upon parting company is, "I'll see you soon, if we're still alive". Most people say the results of the August election were a foregone conclusion anyway—Karzai will win again; the election will be a sham, manipulated by hundreds of thousands of fraudulent votes; and Kandahar will muddle on towards an uncertain future.

Ideas for southern Afghanistan emanating from Washington and the new Obama administration over the past months have been manifold and vary widely in quality. There have been many attempts to find tribal solutions to local problems: one suggests the formation of large consultative bodies, another proposes the formation of tribal militias along the lines of Iraq's Awakening Council or Sons of Iraq movement. This is not the place for a full discussion of the respective merits and confusions of these plans, but this book should serve as a historical yardstick alongside which these efforts should be measured.

My Life with the Taliban, then, offers a personal and privileged insight into the life of Pashtun village communities, into the perceptions and insights of the religious clergy, into the movement now known as '*Taliban*', and into a country bitterly afflicted by war. This first person, participant account of a thirty year conflict is also a cautionary tale for anyone seeking to categorise or simplify southern Afghanistan.

Alex Strick van Linschoten   *Kandahar City, July 2009*
and Felix Kuehn

EDITORS' ACKNOWLEDGEMENTS

This book has been almost four years in the making. We are grateful to have been helped by a small coterie of scholars, journalists and experts from outside Afghanistan, as well as a wide host of Afghan friends and colleagues from Kabul, Kandahar and elsewhere in southern Afghanistan.

Many such friends cannot be named—the war in Afghanistan continues, and their lives might be endangered by inclusion here.

For working long, hard hours on the bulk of the translations from Pashtu into English, and for helping with the follow-up interviews with *Mullah* Zaeef, thanks must go to Hamid Stanikzai, Mirwais Rahmany and Abaceen Nasimi.

For help with proofreading drafts of the text, sometimes in poor conditions and given little time, we wish to thank Dominic McCann and Graeme Smith (*Globe and Mail*). Katherine Ganly, Lisa Weiszfeld, Anna Patterson and Bidjan Nashat also contributed to this process.

A book of this kind requires lots of fact-checking, small pieces of information, and the occasional "big idea" thrown into the mix. Scott Peterson (Christian Science Monitor), Josh Foust (Registan.net), Naeem Rashid and Professor Anatol Lieven (King's College, London) were extremely helpful in this regard, and all are true experts in their fields of study. Special thanks are due to Anatol for introducing us to Michael Dwyer at Hurst.

In Kabul we were fortunate to share ideas across dinner with Joanna Nathan (International Crisis Group), Soraya Sarhaddi Nelson (National Public Radio), and Richard Scarth and Jessica Barry (International Committee of the Red Cross).

A.G.S. has driven us around town since we first arrived in Kabul in 2003 and we would like to thank him for his help and friendship.

EDITORS' ACKNOWLEDGEMENTS

Jean MacKenzie (Institute for War and Peace Reporting) was especially helpful with the introduction, also offering food and hospitality over the years we worked on this book.

In Kandahar, we received assistance from almost everyone we spoke to, often in difficult situations and where there was no need for them to help us. We owe a great debt to the people of Kandahar, including, but by no means limited to: *Hajji* Mukhtar Rashidi, Neamatullah Arghandabi, Baqi Agha, *Hajji* Karam Khan and *Hajji* Abdul Ghani.

Jason Elliot was particularly instrumental in ensuring that this book ever saw the light at all; he encouraged us and offered useful counsel throughout, and we must offer him special thanks. Jere van Dyk and Paul Fishstein were patient and kind, regularly offering advice and support throughout the final two and a half years of working on the book. We must also express our gratitude to N.P., E.R.W., K.D., and Z.D.

Michael Dwyer, our publisher at Hurst, has been an especially pleasant editor to work with on our first book, both in terms of his considerable expertise and his patience with our late delivery of manuscripts.

Finally, and most importantly, we wish to thank *Mullah* Zaeef, for trusting us to work together with him, and for not losing patience with us two or three years ago while we tried to find a home for his book. We are truly humbled by the experiences of his life, in the face of which he has maintained his humanity, kindness and decency.

EDITORS' NOTES

How to read this book

While translating and editing *My Life With the Taliban* we assembled a wealth of materials to help us understand *Mullah* Zaeef, southern Afghanistan, and the historical events through which he lived. In an attempt to make this book accessible to the general reader, we have condensed some of that information throughout the text.

For those who have little knowledge of the complicated twists of politics and conflict in Afghanistan—bringing tribes, religion, money and ideology into play—don't be alarmed. As a first point of reference, we advise you to consult the footnotes that follow the first appearance of each character or religious term. We tried to write a footnote for any element that may be foreign or unfamiliar.

We have included a list of prominent recurring characters for your reference at the beginning of the book, but the biographical details given for each are condensed. These are organised by location. If you forget who a particular character is while reading, you can also refer to the index, which lists the various instances of that character's appearance in the text.

All Islamic and local-language terms are defined in the footnotes, but we have included all of these at the back of the book in a separate glossary.

Maps have been provided to give a sense of the location and distances of places that are described throughout the text, particularly those in southern Afghanistan. We have also included some more general maps of Afghanistan and the region at the beginning of the book.

While the events that this book describes coincide with most of the major historical moments in the past forty years of Afghan history, it is not intended to serve as a history of Afghanistan or of the region.

For readers wishing to see what was happening at the time that certain events happened in *Mullah* Zaeef's life, please consult the chronology at the back of the book. It lists the important junctions of *Mullah* Zaeef's life side-by-side with other important events in Afghan history.

If you want to learn more about the background to some of the events described here, please consult our "Suggestions for Further Reading".

Composition and sources

The original idea to try to publish this book dates back to 2006. Since then we have worked extensively together with *Mullah* Zaeef on the text. The basis of this was a manuscript written in Pashtu, to which we added material from dozens of interviews with him and those involved in events he describes. We also made an extensive search for any and all available written materials relating to these events.

All footnotes are the sole opinion of the editors and were added to enable the lay reader to understand the context of people and places he describes.

Orthography

We have generally used spellings that reflect how a particular word is pronounced. Most names, places and Islamic terms used in this book are thus written exactly how someone from Afghanistan would pronounce them. As such, there is no rigorous system aside from a healthy dose of common sense combined with a use of some of the common spellings of places and people.

CHARACTER LIST

Kabul

Abd ul-Rabb al-Rasul Sayyaf—Pashtun Islamic scholar and founder of the *Ittehad-e Islami* political party; still active and influential in Afghan politics.

Babrak Karmal—Tajik President of Afghanistan (1979–1986) installed by the Soviets at the time of the military invasion.

Daud Khan—Pashtun cousin of King Zahir Shah; Prime Minister (1953–63) and President (1973–78) after seizing power in the 'Saur' coup.

Hafizullah Amin—Pashtun Communist ideologue who served as president in 1979 before being assassinated later that year by Babrak Karmal who took his position.

Mawlawi Ahmad Jan *Saheb*—Pashtun Minister of Mines and Industries towards the end of the *Taliban*'s rule; *Mullah* Zaeef served under him.

Mawlawi Wakil Ahmad Mutawakil—Foreign Minister in the final years of the *Taliban*'s rule; originally from Kandahar and the son of a well-known local poet.

Najibullah—Pashtun President of Afghanistan (1986–1992) who presided over the departure of the Soviets from the country only to be forced to live as a prisoner in a UN compound in Kabul.

Noor Mohammad Taraki—Pashtun *Khalqi* communist leader and President of Afghanistan (1978–9) prior to execution by his successor Hafizullah Amin.

Sibghatullah Mujaddidi—Pashtun Islamic scholar (educated at Cairo's *Al Azhar*) and interim President in 1992, he founded the *Jamiat-e Ulema-ye Mohammadi* political party; he continues to play a role in Afghan politics.

Zahir Shah—Pashtun King (1933–73) who presided over a period of relative stability in Afghanistan's history; he died in July 2007.

Southern Afghanistan

Abdul Ghaffar Akhundzada—important commander of the 1980s *jihad* in southern Afghanistan; he resisted the *Taliban* when they tried to take Helmand in 1994.

Abdul Hakim Jan—highly influential commander and colourful character in Kandahar province from the 1980s *jihad* onwards; he was assassinated in February 2007.

Atta Mohammad Sarkateb—prominent Kandahari *mujahedeen* commander during 1980s; former *Hizb-e Islami* commander; he fought against the *Taliban* in 1994 but was expelled from his positions and checkpoints in the city.

Azizullah Wasefi—Alikozai tribal elder who supported the return of King Zahir Shah from exile. He is still alive.

Baru—*mujahedeen* commander with an exceptionally bad reputation for extorting and terrorising locals in Kandahar during the early 1990s; he was hanged by the *Taliban* on the first day they took control of the city.

Commander Abdul Raziq—commander of the 1980s *jihad* and based in Nelgham, although he is originally from Arghestan district of Kandahar province.

Hafizullah Akhundzada—prominent commander in southern Afghanistan during the 1980s *jihad*.

Hajji Ahmad—prominent commander in Kandahar during both the 1980s *jihad* and the aftermath of the 1990s during which he seized large parts of the city.

Hajji Bashar—senior Noorzai tribal elder from Kandahar who played a significant role during both 1980s and 1990s; supported the nascent *Taliban*'s rule in the mid-1990s; convicted of drug trafficking charges in the USA in 2008.

Hajji Latif—known as "the lion of Kandahar"; highly influential *jihadi* commander and tribal elder prior to his poisoning in 1989; he is the father of Gul Agha Sherzai, the current governor of Nangarhar.

Hamid Karzai—President of Afghanistan since the fall of the *Taliban*.

Hajji Karam Khan—*mujahed* during the 1980s and Achekzai tribal elder in the years that followed.

Mawlawi Niaz Mohammad—religious cleric in Sangisar who supported the communists in the late 1970s; he was later assassinated for his views.

Mawlawi Pasanai *Saheb*—influential *Taliban* judge known for presiding over courts during the 1980s in Kandahar; also prominent following the *Taliban*'s seizure of power post-1994; *Mullah* Zaeef worked together with him for several months.

Mullah Abdul Rauf Akhund—originally from Helmand, he presided over one of the first large meetings of *Taliban* in 1994 to discuss forming a group to secure southern Afghanistan; he has been held in Guantánamo prison since his capture in 2001.

Mullah Burjan—prominent *jihadi* commander from Kandahar, he was killed in 1996 following the *Taliban*'s capture of Kabul.

Mullah Dadullah Akhund—one-legged *Taliban* commander known as much for his bravery as for his brutality; he was killed in May 2007 by ISAF forces.

Mullah Feda Mohammad—fought during the *jihad* in Kandahar but killed towards the end of the 1980s.

Mullah Marjan—commander during the 1980s *jihad* who fought on the *Taliban* front lines; he was killed in the late 1980s.

Mullah Mazullah Akhundzada—senior commander during the 1980s *jihad* in charge of several *Taliban* front lines; he retained his influence until his death in the mid-1990s.

Mullah Mohammad Hassan—there are two people from Kandahar with this name, both of whom were governors of Kandahar during the late 1990s under the *Taliban*; they are to be distinguished from each other by the fact that one lost a leg in the 1980s.

Mullah Mohammad Omar Akhund—prominent commander during 1980s *jihad* and leader of the *Taliban* movement that emerged in 1994; believed to be alive and hiding somewhere in Pakistan.

Mullah Mohammad Sadiq Akhund—highly prominent commander of *Taliban* forces during the 1980s *jihad*; he was captured in 2001 and taken to Guantánamo prison where he continues to be held.

Mullah Naqib—one of the biggest of southern Afghanistan's *mujahedeen* commanders, he continued to play a prominent role in local politics until his death in October 2007.

Mullah Nek Mohammad Akhund—close friend of *Mullah* Mohammad Omar and *mujahed* from Kandahar well-known for success in defending and fighting on a small stretch of road near Pashmol until his death at the end of the 1980s.

Mullah Nezam—one of *Mullah* Zaeef's uncles, killed in 1962 by government forces in the Zheray desert.

Mullah Nooruddin Turabi—*mujahedeen* commander from Uruzgan later appointed as Minister of Justice during the late 1990s; he is still alive.

Mullah Obaidullah Akhund—well-known *mujahedeen* commander during the 1980s later appointed as Minister of Defence; still alive and believed to be in Pakistani custody.

Mullah Mohammad Rabbani—*mujahedeen* commander in Kandahar during the 1980s; he served as deputy leader of the *Taliban* movement until his death in April 2001.

Mullah Sattar—*mujahed* during the 1980s who became a commander during the late 1990s; he was killed in 2004/5 while attacking the airfield in Kandahar.

Musa Jan—uncle of *Mullah* Zaeef (mother's brother).

Nur ul-Haq Ulumi—Afghan government member and former communist governor of Kandahar, Ulumi presided over the south during the early 1990s; he continues to hold a position in the Afghan government.

Saleh—criminal and murderer; well-known for operating a checkpoint in the turmoil of the early 1990s.

Shah Baran—*mujahed* who switched to the government side with Esmat Muslim in the 1980s; in the early 1990s he ran a checkpoint in Kandahar manned by thieves and feared by many.

Ustaz Abdul Haleem—one of the prominent *mujahedeen* commanders of the 1980s in southern Afghanistan; he continues to play a role in local politics and is one of the last of his kind still alive.

Northern Afghanistan

Abdul Basir Salangi—Tajik military strongman in northern Afghanistan who was involved in 1998 when the *Taliban* were surrounded in Salang; he was fired as Kabul police chief in 2003 after an illegal land-grab scandal erupted in parliament.

Ahmad Shah Massoud—known as "the lion of Panjshir", Massoud was a significant 1980s *mujahedeen* commander operating in the north-east and who also fought against the *Taliban* in the 1990s until his assassination on 9 September 2001.

Bashir Baghlani—*Hizb-e Islami* commander in Baghlan during the 1980s who later served as a *Taliban* commander in the same province.

Abdurrashid Dostum—Uzbek commander notorious for switching sides numerous times during the 1980s and 1990s; he led the largest Soviet militia during the 1980s and early 1990s before being awarded a position in the *mujahedeen* government. He continues to play a prominent role in Afghan politics, both in Kabul and in the north.

General Malik—Dostum's second-in-command in northern Afghanistan, he broke a promise of safe passage to the *Taliban* in 1998 and attacked troops moving through and around the Salang Pass.

Gulbuddin Hekmatyar—leader of *Hizb-e Islami* political party, he fought during the 1980s *jihad* and received the lion's share of US-Saudi funding channelled through Pakistan's intelligence services to the Afghan resistance to the Soviets; he is still alive and believed to be engaged in talks with the US administration and Karzai government.

Western Afghanistan

Ismael Khan—the most important *mujahedeen* commander in western Afghanistan, he was affiliated with *Jamiat-e Islami* political party; he continues to play a role in Afghan politics as Minister of Power.

Mohammad Anwar—brother of Ismael Khan.

Pakistan

Abdul Sattar—Pakistani Foreign Minister (1999–2002).

Aziz Khan—director of Asian desk in the Pakistani foreign ministry.

General Jailani—deputy director of ISI (-2001).

General Mahmud Ahmad—director of ISI (1999–2001); he was in Washington on 11 September 2001 and went into meetings with the US authorities following the attacks on the Pentagon and World Trade Center.

Mawlawi Abdul Qadir—*Mullah* Zaeef's religious instructor in Quetta before he returned to Kandahar to fight for the second time.

Mawlawi Nabi Mohammadi—Islamic scholar and founder of the traditionalist *Harakat-e Enqelab-e Islami* political party; many of its members went on to make up a significant proportion of the 1994 *Taliban* movement.

Mawlawi Sayyed Mohammad Haqqani—*Mullah* Zaeef's predecessor as *Taliban* ambassador to Pakistan in 2000; currently wanted by

Pakistani and Afghan governments for attacks on police and foreign forces.

Moinuddin Haider—Pakistani Interior Minister (1999–2002).

Muhammad Rafiq Tarar—President of Pakistan (1998–2001).

Paula Thedi—Political affairs officer to the US ambassador to Pakistan.

Pervez Musharraf—President of Pakistan (2001–2008) following a *coup d'etat* in 1999.

William Milam—US ambassador to Pakistan (1998–2001).

Europe and USA

Francesc Vendrell—Spanish diplomat; Personal Representative of the Secretary General for Afghanistan and Head of the United Nations Special Mission to Afghanistan (UNSMA) (2000–1); also Special Representative of the European Union (2002–8).

George Bush—President of the United States of America (2001–2009).

Kofi Annan—UN Secretary General (1997–2007).

Central Asia

Noor Sultan Nazarbayev—President of Kazakhstan (1990–).

Arab States

Osama bin Laden—Saudi Arabian patron of terrorism; spent time in southeast Afghanistan during 1980s *jihad*, followed by time in Saudi and Sudan, before ending back in eastern, then southern, Afghanistan from 1996 where he organised and planned several terrorist attacks on US interests culminating in those of 11 September 2001; he is believed to be still alive.

Guantánamo

Badrozaman Badr—Pakistani imprisoned from 2001 to 2004; he then wrote a memoir of his time in detention—*The Broken Shackles of Guantánamo*—together with his brother; Badr is believed to be in Pakistani custody currently, and his brother is believed to have been recaptured and brought to Guantánamo.

Colonel Michael Bumgarner—senior military commander of Guantánamo prison (2005–6).

General Geoffrey D. Miller—senior military commander of Guantánamo prison from 2002; many link his counsel to "soften up" prisoners in Iraq to the Abu Ghraib prison scandal of March 2004.

Mullah Mohammad Fazl—resident of Uruzgan province and *Taliban*
Deputy Defence Minister in the final days of their rule; he was captured in 2001 and is currently still being held there.

Sheikh Shakir—Saudi prisoner in Guantánamo since 2001 who was the
lead figure in negotiations between hunger-striking detainees in 2005
and the prison administration; he is still being held in Guantánamo.

FOREWORD

The United States and its allies have been fighting against the *Taliban* for over eight years now, yet we still know very little about them. In the assessment that he prepared for President Obama in June 2009, US General Stanley McChrystal endorsed the description of the struggle in Afghanistan as "a war of ideas," and rightly added that Afghanistan "is a 'deeds-based' information environment where perceptions derive from actions."[1] Yet beyond a few labels such as "Islamic extremism" and their most newsworthy misdeeds—banning girls from school and women from the workplace, refusing to hand over Osama Bin Laden to the US, and, increasingly, their progressively bloody insurgency in Afghanistan—few know what their ideas are and how they have put them into practice.

For this reason, if for no other, everyone concerned with the fate of the US and international efforts in Afghanistan should read and study this book. With the help of his gifted and brave editors, *Mullah* Abdul Salaam Zaeef has presented us with an unapologetic—indeed proud— glimpse inside the world of that movement from its founding in the crucible of the anti-Soviet jihad, through its rise to power amid the anarchic bloody strife that followed the Soviet withdrawal, its five years in power, to its overthrow. From his childhood of deprivation and study in a remote village through his appearances on CNN, his imprisonment without charge in Guantanamo, to his life in Kabul today, *Mullah* Zaeef was there.

[1] COMISAF's Initial Assessment, Unclassified Version, Secretary of Defense Memorandum 26 June 2009, Subject: Initial United States Forces – Afghanistan (USFOR-A) Assessment, Headquarters, International Security Assistance Force, Kabul, Afghanistan, 21 September 2009, Washington Post. http://www.washingtonpost.com/wp-dyn/content/article/2009/09/21/AR2009092100110.html.

Today *Mullah* Zaeef lives peacefully in Kabul. As you will see from his book, he is eloquent. He does not always say what one might want to hear. From 2001, when he was Ambassador of the Islamic Emirate of Afghanistan to Pakistan, until now, internationals have suggested that Zaeef, who helped found the *Taliban* movement even before *Mullah* Muhammad Umar joined it, should help lead "moderate" *Taliban*. He rejects such distinctions in private and in this book, where he writes (p. 153), "The thought of dividing [the *Taliban*] into moderates and hardliners is a useless and reckless aim." When the authorities at Guantanamo asked Zaeef as a condition of his release to sign a paper stating that he had been a member of *al Qaeda* and the *Taliban* and would henceforth cut all ties with them, he refused: "I was a *Talib*, I am a *Talib* and I will always be a *Talib*, but I have never been a part of *al Qaeda*!" By his account, they allowed him instead to sign a statement in which he proclaimed his innocence, protested his imprisonment, and promised not "to participate in any kind of anti-American activities or military actions."

These statements will raise questions in the mind of some readers about what Zaeef and those like him would do if they once again had access to power. Though Zaeef claims no longer to have links to the *Taliban* (and the *Taliban* have made public statements to that effect), and he lives openly in Kabul where he is the subject of constant scrutiny, so steeped was he in the ethos and origins of that movement that his answers may nonetheless give some valuable clues. Readers may find themselves frustrated by Zaeef's many silences—he never mentions the decision to suspend the education of girls and refers only once, offhandedly, to the fact that after the *Taliban* captured Herat, "women were no longer working in government departments." (p. 84.) If *Mullah* Zaeef ever met Osama Bin Laden or any other members of *al Qaeda* before being incarcerated together with some of them in Guantanamo, he never mentions it. He writes that he wept to see the television images of the burning twin towers on 9/11—certain that "we will have to pay the price for what has happened today," but never clearly stating where he places the responsibility. His hatred for the Pakistani state—and most especially its intelligence agency, the ISI—far exceeds his contempt or distaste for the *Taliban*'s other enemies, but he offers only hints of how the ISI backed and manipulated the *Taliban*.

But more important than the answers he may give to our questions are the questions he poses—and answers—himself, about where he and the *Taliban* came from, where they intended to lead their country, and what type of men they were and are. Even if he rejects the label of "moderate," they are clearly not all like *Mullah* Zaeef. But he was one of their founders, and in his own view he has not compromised his core principles.

The *Taliban* were not created to oppose or outrage the West, however they have done so. They were born for different purposes, in a different place, in Kandahar, a place few outsiders know, however many may now have passed through it in armored vehicles. And that is where Zaeef starts his tale.

Barnett R. Rubin is employed by the US Department of State. The views expressed herein are his own personal opinions and are not necessarily those of the Department of State or US Government.

Barnett R. Rubin
Center on International Cooperation, New York University

PREFACE

Kandahar: the land of my birth. There are no words for the love I feel for my home; no other place on earth will ever mean as much to me. Gazing on its mountains and landscape, my spirit rises. No possession, no palace can take its place in my heart. I pray to almighty *Allah* that when the time comes he will take my soul there, and that I will be buried beside my heroes, brothers and friends in the *Taliban* cemetery.

In the last days of 2001 when America launched its attack on the zealous land of Ahmad Shah Baba[1] and Mirwais Khan[2] like so many colonizers before her, bringing fire and destruction, I returned to Kandahar.

When I arrived, I could see sorrow on the faces of the people. No one knew what was to come. Many feared that the warlords would return; others were reminded of the Soviet invasion some thirty years back. Yet others were dancing to the drum of the Americans; they failed to understand what the future held for them.

American jets were carpet bombing the city and the surrounding area as I said goodbye to my homeland, and I knew that much time would pass before I would return. Black smoke rose from the city, billowing into the sky. People were on the move, trying to save themselves and their children from the merciless American bombs.

Six years were to pass before I saw Kandahar again. It was in late 2007 when I arrived on an Ariana plane from Kabul. As the aircraft touched down I could see what had become of Kandahar airport. Trapped in the middle of a buzzing hive of foreign troops, everywhere one looked were the red faces of American soldiers with their tanks and armoured vehicles, their helicopters and planes, their trenches and installations. But I could still make out the mud-walled prison into which I was thrown by them, where they tried to degrade and humiliate me. Back then I was treated as an outcast by people who were outcasts themselves.

This vision of Kandahar reawakened many bad memories, making me feel sad, even desperate. At that moment, I seemed to be in another country. Afghanistan did not feel like home; like a wounded bird, I had crash-landed into unfamiliar territory.

I was both terrified and stunned. Most of the other passengers looked just like I felt.

Kandahar airport had been transformed, completely. It looked like the front line in a war. Afghans were restricted to one road which took them directly from the airport onto the Spin Boldak[3]-Kandahar road. Watchtowers were manned by suspicious Americans who scanned your every move.

A government vehicle collected me from the airport and soon we were on our way towards Kandahar. I was curious to see what had changed; my American interrogators in Guantánamo had often told me that the city "was just like Dubai now". But apart from the paved road we were driving on, everything seemed the same.

In Kandahar, a few new buildings had sprung up and there were signs of private investment. The city itself had grown but there was little evidence that either government projects or foreign aid had had an impact. Paved roads now led to the districts—Spin Boldak, Arghandab, Dand, and Panjwayi—that I visited from Kandahar, but apart from that not much else had changed. Many people thought that the Americans were only paving the roads for their own security, to reach the front lines as quickly as possible and to avoid roadside bombs. Many Kandaharis were suffering. There is little work, and unemployment is a big problem, they complained. The Americans are only here to spend donors' money on themselves, and only the Afghans who helped facilitate this are making a profit. Foreign aid is killing Afghans, they said.

Many people talked about Gul Agha Sherzai[4] and compared him to the then new governor Asadullah Khaled[5] and other leaders. The consensus was that Sherzai had been good for Kandahar. Even though he was fond of music parties and had other bad habits, he did many things for the people. While other politicians kept all the money for themselves, he put at least fifty per cent into reconstruction. Kandaharis were very sorry to see him go.

Security remains the major concern for the people of Kandahar. During my brief stay many residents complained to me about the situation and said that the foreign soldiers had failed to bring security. Even the city itself was being plagued by growing numbers of criminals and thieves. Foreign forces used to raid the houses, and people could not sleep at night.

In district three an incident occurred at a butcher's house that sent shockwaves of fear throughout Kandahar. Everyone was talking about it, reliving the description given by the butcher's children. In their words, "the foreigners blew out the front gate of our house, and everyone just jumped up from their beds. My two elder brothers woke up and screamed 'oh my God!' First our elder brother ran into the courtyard to see what had happened. He did not realize that the American soldiers were already there, on the roof and in other spots around the house, just waiting for somebody to come out. The Americans riddled him with bullets; they did not try to ask him any questions or to see if he was involved in anything. They just opened fire without mercy".

The second brother also ran into the courtyard when he heard the shooting; he met the same fate. After that the Americans entered the house. The women and children were still inside. The soldiers behaved like wild animals, throwing all their belongings into the courtyard, breaking locks, smashing boxes and searching every inch of the building. They found nothing but clothes and household goods.

The men lay in the courtyard, in full view of their wives and children, who were shaking in fear. Nobody could help them because of those merciless American soldiers. Not even the government could get to them.

As they left, the Americans offered their "condolences" to the members of the household. "Just go back to sleep", they said. "There's no problem". But only a few metres away lay the bodies of the men they had just killed, swimming in their own blood.

The people complained bitterly about the inhuman behaviour of the foreign troops. When the *Taliban* fighters killed some of them, they would take their revenge on civilians. I felt the people's hatred grow day by day.

I was an eyewitness to such scenes when driving with another Kandahari man to Arghestan to see the new paved highway. On the way back, near Shurandam, without warning all the vehicles stopped at the side of the road. The passengers in the other cars looked anxious and my driver also pulled over. I asked him what the problem was and he replied, laughing, "Nothing. Its just a convoy of foreigners. When they travel around Kandahar, all other cars have to leave the road and stop. You even have to turn your face away or they get angry".

We were still waiting by the road when I saw the tanks coming, firing flares into the sky. Burning debris fell all around us, hitting cars here and there. They pointed their guns at the cars along the road, screaming at people like animals.

This was the first time I had seen a convoy in Kandahar. It was very strange, and worrying. I asked my friend whether it was always this bad. "Today was a good day", he said. "This is our daily routine, and many times lives are lost when they pass through the city".

It upset me to see the foreigners behave in this way. There is no need for them to be here; they regard every person, donkey, tree, rock and house as an enemy. They are afraid of everything, and can do nothing except shed blood, kill people and provoke more hatred against themselves and the government.

I worry about the people of Afghanistan, especially those of Kandahar: how much longer will they have to suffer? The situation in the rural districts was far worse. There was fighting every day on the Herat-Kandahar highway. Panjwayi, Maiwand, Khakrez, Shah Wali Kot, Miya Nisheen, Maruf, Arghestan, Shorabak, Dand and some areas of Daman[6] were not under the control of the government or the foreign troops aside from the district centres. There were clashes every day, bombings, more destruction and more murder. Most of the victims were civilians. A resident of Sperwan told me that on the night before *Eid*,[7] American planes had bombed a group of refugees leaving a village, just trying to get out of the area; they were heading for Registan. In one hour, they killed more than two hundred women and children, he told me.

"When we went to the area the next day to collect the bodies", he said, "we found their hands coloured with henna for the *Eid* celebration". Their hopes for *Eid* were scattered with their bodies all over the desert.

It was the same thing, every day—more killing and more death.

The gap between the people and the government was widening and still is, largely as a result of the indiscriminate bombing by the foreign troops. Locals were accusing the governor and the rest of the authorities of turning a blind eye to what the foreigners were doing. The foreigners, for their part, were trying to downplay the number of civilian casualties.

They are killing people because they are being fed incorrect information—and sometimes these traitorous informers are acting for money. They would give false information to the Americans, and then they would pocket the money. They take funding for construction projects, but never build a thing. They don't even want to give jobs to people to work on their projects.

Although I had gone to Kandahar with the permission of the central government, I did not have any problems with the *Taliban*, and my friends were very eager to meet me. Soon I realized, however, that most of my hosts felt uncomfortable when I stayed with them in their village. They feared for their lives.

No one could guarantee that they would not be bombed or that an operation would not be carried out; they were always on edge. Sometimes this tension was because of me, and sometimes it was just the way things were. When I asked the elders about it, all they would say was, "God is merciful". But everyone else was in despair.

After an eight-day trip, I returned to Kandahar airport with a young man who had an ISAF[8] ID card that allowed him access to the airport.[9]

From the airport entrance up to the terminal, I could see many passengers, all of them making their way through the many checkpoints on foot. When we reached the terminal, various people came to greet me. Some asked how I was, and some just said hello. I spread my *patu*[10] on the ground and sat down; many passengers gathered around me. It was getting crowded, and I knew that the Americans would not like this. The passengers from two flights—Ariana and Kam Air—were all together. I couldn't just tell them to go away, but I was worried that the Americans might be afraid of such a big gathering.

A few minutes later I saw the heads of Americans appear behind the windows on the left of the terminal. Others came onto the roof, with their guns. Soldiers approached us from two sides. The people around me turned to see what was going on, and I told them all to leave. They went away, and the Americans came towards me. They stopped a few metres away and began speaking to each other.

"Yes, that's him", I heard one of them say. "He's a good man. Yes he's a very honest man". Then they just left. The soldiers on the roof also disappeared.

The flight was supposed to leave at one in the afternoon, but we did not board the plane until six. Then we waited inside for another half an hour. The runway was blocked by American tanks. The pilot came on the announcer every five minutes to apologize for the delay and eventually ISAF gave us clearance to depart.

* * *

Praise be to God, to Whom the angels and all the universe pray. Praise to God Who gave them life. Praise to God Who created the order of the universe. Praise to God Who has bestowed on His creatures life, food, and consciousness. Praise to God Who has guided humans through His prophets, and ordered them to honour the ultimate and most beloved Prophet, Mohammad, peace be upon him. Many honours to him and to his close aides and friends, his family members and his followers, from now until the day of judgement.

Life in this universe has an importance far beyond our understanding, because it is life that created us from nothing. It is life that has given us the ability to survive. It is life that has given so much beauty to this earth. It is life through which God has given the ability to humans to be guided by his prophets through the books that he has given to them.

Life is God's natural gift to humanity. People owe their life to God. Each minute of life is being counted and is valued as much as gold. Life is a gift that nobody can take from another, not at any price. You should take care, treat life the way you would treat the most precious object, and be careful to use it the right way.

As important as a leader's life is, as important as a king's, minister's or governor's life is, as important as Bush's, Obama's, or Blair's life is, as important as Osama's, Zawahiri's or *Mullah* Mohammad Omar's life is, so too is the life of every woman and child, and, finally, of every human being on earth.

Every human being has an obligation to avoid shedding the blood of other humans without a valid reason. Every human has to understand the significance of another person's life as if it was his own. Every human has to understand the importance of the lives of every sister, mother, father, brother, and animal as if they were his own sister, mother, father, brother and animal. And finally, the importance of every human's life should be appreciated like the life of one's own brother or relative; this gift of God must be respected and preserved.

We should ask everybody, in this world and the next, why his life or the lives of his children are more important than that of anyone else? Why should he use each and every possible means for his own preservation only to play with precious lives of others?

After the attacks on the World Trade Centre on 9/11, President Bush, in order to save his own life, was living in the air. He would land for short periods only, for a press conference or some other important event, and wore a flak jacket in the White House. But how many lives did he play with in Afghanistan? How many people did he murder? How many homes and villages did he destroy? This will never be forgotten!

Likewise, when President Obama won the US Presidential election and, stood with his wife and daughters on Capitol Hill, he delivered his inauguration speech behind sheets of bullet-proof glass. But now, with the invaders' surge, he will take the lives of many Afghans. President Obama! You should know that the lives of our children are just as important to us as your daughters' lives are to you!

Your life is important to you, and that blackguard Bush's life is important to him. This is why I wrote this memoir, so that people should understand that the lives of others are also important.

There are four main things that I wish to achieve by writing this book.

First: It is everybody's responsibility to know that his or her life is no more important than the life of any king or beggar, young or old, man or woman, black or white.

Second: Whoever thinks that it is his or her right to defend himself, his territory and his honour should also know that other people in other places on the earth also have the right to live and defend their lives, their territory and their honour.

Third: That those who are unfamiliar with the real culture of the Afghans might do well to increase their knowledge and understanding.

Fourth: The world should realise how bad the situation for Afghans is, and how oppressed they are. People should be kind and compassionate to them.

I am a part of Afghan society, and have lived through various episodes in its recent history. I am familiar with it. I have had the privilege to take positive and negative memories with me from every decade I have seen and from every person I have talked to. I had a rich life and I hope that others can learn and benefit from my experience.

May God grant that this book will benefit present and future generations.

Mullah Abdul Salam Zaeef   *Kabul, March 2009*

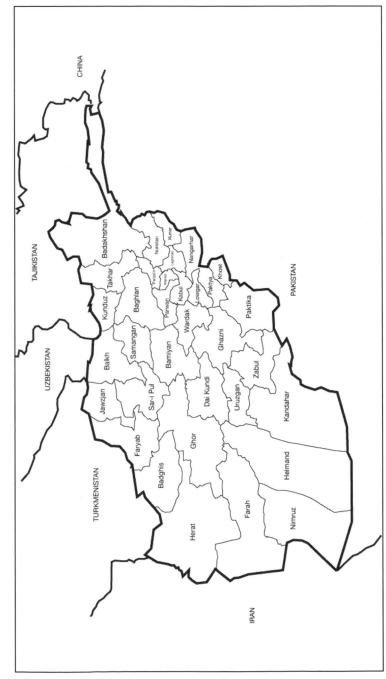

Afghanistan's provinces (as of October 2009)

Southern Afghanistan

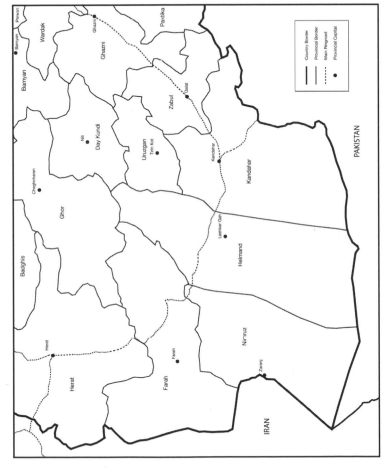

		Country Border
		Provincial Border
•		Main Ringroad
		Provincial Capital

Parwan
Bamyan •
Bamyan
Wardak
Ghazni •
Ghazni
Paktika
Nili •
Day Kundi
Zabul
Qalat •
Uruzgan
Trim Kot •
Chaghcharan •
Ghor
Kandahar •
Kandahar
Badghis
Lashkar Gah •
Helmand
Herat •
Herat
Farah •
Farah
Nimruz
Zaranj •
IRAN
PAKISTAN

1

DEATH AT HOME

I was born in the small village of Zangiabad[1] in 1968. Zahir Shah,[2] the Pashtun King who ruled from 1933 to 1973, was still on the throne, and the country was peaceful. Under his reign students flocked to the universities and foreign tourists travelled throughout the country. Fate had withheld its judgement: the government was strong and the people were content.

My family isn't originally from Kandahar. We had only moved to its western district of Panjwayi[3] a few years before I was born. Tribal clashes over land had broken out in our home village of Jaldak,[4] half-way between Kandahar and Kabul, and dozens had perished in the fight. One of my uncles, *Mullah* Nezam, was accused of killing sixteen people. The government set out to catch him, dispatching troops to Jaldak, and he went into hiding.

When blood is spilled in a tribal feud, the Pashtun code of honour demands revenge. My family was scared; the government was looking for *Mullah* Nezam, and the fighting between the tribes was likely to continue. Along with his two other brothers and the rest of the family, my father decided to leave our birthplace in Zabul[5] to try to avoid further bloodshed. This is how my family came to live in Zangiabad, the village where I was born.

For *Mullah* Nezam, the events in Jaldak proved to be fatal when government forces caught up with him in 1962. He was hiding out in a small village in the Zheray desert together with others involved in the clashes. Government forces moved in on them during the night. Some escaped, but *Mullah* Nezam died along with three or four others in the ensuing fire-fight.

Tribal clashes and feuds, large or small, have cost many Afghan lives. Each Pashtun is a tribesman and, just like my uncle and father before

1

me, I was born into the Ghilzai tribe.[6] The area where the Pashtuns live, home to our many different tribes, stretches from the north-east of Kabul down to the south and the east across the border into Pakistan.[7] As an Afghan you are always more than one thing: your kin, your tribe, your ethnicity and the place you were born; all are part of you. Pashtuns who emigrated long ago to the big cities of Afghanistan, Pakistan or abroad might have forgotten this, but their true identity lies with their tribe, their clan, their family and their relatives. As a foreigner, you can never truly understand what it means to be an Afghan.

My mother was from the same family as my father, as is the custom in the rural south. She had four children with my father, two girls and two boys. I was the second son and her third child. Like most, I remember little of my early childhood. We lived in Zangiabad for a while, but exactly how long I do not know.

My mother was not old when she died, of what I cannot be certain. I have no recollection of her, as I was very young, maybe a year or two old, when it happened. My elder sister told me about her and her death later. There is one thing that I recall from this time, though. The first memory that I have is of my father. He came to his children, took us in his arms, and cried silently. Even though it seems impossible, I still believe this occurred the day my mother died.

My father was a compassionate man. He did not beat or yell at us. A religious scholar who had devoted his life to the study of Islam, he was known for his generosity and kindness. My grandfather had made great sacrifices so that he could attend good religious schools, learn the way of Islam and become a true scholar and man of God. He did the same for us. Even though we talked little about my mother after her death, I know that she was an educated woman. She had grown up in a family that allowed and wished for all their children to learn and study the teachings of the Holy *Qur'an*[8] and *Sunna*.[9] Both of our parents placed a high value on education and tried to present us with as many opportunities as they could.

After our mother died, we first moved in with another uncle, Musa Jan, whose wife took care of us children. My father was teaching at a local *madrassa*[10] and was very busy so we did not see much of him. Life at my uncle's house was good even though the loosely woven threads of history had already started to unravel around us.

* * *

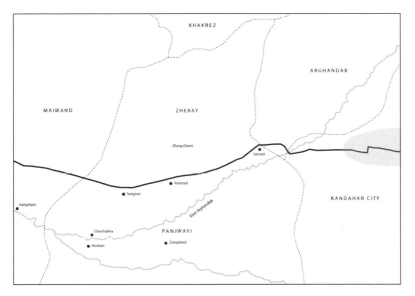

Districts west of Kandahar City

My father, my sisters and I left Zangiabad and my uncle's house to move to another village, Mushan,[11] when I was two years old, my brother Rahmatullah, who was a few years older than me, having already left home to pursue his studies in Pashmol.[12]

My father had become the *mullah*[13] in a local mosque and was working long hours teaching and studying. The women of the village took good care of us, but at night we were often lonely and scared in the mud brick house with its small courtyard. Wolves would howl around the village in the orchards and fields. There was no electricity or running water. Darkness fell swiftly and covered the land like a black veil. Packs of dogs roamed the cramped alleys between the houses, barking and fighting for the little food they could rummage for outside the houses.

Once, late at night, when my father still hadn't come home from the mosque, I sat huddled together with my sister in the courtyard. The wolves had been howling near the village since dusk, and now night had fallen. Each time one of them roared at the moon, they seemed closer than before. We shrieked in fear, on edge for every sound. Holding each other close and listening in the darkness, we thought we could hear the wolves scratching at the gate, moving from one corner of the house to the other along the low mud brick walls. We screamed out in panic until a neighbour came rushing into the yard. She shepherded us into the house and we snuggled up to her while she stroked our heads and told us stories of kings, princes and princesses. I still remember one of the tales from that night. She stayed with us until our father returned.

My younger sister died in Mushan, although I am not sure what she died of. There were many deaths in the villages in 1971 and 1972, after a drought, and some families lost their entire harvest. The famine[14] was worst in central and northern Afghanistan, where thousands perished of starvation and many more left their villages in search of food and water. My father was heartbroken by the loss of his wife and child. We moved to Rangrezan, where he became the *Imam*[15] of a small mosque.

* * *

Rangrezan[16] was—and still is—a small village, smaller than Mushan. It had no paved roads, no running water and no electricity, not even a generator. A few houses, each fortified with mud brick walls huddled close to each other, that was Rangrezan.

The gardens and fields of the arid land in and around the village were irrigated through a system of channels and basins fed by little rivers and streams that run down from the mountains to the north and the east. Pomegranates and grapes were the main crops. Centuries ago, medieval Arab historians referred to them as being the best in the world.

We moved there in the final days of the reign of Zahir Shah, before the Communists came to power and Afghanistan started to drown in the swell of agony that washed through the country, destroying the basins and channels, leaving its fields and gardens dry.

Even though my father was an educated man and a scholar of Islam, my family was no different from any other rural family. My own situation was also the same as that of any other boy. Life was difficult; we were poor and my father struggled to put food on the table. As the local *Imam*, the tuition and guidance of the community were his principal obligations. He would recite each of the five daily prayers in the mosque, leaving at dawn for *fajr*, the morning prayer performed at sunrise.

Most days he would return a few hours later. After we had eaten breakfast together, my sister and I would accompany him to the mosque for the rest of the morning to study. Like every Afghan child, we used the *Al Qaeda* textbook[17] in order to learn how to read and write. In the afternoon we would return for lunch. My father would often lie down for a while before we all went back to the mosque. He was already very old by then, but he still hoped that he would get married again and give us a new mother. He would tell us, "Just you wait! Soon you will have a new mother and I a new wife. Maybe even new siblings". But he never remarried.

In the afternoon we continued our studies. When my father had no time to teach us himself, one of his apprentices would help. The traditional religious education started with basic reading and writing exercises followed by closer study and memorisation of key religious phrases and texts. At the time I was learning the basics of the Pashtu[18] alphabet and some arithmetic from textbooks.

Winters in Mushan were freezing. We had no proper winter clothes and often not enough firewood to heat the small room we all lived in during the cold months. Once I dropped my *Al Qaeda* textbook into the fire; it had been so cold that I was sitting too close to the glowing embers. My book went up in flames and I helplessly sat and watched the pages curl, brown and blacken at the edges.

My father was a well known *Imam* and people from distant villages sought his help and guidance. He often brought home the sick or the possessed, and would perform rituals and pray together with them, reading *suras*[19] from the *Qur'an* or writing them *tawiiz*.[20] There are times when faith works where medicine cannot.

He earned very little, but even though we didn't have much, my father would still not take money from the people, not even the *zakat*.[21] Nevertheless, people would find a way secretly to slip some money into his waistcoat pockets or to leave it under pillows, blankets or in empty food-bowls. Each night when he came home, or when guests left, we would rush up to him and go through his pockets, turn over every pillow and search under every mattress. Most times we found a few rupees and would run around him, waving the money above our heads.

Sometimes one of our uncles would visit us along with their children. I had many cousins but liked Mohammad Aslam and Abdul Bari the best. We were all the same age, and would play for hours in the yard or outside on the street in front of our house next to the little stream. We led our armies into fierce battles, slaying our enemies to defend our kingdoms. We ruled our land just like ministers and kings, at times demanding tax for the right of passage, or negotiating deals and truces. I think this is what all children do around the world.

Looking back now, after almost forty years, I have to smile sadly when I think about those games I played with my cousins. I never would have thought that our clowning around in the shade of the pomegranate bushes and among the dusty alleys in Mushan would be enacted in reality some years later, or that the battles we imagined would soon sweep over us, the country left a ruin in its wake.

As much as we celebrated when an uncle came to visit, we were sad when they had to leave. We would beg them to stay, or we would beg our father to allow us to go with them. We would stamp on the ground and kick against the door, crying and screaming. Of course it did not help.

* * *

In the summer of 1975, my father died in Rangrezan. He got up in the middle of the night, earlier than was his habit. Later, when it was time for the night prayer, I woke up and lay still, listening to my father in the moonlit darkness. I could only make out parts of the words he was whispering, and I saw tears running down his face.

He was praying for us children, asking God for our safety, for our futures and for our health. I had never heard him pray like that before, but I did not think much of it at the time. He left the house early to pray *eshraq*[22] at the mosque.

When he returned, he seemed to be in pain. I could see tears in his eyes when he looked at us, but he said nothing, turned away, and went into his room. I was scared. An hour passed before he called for my sister. He asked her to go and get the neighbours. Neither I nor my sister understood what was happening. I looked at my father lying on his bed, his face moist with tears and strained with pain. The neighbours came, an old woman and a man. We knew them well and often played with their children.

The man went straight to my father and took his pulse at his wrist. Immediately he started to recite *Surat Yasin Sharif*:[23]

$$ إِنَّا نَحْنُ نُحْىِ ٱلْمَوْتَىٰ وَنَكْتُبُ مَا قَدَّمُوا۟ وَءَاثَـٰرَهُمْ ۚ وَكُلَّ شَىْءٍ $$
$$ {}^{24} أَحْصَيْنَـٰهُ فِىٓ إِمَامٍ مُّبِينٍ ۝ $$

He turned to us and told us to leave the room. After a short while the old woman came out of my father's room. Her face was pale when she walked over to my sister and I. Stroking our heads all the while, she burst out in tears, and cried out loud. Then all of a sudden she fainted and collapsed on the floor.

We were shocked and ran to my father's room to tell him what had happened. We called out to him: "Father! Father! Come quick, look what happened to the aunt!"[25] But my father did not answer. When we looked at him we saw that the neighbour had bound his lower jaw to his head with a white strip of cloth as is the custom once someone dies. We shouted again: "Father! Father!" But it was only his body that was lying on the bed. He had died a few moments earlier.

The man tried to shoo us from the room but we screamed and cried, rolling in the dust on the floor. Soon he too started to cry. None of our relatives was there to console us. Not even an uncle or an aunt, nor my older brother. We were alone. My father had died. I was seven years old.

Soon the house was crowded with men and women.[26] Another woman took us to her own house, away from the milling villagers. She spoke softly and took pity on us.

"Your father is alive", she said. "He is only a little ill. He will get better soon".

She told us not to cry, and to be patient. She produced some sweets from the folds of her clothes and tried to cheer us up.

My brother was in Mushan, and some cousins were staying in Pashmol and Charshakha. Our maternal uncle was in Zangiabad. I still don't know how they were informed about my father's passing, but by the time of the afternoon prayer they had all arrived in Rangrezan. My sister and I were back at the house, sitting in the corner of the room, now crammed with our relatives. My brother, cousins and uncles came over to us from time to time, giving us money or sweets, trying to make us forget.

Later that same afternoon, one of our cousins took us back with him to his house in Charshakha.[27] That morning was the last time I saw my father. His body was buried in the cemetery on the riverside, near to other relatives of ours who had passed away. The burial ceremony took place in my cousin's house. Soon after, friends and family returned to their homes. Our brother went back to pursue his studies, and my sister and I were left alone at my cousin's house in Charshakha.

***

We stayed with them for one and a half years. In the mornings I would go to the mosque to study and in the afternoon I helped out at home. I looked after the sheep, goats and cows, cleaning out the barn and feeding them. It was a small house but there was enough space for all of us. I slept in one room with my aunt, and my cousins[28] shared another room.

My father had promised my sister in marriage to one of our relatives at a very young age. After his death, the family of the groom thought it best to hold the wedding earlier so that she could move in with her new husband and family. A wedding party was held at the groom's house. On the day of her wedding I was upset and cried a lot. My sister was the only person left that truly cared about me, and with whom I had grown up.

When the party was over we returned to my cousin's house. I felt abandoned and worried about what would happen to me. I did not eat or drink, and stopped studying altogether. Nothing seemed to make sense. I did not know what I should do, or what would come next. Each time my elder brother Rahmatullah came to visit I begged him to take me with him, but each time he refused. He was still studying and living with relatives. Back then, I didn't understand him.

Some time passed before my cousin brought me to my maternal uncle so that I could continue with my studies. I don't remember how long I stayed with them. My uncle was a cruel man. He would often raise his hand against me or put a stick to my back. His wife, however, was kind and cared for of me.

I was studying at a local *madrassa* in Sangisar[29] and enrolled in a class led by *Mullah* Neamatullah. He had been one of my father's apprentices in Mushan and had great affection for me. The senior religious instructor at the school was *Mawlawi*[30] Niaz Mohammad.[31] He too had known my father, and bought clothes for me and the textbooks I needed to continue my education.

Mawlawi Niaz Mohammad was a prominent provincial supporter of Noor Mohammad Taraki,[32] a dominant figure of the Communist *Khalq*[33] faction that had formed following a split from the Afghan People's Democratic Party[34] in the late 1960s. When Taraki came to power in the spring of 1978, Niaz Mohammad switched allegiances and became a vocal supporter of the Communists. He even said that Taraki was an associate and envoy of the *Imam-e Mehdi*[35] at that time. All his students left him soon after he started to support Taraki. Most of them went to Pakistan, others to different *Mawlawi*s elsewhere in the region. I went to school in Kandahar City as my relatives thought it best that I receive a secular education while pursuing my religious studies at the *madrassa*.

I passed the examination for the fourth grade and enrolled in primary school, attending classes in Kandahar for a year. The city was alive at that time: the granary was full, water was plentiful throughout the province, and I remember people loved to play volleyball (we did not start playing football in Kandahar until much later).

One day I returned to Sangisar to see *Mawlawi* Niaz Mohammad. *Mawlawi Saheb*[36] had changed. His support for Taraki had grown even stronger. As soon as we sat down and tea was served, he asked me: "Son! Have you filled in the form or not?".

After the coup, Taraki had moved fast, introducing legislation for land reform[37] as one of his prized projects. He wanted to redistribute the land among the people. Everyone could apply and would receive up to ten *jeribs*[38] per person. *Mullah* Neamatullah had talked about it in Kandahar. He had told us that we should take great care. It was un-Islamic, he said, to take the land and we should resist the temptation of wealth. So I answered: "*Mawlawi Saheb*! Other authorities have told us that the land belongs to other people. And to take property from others is a sin. How can I take this land?".

"This is the last share of the world's wealth, son", he replied. "Those who don't take part now will remain landless forever". As I was young, he said that he would help me. "You should most definitely do this!" he insisted. "The King," he said, "is in charge. If he decides something then we should not doubt it. We must obey." I stayed there overnight and left the next day for the city without saying goodbye to *Mawlawi Saheb*.

Mullah Neamatullah Akhund, my instructor, and all the other scholars had fled to Pakistan. No one I knew had stayed. *Sayyeds*,[39] *Khans*,[40] *Maliks*[41] and *Mullah*s were all being persecuted by the government. Educated people living in the districts had advised the Communists that the best way to retain control of the countryside would be to imprison the local power holders. Many of them ended up in jail, but few were ever seen again.

* * *

It was 1978, and I was barely ten years old when the Communists— led by Taraki and Hafizullah Amin[42]—took power in a coup. They

9

started introducing Communist ideas and policies early, and the pace of reform was brisk. One of their first edicts addressed the issue of land reform that *Mawlawi* Niaz Mohammad had urged me to take advantage of. Fighting had already broken out around the country. They tried to capture prominent commanders and were persecuting the *Taliban*.

There is a common misconception that "the *Taliban*" only came into being in 1994. In fact, the word *Taliban* is the plural form of *Talib*, meaning 'student'. As such, as long as there have been *madrassas*, there have been religious students or *Taliban*. The *Taliban* mostly eschewed politics, but the government tried to draw them in by pressuring them to be involved in the land reform, or by threatening them in other ways.

In turn, the *Taliban* started to target government supporters and *Mawlawi* Niaz Mohammad and *Mawlawi* Mir Hatem[43] were both killed in this way. I was studying at the time and wasn't particularly interested in what was happening around me, but I heard people talk about these things, about the time of *kufr*.[44]

The Soviet Union was supporting the new government formed by the *Khalq* faction and an agreement of friendship, cooperation and good neighbourliness was signed. There was talk among the elders and my cousins; people were scared. Rumours about spies were rife and people disappeared without trace. The government ruthlessly suppressed the opposition.

The *mujahedeen*[45] began a guerrilla campaign against the government forces, and Taraki and Amin sent fighter planes to attack the *mujahedeen* strongholds in the Registan desert south of Kandahar city and the lush fields of Panjwayi, the river valley where I grew up. We heard the planes every day, and the fighting spread. Thousands started to flee Afghanistan, seeking refuge in Pakistan, Iran, and beyond. The efforts of the *mujahedeen* were organised from the areas bordering Pakistan, and the early days of the campaign were difficult as the Communists fought with overwhelming force.

I moved with my sister to Sanzari,[46] a *mujahedeen* hideout a few kilometres west of the city, as the fighting continued to spread from village to village. Supporters of the new government were clashing with the *mujahedeen*, while Taraki's men were arming villages and small militias, handing out weapons in local markets. *Mujahedeen* and *Taliban* who passed through often fell victim to an ambush in the middle of a village.

The fighters sometimes lasted all night. I would lay awake in my bed listening to bursts of machine gun fire and the explosions of shells and bombs. The Pashtuns were rising against the interference of Kabul and Taraki's puppet government. The south was at war.

Word reached me that I should return to my cousin's house in Zangiabad. All of my relatives still living in Afghanistan had gathered and were preparing to flee over the mountains into Pakistan. They said that the situation was getting worse each day and that fighting would soon dramatically escalate throughout the south. We decided to leave as soon as possible. Two of my uncles joined the *mujahedeen*. The conflict spread and the river of blood swelled to a stream that flowed from one village to the next, from one district to the other, and from provinces to regions until Afghanistan was finally submerged.

2

THE CAMPS

After the Communist coup of April 1978, more people began fleeing to Pakistan, Iran and other countries. A number of Afghan politicians also took refuge there in order to campaign against the Afghan government, with the active help of the Pakistani authorities. Edict no. 8—which legalized the confiscation and sharing out of other peoples' lands and properties—and edict no. 7—which ordered women to be educated and imposed a maximum wedding dowry of three hundred Afghanis—were rejected by the people as being inappropriate and *haram*.[1]

The Afghan refugees[2] were settled in various camps in the border areas of Pakistan as well as in Baluchistan. The political parties that later developed issued identity cards for party members which gave them freedom of movement throughout the country. Residents did not have any problems doing business or commerce. Pakistan became rich off the refugees, both economically and politically.

Charitable institutions like the UN and NGOs rushed to Pakistan and opened many offices there. America was especially active as the main player in the game. In order to defeat its rival, the Soviet Union, which backed the Communist regime in Kabul, became extremely close to Pakistan, but when the Red Army started to lose its foothold in Afghanistan the assistance and attention of the West also waned.

With the decline in western assistance, Pakistan's attitude to the refugees also hardened. Our problems with the government in Islamabad increased; some refugees were even forced to leave certain regions and forcibly repatriated into Afghanistan, or were displaced to arid regions to build new houses for themselves.

I remember little about our decision to flee to Pakistan and leave our birthplace behind. I remember only the biting cold and hunger, that the

13

journey was difficult and it feelt scared. We left in January 1979, when the fighting in southern Afghanistan had intensified. The first wave of refugees had begun to leave, and it didn't seem that things would improve in the near future. The land reform bill had been passed a month earlier, and two of my uncles had joined the *mujahedeen*. It was clear that we could no longer stay in Afghanistan. Our convoy of seven vehicles left Zangiabad in the middle of the night, heading south for Pakistan. We had packed up a few of our belongings, but had no space to take my father's books. Our trip took us down into the Reg desert before we reached Sre Tsahan. It was the first time I had crossed the border into a different country.

It had already become dangerous to travel on the roads, so our small convoy moved only during the night, with our lights switched off to avoid being spotted. Driving slowly through the back roads, we stayed away from the major highways. When we reached the slopes of the mountains we would get out and walk alongside the cars, even abandoning them altogether at some points. Motorcyclists carried us part of the way, with up to four people squeezed onto one bike at times. The dust and dirt tracks became smaller and smaller as we edged our way across the ancient smuggling routes that have always existed between Afghanistan and Pakistan. It took us three days and three nights to reach our destination.

On the other side of the border a camp had been set up outside Chaman.[3] The Pakistani government would use it as a hub for the millions of Afghans who streamed into their country over the coming years. Refugees got further instructions about where to go, or were brought to other camps. We arrived in the early morning and stayed for a few hours in the camp before climbing into the back of a truck along with several other families. We stood side-by-side like cattle, pressed into the back all the way to Quetta. From there we were brought to Nushki.

Pakistan had realized that it would face a major wave of Afghan refugees and was assigning areas like Nushki in which they could settle. Other relatives of ours had arrived at the camp a few days before us, and we moved into the area next to their tents. Even though the camp was new, several distinct sections had already been established. Despite being run by the Pakistani government, the refugees in the camp had their own form of administration; camp and section leaders were elected—one of whom was my cousin—and appointed on the basis of seniority. They sought to maintain order and talked to the Pakistani authorities on our behalf. When we arrived the camp lacked even the most basic facilities, and Pakistan's government agencies were slow to provide them. There was no proper water supply system, no health services and no clinics. The camp lay in the middle of a desert, and the sun bore down on our heads. The heat was oppressive and at times unbearable. Our tents became ovens; some even burned their hands just by touching the tents' canvas walls.

There was a rationing system for water. At times the government would bring potable water in trucks, but it was never enough and we were forced to fetch water from the nearby villages. The local Baluch people have a different culture from ours, and the relationship between them and the Afghans came under serious strain soon after the camp was established and began to expand.

The growing number of refugees scoured the surrounding area for water and brushwood which started to anger the Baluchis who felt threatened by the ever-expanding camp. Hostilities took on their own momentum and the Afghan refugees and local villagers were soon engaged in bloody clashes. Two refugees and four locals were killed. The Pakistani government surrounded the camp, and sealed off all the entry and exit points.

They also tried to mediate between the Baluch villages and the refugees, promising to supply the camp with the much-needed water in tankers. Unfortunately the water was of such poor quality that we could not drink it. The atmosphere in the camp—which was still sealed off—deteriorated inexorably and it slowly became apparent that no solution could be found to the problems. It is hard to say what the real reason for these hostilities was. I personally believe that the Baluch people never accepted the fact that the government had decided to establish a camp in their area from the outset. But in the end they were the victors, as the authorities closed the camp and transferred all the refugees to a new area several kilometres away.

Government trucks pulled up at the camp in the middle of the night. We were given only a few hours to pack up our belongings before being transported to Sher Jan Agha, the site of a small desert oasis and *ziarat*.[4] We stayed there for two days while the Pakistani authorities prepared a new refugee camp for us. I remember Sher Jan Agha well; I spent my time swimming and even found a ten rupee coin in the sand. On the third day we were brought to the new camp which was called Panjpayi.[5]

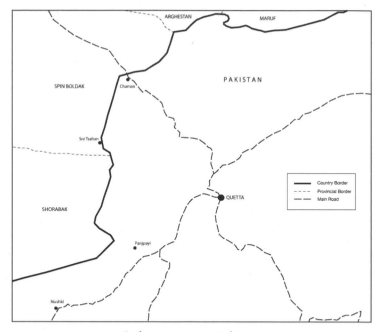

Refugee camps in Pakistan

When we arrived there, some 75 kilometres west of Quetta, we found nothing but wilderness. The sun was already setting when the truck finally came to a stop at the end of a small dirt track. We tried our best to improvise for the night. In these first days everyone was busy cutting down trees and clearing the ground, building small huts and a mosque out of wood. We set up the tents we had brought with us and tried to settle down as best we could. Around our makeshift huts we laid fences made of *osh murghai*, a type of thorn bush.

The land was dry and the weather as hot as in Nushki. We found nests of scorpions, snakes and tarantulas everywhere. Every night when we lit the small kerosene lamp in our tent three or four scorpions would come out of the dark, scuttling towards us. There was no water and during the first days we were forced to ration what we had brought in buckets and canisters. We even used earth and sand for our ablutions[6] before prayer.

The nearest wells were several kilometres away from the camp at a local village. I was sent to fetch water along with the other children. Each morning we would go to the well with our buckets. By the time we returned it was already time for the afternoon prayer. It was a long way and the buckets were heavy. We were usually exhausted when we we reached the camp.

* * *

Fifteen families of my relatives, uncles and cousins were living together in the camp. We organized a complete *jama'at*[7] for congregational prayers in the brushwood mosque. Every day new refugees arrived; the stream was seemingly endless, and the camp grew fast. Soon Panjpayi grew from a few hundred refugees to a few hundred thousand, complete with dozens of makeshift mosques. The camp became an Afghan city in the middle of a barren land and the Pakistani authorities were soon overwhelmed by the sheer number of refugees.

While food and basic necessities like flour, soap, tea, matches and milk powder were available and distributed to all, there wasn't enough water. There was no local supply and the number of trucks was limited. The wells were far away, and even though some had brought their donkeys with them we never managed to bring enough water for everyone. Across the camp people began digging wells, searching desperately for water.

At a depth of 31 metres, we finally found water. The news spread quickly throughout the camp and people were overjoyed; it felt like *Eid*,[8] the holiest of our religious festivals. Friends and relative went around the camp congratulating each other on the success of the wells. It took a few days to complete the work to regulate the flow, but soon everyone was able to take water from them.

Many of those who came from Afghanistan brought news about the Russian invasion in December 1979. Outside the capital, Kabul, uprisings were increasingly common. These took place first in Kunar in the north-east and then in Herat in the west. In Kandahar there were some demonstrations against the Soviets, initially in Panjwayi. Although these were peaceful the Russians did not tolerate such open dissent and dispersed the demonstrators, opening fire and bombing them. By now, the *mujahedeen* were operating from the desert in Registan, conducting operations at night and retreating back to their bases during the day.

There were many *mullah*s among the refugees and we studied at the mosque twice a day. Later, a *madrassa* was established by Sher Mohammad Khan.[9] He founded and managed the Imam Abu Hanifa *madrassa*.

The building doubled as a school and offered classes up to the tenth grade. Some of the children from our camp attended classes there and I also took the admissions exam and passed for entry to the sixth grade.

We went there every morning to study. The school was far away and we had to get up at six in the morning, walking for over an hour to reach it. In the afternoons we would gather together in a small assembly with *Mawlawi* Hanifa *Saheb* who attended to our religious studies. I was one of a group of seven from Panjpayi camp who attended the *madrassa*. I studied hard at school and passed the sixth and seventh grades. I still remember that I received 480 points in the final examination of the seventh grade, the best result of the entire class. For the eighth grade, I was appointed class captain.

I liked my time at school and enjoyed studying. My instructors were happy with me, and in turn I was happy with them. I followed their advice and instructions and behaved well in class. My love of learning never deserted me, even when I was fighting the Russians.

* * *

Many small villages or settlements lay along the way to the *madrassa*. The largest of these was Mushwanu, from which thirty or so other students of different ages were studying together with us. One of these was the captain of the ninth grade, a young man of about sixteen or seventeen years of age. They did not like us, and we did not like them. Each day little fights and scuffles would take place because some boy had insulted another.

One day when we were on our way back to the camp we saw the Mushwanu boys waiting for us, shaping for a fight. All we had were the wooden boards on which we used to rest our books when taking notes, while the Mushwanu boys had come armed with sticks and chains. They were making obscene gestures and shouted encouragement to each other, which was hardly necessary given that they outnumbered us four to one. As we approached them, I started talking to my friends. We all agreed that we should stand our ground. I would attack the biggest of them, and the others would simultaneously attack each of the other boys. We all knew that we needed to strike our opponents with the first blow. When you become weak you need to prepare yourself, you need to use whatever you have. That day all we had to do was to scare the Mushwanu boys away by hitting a few of them as hard as possible. As we drew closer they started cursing us and calling us names. We tried to reason with them, telling them that swearing and cursing were sins. When the biggest of the boys came within my reach, I raised my school-board and without warning or further argument hit him as hard as I could on the head with the sharp edge. He fell backwards to the ground; his head was badly injured from my blow and blood was gushing out of the wound. As he fell to the ground he screamed and cried: "He killed me! He killed me!"

I turned to the boy next to me. Out of the corner of my eye I could see that all my friends had stood firm and attacked the enemy, who fled for their village. None of my friends was hurt, and we continued on our way home, bursting with excitement as we re-enacted scenes from the fight. We told all our friends about the fight, but soon elders from Mushwanu village arrived to complain.

Seven of their boys had been injured. The boy I had hit on the head had been hospitalized. Even though the dispute was arbitrated by the elders, we were not allowed to go back to school and nor to attend the *madrassa*, but continued our religious education at the local mosque in the camp.

* * *

Panjpayi was soon divided into several sections. In our area everyone was from Kandahar, while Camp 2 was filled with people from the south-eastern province of Ghazni and so forth. By this point the Pakistani government had appointed a commissioner to oversee the camp as a whole.

I would see *mujahedeen* heading to Afghanistan to fight, or sometimes coming back with their wounded. The conflict in Afghanistan between the Soviet Union and their puppet government on the one side, and the *mujahedeen* on the other, had been raging for four years already. Many who had left the camp and crossed the border had not returned. Every family had lost relatives, martyred in the fight for their homeland. Many of my relatives joined the *mujahedeen* fronts[10] in rotation.[11] At the mosques the *mullahs* were preaching to us about the holy *jihad*,[12] about the obligation to all Muslims, about paradise, and about our homeland.

Mawlawi Ubaidullah,[13] who was a member of Sayyaf's party,[14] was one of the elders of our camp. He led a large number of *mujahedeen*, many of whom had affiliations with other parties and groups as well. Some people joined the *jihad* on the *Taliban* fronts, some with other factions. One well-known *mujahed* from our village was *Mullah* Shahzada,[15] later to be martyred on the front lines. He participated in the *jihad* together with the late *Qari* Shahzada[16] who was active on the front of *Mullah* Mohammad Sadiq Akhund[17] in Nelgham.

Like most young men at that time, I was eager to join in. We all wanted to fight the Russians. I often talked about it with my friends when we saw the *mujahedeen* leaving. I wanted to fulfil my obligation to *Allah* and free my homeland from the godless Soviet soldiers. But I had no money to get there, and my relatives and instructors at the *madrassa* would not allow me to join in the struggle. They believed in the idea of *jihad*, but weren't willing to risk the life of one of their sons.

My cousin advised me to focus on my studies for now, and that maybe we could join the *jihad* later. "You will see", he would tell me. "Studying is good for you. It gives you a future". I started to save all the money I could get my hands on. All in all I saved perhaps one hundred Pakistani rupees,[18] which took me about three months. I was fifteen years old when I left for Afghanistan. I didn't tell any of my relatives or friends.

I had started my *jihad*.

3

THE *JIHAD*

I left for Chaman in a bus with nothing but the clothes on my back and one hundred rupees in my pocket. It was the summer of 1983, and the passes were clear so many *mujahedeen* moved from the camps to Afghanistan and back. I joined a small group that was heading for Kandahar. One of my religious teachers, Salam Agha, was there so he took me with him across the border. We walked all the way, taking the smuggling routes in the middle of the night.

The border wasn't marked so I don't know exactly when we crossed over into Afghanistan, but I remember that I was happy. We walked through Registan's desert till we reached Bolak Neka and from we rode camels through Naieb Wali and Tangi. After three days and two nights we arrived in the Pashmol valley, lush with wheat fields and grape vines.

By this time, the *jihad* was at least three years old, and the *mujahedeen* had found their battlegrounds in the districts of Kandahar. Soviet troops and *mujahedeen* fighters were fighting on a regular basis, moving from one district to the next. While we used the advantages of our mobility and knowledge of the local terrain, the Russians relied heavily on their superior firepower and air support. I later learned that it was around this time that the Russians brought in extra troops[1] specifically trained to fight our style of war, but I'm not sure how much this made a difference.

I had heard that Commander Abdul Raziq[2] was leading a front in Pashmol and joined up with him and his men. At the outset I thought that he was a good commander and a good man, but it didn't take long for me to realize that his primary concerns were protecting his own land and property.

21

I stayed with Raziq for nearly two months and carried out two operations with him and his men. I spent the rest of my time taking care of his private affairs and those of other *mujahedeen*. We would clean our guns once every week, and sometimes do target practice. Even though I had my first taste of *jihad* with Raziq and his fighters, learning how to handle weapons and how to behave under fire, I soon became disillusioned. I came to Afghanistan to take part in *jihad*, but found myself carrying out mundane tasks for other people. It was time to leave Raziq. Furthermore, there were no teachers among his men, and I worried that I was learning nothing apart from weapons skills.

I knew that the *Taliban* were fighting in Nelgham[3] under the command of *Mullah* Mohammad Sadiq Akhund but I was afraid to join them. I had some relatives in that same area, some even fighting with *Mullah* Mohammad Sadiq, who would inform my family about my whereabouts if I went there. If my family found out where I was, I would surely be dragged back to the camps in Pakistan. Many people talked about the *Taliban*, even back then. They were respected by other *mujahedeen*. Some of them even consulted the *Taliban* courts to settle their disputes or came to seek advice.

Jihad was not just about fighting; in our view, there had to be a strong educational perspective as well as a provision for justice. People came to the *Taliban* to help them in their disputes. *Mawlawi* Nazar Mohammad[4] was initially the senior judge, but after he was martyred *Mawlawi Sayyed* Mohammad Pasanai *Saheb*[5] took over. A *Taliban* prison in Pashmol was established along with other holding cells throughout the districts under our control.

Most of the *mujahedeen* fronts were very homogeneous, with most people coming from the same background, same tribe, same family, or from the same area. The *Taliban* were different. A group of religious scholars and students with different backgrounds, they transcended the normal coalitions and factions. They were fighting out of their deep religious belief in *jihad* and their faith in God. *Allah* was their only reason for being there, unlike many other *mujahedeen* who fought for money or land.

By the time the orchards were green and the summer was at its peak I decided to go to Nelgham to join the *Taliban*. At least there I could be sure that while fighting I also would receive an education. I asked around for directions and walked to Nelgham. After I arrived I soon ran into *Hajji*[6] Mohammad Gul Aka,[7] a former neighbour of ours from

Panjpayi. Other relatives of mine were fighting for *Mullah* Mohammad Sadiq. We were happy to see each other even though I was still afraid that they would inform my family.

* * *

I had only been in Nelgham for a few days when Soviet forces and the Afghan army encircled our position. Their artillery fire and air raids turned night to day; the shells and bombs tore apart the land, leaving only ruins behind. There were graves everywhere. I remember the contorted faces of men and women screaming at the countless funerals. The few civilians still living in the area fled, leaving their houses and farms while the Russian airplanes poured bombs like water.

It seemed that the Russian tanks and artillery could attack our position forever while we stayed put. The earth shook for ten days straight. By then we had run out of everything, with just a handful of bullets and one grenade left. The Russians stood firm and held their positions. We decided to retreat and made a run for Zangiabad. It was a rough business and four *mujahedeen* were martyred during the escape.

There were about seventy *mujahedeen* in Zangiabad, who had between them three Kalashnikovs, one rifle, one Balazan, one Jaghuri[8]

Western Kandahar province during the 1980s *jihad*

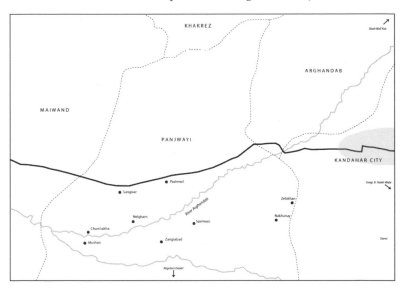

23

and one RPG, which was not even an original.[9] I had one of the Kalashnikovs and thanked God for it. The Soviet forces had already encircled the entire region and the fighting began in Zangiabad.

In Registan, Rud Panjwayi, Charshakha and from Mushan, the Russians and Afghan government forces strengthened their positions by establishing encircling belts. Planes carried out missions the entire day. Groups of four or six Russian planes would attack our positions. At one point we even counted fourteen planes unleashing hell on the tiny region. Tanks could be heard everywhere, and the hills were blackened by explosions and gunpowder. Everyone who was able to tried to flee. The village of Sperwan and the district centre of Panjwayi were flooded with refugees; several families often shared the same house, with more than twenty people pressed into one tiny room.

After ten or so days the Russians left Panjwayi and moved on Pashmol. Hundreds of *mujahedeen* and civilians were killed in the battle of Zangiabad and many houses and orchards were destroyed. A few *mujahedeen* followed the Russians and joined the front in Pashmol. We put up strong resistance there in Pashmol, and fighting continued for almost two weeks. Both sides sustained heavy casualties, and many *mujahedeen* were martyred. Dozens of tanks were set on fire. Finally the *mujahedeen* were driven out of the region again.

Among the many *mujahedeen* and civilians killed in the fighting in Pashmol, two senior *mujahedeen* commanders, *Qazi Mawlawi* Nazar Mohammad—the first *Taliban* judge who preceded *Mawlawi Sayyed* Mohammad Pasanai *Saheb*—and another strong *mujahed*, *Mullah* Khawas Akhund,[10] were martyred. His *mujahedeen* kept on fighting, however, not giving an inch of land to the Soviet forces without a battle, moving from village to village, from one region to the next.

The battles of Pashmol and Zangiabad were typical of the war between the Soviets and the *mujahedeen*. The *mujahedeen* always had fewer troops, less training and used antiquated weapons, but still we managed to wage a guerrilla war that exploited the weaknesses of the large immobile 40th Army.[11] We established resupply and retreat routes. If the Russians drew too close or if the *mujahedeen* sustained too many casualties, they withdrew towards Arghandab, Sangisar or Zangiabad, and if they came under pressure in Arghandab they then withdrew towards Mahalajat, Shah Wali Kot and Panjwayi. Later, when the Russians removed their forces, the *mujahedeen* would return to their original positions. Many times we moved, engaged, fled and regrouped, much like the "*Taliban*" do nowadays.

Throughout Afghanistan, the *mujahedeen* had special cemeteries reserved for martyrs. Many of the casualties of the battlefield could not be treated, however, and often it could take as long as ten to fifteen days until a doctor or medic could treat the wounded. The Russian tactic of encircling the *mujahedeen* positions made it difficult to transport our wounded out of the area. Wounds would become infected, and thus even small injuries killed many fighters. I remember seeing ten to twelve wounded *mujahedeen* in the small crowded rooms they used as a base. Those who had attended a medical training course[12] would do their best to treat the wounded.

When the Russians finally pulled out of Pashmol and the *mujahedeen* and villagers returned to their houses, they found a devastated landscape. The Russian operations had been brutal, and the scenes there belied any traces of humanity.

Even though the *mujahedeen* had left Pashmol, some civilians had stayed in their houses to protect their livestock. The Russians had killed everything they found. The air was heavy with the reek of decaying flesh, and dead bodies of men, women and children were scattered among the remains of cows, sheep and chickens. The villagers who returned were busy for days, trying to bury relatives, friends and carcasses.

* * *

The Russians had established a big army base in the Zheray[13] desert that held DC guns, BM40, BM16, Ouragan and other heavy weaponry and artillery. They would target the villages and houses on the riverside throughout the day and night for no particular reason. When they launched operations they would set the earth on fire: artillery shells would rain down on the houses and villages, and bombs dropped from the sky. They smashed their way through Arghandab, Mahalajat, Zalakhan and towards Nakhunay. When they started their operations they were met by a unified front of several *mujahedeen* groups, in which the individual fronts supported and re-enforced each other. It was always this way: whenever fighting started anywhere in the south, *mujahedeen* from neighbouring areas would hurry to support one another.

We travelled on foot, each carrying our own ammunition, although later we occasionally found tractors and cars as transport. Back roads and smuggling tracks through valleys and mountains bypassed Soviet or Afghan Communist checkpoints and we sometimes rode motorcycles or horses on longer journeys. The *mujahedeen* were also very mobile and put their detailed local knowledge of the terrain to use every day. There are hardly any good maps of Afghanistan's south. Not even a satellite picture will tell you where a mountain pass is, or if one route is quicker than another. In this way, local *mujahedeen* guides were instrumental against the Soviet Union. These wouldn't usually be from your group, but the spirit of cooperation was very much part of the *mujahedeen*'s style. It wasn't difficult to find someone to help with local directions and information.

We fought on regardless of exhaustion, hunger and thirst, walking from Maiwand to Dand, from Shah Wali Kot and Arghandab to Panjwayi and other regions. We would even walk the hundred kilometres or so from Nelgham to Helmand or to Tirin Kot in Uruzgan. We would wear the same clothes for months at a time, surviving on just a loaf of bread or a few dates each day. Many were eager to fight, eager to die, especially young *mujahedeen* like myself.

We lived off the land and thanked those who donated food and money. People wanted to help just as we wanted to fight. If a commander left somebody out of an operation, that fighter would feel angry and disappointed. Just as normal people are eager to get married, we were desperate for martyrdom. At times you could hear *mujahedeen* cry out in the midst of battle, but not out of fear. Even though many of our friends were martyred, one after another, we weren't scared. We would have leapt at the first opportunity to run into open fire during battle, if only our commander hadn't reigned us in. It is hard to believe, maybe, but we were happy. From time to time we danced the *Atan*, such was our elation.[14] At other times we suffered grievously, but it was the true path: if one died, it was meant to be. What a happy life we led! At the end of an operation we would return to our positions and hideouts; we would sit in our rooms, relieved and comforted that we had succeeded in damaging the enemy's military machinery—until the next operation, that is.

Fighting alongside the *Taliban* meant more than just being a *mujahed*. The *Taliban* followed a strict routine in which everyone who fought alongside us had to participate, without exception. We woke before sunrise to perform the *fajr* or morning prayer in the mosque, and afterwards sat together before returning to the camp. We would recite *Surat*

Yasin Sharif every morning in case we were martyred that day. Some would then leave to strengthen some front or other, or to carry out a raid, while others would tend to prisoners, the wounded or spend some time studying.

Even though a large number of common people took part in the *jihad* along the *Taliban*'s front, all had to follow the group's basic principles. Apart from dire emergencies during operations or enemy assaults, the *mujahedeen* were engaged in study.[15] Senior *Taliban* members would teach the younger seekers, and the senior *Mawlawi* would instruct other older *Taliban* members. In this way, a common and illiterate *mujahed* could become a *Talib* within two or three years. I carried out both duties on the front; I would learn from my instructor and I would teach others the basics of reading and writing.

We all studied, and so I was able to continue my religious education. People who did not want to study went to fight under other commanders. Not all the fronts worked this in this manner, but we were *Taliban* and this was our way. We wanted to stay clean, to avoid sinning, and to regulate our behaviour.

***

I had spent close to a year at the *Taliban* front under *Mullah* Mohammad Sadiq Akhund when I was ordered to return to Pakistan. Bur Mohammad, a *mujahed* known as *Mullah* Burjan,[16] had been wounded in the leg by a tank shell. He could not walk and it would be difficult and dangerous to get treatment. Pakistan and the International Committee of the Red Cross had established mobile clinics on the border, but it often took weeks to reach them.

At times, vehicles and trucks could only inch forward along the passes and dirt tracks. The *mujahedeen*, refugees and others would cross the border into Pakistan, and return to Afghanistan by camel. The sick and the injured were transferred in the same way to Chaman. The fighters nowadays have the same options open to them, and mostly take the very same routes that we took to return to Pakistan to recuperate.

The smuggling route was the only way into Pakistan for us. Any male from fifteen and forty-five years old who crossed into Pakistan over the Chaman-Kandahar highway was captured and drafted into the puppet Afghan army. But it wasn't just *mujahedeen* who would make the treacherous journey through the mountains. For many it was the only way to get in and out of the country. Many civilians, families, foreigners and journalists used the smuggling routes.

I met *Mullah* Burjan in Nelgham where we started our journey. Roughly thirty years of age, *Mullah* Burjan was a strong and tough man with a big black beard. From Tangai we made our way through the mountains of Reg on camels. I led our small group of five, moving slowly towards the border. By sunset we were joined by two other *mujahedeen* from the front near to *Mullah* Mehrab.[17]

Mullah Khanjaryar was a good *mujahed* who fought along a small front in Mahalajat. When he was martyred in a battle with the Russians, his brother took his place. Khanjaryar, however, had deviated from the path of his brothers and was running a small arms ring. They were making the crossing with a camel laden with goods. Even though I asked them, they never told me what their camel was carrying.

We eventually reached a place called Do Larey. Only two days earlier the Russians had martyred thirty people and killed seven camels in an ambush in the area. I was convinced that there were Russian forces around and that we would fall into the same trap if we did not prepare ourselves. But we had no weapons with us. There was no other way; another smuggling route would add several days to our journey, and *Mullah* Burjan was badly injured.

The news of the Russian ambush was extremely worrying to the members of our convoy. We could not return, and Russian troops were waiting in front of us. By then there were about thirty or forty of us travelling together, not one of whom had a weapon. As we walked in darkness towards where the Russians were lying in wait, one of the brothers of *Mawlawi* Khanjaryar approached me and told me that they had one RPG[18] and five Kalashnikovs loaded on their camel. "We will give you three Kalashnikovs and one RPG", he said, "but we will keep the other two Kalashnikovs for ourselves".

This was good news, I thought, and I told him to hurry up. Our time was running out, and we needed to prepare for what lay ahead.

They stopped their camel and unloaded the weapons, handing us three Kalashnikovs and the RPG launcher. When the people saw the weapons, many sighed with relief. I drew up a plan, telling the men of *Mawlawi* Khanjaryar's brother that we should split up. I would go with my friends and lead most of the people over one of the smaller side passes, and he and his men would take another pass.

The injured and elderly would follow at a distance, so that they could retreat quickly in case of an ambush and could try to find another way around the Russian forces. This was important as the Russians would often use *Roxana*s during engagements. These were bright flares that would turn night to day, putting everyone in danger of being targeted.

Just as we were preparing our plan to face the ambush ahead, a convoy coming from Pakistan into Afghanistan was attacked just over a kilometre in front of us. We could hear whistling RPGs and machine-gun fire. The *Roxana*s created a bright summer day. Helicopters circled in the air, and when the *Roxana*s were fired, they would sweep down over the ground. We hid under bushes and desert scrub and hoped that the darkness would cover us. Lingering there, we waited until the fighting was over.

We regrouped and proceeded onwards, taking a different route to avoid the ambush site. At dawn we arrived in the mountains of Tangi. At the bottom of the mountains Kuchis[19] had dug wells. We reached the Kuchi camp by sunrise. The village was called Shiin Aka and consisted of some tents and a few houses. Our party split up and went to different houses to rest for the afternoon. The Kuchis were very hospitable, giving us food and water, and we continued our journey at sunset through Naieb Wale to Chaman. Near Bam Bul Tanna we heard of another ambush, so we took a longer way, slipping around it. Arriving safely in Chaman, it was as if nothing had even happened during our journey, and the fear we had felt seemed but a distant memory.

I hurried to bring *Mullah* Burjan to the clinic, but unfortunately his wound had become infected. Even though he was brought to the Red Cross hospital in Quetta, he soon died a martyr.

There was nothing left for me to do but to see my family. I went to Panjpayi, but the people in the area said that my family had moved to Quetta. I spent the night there, and travelled on to Quetta the following day. It was the summer of 1984 and I had been in Afghanistan for thirteen months.

My family had not heard from me since I had left to join the *jihad*. But at the time the happiness of seeing each other again was greater than their anger at my leaving without their permission.

4

LESSONS FROM THE ISI

Quetta had changed since my departure a year earlier. Many of those who had been living in the camps had moved to the city, and even though my family was happy to have me back, they were worried that I would eventually return to Afghanistan and continue to fight.

They urged me to stay in Pakistan and to go to school. I took the entry examination for the ninth grade and started classes. For the next nine months I spent most of my time at school or at the local mosque. When the school year came to its end I passed the entry examination for the tenth grade.

I was still eager to continue my Islamic studies, though, and decided to join a group of students in Quetta taught by *Mawlawi* Abdul Qadir,[1] who had opened a *madrassa* as part of the Kandahari mosque,[2] holding his classes in a simple room in the Burma Hotel on Saryab road. Back then, *Mawlawi* Qadir was still a young man with light-brown hair and dark skin who always wore a white turban. I still remember our first meeting.

As a religious student, it is normal to fulfil certain tasks in the service of your teacher. Students would collect *zakat*, look after the animals, prepare food and so forth. When I first met *Mawlawi* Qadir, I told him that I wouldn't accept this, that I had not come to tend to animals or collect money. It was I who would set the conditions and not him. He laughed when he heard what I had to say, and then he looked straight into my eyes and said, "Zaeef, all these tasks you are talking about, they are made for you. This is how you take care of your teacher and your fellow students. You should do them. Isn't it right that if I make the effort to teach you, you should take care of me?"

I enjoyed studying under *Mawlawi* Qadir and excelled at it. I wanted to focus on my studies so I told none of my *mujahedeen* friends where I was, and stayed out of sight.

After three months Mir Hamza[3] and a few others came to the mosque and we started to discuss the situation in Afghanistan and the ongoing *jihad*. It was 1984 and the Soviets regularly engaged us in battles or largescale assaults on *mujahedeen* strongholds. Our numbers had increased, but we were no closer to winning the war.

My friends tried to convince me to leave my studies and to return to the front. *Mawlawi* Abdul Qadir would have none of it, but my friends were unrelenting and soon we were having heated debates: on the reasons for returning, on the duty of *jihad*, and on the latest battles between the *mujahedeen* and the Russian troops in the south.

Mawlawi Abdul Qadir was not against me returning to Afghanistan. He believed in the *jihad*, and supported people who wanted to join— even young people like me. Over the months, however, we had become close friends and he cared about me; he feared that I would be martyred. In the end, my friends helped me convince him that I needed to return to the front. We left soon after this. *Mawlawi* Abdul Qadir walked together with us part of the way to the border before blessing us and heading back to his *madrassa*.

I did not tell my family about my plans. After my first return they had pleaded with me not to go back. I could have a house, a wife and a business, they said, if only I would stay in Pakistan and not return to Afghanistan. But I was eager to rejoin, eager to follow the call of *jihad* in my country. So our small group of *mujahedeen* went to Zangal camp and to the house of *Hajji* Karam Khan[4] who was managing our front. We started to prepare for our return to Afghanistan.

Mullah Mohammad Sadiq was the commander of our front, while Karam Khan was the manager.[5] Karam Khan was responsible for what happened on the ground most of the time—he was second-in-command—while *Mullah* Mohammad Sadiq was the actual commander. He usually spent half his time at the front and the other half in Pakistan.

It was complicated to run a front. You had to work in both countries to lead a successful group. Relationships with other *mujahedeen* groups and political parties needed to be established and maintained to ensure financial and political support, while the fight in Kandahar depended on local leadership on the ground. Both sides worked as a unit, raising funds and weapons, maintaining communication, organizing transportation, training and preparing new *mujahedeen*.

In the early days of the *jihad*, the *mujahedeen* could not properly engage Russian tanks and helicopters, let alone the MiGs and long-range bombers. The Russian helicopters that swooped down otherwise inaccessible valleys were a great threat. In the early 1980s the ISI[6] began to run a special weapons training programme for the *mujahedeen*. The new weapons, so we were promised, would allow us to destroy Russian tanks and shoot their helicopters out of the sky.

Mullah Mohammad Sadiq chose me along with several other *mujahedeen* to take part in the training programme.[7] We went to Sayyaf's office in Quetta where Commander Abdullah,[8] the head of the office and responsible for south-eastern Afghanistan, introduced us to Pakistani officials.

Mullah Mohammad Sadiq had recently established close relations with Sayyaf's newly-founded *Ittehad-e Islami*.[9] Our front had previously been associated with the *Harakat-e Enqelab-e Islami*[10] of *Mawlawi* Nabi Mohammadi,[11] but Sayyaf and his new party had gained influence with the ISI. It was common knowledge that most of the support, weapons and training provided through the ISI was distributed through Sayyaf.

Pakistan was very different from Afghanistan. In Kandahar, at the fronts and in the midst of battle it was hardly important which faction you were with; the *mujahedeen* would support each other no matter what. Among the different *Taliban* and semi-*Taliban* fronts people were especially known for cooperating as equals and brothers. It was only later in the *jihad* that factional and tribal disputes erupted; *Mullah* Naqibullah[12] and Sarkateb Atta Mohammad[13] frequently fought with each other, for example. Across the border, though, the factional politics were everything.

Pakistani government officials picked us up with a truck from Sayyaf's office. We were huddled into the back so we could not see where we were going. The drive lasted nearly three hours and we all expected that we would be brought to a secret facility somewhere in the mountains. When we stepped off the truck in the middle of a yard, however, we all recognized the place straight away. We were in an area called Tratt, between Pashin Bazaar and Surkhab camp. The river of Pashin Dab Alizai ran in front of the building, and behind it a narrow stream flowed behind Surkhab along the Pashin road up to Pashin itself.

Mullah Mohammad Sadiq had sent twelve people from our front, but there were over eighty *mujahedeen* standing in the yard in Tratt. The instructors gave their lessons in Pashtu so we had to translate for some of the Dari-speaking *mujahedeen* from the north who couldn't understand.

Training started the next day. The first weapon we learnt to use was the BM12, a multiple rocket launcher. This ground-mounted weapons system could fire 107mm rockets to a distance of over eight kilometres. This weapon was made out of aluminium in China, and was very light and effective. The course had a theoretical component that was held in a classroom, and a practical one that took place with the actual weapons to hand. The theory introduced basic weapons handling and maintenance, the different parts and problems of target calculation, range and impact. We would study from 7 a.m. to 12 noon. In the afternoon I would read or review the day's lessons. The theory section lasted for ten days before we actually got to handle the weapons.

We had seen the weapons when we arrived, and everyone was trying hard to understand all the different elements we were taught. We knew that what we were learning there in Tratt could have a decisive impact[14] on our future battles and on the success of our *jihad* against the Soviet Union.

For the practical component we were divided into groups of ten to twelve people, each of which was given a weapon as we attempted to use the lessons we had learned over the previous ten days. We set up the tripod, adjusted the wires, took aim, taking account for wind and other factors for calculating potential targets.

After the BM12 we learned about the BM14. The initial training lasted one month. Once again we climbed into the back of a truck and were brought to a new location. The drive lasted six hours, and it was dawn when we stopped. Getting off the lorry, we were standing in a vast desert leading up to a mountain ridge that climbed into the sky some kilometres away. The entire area was barren; there were no houses or gardens, only some barracks that looked like a military outpost. Some five kilometres away in the mountains to the north we could see a white object shaped like a square. There were BM41s, BM12s and a few rockets on the ground outside the barracks. The Pakistani instructors were sitting on a bench in front of the building. We were ordered to stand in a line and the instructors explained that we were going to use the weapons in practice. This, they said, would be our first chance to actually fire the new weapons that would help us to destroy the Russian helicopters and tanks.

There were other groups of *mujahedeen* from Herat, Kunduz, Jalalabad, Gardez and Kabul. Each operated the weapon, first carrying the apparatus itself, then setting it up and finally firing it twice after adjusting the aim if necessary. Our instructors reiterated the three main points we had learned during the previous weeks' training: the installation and preparation of the weapon, the polishing and loading of the projectiles, and the aiming and actual operation of the firing mechanism.

We were the third group to take part and began by hastily setting up the weapon. I was responsible for the tripod, the optical aim and the spirit level metre. After we were given the command, we fired the weapon but missed the target by ten metres. The second shot was aimed at the distant target at the foot of the mountains. We unpacked the weapon, set it up and fired. We missed again, and in fact only the group from Kunduz managed to hit the target at all. All the other groups missed; the rocket launched by the group from Herat flew over the mountain.

After the second practice run, the training ended. I wasn't very pleased with the outcome and many others were also disappointed that we had not been more successful. We tried to forget about it on the way back to Quetta, squeezed into the back of the truck. Back in Quetta the Pakistani officials gave us one BM12 for the front of Hafizullah Akhundzada[15] and one BM1 for *Mullah* Mohammad Sadiq Akhund.

I joined a group of thirty-four *mujahedeen* heading to Bughra camp in Chaman. It was the first stop on the route to Kandahar, and *mujahedeen* would usually gather there before following on to Shna Narai Kose into Afghanistan and onwards. We were given a tractor from an Arab-funded organization headed by Abu Khabib. There were stocks of weapons in the camp and we loaded up the tractor. Twenty-three of us climbed into its trailer and we started on our way towards Afghanistan. Soon after, we were joined by another tractor belonging to *Mullah* Abdul Ghani in Bala Zhalai.

Some members of our front had befriended others in *Mullah* Abdul Ghani's group and we continued our journey together. After two days we reached Wandooz, where we rested during the day. Before the late afternoon prayer, we sent Karam Khan and *Mullah* Wali Mohammad[16] ahead of us on their motorbikes. They had orders to scout the road ahead for possible ambushes or other problems. The rest of our group with the two tractors followed them at a short distance. It was not even sunset when we started to move forward again. Crossing into Afghanistan was dangerous and we normally only moved under cover of night. We passed Habib Qala and crossed the asphalt road. At Sultan Mohammad Khan *Kareez*[17] the route was blocked by stones and rocks.

A man was standing by the road. He told us that the Russians had come through earlier with tanks and transporters. They took the same route as you are planning to take, he said. There might be an ambush ahead. *Mullah* Abdul Ghani[18] was sure that since Karam Khan and his companion had gone along the same path, they would have come back and informed us if there was an ambush ahead. I disagreed; there could be many reasons why they hadn't returned to warn us. They might have had serious problems or could have been killed. I was sure there was an ambush and we had a long argument. But *Mullah* Ghani was in command and he decided that we would continue on our way. A small group of five *mujahedeen* including myself walked ahead of the rest. We had four Kalashnikovs and an RPG with us.

From Sultan Mohammad Khan *Kareez* we made our way to Garai *Kareez*. We stopped at a small pool of water, a basin of the underground *kareez* close to the village. I knelt down to drink some water while I looked around me. There were torn strands of turbans and clothes hanging in the branches of bushes and trees. The ground was black with gunpowder; dried pools of blood and charred hunks of human flesh were scattered all around. It was about one in the morning and everything seemed quiet.

I remember feeling dizzy as I knelt next to the water; it was like I was dreaming. Only two days before, twenty-three of *Hajji* Babai's fighters had been martyred in a Russian ambush here. I stood up and after a few steps two PK[19] tracer bullets whizzed through the air close to my ear. There was another burst of gunfire. Nazar Mohammand[20] and Mir Hamza were hit and fell to the ground. Another PK bullet pierced my torso at the waistline. The Russians fired *Roshanandaz*[21] and RPGs; grenades and bombs exploded all around us; smoke and dust filled the air. For a second it felt as if doomsday had come upon us. Nazar Mohammand and *Mullah* Mir Hamza had been martyred, but I knew they had been carrying two RPG grenades with them. I had the third and another was with *Mullah* Nasrullah.[22] Shah Wali had been accompanying our tractor; he was martyred. *Mullah* Abdul Ghani and Abdul Ghaffar were injured. Blood was streaming from my waist. I fired my rocket at a spotlight that seemed to be on top of a roof in the nearby village. The rocket hit the roof of a house and lit up the entire village. When the flames rose up into the sky, I ducked down and picked up another of the RPGs.

The Russian were only a few metres away from us; all their grenades had missed us and flown over our heads. After my rocket hit the house they stopped firing at once. It was dark, the flames had calmed and we took the opportunity to pull back. We had retreated only ten to fifteen metres when the Russians opened fire on us again; again we dropped to the ground, rolling backwards into a ditch. We looked at each other and took a deep breath. Our martyred friends lay dead beside us as we returned fire with our Kalashnikovs. The Russians were still firing and had started to move forward. All we had left was one case of Kalashnikov bullets and one RPG. I noticed tanks appearing between the houses and aimed the RPG where I thought they were. Flames and smoke rose up and the Russians stopped firing again. We ran from our position, getting as far away as possible from the site of the ambush. We did not know what had happened to the tractor and the people who had stayed behind. After a few hundred metres I dropped to the ground. I was bleeding heavily and could not move any further.

I turned to *Mullah* Nasrullah and told him that I couldn't move. He shouldn't risk taking me to a safe place, I said. I told him to leave a Kalashnikov with me and run as fast as he could. I would stay behind and fight the Russians until I succumbed and became *shahid*.[23] I had just started to explain how I could not risk getting captured by the Russians when he grabbed me by the waist and hoisted me over his shoulder with his Kalashnikov in the other hand.

Time seemed to stand still as I hung off *Mullah* Nasrullah's shoulder. When we finally reached the tractor the engine was still running, the driver and the other *mujahedeen* having abandoned it. *Mullah* Nasrullah did not know how to get the tractor moving so I told him to put me in the driver's seat. As soon as he had set me down, the Russians who were following us started to shoot. Again we were blinded by the light of the *Roshandaz*, and only with God's blessing did I somehow manage to summon the strength to turn the tractor round and escape. I stopped to pick up others along the way who were fleeing from the Russians. When we finally arrived in Sultan Mohammad *Kareez* all strength left me and I could no longer move a muscle in my body.

Someone else took over the tractor and by dawn we reached *Hajji* Habib's village.

Upon our arrival the villagers told us that the Russians would follow us, and that we did not have long before they arrived. They brought us to some ruins outside the village where we unloaded the ammunition and spent the day hiding. The empty tractor was sent back to the village. A doctor came to bandage my wounds and gave me an injection as a precaution against infection. Just before noon, helicopters started making passes over the ruins and we could see tanks taking up position. The Russians went into the village and searched house-to-house, with tanks moving towards the ruins from the west and the north.

They stopped only a few hundred metres short of our hideout. Everyone was getting ready to fight, setting up weapons, RPGs and laying out the magazine clips. I tried to move and get myself ready to fight, but I felt dizzy and could hardly see. Soon after, I lost consciousness.

It was late afternoon when I woke up. Some *mujahedeen* were sitting at my side and I asked them what had happened to the tanks. They said that they had not come any closer, only holding their positions for an hour or two and then turning away.

By nightfall the tractor returned from the village and the other *mujahedeen* loaded up the ammunition and put me on the trailer. They found another driver and we left *Hajji* Habib's village behind us, heading for Commander Abdul Raziq's camp, which we reached late in the evening.

A small incline led up to the gate, and the old tractor struggled to climb it even though everyone except me had climbed off. When the tractor started to roll backwards the driver jumped off as well. The trailer disconnected and picked up speed quickly. I was still immobile so when it flipped upside down I was tossed through the air. I was only saved from being crushed by the trailer when an RPG box got caught under one of the sidewalls. The others rushed to my aid and pulled me out from under the trailer. I had witnessed everything without being able to move.

I was brought back to Pakistan. Seven or eight days had passed since I had left.

5

BITTER PICTURES

At the height of the war, there were over 100,000 Soviet soldiers in Afghanistan.[1] Millions of civilians fled to neighbouring countries and around a million *mujahedeen* sacrificed their lives.[2] The last few years of the war[3] were marked by increased brutality by Soviet and Afghan soldiers, aerial bombardments and massive battles involving thousands of *mujahedeen*.

The war was a matter of life and death; often chance was all that separated the two. I was caught nine times in Russian ambushes while fighting and trekking back and forth to Pakistan. Eight times God saved me from certain death, just once succumbing to injury. In Khushab, a bomb blew me through the air away from a spot that was riddled with bullets a split-second later. Two of my friends died in a mortar explosion in Nelgham that I also barely avoided; the Russians had booby-trapped a stash of mortars they left behind in a fort. Although I stood only a few metres away when they exploded I was left without a scratch on my body.

When I first joined the *jihad* I was fifteen years old. I did not know how to fire a Kalashnikov or how to lead men. I knew nothing of war. But the Russian front lines were a tough proving ground and—at different times—I eventually commanded several *mujahedeen* groups in Abasabad, Mahalajat, Arghandab, Khushab and Sanzari.

Many times we were surrounded by Russian forces, as happened once in Mahalajat.[4] The Russians had trapped us, cutting off the only retreat with several overlapping security belts, while holding the high ground all around us. They inched closer as they shelled us from the mountains and from the Sufi *Saheb* desert area. We could not find a way out and there were certainly not enough of us to break through the Russian lines. Even though they had moved a significant part of their ground forces from Bana to Wokanu we still struggled just to hold our ground. We were not far from the nearby *mujahedeen* fronts of Panjwayi, Nakhunay and Zalakhan, who would all be able to send us aid quickly, but still we had no way of getting word to them, and we were running short of ammunition. Time was running out; nine *mujahedeen* had been martyred and ten others from different groups were injured.

The situation grew increasingly desperate and we realised that we could not hold out much longer without new supplies and reinforcements. We needed help urgently. *Mullah* Mohammad Sadiq and I decided that it would be best if I tried to slip through the lines. I knew many *mujahedeen* in Panjwayi and had the best chance of getting the support we needed. I could gather troops and return to attack the Russian cordon from the rear, opening a passage to withdraw the injured *mujahedeen*.

But how could I get out? The only option was to pass directly through the Russian lines. We decided that I should go with one of the villagers and pretend to be a farmer. In a nearby village my friends searched all my pockets and took out anything that could identify me as a *mujahed* fighter. A villager agreed to take me on his motorcycle and we set off towards the Russian lines. When we arrived at Sarpoza[5] from Chilzina,[6] an Afghan army soldier stepped out onto the road and pointed his Kalashnikov at us.

The soldier shouted from a distance. "Welcome, *Ashrar*![7] I saw you in the village when your friends were preparing you". I explained that we were civilians; "our houses are over there", I said, pointing to some houses further up the road. "We are going to Mirwais Mina, we don't know what you mean". The soldier seemed confused and told us to get off the bike.

Without any warning, he stabbed me in the arm with his pen and started to search me. The pen broke off and one half was left stuck in my arm. Blood gushed out of the wound and my sleeve slowly darkened to a shade of crimson. He searched me all over but couldn't find anything. The driver swore that I lived in his village and had been living there for a long time. My arm throbbed and I could see the tip of the broken pen sticking out. I repeated my story to the soldier: how I lived in Ghani village, how my home was there, and how I had nothing to do with the *mujahedeen*. I was just a farmer.

When the soldier finally allowed us to get back on the motorcycle, the villager hastily sped off. The villager shouted over his shoulder that the soldier's name was Bismillah[8] and that he was known for his cruelty. "In the past months", he explained over the noise of the engine, "thirty-five people have been shot in their backs". Bismillah was responsible for most of those.

We arrived safe at Panjaw Wali, but I remember feeling tense the whole way. Not a single shot was fired at us. At Jendarma[9] we saw more soldiers and took the long way round. I reached Panjwayi the same day, arriving finally in the village of Mirwais Nika. It took me three days to gather together over two hundred *mujahedeen*. On the third night we moved to Zalakhan and went onwards to Anguriyan and Taymuriyan. Approaching the enemy from the rear we fought our way towards *Mullah* Mohammad Sadiq, attacking several government positions and breaking the security cordon. The Afghan government forces and their Russian allies were now separated into two groups. Some of the enemy soldiers threw down their weapons in surprise and fled. We managed to secure a path out of the confusion, and evacuated the wounded *mujahedeen* and the bodies of the martyrs. Our attack had caused consternation among the enemy and they pulled back, thus ending the siege of Karesh.

* * *

Not long before the Russians withdrew from Afghanistan, they carried out a wide range of operations in Panjwayi, Maiwand, Dand and Arghandab. These were their last attempts to regain control of the province but instead turned out to be their final defeat. Russian soldiers tried to enter Sangisar in Panjwayi for one last time but were faced by all the *mujahedeen* of the region, who came together to mount a common defence line. The well-known front of Hafizullah Akhundzada was in Sangisar and he commanded many strong and experienced *mujahedeen*. A second, newly-established, front was being directed by the late Major Abdul Hai.[10] Various other small *mujahedeen* groups joined us.

We faced rockets, artillery fire and bombardment for three days. Planes crisscrossed the skies and their ordnance shook the earth, striking fear into our hearts. Tanks rolled into Panjwayi, and ground forces followed soon after. Despite their overwhelming power, however, the

Russians and their Afghan allies faced strong resistance. After four or five days the Russians had surrounded our positions from Nelgham road, Nelgham hill and Kolk. Once again all the routes were cut off; we had no access to supplies and we couldn't evacuate our injured or martyred.

We were also running out of food, and soon only bread and dates were left. *Mawlawi Saheb* Dangar[11] was the logistics officer of the *mujahedeen* and tried to stretch our thin reserves out to last as long as possible. By the end we were only receiving three dates per meal. The Russians gained ground each day. We started to prepare for a close-range fight and dug trenches outside the houses we slept in.

We reorganized into a new group led by the late *Mullah* Mazullah Akhund.[12] Our commanders were Khan Abdul Hakim[13] and Karam Khan, whom we called the "twin brothers". We had Karam Khan as our commander, and Khan Abdul Hakim commanded the front of the late Hafizullah Akhundzada. They were skilful men and brilliant tacticians who fought with great courage. *Mullah* Mohammad Omar Akhund,[14] who later became the leader of the *Taliban* movement, was the commander of our fronts in the north. *Mullah* Mohammad Omar Akhund, *Mullah* Mazullah, *Mullah* Feda Mohammad[15] and *Mullah* Obaidullah Akhund[16] were the main leaders of that battle in Sangisar.

The Russians pushed forward, and soon we could see them from our trenches. By the late afternoon they were only a hundred metres away. The clash was brief but the fierce fighting left the battlefield littered with bodies. We seized two PKs and many light weapons. Jan Mohammad took one of the PKs and *Mullah* Mohammad Omar Akhund took the other. The battle turned into a hand-to-hand fight, with grenades flying over our heads. Some *mujahedeen* managed to catch them in midair and throw them back, though in one case a *mujahed* was martyred when a grenade exploded in his hand before he could throw it back. The Russians pulled back and started shelling our position with DC guns. The ground shook with the explosions and the air was heavy with the smell of gunpowder. Smoke and dust rose up all around. Their air forces bombed our positions; every house and trench was hit. Four *mujahedeen* were martyred and another four injured.

Mullah Najibullah[17] was hit by a bomb, and the blast knocked him out. His hand was injured and when he came to he could no longer hear. Shrapnel, pieces of stone and wood flew through the air. *Mullah* Mohammad Omar was only twenty metres away from me taking cover behind a wall. He looked around the corner and a shard of metal shrapnel hit him in the face and took out his eye.

Soon every room was filled with injured *mujahedeen*, but none of them lost their composure. The bodies of the martyred *mujahedeen* lay on the ground, a jarring reminder of the battle outside. *Mullah* Mohammad Omar busied himself bandaging his eye. On that same night we held a marvellous party. The late *Mullah* Marjan[18] sang and we accompanied his sweet voice with percussion on whatever we had to hand. I can still remember the *ghazal*[19] that *Mullah* Mohammad Omar Akhund sang:

> *My illness is untreatable, oh, my flower-like friend*
> *My life is difficult without you, my flower-like friend*

Even though he was injured, *Mullah* Najibullah amused us a lot. He still could not hear a word but we kept on trying to talk to him. A bomb had also injured Khan Abdul Hakim, the commander of the other front.

May God be praised! What a brotherhood we had among the *mujahedeen*! We weren't concerned with the world or with our lives; our intentions were pure and every one of us was ready to die as a martyr. When I look back on the love and respect that we had for each other, it sometimes seems like a dream.

The next day we left and made our way to Zangiabad through Sia Choy. We rested for a couple of days while the Russian and government forces moved to Pashmol. The *mujahedeen* in Pashmol soon sent word that they needed our help, and we left immediately. *Mullah* Mohammad Omar picked up his PK, ready to head out to Pashmol with us, but we urged him not to go. He argued with the late *Mullah* Mazullah but in the end he didn't come. He went back to Nelgham and then on to Pakistan for treatment.

The clashes dragged on and on in Sangisar, Nelgham and Nahr-i *Kareez*. In Pashmol they had us pinned down for some three weeks before heavy casualties forced them to withdraw. Blood was spilled over every inch of contested ground, and the enemy forces moved to Mahalajat, Suf Zalakhan and Mashur. The *mujahedeen* who did not take part in the fight in Pashmol went on to help out in Mahalajat. With the support of the new forces, they were able hold the line against the Russians.

The siege of Arghandab[20] was the last big operation the Russians carried out in southern Afghanistan. Over four thousand tanks came over the mountains into the green and fertile valley, and the battle lasted for more than five weeks. *Mujahedeen* from all over the south came together to defend the district against the Russians. Hundreds were martyred; in our front alone we lost over seventy fighters. The *Taliban* fought alongside the Alikozai tribe led by *Mullah* Naqib.[21] The Russians finally retreated and pulled back to their main base at the airport.

Aside from the camp at the airport, they maintained some checkpoints along major roads and highways. Their helicopters routinely patrolled and conducted searches, and single cars on the road at night would be stopped or sometimes shot at. Russians units set up ambushes along the major smuggling routes, often flying troops directly onto the remote mountain passes used by the *mujahedeen* to go back and forth between Afghanistan and Pakistan.

We attacked one checkpoint after another, gradually forcing the Russians out, and soon parts of the region came under the control of the *Taliban*. The Russians continued to attack the area from afar using their heavy artillery and air force, while we busied ourselves with extending our judicial system. The courts were working well and started to settle disputes among the communities.

Mullah Nek Mohammad Akhund[22] was a well-known figure from this time. A close friend of *Mullah* Mohammad Omar, he was most closely associated with a stretch of road near Pashmol where he fought his *jihad* against the Russian convoys on his own. He would hide in the stream next to the road—breathing with the aid of the air in an inner tube of a bicycle tire—rising to ambush passing columns of tanks with his RPG.

The Russians came to hate that part of the road, and tasked their airplanes to kill him. He was eventually martyred in a bombing raid, but before dying he was said to proclaim that the Russians would never dare to drive up the road even after he had died. He was buried beside the road, as he wished, and three days later the Russians withdrew to their base in Zheray desert. They never did drive up that road again.

* * *

Many great battles were fought against the Russians and the government forces by the *mujahedeen* but none was as intense for me as the final assault on Kandahar Airport near Khushab in 1988. The Russians had already retreated to their main base camp and were preparing to withdraw when we decided to make a final push. It was summer and the grapes were not yet ripe when we gathered our forces together. It was the biggest operation I personally took part in, with some five or six hundred *mujahedeen* led by *Mullah* Mohammad Akhund[23] and myself. I commanded a group of fifty-eight approaching the base from the northeast, while *Mullah* Mohammad Akhund attacked the camp from the north with the rest of the fighters.

The Russians fought back aggressively—no holds barred—in a way we hadn't seen before. There was no way for them to retreat and it was their last base in the south. We fought for three days and three nights. I did not sleep or eat. It was the month of *Ramazan*[24] and I was fasting, but the attacks did not cease and went on all throughout the night. The *Ulemaa'*[25] advised me to break my fast, but I was afraid that I would die any minute in the storm of bombs and rockets being launched at us, and I did not want to be martyred while not fasting. In only three days, I lost fifty of the fifty-eight men under my command.

We came under attack from Dostum's men[26] and his government forces. In all my life and out of all the fights I saw and took part in, the battle for Khushab was the fiercest, most dangerous and hardest of all. We faced a huge number of troops, and were so close to the airport that our enemies threw their entire might at us. Every centimetre of ground was flooded with soldiers and war. *Mujahedeen* fronts from the entire region joined the fight.

Military operations took place every day; villages and houses were bombed; people were killed and the land was turned to ruins. But the government and Russian forces were stretched and engaged on every front by the *mujahedeen*.

There were a large number of *mujahedeen* fighting in Mahalajat, including many famous commanders and strong fighters. *Mullah* Nooruddin Turabi,[27] the late *Mullah* Ahmadullah Akhund,[28] *Mullah* Abdul Ghani Akhund,[29] Ghani Jan Agha and many *mujahedeen* from other groups were fighting alongside each other.

These final battles with the Russians cost us dearly.

At the end, I remember one house where there were ten *mujahedeen* laid out in a line. *Hajji* Latif Akhund,[30] known to western journalists as "the Lion of Kandahar", came the same day to pay his respects in person. The *mujahedeen* lay there like lambs, and tears rolled down his face. *Hajji* Latif, who was the commander of the joint front at this time, told *Mullah* Burjan,[31] "*Mullah Saheb*! Fear God! You should not sacrifice our young *Taliban* to the Russians". "*Hajji Saheb*!" *Mullah* Burjan responded. "There is no other option. If we don't fight the *jihad*, then the Russians will conquer our homeland. To fight the *jihad* means that martyrdom and losses are inevitable".

This didn't satisfy *Hajji* Latif. "*Mullah Saheb*! I don't mean that we should not fight the *jihad*, but I am concerned about the *Taliban* and the *Ulemaa'*, for they are the spiritual heart of our country and they need to be protected. Most of the fighters I have on my fronts smoke hashish, shave their beards and know little about Islam. They would fight against the *mujahedeen* if I let them. Making them stay stops them from joining the government forces. If they die along the way, well then they will be martyred and enter heaven. The *Taliban* have a greater role in society".

The *Taliban* encountered *Hajji* Latif and his men later, at a meeting of commanders in Nelgham. *Hajji* Latif had arrived at the meeting escorted by rough-looking, hashish-smoking boys. They were young, wore western-style clothes and carried small Kalakov machine guns slung over their shoulders. The difference between them and the *Taliban* was clear and plain to all. They stood outside our door with their hair all slicked-back, and soon the *Taliban* were gathered around them, staring in their direction instead of showing them hospitality.

Hajji Mullah Ali Mohammad Akhund[32] voiced his concern about the young men *Hajji* Latif had gathered around him. They were all hashish smokers and "cinema boys",[33] he said. *Hajji* Latif was embarrassed and promised that he would order his men to shave their heads and take a haircut. He would, he said, teach them the *suras* of Yasin, Tabarak al-Azi and Amm.[34] "I will make them become like the *Taliban*", he pledged whole-heartedly.

As soon as he left the meeting he started teaching his men, but we later heard that a woman had visited him. "What are you doing, *Hajji* Baba?"[35] she asked. *Hajji* Latif told her that he wanted to turn his men into *Taliban*. "But *Hajji Saheb*!" she said. "They will not become *Taliban* this way. Leave them be. They are young and have desires. They only have a two-day life. Let them pass it in happiness". This woman apparently made *Hajji* Latif change his decision. God knows better!

6

WITHDRAWAL

It took us ten years, but by the end of the 1980s we finally managed to turn the tables on the Soviets. The war had become too costly and Moscow knew it could no longer sustain the occupation. The *mujahedeen* had gained ground not only on the battlefield but also internationally. Since the Russians first sent troops into Afghanistan in 1979, the UN passed successive resolutions condemning the operation as an act of violence against a sovereign country. Journalists started to travel from Pakistan to "the other side" to witness the fighting, and supportive groups and societies were formed in American and Europe.

A number of western countries had actively supported the *mujahedeen* almost since the beginning of their struggles. By the mid-eighties this access to financial resources and sophisticated weapons made it clear that the Russians were fighting a losing battle. The international isolation of the Soviet Union in turn also led to growing internal pressure from citizens and veterans. As a consequence of all this, the Soviet Union announced its intention to completely withdraw from Afghanistan in 1988 as part of the UN-sponsored Geneva Accords. Babrak Karmal[1] was replaced by Najibullah.[2] Karmal's promises to turn Afghanistan into the 16th Republic of the Soviet Union hadn't come to pass. The Kremlin installed Najibullah and a puppet government of supporters in Kabul. He had less power than his predecessor and he was young, but as former head of the KhAD[3] he was able to secure his ascent.

Under the shadow of this new government, the Russians announced their intention to withdraw their troops from Afghanistan. When I first learned about this I was very happy. The *jihad* seemed to be over, and we had won. I had never thought that I would live to see the day when

47

the Soviet Union left Afghanistan. I was sure I would be martyred by one of their bullets: I even wished for it. Every time I went on an operation I believed I would not return. With the defeat came new hope, though, and I found myself praying to God that he would let me live to see Afghanistan as a free and independent Islamic country with an Islamic government.

But the loose alliance between the different *mujahedeen* groups crumbled before our eyes as everyone started to pursue their own goals. What came next obliterated what we had fought for, and defamed the name and honour of the *mujahedeen* and the *jihad* itself. Russian operations decreased rapidly after their declaration of withdrawal. They stopped most of their patrols in the mountains and deserts, soon also abandoning the cities and highways altogether to focus on the airports and airstrips where the bulk of their forces were located. They continued to carry out air raids and bombardments.

With Russia retreating, life improved considerably in the villages. But it also created new problems. The United States started to de-escalate their funding of the *mujahedeen* in 1990[4] and the commanders started to run out of money and weapons—so started looking elsewhere for resources. Many turned to Najibullah's new government. Some of the commanders had even been paying their *mujahedeen*, and without a steady income they would lose their men.

At the same time as these commanders looked for new partners to finance their operations, Najibullah started to register *mujahedeen* fronts with the KhAD. When they received approval these fronts would receive money from the government, making them a virtual extension of the intelligence services and no longer a threat to the government.

The groups collaborating with the Communist government started to operate against fronts like ours who were still continuing the *jihad* against the Communists according to its original principles. Kandahar's governor at the time, Nur ul-Haq Ulumi,[5] was handing out truckloads of money to various groups, in exchange for which they would conduct staged and pre-announced attacks on each other in which there would be no casualties. With many of the prominent commanders siding with Najibullah, an Islamic government in more than just name started to seem out of reach. Even though the Russians were defeated, the Communists would remain in power by buying off the *mujahedeen*. This tactic was extensively funded by the Soviet Union, notwithstanding precise clauses in the Geneva Accords which forbid it. The fragile alliance between the *Taliban* and other Kandahari *mujahedeen* groups began to crumble.

* * *

Nevertheless, once the last Soviet soldier had left Kandahar in August 1988, we celebrated without a worry in the world. *Mullah* Marjan sang in joy using the top of an old stove as a drum while the rest of us danced the *Atan*. We still hoped that the *mujahedeen* would share the power among themselves and establish an Islamic government, so we could honour our dead, feed our orphans and support our widows. But the new government held on to power.

President Najibullah broadcast on the radio, talking about peace, security and brotherhood. He quoted verses from the holy *Qur'an* and the Prophet Mohammad's (Peace Be Upon Him) *hadith*s.[6] His solution for reconciliation was forgiveness, not true reconciliation. We were just to forget what had happened, to block from our mind the hostilities and clashes that had taken place. "You haven't done anything, nor have I", he would say. He urged all sides to join him to establish a government together. What he said made sense, but we knew that he was weak and that his government did not have the power or the support to last.

The *Taliban* reduced their operations considerably once the Russians left Kandahar. Many others like myself focused more on their religious studies again, while maintaining security and conducting a few operations against the Communists in remote areas. I continued teaching villagers and religious students in Nelgham along with other *mujahedeen*, but we soon decided to settle somewhere else. The village was too far from the main road, and news about the government and the fighting often took days to reach us. We went to Hawz-e Mudat, a village on the highway on the top of the Wazir Qala Pasao and started work. I lived at the construction site, helping to build the camp with its four corner towers. Eventually we all moved from Nelgham to our new residence. It looked very much like a *madrassa*. At the time we had two vehicles, so to cover the costs of the building and food we rented out a tractor.

The *Taliban* leadership held a meeting[7] at the grain silo in Kandahar, the same building that still sits on the western outskirts of the city, pitted by rocket and mortar blasts. The most prominent commanders had all come together to discuss how to divide the city up among the *Taliban* and the other *mujahedeen* factions now that the Russians had abandoned it. At the very moment they were holding their meeting, though, other *mujahedeen* groups were speeding towards Kandahar. The commanders who now sided with Najib's government had decided that the *Taliban* should be excluded from the new administration. They had divided the city, and while the *Taliban* sat in the silo discussing what should happen next, commanders took positions throughout the city.[8]

I had been on my way to Mirwais Mina from the silo on my motorcycle when I saw scores of armed men taking the checkpoints and entering the city. I hurried back as fast as I could and burst into the meeting. "While you are busy here, the city is being occupied by the alliance!" I told the commanders. No one had noticed the silent assault. When the commanders finally left the silo and moved towards the city it was too late.

The *Taliban* had carried out many military operations against the Russians and had been one of the most important pillars of the *jihad*, sacrificing their lives and sustaining thousands of casualties, but we had been betrayed. Only the old Russian family barracks[9] outside the airport came under our control; the late *Hajji Mullah* Yar Mohammad Akhund[10] was responsible for that. Even so, we no longer wished to fight, and most of us returned home to continue our studies. We contented ourselves with the fact that we had driven the Russians from Afghanistan.

* * *

All over Afghanistan the *mujahedeen* parties were taking control. Najibullah was forced to resign and took refuge at the UN compound in Kabul on 16 April 1992. Two weeks later a transitional government, chaired by Sibghatullah Mujaddidi,[11] was installed by the ISI in Peshawar. Mujaddidi was appointed as the president for a term of two months, after which Burhanuddin Rabbani[12] would take over for four months. Even though a term of two months for the transitional president seemed strange—not even a shepherd would agree to work less than four months—we still considered it good news, and were happy.

One day while I was listening to a radio transmission being broadcast from Kabul, from the very same radio channel that had previously

accused Mujaddidi of being a servant of the ISI and America, I gasped
in astonishment. It was a recording of Mujaddidi, and the introduction
by the correspondent explained what had happened. "His Excellency
Professor Hazrat Sibghatullah Mujaddidi, the leader of *Jabha-ye Milli*[13]
and the president of the Islamic government of Afghanistan…" the
speaker intoned. This moment might be the happiest moment of my
entire life. I had many experiences of happiness: I had seen Mecca and
the *Ka'aba*[14] performing the Hajj in 1989; I had married; experienced
the pleasure of learning and knowledge; had felt the blessing of memo-
rizing the holy *Qur'an* in Arabic and even later held a government
position, but nothing has ever matched the joy and happiness I felt on
that day.

At the time I was happy that the wishes of the people would finally
be granted, that our sacrifices, our suffering and seemingly endless
endeavours had reached their culmination and had not been in vain. I
remember thinking all this while listening to the broadcast. Mujaddidi's speech that followed the introduction held one disappointment
after another, however. He announced that his new permanent Defence
Minister would be Commander Ahmad Shah Massoud[15] from the
Panjshir,[16] a fertile valley northwest of the capital. Anyone with any
sense could see that his appointment was a potential source of conflict
and I did not understand how Hazrat Mujaddidi could permanently
hand over the defence ministry to a province-level commander while
he himself was only in office as president for two months.

Why did he appoint Massoud? Why would he take a decision like
that? I knew Mr Mujaddidi was a *jihadi* leader, who himself had
fought against the Russians and the Communists. He had suffered and
sacrificed in the name of God. Why would he now do something that
would cause even more suffering? What was in his heart? In a split-
second my happiness left me, my eyes turned red from the tears that
came pouring down my cheeks and my cry turned into a scream.

Some *mujahedeen* turned to me and asked, "Why are you crying on
this happy day? Afghanistan has been freed and our wishes have come
true". I answered that they were right, and that I was happy, but that
I was sad at the same time. I had to think about all my friends who
were martyred. All of them had shared our dreams and hopes for this
day, but they had paid the ultimate price. In particular I had to think
about *Mullah* Marjan, who had always wondered when the time
would come when he could walk around the Shahidan Chawk[17] in

51

remembrance of the victory of the *mujahedeen*. We made that walk often together, but he died before the war ended.

In Kabul, fighting soon broke out between Massoud and Hekmatyar.[18] Massoud had demanded full control of the city but Hekmatyar—as Prime Minister—didn't accept this. The old Communist party splits between Khalqis and Parchamis were being played out again, and while alliances were never clear, the Khalqis sided with Hekmatyar while the Parchamis seemed to support Massoud. Soon the fighting reached Kandahar, where rival commanders clashed in the city. *Ustaz* Abdul Haleem,[19] a commander of Sayyaf's faction, had taken the provincial police department, but *Mullah* Naqib's forces turned it into rubble. Abdul Hakim Jan[20] was the commander at that battle, which lasted just one day before *Ustaz* Abdul Haleem fled. Most people in the building were killed, but some escaped towards Sarpoza and to the main base of *Ustaz* Abdul Haleem.

The *Taliban* didn't involve themselves in these disputes, and in any case most had returned home by now. *Mullah* Mohammad Omar turned our old *mujahedeen* base in Sangisar into a *madrassa*. I briefly considered staying there as well, but without any work it would be difficult. I decided to return to my wife and children. I had married in 1987 and we had moved in with my father-in-law in Deh Merasay. My wife had given birth to our children by then. I discussed our situation with her and my father-in-law and we decided that I should start to look for work.

I had never worked in my life, had no money to start a business and didn't know what to do. My own family was living in Pakistan; they could help me to find work or start a business, but I did not want to leave Afghanistan. I had heard there was a foreign organization operating along the Salawat-Panjwayi road where people had found work, so the next morning I went to register with them.

I was given a shovel to dig water channels along the road and started work straight away. Everyone there was given 250 Afghanis and seven kilos of wheat per day. It was the first time I had worked and I wanted to make a living for my family, so I enthusiastically took to the task. The other workers stopped digging as soon as they were left alone or when no one was watching them. They sat down and chatted amongst themselves, and even told me to stop digging. I shouldn't bother doing any work, they said, if no one is watching. And even when they're watching I could apparently get away with looking busy and not really doing anything. Work hours were from eight in the morning until one in the afternoon.

It was almost noon on my first day when *Hajji* Bahauddin, a tribal elder from my village who had been a student and friend of my father, drove by. He was on his way from Salawat to Deh Merasay when he caught sight of me among the other men. He stopped his car and walked over to me.

He put his hand on my shoulder and asked, "*Hajji Mullah Saheb*, what are you busy with?" I greeted him and he glanced at my hands. I had only been digging for half an hour but already blisters had broken out on my hands and had even started to burst. My hands were smeared with blood; my hands were not used to digging.

Tears welled in his eyes as he looked at me: "Such hands should not work", he said and took the shovel from my hands and drove me home. When we arrived at my house I had nothing to offer him so eventually he went on his way. We had neither food nor tea, and my six-month old son was ill. I was deep in thought, trying to find a way out of this dire situation, when someone knocked on the door calling my name. Noor Ali, the son of *Hajji* Bahauddin, was standing there holding a sack of flour. He asked if he could bring it into the house. After he put the sack in the yard he took some money out of his pocket and handed it to me. "My father said you should take this money and solve your problems for now", he said. I counted out sixty thousand Afghanis, at the time an unthinkably generous amount of money. I will never forget the goodness of *Hajji Saheb*.

The next day I took my son to see a doctor in Kandahar city. *Ustaz* Abdul Haleem and *Mullah* Naqib were still fighting when we passed through the area near the prison. A group of shaggy, dirty-looking men stopped us and told everyone to get off the bus. They ordered us to start digging trenches. I told one of them that I had my six-month old son with me who was ill. "We are on the way to the doctor", I explained, "and his mother is not with me". But the man just shouted at me, telling me to get to work and not talk about things I wasn't asked about. If I spoke one word more, he said, he would riddle my body with thirty bullets. He cursed me, and asked why I didn't want to help the *mujahedeen*. Shame on this kind of *mujahedeen*! They brought a bad name and embarrassment to the whole *jihad*!

I did not know anyone on the bus, so I gave my son to an old man saying, "Brother! Take this child to the driver, and when I am finished with the work they force me to do I will come and get him. If anything happens to me, the driver knows my village and will bring the boy back to my wife".

We were in between *Mullah* Naqib and *Ustaz* Abdul Haleem's areas of control. Many travellers had been martyred or had disappeared while they were held up and forced to dig trenches. On many occasions innocent passersby would be shot by one side or another, and they would be thrown into the ground disrespectfully, without consideration for the proper religious burial rites and without informing the family to alert them of the death. I had not yet reached the place where I was supposed to dig when someone put his hand on my shoulder and said, "Oh *Mullah Saheb*! What are you doing here?"

I told him that I had been commanded off the bus and forced to work. Without replying he turned to his friend and shouted, "Motherfucker! Don't you know what a *Ghazi*[21] looks like? You've been taking them off the bus. Look, my son! This is *Mullah Saheb*. He is a *Ghazi* from the Russian time. You should know him!" He told me to get back on the bus. The man who had forced me off the vehicle apologized. "My son! How could I have known who this father of mine is?"[22] I was glad to be spared this work and got back on the bus. Only a couple of minutes further down the road the bus was stopped again. We had reached Hindu Kotai and now it was the turn of *Mullah* Naqib's men. One of them got on the bus, looked around and got off again. He said nothing. Another man got on carrying a bag of fruit. He was one of *Mullah* Naqib's men and worked at the checkpoint.

When the bus drove off I turned to the man. "Brother! How much did you pay for this bag of fruit?" I asked. He laughed and explained. "We take commission from the trucks that transport fruit on the highway". I asked him how many bags of fruit they took from a truck. Ten bags, he said. "You must be responsible for the vehicles' security till they arrive in Pakistan then", I said. I had presumed that they accompanied the vehicles all the way until Pakistan. "No, brother. They travel only till Hazaraji Baba without fear. After that, Lalai[23] controls the road and his men take their own commission", he replied. Hazaraji Baba was only three or four kilometres away from Hindu Kotai. Trucks must have been losing most of their load travelling through the checkpoints.

In the evening I returned home from the city together with my son. I told my family that I thought that Afghanistan was no longer safe for them. Even though the district administrator of Panjwayi was *Moalem*

Feda Mohammad,[24] a good man and *mujahed*, nonetheless travelling to the city had become a dangerous and troublesome business. *Moalem* Feda was strict and did not allowing any thieves, gamblers or wine-drinkers in his district, and had always been helpful to us. But how long would he be able to defend his district?

Once, during the days of *Eid*, *Ustaz* Abdul Haleem had come to Panjwayi with his men. They held dog fights and were corrupting the people. When he first arrived his men got into a fight with the district security personnel even before they had started to gamble and stage their dog fights. Soon the *mujahedeen* of the district gathered together and turned his pleasure into grief. Several of his men were killed or injured but *Ustaz* Abdul Haleem managed to escape.

So I took my family and we fled to Pakistan. We avoided all the main roads and used smugglers' routes and back roads to avoid the criminal gangs that were holding up travellers, robbing them and raping their wives all over southern Afghanistan. There was no security and there was no law. Gangs of former *mujahedeen*, thieves and thugs were bleeding the people. No one was holding them accountable and travel had become dangerous and expensive.

I was relieved when we arrived in Pakistan without incident. My cousin Obaidullah in Sumungali near Quetta gave us a room to stay in. The money from *Hajji* Bahauddin soon ran out, and once again I found myself in a difficult situation. I first opened a small shop with the money I borrowed from my cousins, but it made hardly any money. Nevertheless, I rented a small house and began to study and teach again.

Soon I began to forget about Afghanistan. I started to develop land, borrowing money to buy small plots on which I built houses. It took several months, but once the houses were ready I sold them off for a profit, paid back the money I had borrowed and bought another piece of land to develop. My portfolio of houses grew and the financial situation of my family improved. I worked hard and used every waking minute to work or study.

Business was good and soon I was able to leave for Peshawar to focus on my Islamic studies and finish my education. It was there that I started to develop and cultivate an interest in politics.

7

TAKING ACTION

For the next few years I lived in Pakistan but frequently visited Kandahar. In the early 1990s, after the fall of Najibullah and the arrival of the *mujahedeen* government, Afghanistan seemed to disintegrate. Fighting had broken out in Kabul but soon swept down through the south. Local commanders such as *Ustaz* Abdul Haleem, *Hajji* Ahmad,[1] *Mullah* Naqib and others were clashing within the city limits and in the surrounding districts for power and control. Fighting became so intense that it was impossible to live a normal life.

During one of my trips, I was stuck in the house of Gul Ahmad in Deh Khuja, the area to the east of Kandahar city, for six days before I could continue on to the city itself because of the fighting. On that occasion, the people of the city gathered after Friday prayers and staged a demonstration against the commanders. Thousands of people poured onto the streets, marching through the city from Eid Gah Darwaza to Charsu, the old bazaar dating back hundreds of years to the time of Ahmad Shah Baba. But the demonstration came to a stop at Kabul Darwaza square, where Baru,[2] a former *mujahed* who had gathered a few men around him, had taken position with a tank.

Without warning he fired into the demonstrators. Dozens were martyred by Baru, and the demonstration ended. For the next few days every house seemed to be mourning the loss of a family member or a friend. But even attending a funeral was almost impossible, because each lane and street had been fortified with trenches; the city had become a battlefield. On the sixth night, the parties to the conflict agreed to ceasefire terms. People slowly emerged from their houses, still afraid to go to the bazaar. The city had changed; the roads were in ruins and pocked with bullet scars. Walls were blackened by gunpowder and houses were burned to the ground. Dead bodies lay scattered in the streets; houses and squares, walls and roads were stained with blood everywhere. Hundreds of shops had been looted during the fighting, but people were still grateful for having survived.

I spent the night in *Qazi Kareez* and on the second night I arrived in Kandahar city.

Checkpoints had sprung up all over the south like mushrooms, with chains across the street, and demands for money and goods were being made from passing busses, cars and trucks. On our way to the city we were stopped near *Hajji* Lalak Mama Saray yard by a young boy who looked like a fifteen year-old virgin girl wearing an expensive Chaman hat.[3] He was carrying a semi-covered Makarov pistol and smoking an LM cigarette.[4]

He told the driver of our car to hand him a cassette of Naghma.[5] "Son! I would happily give you a Naghma cassette if I had one", the driver replied. "I don't have the tape. I don't even have a tape player in my car. I am sorry". The boy became furious and snatched the car keys out of the car—turning off the engine—and started walking away.

No one said anything as we waited by the side of the road. There were three men with shaved faces next to the boy. The bus driver muttered under his breath, "God! How insulting are the times in which we live! Look what this boy is doing. And no one can stand up and teach him a lesson!" But the boy heard him, and wheeled round, demanding to know what he had said. The driver looked nervous and answered that he had said nothing. The boy started swearing at the driver, cursing him and making foul remarks about his mother and sisters. He drew his pistol and cocked it. We were filled with terror, and begged him: "Blessings, Blessings! Don't do this! For the sake of God! What do you want to do?" But the boy got more and more agitated, swearing and talking himself into a rage. The men who were with him came and grabbed him by the arm, pleading with him to get a hold of himself. One of the men stood close to me and I spoke with him briefly and slowly. "Brother!" I said. "You can see that there are old men, women and children on the bus and it's standing in the middle of the road blocking all traffic. You meanwhile are trying to reason with this boy. You should slap him and take the keys from him. He is not a commander. Take his gun from him. Why do you beg him? You are elders and this is a shame for all of us to see".

The man looked at me helplessly. I could see the whites of his eyes: "*Mullah Saheb*! We cannot do anything. We need to be very careful.

He is Baru's boy.[6] Baru loves him a lot. If we slap him around, or even if we tell him off, Baru will be angry", he replied. They spent a long time talking and entreating him until finally the boy relented, returning the keys and allowing us to pass.

I stayed for a few days in Kandahar before returning to Pakistan in a shared taxi. The roads were full of checkpoints. Every few kilometres a different gang or commander demanded money or goods. Even nowadays when people talk about that time, they call it *topakiyaan*.[7] The time of the men with guns.

At Meel bridge we arrived at Shah Baran's[8] checkpoint. He was an infamous thief and con man, and Meel bridge was where all the thieves from Zangal refugee camp had come together under Shah Baran's banner to rob travellers and merchants. They looked rough—even not quite human—with long unwashed hair falling across their faces, black with dirt and their thick brown lips and teeth stained from tobacco, hashish and snuff. Enveloped in huge woollen cloaks, they squatted in the road with a large *chelam*.[9] Each would take his turn, walking over to the pipe to take long deep drags. Their gaze would lose focus and they soon started to talk gibberish.

We had stopped directly in front of the checkpoint, but his men did not notice us at first. None of my fellow passengers in the car dared to get out and let them know that we were waiting. There was hardly any traffic so we sat in the car anxiously watching the men smoking and chatting. It took them more than fifteen minutes to notice us. Shah Baran looked over at our car and then at his men.

"Go and allow these husbands of our mothers to go!" he told his men. We had been very lucky. Often Shah Baran and his men would pull passengers out of their cars, shave their beards or make them break their fast. At times they would even kidnap young boys.[10]

* * *

In 1992, I returned to Afghanistan and became the *Imam* of the mosque of the late *Hajji* Khushkiar Aka[11] in a tiny village inhabited by no more than ten or fifteen people located on the way to Panjwayi district centre. I felt calm and for once life passed easily, allowing me to keep busy with my studies. I avoided the city altogether and never went anywhere near the various checkpoints and known hangouts of local criminals and gangs. Whenever I needed anything I would ask a member of my congregation to bring it for me. I spent little time with my friends from the *jihad* period, just meeting them occasionally when they happened to pass through the village.

Many of the people who went to the city would come back with tales of anarchy and chaos, and often I heard artillery fire in the distance. The stories made me feel uneasy; I remembered the *jihad* and the sacrifices we had made. It seemed that it had been for nothing, but I still remained patient and gave the same advice to my congregation.

Two old friends came to visit me at the mosque. Abdul Qudus[12] and Neda Mohammad[13] were both *mujahedeen* and we had fought side-by-side during the *jihad*. They stayed for dinner and we talked till late at night. Abdul Qudus, who was later martyred in northern Kabul, said that life had become unbearable. Stealing and looting were unavoidable. Homosexuality and adultery were everywhere. People acted without any thought of morality. "What shall we do, *Mullah Saheb?*" he asked. "We have lost our way".

This was not the first time old friends and people from the village had come to me. For months I had heard them telling me how helpless they felt with no one to turn to, no court or police who would help them. I myself felt helpless as I listened to them, and it affected me deeply. I spent a lot of my time wondering whether it was my religious duty to act, if this was still part of my *jihad* to fight against Afghans who were squeezing the life out of their own people for the sake of money and power.

My friends were young; they were part of a new generation that spoke easily about the intolerable situation but who did not think of the consequences of taking action. I told them to be patient, to wait. God is great, I told them, and things might still change. But the two young men, Abdul Qudus and Neda Mohammad, said they could not just sit around and wait.

In Pashmol near their home, Commander Saleh[14] operated a checkpoint on the Kandahar-Kabul highway. He and his men were not just harassing people and robbing them of their money but had been raping women as well. They planned to ambush him at the Arghandab river. Saleh had become engaged to a girl in Sperwan and travelled every day to her across the river. They wanted to make their move at the river and kill him there. At least then the people will be rid of him, they said.

They had put together a serious plan and I heard them out, but I could not agree with it. All over Afghanistan people faced the same situation; the entire province of Kandahar was crawling with rogue commanders and bandits lingering along the roads and cities. Just killing one of them would make no difference, I said. I turned to my friends and scrutinized their plans.

"So let's suppose you kill Saleh", I said. "Don't you think there are other people already waiting to take his place and continue what he is doing? And when Saleh's tribe learns that you have killed him, do you think anyone in Kandahar will protect you from their thirst for revenge, or even to get you in front of a *shari'a*[15] court?"

They had no answers to my questions and sat silent for a while before they replied. "So what should we do then? What should be done *Mullah Saheb*?"

"The things that should be done are out of our hands now", I said. "Of course the things that we do are our duty and responsibility, but we should leave it to God. We don't know anything at the moment. Things could get better, they could get worse".

We were still discussing the situation when Abdul Mohammad came into the room. He was a young man and a member of my congregation. He had just returned from the city and I invited him to join us for a cup of tea. I asked him about the situation in the city.

Abdul Mohammad looked surprised. "*Hajji Mullah Saheb*", he said. "Why are you asking about the situation in the city? Just a few minutes ago we were nearly killed right here on the road!" I asked him what had happened, if there had been a car crash.

"No! There were bandits on the road", he explained. "They came with a motorbike and stopped our car. One of the men pointed his gun at us, while the other told us to hand over our watches and money".

Abdul Mohammad continued his story. He had confronted the armed men and shouted at them. "What are you doing, robbing people in broad daylight while our country is falling apart!" They told him to shut up.

Instead of handing over his money, though, he was quick to act and attacked one of the men. They were wrestling in the middle of the street and Abdul Mohammad called on the other passengers to attack the other bandit, but they did not move.

The second man raised his Kalashnikov. He wanted to shoot Abdul Mohammad but he couldn't get a clear shot while the two grappled with each other. He could not shoot him without risking his friend's life. He stepped back and shouted, "If you don't let him go I will kill you all". The other passengers in the car were afraid and asked him to let the man go. Abdul Mohammad released him and the bandits escaped on the motorbike.

Everyone became animated when they heard the story. They were already talking about tracking down the men and going to their houses. I stayed silent until Abdul Mohammad had left. Then I spoke.

"First, we need more men, a force big enough to be able to hold its own ground and defend itself. We need enough men to stand up to other groups of bandits and robbers, a group that cannot just defend itself, but also other people's rights. We need the support of the people and we need to find a solution together with the people. We should not only focus on our own problems".

I continued. "I think we need to consult our friends. We need to learn more about their opinions and learn from their points of view to find a way that combines all our opinions, and can lead to success". They both agreed with me, but said that we needed to put the plan into action as soon as possible.

* * *

We started to meet other *mujahedeen* and *Taliban* from the time of the Soviet *jihad*. After a few days we decided to hold a meeting in Pashmol. Thirty-three people came to the mosque to attend the meeting which was chaired by *Mullah* Abdul Rauf Akhund.[16]

The discussions lasted for several hours before we reached a plan of action: we would seek the support of other *mujahedeen* and *Taliban* and together with them we would clear the streets of the rogue commanders and checkpoints. We decided to send out three groups. The first group would talk to those religious *mujahedeen* who were playing no part in the looting and robberies, and who were pious and virtuous men.

A second group was to meet with the *Taliban* and other virtuous people to gain their support, or at least to gain their assurance that they would not stand against us. The third group would go and meet with the *Ulema'*, would consult with them and gain their support. In particular we sought the approval of *Mawlawi Sayyed* Mohammad Pasanai *Saheb*, the respected and well-known judge whom we hoped would issue a *fatwa* to give our movement legal backing.

After all the groups had carried out their tasks another meeting would be convened in Pashmol in which each would present their findings. A month went by before this second meeting took place. The report of the first group was encouraging and it seemed that many *mujahedeen* would lend their support to our plan. The second group, however, came back with only negative responses. The *Taliban* and their commanders had not only said that they would not cooperate, but some had even opposed them. The reply given by *Mawlawi* Pasanai *Saheb* was positive, but he did not agree with all parts of our plan.

We decided that we would stick with the broad outline regardless of his criticisms, though. The meeting continued and the issue of leadership was raised.

People were discussing what kind of person should be selected to lead our group. Most of the people in the room suggested that I should be selected as temporary leader, but I did not think that I was the right person. I suggested that the older commanders, even those who weren't themselves looting, did not support us, and that they would be the first to stand against us. We should, I argued, find a leader who is not a prominent figure, who doesn't have any standing as a commander and thus does not have any political relations from the past with any of the known commanders. According to these criteria I thought I wasn't the right man for the leadership post. We decided to postpone the selection of a leader and would spend some time searching for such a figure.

Groups were sent out to meet with known commanders like *Mawlawi* Abdul Samad,[17] *Mullah* Mohammad Omar Akhund, *Mullah* Obaidullah Akhund and others in Helmand such as Abdul Ghaffar Akhundzada,[18] Chief *Mullah* Abdul Wahed[19] and *Mawlawi* Atta Mohammad.[20]

I was part of the group deputed to meet with *Mullah* Mohammad Omar Akhund and *Mullah* Obaidullah Akhund because I had suggested them for their abilities and leadership qualities. The late *Mullah* Sattar,[21] *Mullah* Neda Mohammad and I went to Sangisar to the house of *Mullah* Mohammad Omar Akhund.

Mullah Mohammad Omar's wife had just given birth to a son, and he was holding the traditional recitation of the *Qur'an* when we arrived. Others had been invited to his house for his ceremony; the *Imam*s of the mosque and all his friends had gathered there. We joined them and also recited a section from the *Qur'an*. The final prayer was uttered and food was prepared. After dinner most guests left. We went to a separate room with *Mullah Saheb* and told him about our previous meetings in Pashmol and about the plan. We told him that he had been proposed as a leader who could implement our plan. He took a few moments to think after we had spoken, and then said nothing more for some time. This was one of *Mullah* Mohammad Omar's common habits, and he never changed this. He would listen to everybody with focus and respect for as long as they needed to talk, and would never seek to cut them off. After he had listened, he then would answer with ordered, coherent thoughts. Finally he said that he agreed with our plan and that something needed to be done. "But, I cannot accept the leadership position", he said. Turning his face to *Mullah* Abdul Sattar and myself, he asked, "Why did you not accept it?" We explained the reasons why we were unable to lead the group, but still he seemed to have his doubts. He argued that it would be a dangerous mission, and asked us what guarantees he could have that everyone wouldn't just abandon him if things became tough. We assured him that all those involved were true *Taliban* and *mujahedeen*.

After this short discussion he told us that other people had also come to him with similar plans. *Hajji* Bashar,[22] the district administrator of Keshkinakhud, shared our opinions and was ready to cooperate. "We will undertake every effort we can", *Mullah* Mohammad Omar told us. He thought that we were obliged to solve the problems of the people to the very best of our ability, and that everything else must be left to God.

"In the end everything that happens depends on God", he said. "I will consult some of the *Ulema'* and we will persuade *Mawlawi Saheb* Pasanai. Then let's see what we can do".

The White Mosque, Sangisar, Kandahar province

All the meetings and consultations we held took place in the four to six weeks after the first discussion in my house with Abdul Qudus and Neda Mohammad.

The founding meeting of what became known as 'the *Taliban*' was held in the late autumn of 1994. Some forty to fifty people had gathered at the white mosque in Sangisar. *Mawlawi Saheb* Abdul Samad, *Mullah* Mohammad Omar Akhund, *Mullah* Abdul Sattar Akhund and *Mullah* Sher Mohammad Malang[23] all spoke, outlining their responsibilities.

The respected *Mawlawi* Abdul Samad was designated the *Taliban*'s *Amir*, and *Mullah* Mohammad Omar was its commander. *Mullah* Mohammad Omar took an oath from everyone present. Each man swore on the *Qur'an* to stand by him, and to fight against corruption and the criminals. No written articles of association, no logo and no name for the movement was agreed on or established during the meeting.

The *shari'a* would be our guiding law and would be implemented by us. We would prosecute vice and foster virtue, and would stop those who were bleeding the land. Soon after the meeting, we established our own checkpoint at Hawz-e Mudat along the Herat-Kandahar highway, and we immediately began to implement the *shari'a* in the surrounding area.

We sent out groups of people to the nearby villages to let them know who we were, and to collect bread and sour milk[24] from the houses. *Mullah* Masoom[25] was in charge of managing the collection and of informing the people. Many of the *Taliban* were well known in the area and respected, and people were eager to help.

The next night the BBC[26] announced the birth of a new movement in Afghanistan, and that the *Taliban* in Sangisar had started it. According to the BBC report, the *Taliban* wanted to cleanse the region of the illegal armed groups that were robbing the people. Members of the *Taliban* had not issued any official announcement or press statement about their objectives; they hadn't even given any interviews. The media immediately started coining names for the movement, though, like "the movement of the *Taliban*", "the Islamic Movement of the *Taliban*", "the *Taliban* faction", or just simply "the movement". Even though the *Taliban* had now taken shape and were an undeniable fact, I was still worried.

I was worried about the old commanders. They would stand against us and their men would not join what was to become a national movement. We had to find some way to include them among our ranks.

8

THE BEGINNING

The first few days of the movement were times of great need. We had a few weapons, but no cars and no money. *Mullah* Abdul Sattar and I each had a motorbike, and I had about ten thousand Afghanis[1] at home that I donated to the group's funds. We pledged our motorcycles to the movement. My bike broke down with an engine problem on the first day, though, which left *Mullah* Sattar's Russian motorbike as the *Taliban*'s only means of transportation. It had no exhaust pipe and could be heard coming from miles away, roaring down the dirt tracks and back roads. We called it "the Tank of Islam".

After *Mullah* Masoom visited the villages, scores of people came to our checkpoint to see the *Taliban* for themselves. There was hope in their hearts for the first time in years, and many were quick to embrace what we stood for. The *Taliban* had given beauty to the region just as a flower can brighten even the most barren desert. Soon dozens of volunteers came to join us, and only a few days after the movement started it had over four hundred members. Invitations were sent out to people who came from all over Helmand and even from Pakistan to join.

Many businessmen and traders began to donate money to support the movement. One man came to the checkpoint lugging a sack of money behind him. I remember when we counted the notes that the total came to over ninety million Afghanis. This was an unimaginable sum of money at the time; I had never even dreamed of an amount that large. We were stunned by the man's generosity and told him that we would give him a receipt that recognized his donation and charity, but he said, "I have donated this money for the sake of God alone. I don't need anyone to know about it. There is no need for a receipt, or for my name to be known". Many others came to donate whatever they could afford.

We travelled up and down the road between Maiwand and Panjwayi from checkpoint to checkpoint, informing all the commanders and bandits that they should stop their extortion and harassment. Most of them ignored us. Many even stepped up the cruel punishments that they inflicted. They would send messages filled with curses and abuse with every car that passed their checkpoints going towards the *Taliban*. They would call us beggars, sons of *mura*,[2] or wild turbaned men. Often worse names and messages would reach us.

The closest checkpoint to the *Taliban* was that of Daru Khan;[3] then came Yaqut,[4] Bismillah,[5] Pir Mohammad,[6] Saleh and Qayyum Khan.[7] This was just Maiwand and Panjwayi. There were also places along the road where well-known thieves would stand during the day demanding money and robbing travellers.

At the time the *Taliban* did not have any plans to extend their activities beyond those two districts. We were mainly thinking about our friends and neighbours, the villages and towns in which we lived. The situation had become so bad that something needed to be done, but no one seemed to be able or willing to try to stand up to the rogue commanders and bandits. We informed only the people along the road. But instead of complying with our calls for them to leave their checkpoints, the situation deteriorated.

Negotiations didn't help, either. We needed to prove that we would act if our demands were ignored. At a meeting we all resolved to attack Daru Khan's checkpoint. A group of ten or twelve *Taliban* armed with one RPG and a few Kalashnikovs approached the checkpoint from a village close by, while another group came down the road. When he noticed us Daru Khan opened fire and the fight began. He was being attacked from two sides and he realized that we were serious: we would neither tolerate his checkpoint nor would we retreat just because he forced a fight on us. A few of his men died in the exchange of fire. Daru Khan started to plead with us.

"For the sake of God! Killing me will not serve you well. I am a Muslim. I fought in the *jihad* side-by-side with you. Just give me a chance to leave this place. I will carry out any order you give me!" he begged. With words like these he tricked us and fled. When Yaqut, Bismillah and Pir Mohammad saw the fate of Daru Khan they, too, abandoned their posts without a fight.

But further down the road, Saleh was boasting how he would defeat the sons of *mura*, how he would destroy us and how not a single *Talib* would escape. Saleh commanded many men, sometimes hundreds at a time. And he was not alone; he was supported by commanders from the city like *Ustaz* Abdul Haleem and Sarkateb. We heard rumours that they had sent him men and weapons. Sarkateb and *Ustaz* knew about the checkpoints of Daru Khan and the others. Saleh was the last commander who stood in the way between them and us, and they knew that we were moving forward. They decided to support Saleh in an attempt to keep the *Taliban* out of the city.

We sent three delegations to Saleh's checkpoint, and finally we gave him and his men a deadline. They had twenty-four hours to abandon the checkpoint or we would attack him. He never reacted.

On the second day after the deadline had passed we still had not received word from Saleh so we moved in. Our forces were split into three groups, the largest of which was led by Abdul Qudus and Neda Mohammad, the two friends who had come months before to my mosque with the plan to kill Saleh by the river.

We covered all the possible escape routes, with one group closing off the way to a nearby village. Our forces approached from the west. Saleh opened fire on us but after a brief fight he and his men wanted to retreat to the village. They ran straight into our trap. He was caught between two fronts, and his men fought for an hour or two before making a run for the city. They had left in a hurry and had abandoned their supplies which included a large stockpile of weapons and ammunition.

We seized the base but soon discovered the naked bodies of two Herati women tossed in a pit behind it. We had heard from travellers that Saleh and his men were forcing women off buses to rape them.

We later learned that the women—whose bodies showed signs of beating and rape—were travelling from Herat on their way to Kandahar. The scene and the deed were monstrous, and everyone was enraged. All those who were previously not convinced of our mission were reassured that what we were doing was the right thing and our support grew further.

***

Hajji Bashar, the administrator of Keshkinakhud, handed his area over to the *Taliban* even though no one had demanded it from him. He had already donated a Toyota Datsun and a Hino truck. Abdul Wasi,[8] a well known and brave *mujahed* who had fought under the late *Mullah*

Abdul Hai and who had become a prominent merchant, had also donated a Land Cruiser.

Hajji Bashar was a good *mujahed* and a commander of a front of the *Jamiat*[9] party during the war against the Russians. Even though he was younger than most of us, he was courageous and generous. He had played a key role during the *jihad* and took part in most military operations with us. He was happy to hand over his district. I remember how he stood in the middle of the main bazaar in Keshkinakhud and asked to be the first to be judged by the *shari'a* that was to be implemented by the *Taliban*. "I am proud to be the first to stand in front of the *shari'a* out of my own free will", he said. He asked the *Taliban* to shave his head[10] first as a lesson for the other people of his district.

Mullah Naqib, the leader of the Alikozai tribe who was known for his battles against the Russians in Arghandab district, also gave his support to the *Taliban*. *Mullah* Naqib was one of the most powerful leaders in Kandahar at the time—maybe the most powerful—and his Alikozai tribe had been undefeated in battle. Many of the other commanders tried to get *Mullah* Naqib to oppose the *Taliban* and prevent us from entering the city. But instead of fighting against us, he unexpectedly handed over Hindu Kotai inside the city border. Hindu Kotai was his main base within the city limits and most of his men were stationed there.

The news of the *Taliban*'s initial success and *Mullah* Naqib's support spread, and many more came to join. The late *Mullah* Mohammad Rabbani Akhund[11] soon followed *Mullah* Naqib and joined the *Taliban*; this brought the south-eastern district of Arghestan under our control.

Soon we were known throughout Afghanistan. One day Azizullah Wasefi[12] and the father of Hamid Karzai[13] came to Hindu Kotai to talk with us. I don't remember if Hamid Karzai himself was with them or not, since I did not take part in the meeting. I was sitting on the rooftop of a house overlooking the front yard. The meeting took place in the room below me, where Karzai, Wasefi, *Mullah* Mohammad Rabbani and *Mullah* Burjan all sat together.

Karzai, Wasefi, *Mullah* Mohammad Rabbani and *Mullah* Burjan were talking quietly and while I wasn't with them I was able to catch fragments of their conversation from the roof. They had come to discuss some plans, but Mohammad Rabbani and *Mullah* Burjan did not agree with them. Sometime they raised their voices in disagreement.

Other representatives from the Red Cross and other institutions would often come to Hindu Kotai as well. Occasionally journalists would turn up, but we did not care much for them. They often came with many demands, and on one occasion a journalist wanted to talk to me. Since we were not allowed to give interviews to the media, I told him that he should talk to our leadership and not to me, but he just took that as an invitation to ask me questions about the *Taliban* leadership for his interview. I told him that *Mullah* Burjan and *Mullah* Mohammad Rabbani were our leaders but that they weren't at the base. The journalists would then try to find someone who would give them an interview but the *Taliban* kept to themselves.

* * *

With Saleh gone, the *Taliban* had cleared most of the checkpoints from the road, and most of them without fighting. Nadir Jan[14] had a checkpoint at the Shah Agha intersection and he initially resisted. We issued three warnings and he did not leave the road, but as soon as he faced a fight, he fled. With Nadir Jan gone, only Sarkateb Atta Mohammad and *Ustaz* Abdul Haleem remained along the road. They seemed to have more men and were stronger than the other groups we had previously faced.

So far we had moved freely through their territory. But there was open animosity between us, and whenever we passed through they would get hostile. We wanted all the armed groups off the roads and highways, and all heavy weapons to be collected, but Sarkateb and *Ustaz* were unwilling to relinquish their to the *Taliban*. There were tensions between *Mullah* Naqib and Sarkateb, and their forces fought every day. The *Taliban* had talked with Sarkateb several times and tried to persuade him to join our forces, but he turned down our demands.

We sent three delegations offering vehicles, Kalashnikovs and free passage if only he would leave, but he arrested our delegates and threw them into his prison. We had given him every chance, but the situation still deteriorated. A report reached us that Sarkateb was planning to assassinate *Mullah* Mohammad Omar. He wanted to attack our leader's convoy on the road from the city back to his house. *Mullah* Mohammad Omar stopped using the road; it was no longer safe for him to travel.

All over Kandahar, the movement had sprung up in different districts at the same time with three different groups operating semi-independently. *Mullah* Mohammad Omar decided that the movement should be united and invited *Mullah* Mohammad Rabbani Akhund and *Mawlawi* Abdul Razaq[15] to a meeting. Both swore on the holy *Qur'an* to follow *Mullah* Mohammad Omar and the three factions of the *Taliban* came together under his single leadership.

We carried out a surprise attack near the Pakistani border on Spin Boldak district centre. Several trucks drove into the main market. Our forces suddenly descended from the trucks in front of the police department. We took the district within fifteen minutes. *Mullah* Akhtar Jan[16] escaped and his men either joined the *Taliban* or went home. On the second day, we removed Mohammad Nabi's[17] posts from Ghra and Ruut and the *Taliban* advanced up to Meel Bridge from Boldak. Shah Baran removed his pipe and his hashish-smoking men before we reached his checkpoint. But the area from Takhtepul up to Bozo Sawkai was under the control of Mansur,[18] and he and his men were prepared to fight.

I was in Hindu Kotai at the time. I had been given fifteen men and ordered to control the area of Naredalai Maktab near to *Ustaz* Abdul Haleem, blocking possible attacks. Even though I had not intended to take any responsibility and made many attempts to avoid it, a fierce fight erupted the same day from the direction of Takhtepul, and I was forced to act. In the afternoon Sarkateb and *Ustaz* Abdul Haleem sent tanks and *dahshakas*[19] to Takhtepul through Mahalajat from the direction of the old city. *Ustaz*'s men underestimated our strength. "If you need any *Pahjs*",[20] they used to boast to everyone, "just come tomorrow and you'll be able to take as many as you want from the dead bodies of the *Taliban*".

They took position with two tanks and a *dashaka* in front of the prison. We only had one RPG and some Kalashnikovs. They outgunned us and we needed better weapons quickly. I rushed back to Hindu Kotai to try to find an 82mm gun. Back at the base I saw *Mullah* Naqib and *Mullah* Burjan sitting together. After greeting them, I explained the problem to *Mullah* Burjan and told him that I needed an 82mm gun because *Ustaz* had brought two tanks.

"Sometimes one person's worries can influence others", said *Mullah* Naqib. "*Talib*! Don't worry! If they have brought two tanks then you should take three".

I said, "*Mullah Saheb*! We don't have tanks!" *Mullah* Naqib looked at me and grinned. He pointed towards the military corps division building.

"It's full of tanks and they are all at your service", he said. I have always been and am still grateful for the encouraging words of *Mullah* Naqib on that occasion. I returned to my position.

Ustaz's men sent a delegation to us led by a man named Moalem. They ordered us to leave. I explained that we had orders to secure the area, and that they would have to talk to our leaders. But the men just started to swear at us, leaving with a shout: "we will deal with you tomorrow!"

After they had left we observed the situation closely, watching for any movement from Takhtepul. It was nearly ten o'clock at night when a messenger arrived telling us that Takhtepul had been taken by our forces and that we should secure the road by stopping anyone trying to enter the city through Sarpoza. At around midnight, a car approached our position from Takhtepul. We could see its headlights in the distance, slowly closing in on our position. Even from far away we heard them shouting, "Oh *Taliban*! Don't shoot! Don't shoot! We have come to talk".

We lowered our weapons and I greeted them. *Ustaz* Abdul Haleem himself had come. He remained in the car and asked where *Mullah* Burjan was.

"He is not with us. Perhaps he is in Hindu Kotai", I said. He said that he wanted to go there to speak with him or any other senior *Taliban*. I replied that I had orders not to let anyone past my position. He looked surprised.

"I am *Ustaz*! Not even I am allowed to pass?"

"I know who you are", I replied, "but I am still not allowed to let anyone pass". *Ustaz* first got angry but when he noticed that his rage did nothing he lowered his voice and spoke softly. But however much he tried, we did not let him pass. Finally he left, but an hour later he returned once again saying that he had an important message and that he was the friend and servant of the *Taliban*, even that he was the *Taliban*'s dog. Still we did not allow him to pass.

After he left I recalled what had happened during the *jihad* against the Soviet forces and their puppet regime in Kabul. *Ustaz* had turned against the *Taliban* and the *Ulema*' to pursue his own interests. There were rumours that he only uttered our name when he cursed. The people said he was robbing civilians and preventing *mujahedeen* from taking part in the holy *jihad* by stealing their weapons.

We had also heard that he had supplied the government with intelligence about the *mujahedeen* troops and had even helped them with logistics on several occasions. It was common knowledge that he had close relations with Jabbar[21] and met him often.

The six *Taliban* fronts[22] fighting against the Soviets all agreed to meet at *Mullah Hajji* Mohammad Omar's residence[23] in Panjwayi, and we reached a swift agreement that *Ustaz* should be disarmed. Somehow he had heard about the meeting and where it was to take place; he showed up without an invitation and entered *Mullah Hajji* Mohammad Omar's house where we were sitting. People were surprised to see him and taken aback when he sat down and started to speak without any pretext.

"This is a good opportunity for all of us", he said. "Honourable people have gathered together. You are the leaders of the six *Taliban* fronts and respected *Ulema'*. I am your humble soldier, your servant, your son even. I follow your orders and respect them whatever they are. If you wish to imprison me, I am ready. If you wish to kill me, I am ready".

We sat in silence after his speech. No one dared say anything. He had interrupted the discussion and no one knew how to react to his intrusion. The room remained silent for a long time, and I remember wondering how he could have found out about the meeting. Who had informed him? He promised us that he did not have any relations with the Communists, and that he was not tormenting the people. Someone, he said, had been telling lies about him, and at the time we believed him.

Later we learnt that *Ustaz* had indeed been working with the Soviets and the Afghan government. There was proof that he had been receiving a regular salary from Kabul. He attacked *Hajji* Bashar, assaulting the villages from the desert and the road with the support of government forces stationed in Keshkinakhud. I was there at the time and I listened to their conversations over the radio.

Standing with my men in Hindu Kotai, though, with *Ustaz* trying to get past us, I recalled how he had deceived us in the past. The rest of the night remained quiet and when the sun came up he and his men had disappeared. The tank and vehicles were gone; they had all run away. That same night *Taliban* forces had taken Kandahar airport, and by 9 a.m. our men entered the city via the Herat Gate.[24] Only some of Gul Agha Sherzai's men resisted[25] the *Taliban* in Shkarpur Bazaar, but the rest of Kandahar came under our control without a single shot being fired.

The area from Bagh-e Pul up to Mirwais Mina was still controlled by Sarkateb however. His men had detained *Hajji Mullah* Burjan

Akhund and *Hajji Amir* Mohammad Agha[26] and they were blocking our routes to Panjwayi.

A message had reached me that one of my family members was ill and that I should return home immediately. I entrusted my command to *Hajji Mullah* Abdul Sattar Akhund and boarded a bus. When the bus approached Mirwais Mina, I could see ten men standing on the road with PK machine guns and bullet belts around their bodies. The men stopped the bus and started searching. One asked the driver if there were any *Taliban* on the bus.

I was petrified. Even though the driver said that all the passengers were residents of Panjwayi and that there were no *Talib*s on the bus, I ducked down, took off my *Pahj* turban and put on that of another passenger. God is my witness that I was scared for my life sitting in the bus, but thankfully the men did not notice me and we were soon on our way to Panjwayi again. I remained in Panjwayi while Sarkateb was defeated.

Kandahar City was handed over to the *Taliban* by *Mullah* Naqib willingly. *Hajji Mullah* Obaidullah was appointed commander of the Kandahar Corps; *Mullah* Mohammad Hassan[27] was appointed governor; Akhtar Mohammad Mansur[28] was appointed commander of the air forces; the martyred *Mullah* Abdul Salam[29] was appointed the provincial Army chief, and the responsibility for government departments was divided between various people. The city was at peace. The old habits of keeping boys, adultery, looting, illegal checkpoints and the government of the gun were over. An ordinary life was given back to the people, and they were satisfied for the first time in years.

* * *

With the fall of Kandahar, the *Taliban* began to re-establish their judicial system throughout the south. Several courts were opened and the judges started hearing ongoing disputes. I was deputed by *Mullah* Mohammad Omar to assist *Mawlawi* Pasanai *Saheb* in his court. He had been appointed high judge of the Appeals Court and had his offices in the Arg[30] behind the *Welayat*.[31] *Mawlawi* Pasanai *Saheb* was known for his impartial judgments and rulings. Whoever was brought before him—even if they were relatives or friends—would receive the same treatment and the same judgement. He followed God's orders as specified in the Islamic *shari'a* law. I remember many of the cases we dealt with, but two in particular stick out.

There is a place near Pashmol called Shukur Hill where most sentences against murder cases were carried out. When a convict was led up the mountain to receive his punishment we would secure the area. Twan, also known as Qurban, had slaughtered a man with a knife in cold blood in my childhood village of Charshakha. He was brought to Shukur Hill. Many *mujahedeen* had gathered there, and the father of the victim and his family were waiting for him. When Twan was brought onto the empty square the people started to beg the father of the victim for forgiveness, as was the custom in these cases.

The *Ulema'* explained the virtue of forgiveness, other people offered money, and some commanders pledged weapons. One of the commanders offered fifty Kalashnikovs and some money on behalf of the condemned man, but the father of the victim could not be convinced to forgive Twan. The on-duty personnel gave him a knife and Twan was brought to him with his hands and legs tied. The father of the victim walked over to him slowly, rolling up his sleeves. He first knelt on the ground then uttered *Allahu Akbar*[32] loudly and put the knife on Twan's neck.

Taking back the knife and raising it in the air, he started to speak. "Look! God has given me this power. No one can release you from me but God. You are the one who brutally killed my son without any lawful reason. Based on the *shari'a*, God has given me the right to take revenge for my dear son or to forgive you for sake of God. Forgiveness pleases God more than revenge. I forgive you, so that God will be pleased with me. Now it is he who shall take revenge when the final day comes".

He threw the knife away and at once people were crying out the *takbir*,[33] others were firing guns and the people were rushing forward to kiss the hands and feet of the father. Someone untied the hands of Twan but he could not move or talk for a full five minutes. People congratulated him on this unexpected chance for a new life and told him that he should devote himself to Islam and the worship of God.

"God has shown mercy. Regret your deeds and never even think of actions like these again", he was told.

I was convinced that the man would never commit another crime, but he soon killed again. I also heard that he himself was killed in a robbery a short while later.

***

Another case that *Mawlawi* Pasanai ruled on was that of the murder of an entire family and their guest. A man called Mohammad Nabi from Girdi Jangal camp had gone to the house of the *baaja* or husband of the sister of his former wife. He was warmly welcomed by his wife's sister and her husband. Another guest arrived and dinner was served when night fell and it became dark outside. Mohammad Nabi and the other guest decided to stay overnight and settled in the guestroom to sleep, while his *baaja* and her family retired to their rooms.

When everyone was asleep, Mohammad Nabi, a trained butcher by profession, took a cleaver and beheaded the other guest in his room. Then he proceeded through the house killing the entire family room by room; there were eleven victims in total: a woman, two men and eight children including a six-month old baby. Before he left the house, he chopped all the bodies into pieces and brought them down to the basement.

He was arrested in Panjpayi Camp in Baluchistan by the *mujahedeen* and brought to Kandahar, where he confessed to the crime but never explained why he did it. During the court sessions and while in prison Mohammad Nabi would often say that he should be killed, but never told us why he had butchered the family of his *baaja*. More than once he said he wanted to be killed. In his dreams he could see the small children, their limbs in his hands, blood everywhere. Every night they would come to him and ask him why he had so brutally killed them. "What did we do?" they would ask him. Mohammad Nabi could not sleep; "my heart is heavy, please have mercy and kill me soon", he often told the judge. He was condemned to death and the sentence was due to be carried out at the riverside between Kushkak and Nelgham.

Relatives and friends of the family had come with their guests. They had selected two men—one from each family—to avenge the deaths of their relatives. The two men were both brothers of a victim. When Mohammad Nabi was brought before them at the riverside no one asked for forgiveness. Neither the *mullah*s nor the people said a word, even though *Mawlawi* Pasanai *Saheb* had instructed the *Ulema'* to ask for mercy and to pray for him. Not even the friends or family of Mohammad Nabi had come to collect his body. I went to Judge *Mawlawi Saheb*. I asked for permission to have Mohammad Nabi perform two *rak'at*[34] and that he should be instructed to utter the *kalima*.[35]

With the permission of *Mawlawi Saheb* I went to Mohammad Nabi. I told him that the relatives had arrived and that they would avenge what he had done. Now would be the time for him to perform a last prayer towards the *Ka'aba* and proclaim the creed of faith. But Mohammad Nabi looked straight at me and said, "Just kill me now. I can still see those limbless children in my hands. I can't pray or proclaim the creed of faith".

I was surprised and astonished by his words. I begged him to reconsider. I tried to change his mind for a long time but all he would say is, "Just kill me". Finally *Mawlawi Saheb* told me to leave him alone. I was pleading with him until the very last moment when he was shot by the heirs of his victims. He died without praying or uttering the *kalima*.

The victims' families became ecstatic after he was shot; people screamed and threw their turbans in the air. For me, Mohammad Nabi was proof that a cruel man will die without even being able to pray or proclaim his faith. If a man is not guided by God himself, no experience or amount of suffering will show him the right path.

* * *

Some time passed and I decided to go to Delaram in Farah province. Most *Taliban* forces had either marched towards Kabul or were busy fighting in the east when Ismael Khan surprised us by dispatching his men to attack us from the west in March 1995.

I was stationed in Sangelan where we repulsed his first advance. On the second attempt his troops were badly mauled and we pushed them back from Delaram to Ab-e Khurma, an area between Shindand and the Farah river. My leg was injured in the fighting in Ab-e Khurma and I was sent back to the Chinese hospital[36] in Kandahar city for treatment.

As soon as I was well enough to leave the hospital I returned to *Mawlawi* Pasanai's courthouse. I was still weak and the wound had not fully healed when I went to see *Mawlawi Saheb*. Since my return he had not visited me and I was wondering whether he I had disappointed or angered him. When I arrived at the office all the judges were there. *Hajji* Baba, *Mawlawi* Ahmed *Saheb* and *Mawlawi* Obaidullah *Saheb*[37] were all sitting in the office with *Mawlawi* Pasanai *Saheb*. As I entered the room he greeted me coldly.

"Abdul Salam!" he said. "You have worked with me for a long time and I have trusted you more than anyone else. Why did you issue a business license to *Hajji* Amanullah?"

Hajji Amanullah had a serious dispute with his brother, *Hajji* Ibrahim, concerning their business. They owned commercial markets and offices in Kandahar, Quetta, Kabul and Peshawar and *Mawlawi* Pasanai had put their business on hold until a decision was reached about their case. Pasanai *Saheb* had become so short-sighted that he was nearly blind, and I spent a good deal of my time supervising and preparing all his decisions, often writing them myself, before he signed them. He did not trust many people with this work. I had been in Delaram for one month and four days and during my absence *Mawlawi* Obaidullah had filled my position.

Obaidullah had written and signed the license for *Hajji* Amanullah that allowed him to resume business. He had then given the letter to *Mawlawi Saheb* who unknowingly signed and stamped it. When Amanullah's brother learnt that he had started trading he complained to *Mawlawi Saheb*.

The brother had brought a copy of the original license arguing that he should also be allowed to restart his business again. Since *Mawlawi* Pasanai *Saheb* was not aware that he had issued such a license, he told *Hajji* Amanullah's brother that the document was not issued by him.

He had asked *Mawlawi* Obaidullah who had issued the license, who in turn had said that I was responsible and that I had issued the document. This all happened while I was in Delaram, even though it was clear that I had not done it. *Mawlawi* Pasanai *Saheb* had kept the document in order to ask me personally about it.

I had never given him a reason to doubt me or my work, but standing there in his office it seemed he thought I was at fault. He was dismissive and did not give me time to react or defend myself against the allegations.

I was surprised by his behaviour and said, "*Mawlawi Saheb*! I have never done anything that could hurt your prestige, trust or dignity over the past years we have known each other. Why would I do it now? I do not know anything about it nor did I have anything to do with it!"

He looked at me, took out the document from the special folder that he used to keep with him and handed it to me. "This is the document!" he said.

When I looked at the paper I immediately saw what the problem was.

I brought a large magnifying glass so *Mawlawi* Pasanai could read the paper for himself. After studying it carefully I handed it back to him. *Mawlawi* Obaidullah seemed worried, and said that *Mawlawi Saheb* should drop the issue. After all, he said, it's not important. The issue, however, was important to me and to *Mawlawi* Pasanai. While he examined the paper, I asked him, "*Mawlawi Saheb*, do you recognize my handwriting in this document? Take a close look at the letters and words. You know my writing for over ten years. Did I write this license or was it written by someone else?"

Mawlawi Saheb looked at the letters with great care, before replying. "This is not your handwriting!" he said.

"Do you know whose handwriting it is?" I asked him. He didn't recognize the script, so I told him who had written the license he was holding in his hand. "It is the work of *Mawlawi Saheb* Obaidullah, sitting right next to you now", I said.

Mawlawi Pasanai became very angry and turned to *Mawlawi* Obaidullah and attacked him. With both hands he threw punches at him and gave him a firm beating, even kicking him. Amidst the cursing and beating *Mawlawi* Pasanai drove Obaidullah out of his office. Obaidullah later sent a letter of resignation, but after this incident I thought it best to stop working with *Mawlawi* Pasanai. I didn't want anything like that to damage my reputation from the past decade. He asked me many times to return and even sent *Hajji* Obaidullah Akhund and the late *Hajji* Abdul Sattar Akhund to convince me, but I refused to go back.

9

ADMINISTRATIVE RULE

I had still not recovered from my wounds when our forces defeated Ismael Khan[1] and entered Herat in early September 1995. I was still recuperating at this time, and I helped out a little at the military corps building, doing some logistics work, or simply manning the radio from time to time. I was working in the radio room one afternoon when *Mullah* Mohammad Omar called me to his office.

"Go home tonight and pack your things. Tomorrow we leave", he said.

I did not ask him where we would be going or for how long, but went back home and packed a few of my belongings. When I returned to the base the next morning, four or five jeeps were waiting and we left Kandahar at once. We drove through Maiwand and crossed the Arghandab river on our way towards Lashkar Gah.[2] In Gereshq[3] we stopped at the military division headquarters where *Mullah* Mir Hamza Akhund[4] welcomed us warmly and served food and tea. After lunch two helicopters landed in a nearby field. *Mullah* Mohammad Omar *Saheb* got into the first one and (the later martyred) *Hajji Mullah* Yar Mohammad Akhund and I boarded the second.

The helicopters took off and headed north-west, passing over Helmand and Farah into Herat province. We passed over the Bakwa desert in Farah and then saw the plains of the west open up with mountains beginning just east of the centre. Just outside the Herat corps building the helicopters swooped down and landed on a small field. A convoy brought us to Bagh-e Azadi[5] and to the governor's guesthouses. Several people were already waiting for us there and immediately a meeting was held in which *Mullah* Mohammad Omar *Saheb* appointed people to several government posts in Herat.

Hajji Mullah Yar Mohammad[6] was given the governorship of Herat, *Mullah* Abdul Salam[7] was appointed as commander of Herat's army corps, *Mullah* Serajuddin[8] was the commander of the military division (*ferqa*), the martyred *Mullah* Mazullah took up the post of provincial police chief, and I was put in charge of the banks. On my second day I was officially introduced to my new position by the governor.

Ismael Khan had ruled over Afghanistan's west and made Herat his capital. Throughout the country he was the only one among the warlords, commanders and tribal leaders who had taken power in the absence of a real government and who had actually served his people. Known as the 'prince of the west', he had run his region through institutions even in the absence of a central government and had used the money he collected by taxing the cross-border trade with Iran to develop the city and its surrounding districts. When I took over the banks of Herat I first conducted a survey to account for all the existing money and goods.

Herat had four banks that were all administered by the central bank. The central bank of Afghanistan, *Pashtani Tejarati* Bank, was a national bank which catered to development and industry, and had considerable financial reserves. Herat's banking system was intact and, in fact, far more advanced than the systems used in other parts of the country. People widely used bank accounts and credit to establish businesses or to finance other investments. The central bank of Afghanistan in Herat alone had net reserves of 40 billion Afghanis, $300,000 (US) and some Pakistani Rupees. In its vaults we also found old currencies, gold, silver and a small amount of platinum.

The civil servants in the bank were ordinary people whose word you could trust and who were running a functioning institution. There were also some intelligence personnel working at the bank, but most of them were former Communists. During the first days most people who worked in the bank or for the intelligence agencies came over and introduced themselves. They explained what their position and responsibilities were; it was through these meetings that I learnt very early on about the brother of Ismael Khan who was also working at the bank. People alleged without proof that he still maintained contact with his brother, and was feeding him information. I thought it normal that they would introduce themselves and explain their positions to me, but it seemed very strange that they would begin immediately to denounce Ismael Khan's brother.

From what I understood about Ismael Khan, I thought of him more as a king than a governor. It surprised me that people so quickly turned their backs on him. Still, soon after my arrival people started to visit me each day in an attempt to persuade me to imprison his brother.

It seemed there was no loyalty after all, and I wondered if I could trust the people I was supposed to work with. I called Mohammad Anwar,[9] Ismael Khan's brother, into my office. He looked worried and uncertain about the purpose of the meeting. I greeted him and invited him to drink tea, telling him that I had called him into my office to get to know him and to get acquainted, and to assure him that no one would harass him or his family.

"Mohammad Anwar", I said. "You are a brother to Ismael Khan but you are also a brother to us. Believe me, we bear no ill will against you. Return to your work. If you have any problems call me and I will help you as best I can". I directed the banks in Herat for almost two years. During that time he worked in the bank like any other and I allowed no one to bother him.

I enjoyed living in Herat. Ismael Khan had invested a lot into the infrastructure and even though the people seemed to fear us at the beginning, they were friendly and welcoming. People were eager to work for their homeland. They were peaceful and valued education. They respected values and principles and had a knack for business. They respected the elders, and the *Taliban* tried to serve them as best they could, maintaining security and upholding the law.

After nearly two years I decided to return home. My wife had sent for me with a message that our son was ill. I went to the governor and begged him to help me find someone who could fill my position at the bank, but he did not want me to leave and nobody new was appointed. Even though I had no official permission, I prepared to leave Herat. I entrusted my deputy with my responsibilities, took a car from the office and drove home. Once back in Kandahar I returned the car to a government office and went to my house in Hajji Khushkiar Qala, near to Salehan.

I had wanted to stop working in government departments for some time and looked forward to following in my father's footsteps as *Imam* of a mosque, where I could spend my time learning and teaching the holy *Qur'an* and Islam. For me, to this very day, it's the life I want to lead and that which fulfils me the most. It is work that has no connection with the world's affairs. It is a calling of intellectual dignity away from the dangers and temptations of power. All my life, even as a boy, I was always happiest when studying and learning things. To work in government positions means a life surrounded by corruption and injustice, and therein is found the misery of mankind.

* * *

After returning from Herat I decided to stay home for a month to reflect on the past few years, while my brother—who had since returned from his studies—stood in for me at the mosque. But before I could return to my mosque *Mullah* Mohammad Omar sent a car for me. His title had changed and he was now called *Amir ul-Mu'mineen*.[10] We sat down in his office and he asked me about my health and my family. "It was a good idea to take a month off", he told me. "It is good to rest. But now you should return to your work".

Kabul had fallen to the *Taliban* and *Mullah Saheb Amir ul-Mu'mineen* wanted me to become the administrative director of the National Defence Ministry. He wrote a letter of official appointment for me, and even though I no longer wanted to work for the government, I could not turn him down. I had taken an oath in Sangisar to follow and stand by him, so if he needed me in Kabul then I would go.

I gathered a few belongings, said goodbye to my family and left for Kabul. The *Taliban* had reached the capital while I was in Herat and by the time I arrived *Mullah*s Mohammad Rabbani and Abdul Razaq had already secured the city, putting an end to the fighting between the *Hizb-e Islami* commander Gulbuddin Hekmatyar and Ahmed Shah Massoud. Like many of my colleagues in the *Taliban*, it was the first time I had visited Kabul.

The *Taliban* had also started to implement *shari'a* law: women were no longer working in government departments and the men throughout the city had started to grow beards. Life in the city was returning to normal. People were coming to the market again and security improved on a daily basis even though there was still a curfew in place. The fighting in the city had taken its toll, though, and many seemed to suffer psychologically. There was little left of the previous administration: most of the offices were looted and the government departments were in chaos. Parts of the city had been completely destroyed and many of the ministries lay in ruins.

Fortunately, the Ministry of Defence building appeared to be intact. When I first arrived to take up my duties there was still no budget in place and no one knew anything about the ministry's expenditures. Most of the offices were empty; many of the former officials had had ties with the Northern Alliance and had fled Kabul, and others were unaware that the ministry was working again and did not show up for work.

It was difficult for me to start work in the middle of such chaos at the same time as trying to settle in a new and unfamiliar city. I had to navigate a minefield of conflicts among ministry officials, but even though I was new to the job it wasn't long before I was promoted and became the administrative Deputy Defence Minister. This made me responsible for all the financial and logistics affairs of the ministry. On several occasions I was even acting Defence Minister.

When *Mullah* Obaidullah, the Defence Minister, was injured in Mir Bacha Kot, a district of Kabul province, and went to Pakistan for treatment, I was the acting minister for a stretch of nine months while *Mullah* Fazl Akhund,[11] the army chief, and his assistants, *Mullah* Khan Mohammad[12] and *Mullah* Mohammad Naeem Akhund,[13] took care of military affairs.

We designed two budgets for the ministry; the annual budget was funded through the Central Bank and was spent on salary payments, administrative affairs and sometimes transitional dealings in relation to other ministries. The second budget was an independent budget submitted mostly in cash from Kandahar and was used for the consumption and supply of logistics, fuel and other requirements of the military divisions at the front lines. The *Taliban* forces trapped in Kunduz, for example, were being supplied with fuel and other necessities through airlifts each week. Other fronts closer to Kabul in Tagab and Nejrab up to Laghman, and near Jalrez in Bamyan, received supplies overland.

Until the middle of September 1998 when Bamyan fell to the *Taliban*, the weekly budget for the fronts was roughly $300,000. Often, however, the amount that reached us was insufficient and we had to make do with less. Money withdrawals or transfers had to be signed for by the defence ministry, the acting minister and the Deputy Minister. We implemented this process to track who was receiving money and to ensure transparency in the ministry. Other expenditure—like travel costs, the budget for military intelligence, operational taxes, the logistical costs of some commanders who had an alliance with the *Taliban*, or charges for the medical care of injured personnel—were all taken from the second budget.

***

Even though we had managed to put a functioning system in place, the ministry of defence still faced many problems. The military constantly complained that they were not being adequately supplied. One of the most testing situations that I faced during my time at the defense ministry was the fallout from the *Taliban* forces' betrayal by Malik[14] in the north. Malik had invited the *Taliban* to join him in his northern stronghold of Mazar-e Sharif and a large force was dispatched there. After they had reached Pul-e Khumri through the Salang tunnel[15] north of Kabul, Abdul Basir Salangi turned on the *Taliban* and attacked them in Gulbahar and Jebal us-Seraj in early summer 1997. Some even came under attack in Salang itself.

The highway was blocked and nearly 6,000 *Taliban* were stuck, surrounded by the enemy between Khenjan and Pul-e Khumri. On the one side they faced Massoud's forces and from the other Malik and *Sayyed* Mansour Nadiri. They fought till they ran out of bullets. Low on supplies and without any food, they could no longer hold their ground and retreated towards Baghlan taking refuge with Bashir Baghlani.[16] With the support of the local population and former commanders like Arbab Hashem Khan and Aref Khan, the *Taliban* forces managed to open a corridor to Kunduz and were able to hold out for years until our troops were able to conquer the north.

Our main way of supplying Kunduz was through the air. Planes would come from Yarganak and try to land on Kunduz's small airstrip, itself under constant attack. RPGs and rockets were fired at the planes when they started to approach the strip. Many of the pilots crashed or had to perform an emergency landing, and soon they refused to fly at all. At times planes would even return to Kabul without having landed in Kunduz. We announced that five million Afghanis[17] would be awarded to all pilots who could land their planes in Kunduz, and soon every pilot was managing to do so—even in the most critical situations. This air support was the lifeline for the *Taliban* in Kunduz; vital supplies were flown in and dead or injured *Taliban* brought out.

The other way of supplying Kunduz was overland, driving through enemy lines by bribing the commanders and men of Massoud and Malik to let transport vehicles through that carried food, fuel and other material. The same was done with other well-known commanders in Takhar and in Mazar-e Sharif. Fuel was one of the most important resources sent to Kunduz. For ammunition, the *Taliban* commanders in the north mostly bought supplies from the enemy's lower-ranking commanders. These commanders who fought against the *Taliban* during the day would sneak out of their bases to sell us ammunition at night. It was cheap to buy bullets and shells in this way, and guaranteed that the *Taliban* forces in Kunduz had a relatively regular and sufficient supply.

On the ground, however, it was the leadership of *Mullah* Dadullah Akhund,[18] as commander of the *Taliban* in Kunduz, that played a key role in their success. Most of those involved at the time agree now that without him the six thousand *Taliban* would have faced certain death as they had done in Mazar-e Sharif.[19] The one-legged commander was always ready to lead each military operation himself, standing among his men on the front line and dashing into the offensive as the first person over the ridge. His style of command was so strict that no one dared to escape or failed to perform their duty.

He would tell his men, "Be killed as men, but do not hand yourself over to the enemy! Don't kill yourself as the others did in Mazar. Only your zeal and confidence as men can save you. If someone wants to fight then he should not retreat, and if that person comes back I myself will shoot him".

His threat was well known; once he had shot a retreating *Talib* in the leg with a pistol, and since that day no *Talib* ever retreated without his direct order. He was a brave young man who never knew fear. Maybe there were others like him, but he was the only one who managed to keep the head of the Northern Alliance, Massoud, in the Pamir mountains. Those commanders could not even stand the sound of his voice.

* * *

While the initial years of the movement were often preoccupied with military operations to expand our area of control, there was always a part of our strategy that stressed the importance of negotiations and that sought to prevent fighting with other commanders. This continued until our fall in 2001. I myself took part in peace negotiations with Massoud's group twice, once face-to-face with him and another time with a group of his representatives.

On the first occasion, Massoud had called *Amir ul-Mu'mineen* and had said that he wanted to sort out their differences through negotiations. They talked briefly over the phone and agreed that I should meet him to have a more detailed discussion. Even though my friends and family were against it, I went to Bagram and then onwards to the region called Sarak-e Naw.[20] It was an area controlled by Massoud and his men; many people had advised me to find a different location on neutral ground, but discussions with him to suggest any other location were immediately rejected as he worried that the *Taliban* would try to kill or capture him in any other meeting place. I told him that I would come to the Panjshir and that *insha'allah*[21] we would reach a peaceful solution.

The negotiations near Bagram lasted for almost four hours, with most of my time spent answering Massoud's questions. I left Kabul with a few security guards in the middle of the night. Massoud and his men were waiting on one side of the road. We spread out our *patus*[22]— with only the light of the moon to guide us—and sat down underneath a tree in the middle of nowhere.

He had brought plans for peace, but among them were his arrangements for a joint military coalition. In our discussion prior to my leaving to meet with Massoud, *Mullah* Mohammad Omar had told me of his concerns on this point; while he would grant Massoud a position in the political or civilian sector, he thought it would be dangerous to share power in the military. From *Mullah Saheb*'s perspective he thought that giving Massoud power over the military would create more problems than it would solve. Massoud, however, continually stressed the importance of sharing military power.

He used to argue that, "We fought in the holy *jihad* as well! It is our right to have an equal share in the government". But *Mullah Saheb* reasoned that, "We respect you. We are also *mujahedeen* and we fought in the *jihad*, but from a military point of view we need to have a united chain of command".

One of the initial reasons for our meeting was to organize an exchange of prisoners, but Massoud tied the issue to a more general understanding and so negotiations ended without a result. The only thing we agreed was to continue negotiations in the future. As we were saying goodbye I told him that, personally as a *mujahed*, I respected his *jihad* and that in which all the people of Afghanistan had participated.

"We both took part in this pious duty to the extent of our abilities", I said, "and we both had to make sacrifices. But as a *mujahed* I must tell you that this is a matter of unity. Unity does not mean questioning who is going to lead—the north or the south—but rather unity means that the interests of the nation are at the centre of all decisions. The needs of the country should take priority or the name of *jihad* and the *mujahedeen* who have become famous for integrity and virtue will be defamed. What happened has already been damaging enough".

Several months passed before the second meeting between representatives of Massoud and myself took place. The situation had deteriorated and Massoud was no longer willing to meet in person. *Mullah Saheb* had deputed me personally to lead the negotiations and I decided to take *Mawlawi* Agha Mohammad[23] and *Mawlawi* Abdul Hai[24] with me. The negotiations took place on the no man's land between the front lines of the *Taliban* and Massoud.

Massoud had sent *Mawlawi* Ataullah[25] and someone else—whose name I can't recall—to lead the negotiations. There was a positive atmosphere at the meeting but a new issue was brought forward by Massoud's men. They wanted to discuss the *Ulema'* and a plan they had for creating a joint council. According to their plan, each side would appoint fifty *Ulema'* to assure that the council remained balanced. He was worried that once again the history of Habibullah Kalakani and Nadir Khan would repeat, so he wanted to remain in power. We, for our part, tried to ensure that these kinds of things didn't happen.

From our perspective, however, the matter was simple. We told them that the *Ulema'* were for discussing religious matters and for deciding on issues of *shari'a* in which they knew best. The role of the *Ulema'* was to engage with more general Islamic deficiencies in our system and to make sure that all our actions and plans were in line with the *shari'a*. If they were suggesting that we divide military power through the *Ulema'* council, I said, then it was clear that their goals had political motivations and were not related to the *shari'a* at all.

"A division of military power", I explained once again, "will cause further clashes and bloodshed, and *Mullah Saheb* will not agree to this". Again they made the issue of the prisoners subject to their political ambitions, and even though I tried very hard to steer discussions back to the matter of prisoner exchange and detention conditions they showed little interest in solving the issue. I spoke my mind and said that linking the exchange of prisoners to a political understanding was cruel and unthinking, but still they dismissed the matter. We had two sessions in this second meeting with Massoud's delegation. The Chief *Imam* of Charikar took part in this second round acting as mediator, but once again the talks ended without any tangible results except for the hope of future meetings.

89

The most astonishing part of these talks for me was the knowledge that both sides in fact agreed that war was not a solution, that it was destructive and did not serve either side. War favoured the enemies of Afghanistan and civil or internal war could not solve the problems we were facing. War was the cause of the breakdown of the tribes, too. We all knew that the Afghan people were tired of war and wanted peace, but nevertheless war continued and no solution was found.

Even though both sides had foreign supporters that fuelled the war and provoked it, the key reason for its continuation was the individuals who took part. I stayed with the Ministry of Defense for over one and a half years before leaving. I had grown tired of my work, and several issues that I had been commanded to look into lay uneasy with me. I had been ordered to search through all the files in the ministry's archives to filter out all Afghan Communists who had received a medal of honour or other awards for the killing of Afghans during the Communists' rule. Another investigation was being conducted into the events of Shomali,[26] the outcome of which was not persuasive to me, and the difficult and hard work had not left me unaffected, so I resigned. I took care of all my responsibilities, handing them over to others, and then I went home.

10

MINES AND INDUSTRIES

I stayed at my home in Kabul for almost three months after resigning from the Ministry of Defence. I later discovered that my old friend Mattiullah Enaam[1] was working at the logistics department in Sherpur and I cycled out to meet and study with him.

It was a difficult time in many ways, and I had financial problems to contend with, but I was still happier than I had been at the ministry. I felt free, and no one troubled me. But starting a normal life all over again, after years spent in government, was challenging. It was financially and politically difficult once I left my job, and my security was sometimes a problem, but I longed for a mundane, normal life. Friends visited my house in front of the Wazir Akbar Khan mosque from time to time, sometimes lending money to keep my family afloat. I kept to myself, spending most of my time at home or praying at the mosque.

One morning I had just performed my *fajr* prayers and was leaving the mosque when a *Talib* approached me. "Today *Mawen Saheb* will come to your house for breakfast", he said. *Mawen Saheb* was how we referred to the deputy leader of the *Taliban*, *Mullah* Mohammad Rabbani.

I went home and prepared tea and breakfast. *Hajji Mawen Mullah* Mohammad Rabbani *Saheb* came to my home just as the sun was starting to rise. He was a patient and kind man who spoke softly. Mohammad Rabbani *Saheb* sat down and enquired politely about my family, my work and my health. Then he asked why I had not come to see him in the past three months. I apologized, telling him that I had been preoccupied with my studies and that I did not want to waste his time for I knew he was very busy too. *Mullah* Mohammad Rabbani said that he had discussed my situation with *Mullah* Mohammad Omar *Saheb*

91

and that they both agreed that I should return to my position at the Ministry of Defence. It was very difficult for me to turn him down, especially as I had great respect for him, but there was no way I could consider returning to the ministry. I waited for him to finish talking, then sat in silence for a long time as I carefully weighed my words.

"Your Excellency *Hajji Mawen Saheb*!" I said. "You know that I have the utmost respect for you, but as regards my work I must tell you the truth. I think that *Amir ul-Mu'mineen* is not satisfied with me right now. I don't really know why and I don't particularly need to know, but I cannot work in an atmosphere like this. As you know, I am not one to work for money, position or career, so I think it should be me who decides. I also faced great problems while I was working in the Ministry of Defence which have still not been resolved. It would be more than difficult for me to return to the ministry to face those same problems and obstacles all over again. They were the reason why I resigned in the first place. And I am tired. I want to pursue my studies and don't want to get involved in the world's affairs any more".

Mullah Mohammad Rabbani said that I should be patient and that he was sorry for the problems I had faced. "We should meet again", he said as he left. "Soon".

After a few days he called me. I should prepare to travel down to Kandahar to meet with *Mullah* Mohammad Omar and talk with him myself. I did not want to go. I made excuses as to why I could not travel, but *Mullah* Mohammad Rabbani insisted. "You can go to Kandahar yourself or I will take you", he said. The next day I took an Ariana² flight from Kabul to Kandahar and went to see *Mullah* Mohammad Omar.

I went directly from Kandahar's airport to *Mullah Saheb*'s office behind the governor's house. He was sitting in his room along with a few of his bodyguards when I entered. We exchanged greetings, but *Mullah Saheb* soon came to the issue at hand.

"You need to return to the Ministry of Defence", he said. I told him that I could not do so but he ignored my reply. "You will return to the Ministry, or I will throw you in jail", he said. I thought about what he had said before I spoke. I looked him in the eyes and told him that I would not return; I was not ready to return to the Ministry of Defence. If he wished to imprison me, I said, then he could do as he pleased.

Mullah Mohammad Omar was surprised and looked at me in disbelief. "Fine", he said. "If you do not want to return to that Ministry then you will take a position in a civil ministry". Then he handed me a chit for over 400,000 Pakistani rupees.[3] He had learned that I was in debt, but I made my apologies and handed the money back to him. I was to return to Kabul, he told me. *Hajji Mawen Saheb* was waiting for me there.

* * *

I was still upset when I returned to Kabul. I had no wish to return to government, but going to prison wasn't a serious alternative and I had sworn in Sangisar to stand by *Mullah* Mohammad Omar no matter what. After two days in Kabul I was appointed the Deputy Minister of Mines and Industries. *Amir ul-Mu'mineen* had written a decree that was announced over the radio. A few days later I was officially introduced at the ministry by members of the Independent Administration of Affairs.

Mawlawi Ahmad Jan *Saheb*[4] was the Minister of Mines and Industries and the first Deputy Minister was *Mawlawi* Mohammad Azam Elmi.[5] I knew both of them prior to my appointment and they were good and pious men.

I settled easily into my new position and soon quite enjoyed working at the ministry. A Ministry of Light Industries was added to the Ministry of Mines and Industry soon after, and together they formed the most important governmental body for the development of the economy. Many expected it to play a key role in the future development and reconstruction of Afghanistan. Our outreach, however, was very limited, with many of the ministry's departments in the provinces acting independently or being used by individuals for personal gain.

There were endless disputes between the provincial governors and the ministries in the capital. The governors sought to control the provincial government departments themselves, and the ministries in Kabul struggled to implement the formal systems of governance. The *Taliban* controlled about 90 per cent of the country, but there were still massive internal disputes over control. The different provincial government branches acted independently from each other; central ministries and the provincial governors feuded over power; all these problems remained unresolved when the Islamic Emirates was ousted in 2001.

During my first days in the ministry I collected information about my actual responsibilities before starting to work. The great bulk of

Afghanistan's natural resources are concentrated in the north of the country. At that time, the chemical factories, a hydropower plant, the gas sector, refinery sector, the cement factory, coal mines and factory, the factory for refining marble and precious stones, salt mines and other heavy industries were all located in the northern provinces and had been divided among various *jihadi* commanders. Due to the war and what often amounted to neglect, all these industries were damaged and run down.

Productivity at the Qudu Barq factory[6] in Mazar-e Sharif was down by over 80 per cent. The commanders in charge of the facilities had not even performed the most basic repairs and maintenance work, and sought merely to exploit the resources for their own profit. The hydro-electric dam, for example, was meant to be producing 18MW of power, but its output had decreased to 6MW. The chemical factory was meant to produce 4,000 sacks of fertiliser, but it only managed around 700. Another example of this neglect and greed were the oil wells in Sar-i Pul. Local commanders would take turns each night to extract as much oil and gas as they could, paying no attention to standards of technical exploitation. Hundreds of new wells had been drilled all over the northern oil fields without considering the damage that this might inflict. By the time I joined the ministry, the wells were in a dire state of decay, badly damaged by earthquakes and tremors. Dostum's commanders in Sar-i Pul had unprofessionally extracted oil under high pressure. Water had started to seep into the shafts, and we felt occasional tremors as the land structure underneath was damaged by this mistreatment.

The other facilities were in an equally bad state so we started to rebuild the industrial complex, and, even though our resources were very limited, it was soon possible to see a significant improvement.

Amir ul-Mu'mineen had given me a second position, too, that of director general of the northern industries. I used to spend half my time in the north, and the other half in Kabul. I effectively became the liaison between the individual provincial departments and the central ministry. One of the many issues that I addressed at the start of my time was that of communication. I decided to distribute radio sets to each province and introduced a schedule for obligatory daily productivity reports.

The production levels of Sar-i Pul and the power output soon reached their previous levels. The brick-baking plant, ice factory and water plant were re-built. The engineers surveyed and repaired the existing wells. The gas network was extended from Sheberghan to Mazar-e Sharif; the production of cement increased; and industrial plants were rebuilt and became active throughout the north. Contracts were signed with foreign investors for new refineries.

* * *

The groundwork for the international gas pipeline through Turkmenistan, Pakistan and Afghanistan had been laid, but the plans were derailed and put on hold when the UN imposed broad sanctions in 1999 because of the continued presence of what it called "terrorists" in the country. Nevertheless by 1999 our ministry deposited $3.5 million into the national treasury, money that had previously been channelled into private pockets.

Afghanistan's greatest assets are its natural gas and oil resources, which are needed not only by the country itself but all over the world. In fact it is specifically the industrialized countries in the West—led by the bottomless consumption of America—who are increasingly looking for new resources to feed their petrol-driven economies. Unocal,[7] an American firm, wanted to gain control of the gas and oil resources of Afghanistan and Turkmenistan and was competing with Bridas, an Argentine company.[8]

Bridas seemed the better choice and eventually won the contract, but Unocal and some other European companies reserved the rights to refine the existing oil resources in Afghanistan. The Islamic Emirate of Afghanistan—especially we at the Ministry of Mines and Industries— actively negotiated with all companies. Bridas opened offices in Kabul in March 1997, and later in Kandahar. Unocal even started primary work at their Kandahar compound.

As for Afghanistan, we wanted to secure a relationship that addressed the needs and fostered the development of our country. We thought that splitting the contract between both companies would be in our best interest, but Unocal insisted on an exclusive contract. I suspect they didn't think that the Islamic Emirates would be able to withstand the pressure, but we put the interests of our country first and acted independently. Bridas would take part in the project, and other European companies would work as subcontractors.

A new refinery began to be built in Kandahar while a Greek company that invested $1 million in a satellite imaging survey discovered that there were significant possible reserves of oil in Kandahar and Helmand. Did Unocal begin to regret its intransigence once these survey results were released? I suspect that Unocal eventually came to believe that the Islamic Emirate of Afghanistan should be given time to complete its projects, which would eventually run into the sand because of our mismanagement. America also later implemented economic sanctions against Afghanistan through the United Nations and companies that expressed an interest in working in Afghanistan were prevented from doing so.

Iran shared a border with all three parties and worked hard to derail our plans. It made every effort to destabilize Afghanistan and to scare off investors. Their idea was that the pipeline should pass through Iran instead of Afghanistan. Noor Sultan Nazarbayev,[9] the President of Kazakhstan, was against this, however, and promoted the pipeline route through Afghanistan as originally agreed. The leader of Turkmenistan was also interested in Afghanistan.

I remember a lunchtime meeting that we had with Nazarbayev in his guesthouse. He would give two gifts to Afghanistan, he said. Firstly, he would give power to some provinces, and secondly, the oil and gas pipeline would remain in Afghanistan, even if it took years for security to be completely re-established.

Iran, in turn, began to assist the Northern Alliance by giving them money, ammunition and logistical support for the fight against the Islamic Emirates.

* * *

While I was with the ministry we built industrial parks in Kabul, Mazar-e Sharif, Herat, Kandahar and approved a site in Jalalabad for more than four hundred small and large projects. One of the key problems that we had was the rocky relationship with Iran and Pakistan. Afghanistan had few domestic markets and exported most of its produce to its neighbours. Even though we had managed to rebuild some factories and establish a few new industries, we were still heavily dependent on imported raw materials from Pakistan and Iran. When they started to introduce export taxes on raw materials they effectively rendered our emerging industries useless; it became more expensive to produce the goods in Afghanistan as opposed to simply importing them.

The situation was replicated with imported goods. As soon as we became ready to produce something ourselves, Pakistan would grant a tax exemption to its own companies that produced the same goods and would crush the emerging industries in Afghanistan. In other cases, Pakistan started to use cheaper materials to produce products of poorer quality that undercut ours. If we look at fertilizer, for example: Afghanistan managed to increase its productivity and started making agricultural fertiliser with the industry-standard 46 per cent nitrogen content. Pakistan and Iran were also producing fertiliser that claimed to be equal in quality but that sold for less. Most Afghan farmers chose to buy this cheaper Pakistani or Iranian fertiliser. We tested these foreign fertilisers in a laboratory for content and quality. The results clearly proved that instead of the advertised 46 per cent they only contained a meagre 20 per cent. This was in turn disastrous for many farmers in Afghanistan, and the poor quality led to disease and pest-prone crops as well as lower production. This was the reason that the harvest decreased from a normal production level.

Soon many Afghans started to complain about the quality of the ghee,[10] plastic and iron from neighbouring countries. Most of the material could have been produced in Afghanistan with the natural resources we had available, but this would have required a far greater investment from the ministry than we could afford. Only the coal, salt and marble mines were developed. The products were sold at low prices—often lower than international prices. Rukham marble[11] was exported to Pakistan, however, where it was polished and resold with a significant profit. We later established our own factories to polish the marble in Kandahar, Herat, Kabul and Jalalabad.

The development budget for our ministry was small; indeed, there was little anybody could have achieved with it, in particular when it came to developing primary industries that require significant financial and resource investment. The *Taliban*'s budget for the entire country each year amounted to roughly $80 million (US). Military expenditures took the lion's share of the budget. From what was left, our portion for development came to 70 to 75 billion Afghanis—about $7 million at the time. The budget didn't even come close to what was needed in order to start any serious development; it was like a drop of water that falls on a hot stone, evaporating without leaving any trace.

In hindsight, I still believe that the things we achieved were remarkable given the limited funds and short time that we had. The success of our programme also heavily depended on the ministry's personnel. The Minister, Deputy Minister, director and the staff were all motivated and went to great lengths to make it work. Money was spent on the actual projects, and *not* diverted into private pockets. A financial council was founded with representatives of all relevant ministries—the Ministries of Finance, Mines and Industry and Transportation and chaired by the Minister of Planning. This met every week to discuss the economic situation and problems, and sought to find solutions. I worked at the Ministry of Mines and Industry for eighteen months.

I enjoyed my work and excelled in my position. At the time nearly every minister wanted me to join their ministry, and many proposals and requests were made for my transfer to the presidency of the ministries and to the central leadership.

Finally, *Amir ul-Mu'mineen* decided that I should take over the general independent administration of transportation. He issued an official decree that gave me the power to change whatever I saw fit within that administration. There were many problems for me to address.

The transportation business was managed through local offices in each city. In some provinces the *Taliban* controlled the local departments and were dividing the profit amongst themselves, while in others places the offices were managed by the private sector. There was no clear government system in place, and my predecessor had been unable to find a solution. Many of the private-led transport offices clashed with local *Taliban* commanders who tried to extend their control. As always in these matters, it was the ordinary people at the bottom who suffered; these uncertain conditions had led many of them to approach the central administration in Kabul to ask us to find a solution.

It was well-known that the administration was beset with these severe problems, and I was aware of many of them even before I started work. God is my witness that I was very worried upon taking the position. How would I be able to achieve changes when my predecessors had failed? And how would I be able to find a balance between the local *Taliban* commanders and the civil systems?

When I was introduced to my new position at the administration I spent many days observing and studying the different dimensions of the problem. I travelled to all the major transport departments throughout Afghanistan and had conversations with the heads of the unions, all the while listening to ideas for solutions and plans from the staff.

Soon another problem among the transport unions became apparent. The system was corrupt and many drivers were complaining.

Traditionally, the transport sector operated a rotation system which allotted every driver his turn. But now some of the transport agents were circumventing it by using just four or five vehicles, giving jobs to relatives and friends, and depriving other drivers of their turn. It was also increasingly common to pay bribes for contracts. The *Taliban* had forced the agents to lower their prices, which had led to increased corruption, with many seeking to gain more contracts to balance out their losses. Work was supposed to be conducted on the basis of fairness and justice, but amidst the confusion a few were profiting while many suffered.

When I finally returned to Kabul I tried to come up with a solution. On the basis of what I had seen on my travels, I adopted a third path that would serve both the transport agents and their income level as well as address the problems of the people. To this end, I introduced a new law that nationalized all transport agents and effectively brought the entire transport sector under the direct control of my administration. I hired department managers who were responsible for depositing the income of their department each day into a centralised bank account. These payments were logged, which reinforced the rotation system and made sure that each driver got his turn. We also established posts for independent commissioners who were themselves supervised by the *Taliban*.

While there still remained a small proportion of transport agents who had special relations with higher-ranking officials and illegally bypassed these new rules, the great majority—at least 90 per cent—were forced to act within the new system. Recommendations, friendship, violence or bribery would no longer be accepted as a way of conducting business.

The new system gave thousands a job in transportation and the complaints soon stopped. The income of drivers and other personnel also began to increase. Some of the private agents, however, complained and said that we had harmed their interests. Even though the law benefited everyone, these agents were only concerned with their own profit. At times I came to think of them as thieves who were neither interested in justice nor in a fair system.

Given the situation, it had been necessary to bring all departments under the control of the government. In order to get rid of the growing problems within the transportation sector, I first needed to get the local *Taliban* commanders—and with them the private agents—under my control. This was a difficult task, and the *Taliban* commanders complained as loudly as the private agents. These commanders told us that the people weren't complaining because they were receiving payments from the private agents, and others argued that they had fought hard for their country in the past and so had a right to the money they earned now. The new system, however, applied to everyone—the *Taliban* commanders and private agents alike. All in all, the first step of my plan was successful, and the people were satisfied with the improvement.

Once I had control over them, I planned to privatize the departments again. The idea was that once a system was in place, the agents who would take over were more likely to adhere to it and the transport administration would have the tools to control and monitor them. During my time at the administration I managed to complete the first phase.

After only three months of putting the new system in place, however, *Amir ul-Mu'mineen* appointed me as Afghanistan's new ambassador to Pakistan.

11

A MONUMENTAL TASK

It was 2000 and I was on my way to Jalalabad and Kunar to evaluate the transport system when I first learned about my nomination as ambassador. We had just left Kabul when I heard the announcement on the radio. As with my previous appointments there had been no discussions with *Amir ul-Mu'mineen*, and the nomination came as a surprise.

God is witness to my unhappiness about leaving Afghanistan again. At the time, the ambassador's position in Islamabad was highly sought after by career *Taliban* in Kabul. The salary was good, and the living standard was higher than in Afghanistan. But even though life was more comfortable in Islamabad compared with my still-ruined homeland, I did not want to leave.

The embassy in Islamabad had a special standing with the Ministry of Foreign Affairs. Following a request by the United States, the UN had imposed sanctions[1] on Afghanistan which placed additional strain on the difficult relationships between members of the international community and the Islamic Emirate. The embassy was our last and only hub for communications. Very few foreigners travelled to Afghanistan, and all foreign diplomats who had business with the Emirate would visit Islamabad.

Only Pakistan opened an embassy in Kabul and had consulates in Kandahar, Herat and Jalalabad. They handled issues directly in Afghanistan. The UAE and Saudi Arabia had offered official diplomatic recognition to the Islamic Emirate of Afghanistan, but they still had not opened embassies; they passed their communications to the Foreign Ministry through the Afghan embassy in Pakistan. France, Germany, Britain and America had all deployed high-ranking diplomats

101

who were responsible for Afghanistan but operated from their embassies in Islamabad. They maintained close contact with our embassy.

Working in the field of diplomacy without any experience in such a fragile and charged environment was a monumental task. I knew about the difficult situation and the role that the embassy in Islamabad played in the events that were unfolding. All this left me concerned upon hearing the announcement of my appointment as ambassador.

After returning to Kabul I headed straight to my home in the south. I stayed there for eight days, keeping to myself while searching for a way to be excused from my new position. I wrote a letter to *Mullah* Mohammad Rabbani explaining the problems and why I would not be able to do good work as ambassador. I hoped that he would help me. Without him on my side, I was sure it would be almost impossible to convince *Amir ul-Mu'mineen* to appoint someone else. But even though I tried my best, *Mullah*s Mohammad Rabbani and Mohammad Omar turned me down. They told me that it was too late; I had been nominated, formally announced, and a decree had been issued. Furthermore, they were confident that I would overcome the problems and that my work would be as good as usual.

After I had come to terms with the fact that I would actually have to assume my new position in Islamabad, I went to the foreign ministry in order to meet with Abdul Rahman Zahed,[2] the Deputy Foreign Minister at the time. He seemed surprised when I came to visit, and pretended not to know of my appointment.

Zahed said that *Mawlawi* Wakil Ahmad Mutawakil,[3] the Foreign Minister, might have been informed about the decree but that he was in Kandahar at the time. When I finally managed to talk to Mutawakil on the phone, I asked if it was he who had suggested me for the position. Mutawakil said that he had indeed proposed to *Mullah* Mohammad Omar that I would be a good candidate to manage the difficult task, but that it had been *Mullah* Mohammad Omar who had finally decided to choose me. Later *Mullah* Mohammad Omar also told me in person that the final decision had been his. I was disappointed, and told him that he should have asked if I wanted to become the ambassador before approving my nomination.

"I don't want to go to Islamabad, and I don't think that I am capable of doing a good job. If you could reverse your decision, I would be very grateful", I told *Mullah Saheb*. He told me it was too late.

There was no one else to whom I could complain, so I resigned myself to the fact that I would soon be leaving for Pakistan. By that time, Pakistan had also accepted my appointment as ambassador and had issued a visa. A diplomatic passport was issued in my name and my fate was sealed.

I boarded a UN flight to Islamabad the next day. The late *Mawlawi* Mohammad Nabi Mohammadi, leader of *Harakat-e Enqelab-e Islami*, was with me on the plane. He had just come back to Lowgar and Kabul for the funeral of his young son, and we talked throughout the journey. He shared some of his experiences in Pakistan. As we landed he assured me that that he would help as best he could.

* * *

It was the first time I had been on a UN charter plane and the first time I had flown into Islamabad airport. After we landed, a small car brought me to a VIP guesthouse in the city. The assistant of the protocol department of the Pakistani Foreign Ministry welcomed me along with the first secretary of the Afghan embassy. Tea was served, and the protocol officer gave a short speech in English.

He introduced himself briefly. "Your Excellency!" he said. "We welcome you to the Islamic Republic of Pakistan and hope that you will enjoy your stay here. The government of Pakistan and the Ministry of Foreign Affairs will be at your service if you require any assistance. Consider Pakistan your second home. You will be honoured guests". I cannot remember the name of this young protocol officer; I only recall that he was Punjabi. After the speech I was brought to my new home, the Afghan ambassador's residence.

For the first few days, however, I stayed in the private guesthouse of *Sayyed* Mohammad Haqqani,[4] my predecessor. He had not formally handed over his position, so I did not immediately take up my responsibilities as ambassador.

Protocol demanded that I be officially installed after presenting my credentials to the previous ambassador, but *Mawlawi Sayyed* Mohammad Haqqani had been in a hurry. Prior to the greeting ceremony and handing over his responsibilities to me, he had already said farewell to the old Pakistani President Rafiq Tarar.[5] In doing so, he had legally ceased to be the representative of Afghanistan while I had not yet been formally introduced. Nevertheless, I started working as soon as I arrived in order to get familiar with my responsibilities and the procedures in the embassy. The embassy staff—official diplomats as well as local employees who would have passed as Afghans—were welcoming and friendly. They introduced me to my new work.

I met the President four times while I was ambassador. The first time was at the ceremony in which I received my credentials. It is customary to be informed a few days in advance of an official meeting in order to give everyone enough time to prepare. Two days before the ceremony was to be held, the invitation arrived. It stated that I should be present at the embassy with my family and staff at 8 a.m. to meet the president of Pakistan. My son Abdul Manan and my nephew Hamidullah came with me, along with *Qazi* Habibullah Fawzi,[6] a judge who was the embassy's secretary, and *Mawlawi* Abdul Qadeer *Saheb*,[7] the military attaché. At 8 a.m. we were brought to the presidential palace by the protocol department of the Pakistani Foreign Ministry.

There were several coaches with colourful horses waiting at the presidential palace. I was placed in the middle coach and the Pakistani and Afghan national anthems were played. After the ceremonial parade we met the President in his office. I handed him the credential letters from *Amir ul-Mu'mineen* and the ceremony ended.

The president welcomed me once again and extended his best wishes. He looked forward to close cooperation and to good bilateral relations between our two countries. With the official recognition of the president, I was now the ambassador of the Islamic Emirate of Afghanistan to the government of the Republic of Pakistan. I invited all the *Ulema'* from the embassy to my home to celebrate my inauguration.

* * *

After I had officially assumed my position, I met with Abdul Sattar,[8] the Foreign Minister, for a second time and was introduced to Moinuddin Haider,[9] the Interior Minister. I did not know better at the time, but I should have met with the head of the ISI and its relevant departments first.

I later came to learn that the ISI played a key role within the Pakistani government and became accustomed to the fact that representatives from other countries also recognized its growing power. The intelligence agency's officers had established a close relationship with Afghanistan and had influenced Afghan politics even before the Soviet invasion. But it was after the Russians had provoked Daud Khan's coup against Zahir Shah that the ISI showed the extent of their influence and ambition. With Russia gaining ground in Afghanistan, the ISI felt increasingly threatened.

In an attempt to stop the Soviets, the ISI turned to some *jihadi* leaders who had already come to Pakistan and who were organizing the resistance to the Soviet puppet regime from outside Afghanistan. By the time the Russians staged the Saur coup[10] in April 1978 against their former ally Daud Khan, the ISI had already established firm relationships with the resistance, even doubling the money, operations and training for the *mujahedeen* in Afghanistan.

Many countries outside the region agreed with Pakistan and openly expressed their concern about the growing influence of the Soviet Union in Afghanistan. Many Arab countries also gave support to Pakistan to stop the spread of communism. In 1980, the *mujahedeen* opened offices in Pakistan under the supervision of the ISI. When Moscow decided to intervene by sending the Red Army to invade Afghanistan, the situation became more and more urgent. The arrival of Russian troops triggered the exodus of the Afghan people, and over the next few years Pakistan welcomed over two million Afghan refugees.[11] What began as small refugee camps soon grew into cities, and the ISI started an extensive programme to assist the *mujahedeen* in their struggle. The ISI was responsible for uniting the *mujahedeen* and forcing them to adopt a united strategy. The agency continued to play a crucial role among the *jihadi* factions until the outburst of the *Taliban*. At the time, even low-ranking Pakistani officials were more popular in Afghanistan than in Pakistan.

As an official representative of the Islamic Emirate of Afghanistan it was important to maintain my independence from this foreign intelligence agency, but I couldn't entirely avoid their influence. In my dealings with them I tried to be not so sweet that I would be eaten whole, and not so bitter that I would be spat out. I attempted to work in an official way rather than clandestinely, and worked mostly with the Foreign Ministry in an attempt to establish an amiable relationship.

General Mahmud,[12] the director of the ISI invited me for lunch one day. It was an official invitation and a few diplomats from the embassy accompanied me. The lunch took place in the guesthouse of the ISI at its headquarters in Rawalpindi. General Mahmud and his deputy General Jailani[13] both seemed to be Punjabi, and various other "Afghan desk" staff attended, including Brigadier Farooq,[14] Colonel Gul,[15] Major Hamza and Major Zia.[16] The heads of the Afghan desk appeared to be Pashtun.

It was the first and last time that I met with ISI officials and entered their black offices. Even though later on they tried to settle our disputes in Afghanistan, I stayed away from them. In my life I hate few things more than clandestine services; for me, spying and shadowy operations are dishonourable. It takes a special kind of person to pursue a dirty profession like this.

I recalled how, when I worked as the acting director of the Ministry of Defence in Kabul, they approached me on a regular basis to try to establish a good relationship. I was offered many things, but I never considered any of them. During my entire time at the Ministry of Defence I gave them one chance and allowed them a visit concerning a tribal dispute. They brought an urgent message about the clashes that were taking palace on the border in the south-eastern province of Paktya, where a conflict had erupted between the tribes. In reality, they wanted to seize Afghan land and push their border into our land at Paktya. The border stayed where it was, though, and an agreement was reached internally.

Throughout my time as ambassador I never agreed nor disagreed with the ISI. I was always careful to use non-committal expressions that bound me to nobody. It was in both countries' best interests to have good relations. A hostile environment would harm us both, and the relationship was especially beneficial for Afghanistan, drained by war and internal conflict.

This cost-benefit equation should be at the forefront of considerations of both countries; the common values, shared cultural, political, economic and geographical situation should clearly outweigh the differences.

Disputes from the past or between individuals who made countries friendly or hostile to each other should not dictate future relations. The interest of the nation should guide all political decisions, especially about neighbouring countries. The relationship should be informed by cultural and economic development, independence and mutual respect.

In short, a country should not be labelled an enemy or a friend, but dealings should be based on moderate policies that adopt moral principles and laws as their foundation. The policy I followed during my time as ambassador and in my private life was always guided by the principles of Islam and the respect for other countries. This was the basis of my foreign policy.

12

DIPLOMATIC PRINCIPLES

The relationship between the Afghan Embassy and the Foreign Ministry of Pakistan went far beyond the normal principles of conduct, as does the relationship between the two neighbouring countries in general. Afghanistan and Pakistan share far more than just a common border: often the same culture, religion, ethnicities and language.

The invasion of the Soviet Union had brought us even closer, with some three million Afghans fleeing across the border into Pakistan to find refuge. This large number of refugees posed multiple problems for the Afghan Embassy and the Pakistani Foreign Ministry alike. It was a momentous task to provide security, organise accommodation and manage the detention of criminals. Then we had to deal with the merchants who imported commercial commodities through Pakistan and Iran. The trade of cereals, fruits and other products between Pakistan and Afghanistan caused further problems, especially relating to security across the border areas.

I felt comfortable dealing with the Foreign Ministry; it was the official reference point for the Embassy, so we would first approach officials there with any concern or problem we had with other ministries. After discussing the issue, the Foreign Ministry would then put us in touch with whatever ministry was responsible.

Even though the ministry had an Afghan desk with a dedicated administration and management through which we conducted all our written communications, I usually met with Aziz Khan,[1] the director of the Asian desk. He was a Pashtun who had previously been posted in Afghanistan and therefore knew about the various problems that we had to deal with from his own experience.

At times I would meet with the Deputy Minister or even the minister himself to discuss specific issues. Aziz Khan would often approach me with advice, suggesting that it would be better to deal directly with the ISI on certain matters. At times it was hard to comprehend the logic behind Aziz Khan and the Foreign Ministry's actions. On one occasion he called and asked me to come to his office. When I arrived he told me that a man wanted to speak with me: this was Abdul Samad Hamid.[2]

Two days before, I had learned that Abdul Samad Hamid had arrived in Pakistan; he was staying in the Marriot Hotel in Islamabad. I had already enquired about his room number and planned to visit him the very same day to invite him to my house for dinner. I had hoped to meet him; he was a well known and respected personality in Afghanistan. Aziz Khan's request made me change my mind, though.

I pretended that I didn't know Abdul Samad and asked Aziz Khan who he was, if he was a minister or a commissioner here in Pakistan maybe. He was astonished. "Why don't you know him?" he asked me in disbelief. "He is a well-known personality in Afghanistan. He was the deputy prime-minister before!" he continued. He criticised me for not knowing this, and for having so little knowledge of my own country.

"Mr Aziz Khan! Of course I know him. He might even know me!" I told him patiently. "My knowledge about Afghanistan is not slight. But why doesn't he contact me directly? He knows where the Embassy is. Why does he need you to contact me? I know he is well-known and respected, but he is from Afghanistan!"

After my conversation with Aziz Khan I decided not to meet Abdul Samad Hamid. I would have understood if some man who did not know better had involved the Foreign Ministry, but I didn't need to receive an invitation from Aziz Khan. That was not the way to receive an introduction.

I met with Abdul Sattar, the Foreign Minister, many times. He was an honest and pious man who often shared his concerns about Afghanistan with me. He told me that many countries had doubts about Afghanistan, and that we needed to pay more attention to their objectives. "You need to be more active in your diplomatic efforts", he would say. "You need to address those issues, in particular those regarding America. You should meet with more diplomats and explain everything to clear their minds".

But at times it seemed that he too didn't understand how to deal with Afghanistan. On one occasion he was approached by the Russian ambassador who had called him to organize a meeting with me. Even though he didn't mention it, I felt that a meeting at the Foreign Ministry with the Russian ambassador would not be in my best interests. I told Aziz Khan that I would be happy to meet the Russian ambassador alone in a neutral location with a translator. Aziz Khan insisted on holding the talks at the Foreign Ministry and participating in them. I told them that I was not interested, and the meeting never took place.

Tripartite talks between Afghanistan, Pakistan and America were also sabotaged by Pakistan. I had not been informed about them and nor did I agree to their taking place. Pakistan told the American diplomats that my absence was a clear sign of the *Taliban*'s reluctance to negotiate. In reality, I only learnt about the meeting from one of my informants days after it occurred.

I often told the US Ambassador that he should contact myself and the Afghan Embassy directly and not try to solve the problems they had with Afghanistan though the mediation of the government of Pakistan or its administration. "Pakistan", I told him, "is never an honest mediator and will control and manipulate any talk they mediate or participate in". I passed on the same advice to all other diplomats and embassies, as well as the United Nations.

When recommendations from a third party were passed to me through the Pakistani administration, I never gave them a straight answer but advised them that whoever submitted the request or letter should contact me directly if they wanted an official reply.

On several occasions other governments approached me about specific issues through the Pakistani administration, but my reservations about Pakistani involvement often meant that matters could not move forward or be resolved. On one occasion a French journalist had been arrested in Afghanistan and the government of France demanded his release. Instead of negotiating directly with us, though, they chose to send officials from the Pakistani Foreign Ministry. I advised the representatives that the French government should contact me directly. It took another three days before the French ambassador called me and I was able to hand over the journalist on the Afghan-Pakistani border.

Pakistani officials were well aware of the general diplomatic principles, but they seemed to think that we at the Embassy were simple minded because we lived simple lives. Furthermore, America was pressuring Pakistan and other countries not to establish or maintain direct contact with us in an effort diplomatically to isolate the Islamic Emirate of Afghanistan.

Even when I was alone with Pakistani officials they were afraid that there was an American hiding behind the next door. They would speak cautiously and always with the utmost respect to any Americans, even when they were only talking about them. They would refer to damned President Bush as "His Excellency, Mr. Bush", or would refer to "Colin Powell *Saheb*". I remember well how much it annoyed me.

* * *

Even though we handled most of our affairs with the Foreign Ministry, we used to deal nearly as much with the Ministry of the Interior. Due to the huge number of Afghans in Pakistan, many security problems arose concerning refugee prisoners, the excesses of the local police and cross-border trade. Moinuddin Haider, an Army General, was the Interior Minister. He was a *Shi'a* and his ministry was responsible for all police affairs and for security within Pakistan. Many Afghan refugees would come to the Embassy to complain about the police who harassed and robbed them. Often visitors were harassed, even outside the Embassy. Policemen would linger on the streets that led to the Embassy and rob Afghans, falling upon them like a pack of wolves.

I complained to the Ministry of the Interior and even the Foreign Ministry, but the situation did not improve. The reply was always the same: an official statement assuring me that the Pakistani police did not bother Afghan refugees but were in fact protecting them. In other words they considered my complaints to be baseless.

One day I had called on the elders and the *Ulema'* from the Afghan refugee camps to gather at the Embassy for a meeting to discuss several issues. On the way to the Embassy the police had stopped them and extorted money even though they were carrying their refugee ID cards. When they were finally released and arrived at the Embassy they told me what had just happened to them. They were angry and agitated, and their anger affected me deeply, for they were much-respected elders. I took one of them with me and left the Embassy. We drove straight to the place where they had been held earlier. The police officer was still there, waiting for new victims. I stopped the car and told him to get in. He tried to escape but I grabbed him and forced him into the car. Then I took back the money that he had just stolen from the *Ulema'* and drove straight to the Ministry of the Interior.

All the way there, the police officer begged me to let him go, repenting for what he had done and promising never to bother anyone again,

110

but nevertheless I handed him over to the Ministry of the Interior. I wanted to prove to the ministry that the accusations had not been without foundation and make them see what the Afghan refugees were facing each day. The Foreign Ministry and the Ministry of the Interior criticized me for my action, and accused me of having violated the diplomatic code.

During my time as ambassador in Islamabad I was also instructed to help Afghan nationals who were in need of medical treatment abroad with letters of introduction and visa applications. *Mullah* Serajuddin, a commander with the Ministry of Defence who was on his way to Germany, was staying at a guesthouse with $10,000 for his journey and medical treatment. He had entrusted the money to the financial officers at the guesthouse and had gone to the local mosque to pray. As soon as he left, the local police, who had earlier seen him arrive and had learnt of his money, forced him into a car and abducted him. The other *Taliban* who were staying at the guesthouse called me. They said that a group of men wearing police uniforms had waited for him outside the mosque and taken him.

God knows I was worried that he would be tortured or killed by some rival. I immediately contacted the Interior and Foreign Ministries, but before anything happened he turned up again. The police had scrutinized and harassed him before dumping him somewhere outside the city. This was a matter of terrorism and we were very serious about following up on the investigation and developments at the Interior and Foreign Ministries. The story was picked up by the press and featured in several newspapers which accused *Mullah* Serajuddin of abusing a Pakistani boy. With each passing day the accusations became more and more outrageous. It reached the point that we thought it would be better to drop the issue instead of pursuing it further.

Instead of trying to shed light on the issue, the Interior and Foreign ministries confirmed the police report and covered up for their policemen. Since they didn't need to fear prosecution by the government, the policemen continued to target Afghans.

A young man who was on his way to Germany was killed. He and his wife were travelling to the airport in a taxi when the police chased after them. It is not clear how much money he had with him, but his wife was wearing very expensive jewellery. The police must have noticed the bracelets and necklaces she was wearing and decided to steal them. When they stopped his taxi, the police forced him to get out of the taxi and into the police car. When other officers got into the car the young man realized what was happening and jumped out of the moving police car. His head hit the road and he was badly injured. The policemen grabbed the jewellery from his wife and took off.

In Pakistan it is a commonplace to say that there is a connection between the taxi drivers and the police. Sometimes, for example, if a taxi driver sees that someone has money with them, they will drive the passenger through a particular police checkpoint and make a signal to the policemen who will then rob the unsuspecting prisoner.

When the woman saw her husband lying on the ground bleeding she screamed in despair until someone stopped and brought her and her husband to the hospital, where he soon died of his injuries. The woman contacted the Embassy and we made an official complaint to the Ministry of the Interior and the Foreign Ministry. They detained the offending policemen for some time, but later released them without any further censure. They were not punished and did not even have to pay *fidya*[3] to the family.

Many similar incidents happened all over Pakistan. In the refugee camps between Islamabad and Rawalpindi, the police used to wait outside the mosques during prayer time and would take anyone who looked like he had money, holding him until they received a bribe. But the security of Afghan nationals was not the only issue that caused trouble.

Afghan merchants and businessmen were facing problems. Afghanistan is a land-locked country so all our imports transit through Iran and Pakistan. International conventions state that imports should not be taxed by transit countries. Pakistan, however, tramped on international law and imposed sanctions on dozens of commercial items. Afghan traders' goods were held in the port of Karachi; many of these expired or spoiled which resulted in losses of millions.

We managed to get some of the foods off the sanctioned list, like ghee and other foodstuffs. The Pakistani police only used the list as a pretext for bribes. It was a business for them to delay the imports of Afghan merchants in the name of imposed restraints, only releasing them after taking bribes from our businessmen. Pakistan would complain that the imported goods were not consumed in Afghanistan but were smuggled back to Pakistan and that the volume of commodities being sold on the black market had started to affect Pakistani industries.

Problems occurred on a daily basis. Some of them I managed to solve, others continued throughout my time as ambassador. In particular, the individual attacks of Pakistani policemen on Afghans increased over time, and problems were mounting not just in Islamabad but throughout the country, even all the way down to Baluchistan.

Although the Embassy had no official authority, the refugees still expected us to come to their aid. Once I made an appointment with the governor of Peshawar to discuss the problems of the refugees in his province. I travelled to Peshawar and met him in his house. He put on a ceremonial welcome for me but when I started to raise some of the issues he cut me off. "Afghanistan has a government and security now", he said. "Your people are able to live in their own country, so now they should return to their own houses in their country. We cannot shoulder them anymore".

He was bitter, and spoke like a military man. But what he said was irresponsible and often differed from the official policy of the central government.

With the growing number of incidents I once again went to the Interior Ministry and complained about the situation. I met with the minister himself and explained the unsustainable situation of the Afghan refugees in Pakistan, the growing number of security incidents, and the behaviour of the police.

I had talked for nearly an hour when I finished. He gave me an answer that I did not expect. "Our police aren't only bothering the refugees", he said. "It's the same for everyone in the country. They aren't targeting any specific group. They target anyone who seems to have money and who cannot protect himself. It's a general problem, not a specific one".

I was startled. "You are the head of the police forces", I said, "and you seem to be telling me that you can't do anything about it. So who can I complain to?"

At that same meeting, he presented me with a list of men that were wanted by Pakistan and that he said were staying in Afghanistan.[4] The list started with Saifullah Akhtar[5] and *Mawlawi* Mohammad Qasem.[6] I glanced further down the list.

"But General!" I said. "I am sorry, but you should give this list to the people it mentions". The General looked at me without understanding and replied. "You are the representative of Afghanistan here in Pakistan, and the men on this list are in Afghanistan. To whom shall I go if not you?"

"General!" I said. "Don't be upset. There is a government within your government where this list belongs: the ISID". He was astonished.

"This list does not concern the ISI", he said. "And why do you talk to me in this manner?"

"General!" I replied. "Yesterday Saifullah Akhtar visited me here in my office in Islamabad when *Mawlawi* Mohammad Qasem partici- pated in the Dastarbandi[7] ceremonies in the madrassa of I-7 area. He had five armed bodyguards with him. I saw him myself. He even gave a speech during the ceremony. So how can I hand them to you, and how can you demand them from Afghanistan, when they move freely through Islamabad bearing arms? And with utmost respect, do you think this request of Afghanistan is fair and just?"

He seemed shocked. Sweat started to trickle down his forehead. "This can't be true!" he said, but I replied, "Believe me it is". He never asked me about the list or anything concerning wanted men again after this conversation.

Moinuddin Haider did not know that Pakistan was a two-faced country. When he assumed his position one of his concerns was to address the persecution of his fellow Shiites by dealing with those ele- ments who had done them wrong. Certain elements in the administra- tion, however, worked to cover the matter up and told him that many or most of the people he was trying to track down were in Afghani- stan. Even though he was the Interior Minister and the national civil department of the intelligence agency was under his command along with the entire police force of Pakistan, he seemed to have little infor- mation about what was really going on.

On one occasion we were on a private plane to Kandahar together; we argued a lot during the flight about all sort of religious and political matters. He said that *Mullah*s often preach on their own merit and that many of their claims cannot be found in the *shari'a* or the *Qur'an*. He thought that they were imposing harsh religious rules and atti- tudes on the people. When I asked him for an example, he said that the case of ablutions would serve to illustrate his point. It is not writ- ten in the *Qur'an*, he said, but the *Mullah*s still instruct the people to perform ablutions.

I asked him if he had read the *Qur'an* and if he knew the meaning of it. "Yes, of course!" he said. "I am a Muslim and an educated man".

"I'm not talking about your education", I replied. "But your com- ments show that you don't know much about the *Qur'an*. And as a Muslim, I advise you not to take matters like God and his prophet (PBUH[8]) lightly". But he was not persuaded. I asked the pilot if he had a *Qur'an* with him. He gave me his copy and I showed the minister the verse in which God ordered the Muslims to perform ablutions. I told him that the main point of contention was not ablutions themselves, but that there were disagreements between *Shi'a* and the *Sunnis*. The *Sunnis* believe that the feet should be washed, but *Shi'a* interpret one of the words written as implying that the feet should only get wet or be wiped by the hands. I added that he should first learn the issues and then raise his objections.

Moinuddin Haider was a straightforward personality. When discussing certain issues he became serious, but sometimes seemed to be out of touch with Pakistan's internal politics. He often listened to what I had to say, and at times he even agreed with me. On the issue of Afghan prisoners, for example, we agreed with the Interior Ministry of Pakistan that a joint Afghan-Pakistani commission should be formed to visit all Afghan prisoners in Pakistan and review their case files. If it was determined that they were innocent, they would be released, while a separate decision should be made over the guilty ones.

This plan, like so many others, was derailed by the events of 11 September 2001.

* * *

My work as ambassador entailed more than just dealing with the Pakistani government. In order to further the Islamic Emirate's interests I involved myself beyond the ministries and established good relations with political parties, well-known personalities and other diplomats. It was important not just to deal with the government but also to involve myself actively in the political process and lead discussion about issues concerning Afghanistan and Afghan refugees in Pakistan.

To strengthen Afghanistan's relations with foreign countries I held regular meetings and discussions with ambassadors and diplomats from around the world, visited charitable organizations and the United Nations, and held press conferences for journalists. I also met with representatives of Pakistan's political parties, well-known personalities, respected *Ulema'*, merchants and others to foster cooperation and establish more links between our countries while drawing their attention to matters that concerned them as much as Afghans.

Throughout my time as ambassador I met with groups like Pashtunkhwa[9] and *Jamiat-e Ulema-ye Islam*,[10] Barelwi[11] and Panjpiriyaan, *Sipah-e Sahaba*,[12] members of the Shi'a and other religious and political groups and movements. But I never got involved in their internal affairs or in the conflicts between them. If a discussion turned to issues regarding their relationships to each other I would advise them to be patient, but told them clearly that the Emirate and myself had no interest in getting involved.

For the Embassy, it was important to have links with people from all strata of Pakistani society. Obviously relations differed from one group to another; the Emirate was closer to *Ulema-ye Islam*, the People's Party[13] and the Muslim League, sharing many of their values, points of view, language and regional interests among other things. So in turn the Baluch people and Pashtuns who had a similar culture and history were closer to us than the Punjabis and people from Sindh.

However we worked hard to maintain good relations with everyone. Most of our own *Ulema'* and *Taliban* members had studied in Pakistan, and many still continued to have close friends among the *Ulema'* of Pakistan. The only party which never got on with us and opposed us up to the end was the Pashtunkhwa Party of Mahmud Khan[14] which fought against the *Ulema'* for a long time. Even though the Awami National Party[15] of Wali Khan[16] was similar to Pashtunkhwa, we met occasionally and held discussions.

Once I was invited by some members of the Awami National Party to take part in one of their sessions to answer questions about the *Taliban*. We discussed a lot at that meeting. I also had many questions since all their questions were about Pashtu and the Pashtuns. I thought we would never hear the end of it. I tried to explain to them that while Pashtuns were in our thoughts, there was more to Afghanistan than just Pashtuns and that the other tribes settled there were just as much a part of our country as the *Taliban*.

As ambassador, of the *Taliban*, my colleagues and I promoted brotherhood among Muslims. This included all Muslims for us; there was no restriction. It did not matter which tribe or country you were from, or if someone belonged to a different sect. If a group is narrow-minded like this it will never become great. Many *Taliban* belonged to the same ethnic group, and often people get confused by this and say that tribal heritage was important to the movement. In reality, it was purely incidental; the movement started in the birthplace of the tribe, but even though the tribe assisted in its rise it never played a role later on.

After the attacks of 11 September 2001, a joint Afghan-Pakistani defence council was held in Islamabad. All the political parties of Pakistan attended, including the People's Party and the Muslim League. Even though we did not meet each other directly, meetings took place between senior-ranking officials of the political parties including well-known personalities like Chawdari Shujat Hussein,[17] Ajazul Haq[18] and some others.

All in all, we had good relations with all the Islamic and religious parties, in particular with those established in the name of *jihad* or who supported it. We worked closely with *Jamiat-e Ulema-e Islam* of Fazal Rahman,[19] *Jamiat-e Ulema-e Islam* of *Mawlana* Sami ul-Haq,[20] *Jamaat-e Islami*[21] of *Qazi* Hussein Ahmad[22] and other parties like that of Shah Ahmad Noorani *Saheb*[23] and Dr Asrar Ahmad. This close cooperation meant that the *Taliban* were very popular throughout Pakistan. At the time, I believe as many as 80 per cent of the people of Pakistan supported the Islamic Emirate of Afghanistan. The dictatorial regime of Pakistan—led by its Chief Executive Pervez Musharraf—disapproved of our close cooperation and our strong relations inside Pakistan. Pakistani officials were very concerned to see this public support for Afghanistan.

At times they would openly voice their objections, but all our activities were within the law. None of them were directed against a person or a country. I used to travel freely to each corner of Pakistan to take up invitations from people from Karachi, Lahore, Quetta and Peshawar, often informally meeting with religious and political parties, tribal elders and the *Ulema'*. From time to time I even travelled to the agencies in the tribal regions of Pakistan where most Pashtuns live. Or, I would travel to the heights of Kashmir.

I never told people where I was going and kept most of my journeys confidential to avoid any problems and raising the suspicions of the Pakistani government. Muslims throughout Pakistan were interested to meet me and other representatives of the *Taliban*. They were eager to know about the *Taliban* and the Islamic Emirate of Afghanistan, and I would hold long discussions sharing our ideas and viewpoints with them. They invited us often to meetings held on the initiative of political and religious personalities. We took part in international conferences such as those in Qartaba[24] and Deoband[25] that were attended by millions of Muslims coming together from all over the world. We would explain the situation of Afghanistan there, and promote unity among Muslims.

I took part in the *Dastarbandi* ceremonies where the *Taliban* were given their turbans of dignity, but of all conferences I attended, I was most interested in the one that took place at Deoband. It was held on the initiative of *Mawlana* Fazal Rahman, the leader of *Jamiat-e Ulema-ye Islam* and took place four or five kilometres west of Peshawar. The management was organised by *Jamiat-e Talaba-ye Islam*. Nearly two million Muslims gathered together for the conference. I was only there for the last day, but I delivered a speech on behalf of the Islamic Emirate of Afghanistan and a recorded message of *Amir ul-Mu'mineen* was played to the audience.

Several prominent personalities of Afghanistan, ministers and deputy ministers attended the conference along with me. *Mawlawi* Abdul Kabir,[26] the deputy of the ministers' council, was also supposed to take part in the conference but he was forbidden by the government of Pakistan from travelling to attend the great historical gathering. They always used to warn me not to travel to the outlying regions of the country where my security could not be guaranteed. They were more outspoken in these pronouncements after 11 September and after America's cruel attacks on Afghanistan.

* * *

Many of the problems that developed between Afghanistan and the government of Pakistan were caused by Pervez Musharraf.[27] After he seized power through a military coup in 1999 he initially emphasized his intent to establish good relations with Afghanistan. He warmly welcomed *Mullah* Mohammad Rabbani for an official visit and reassured him of his support and cooperation. At the farewell send off he even called him the most sincere ruler of Afghanistan, and a good brother of the Afghan people. Only God knows the sincerity of his heart and his promises.

In reality, Musharraf needed to establish a good relationship with the *Taliban* on account of the domestic political situation of Pakistan. The ISI had gained even more power and officially recognized the *Taliban* administration. The *Taliban* were also widely supported by the people of Pakistan. Musharraf needed support from both the people and the ISI if he wanted to remain in power. Some even say that Musharraf's coup and the collapse of Nawaz Sharif's government had only been possible because of the influence of the *Taliban*, who were widely popular. Knowing this, Musharraf welcomed Mohammad Rabbani and stated his good intentions; he hoped to gain the support of the *Taliban* and hence the Pakistani people.

Musharraf might have had other reasons as well. He is a secular man who does not believe in religion with his heart. For him, Islam is a political tool through which he thought he could control and use the *Taliban* to extend his power. He never saw the *Taliban* as a religious movement that actually wanted to establish an Islamic state. Rather, he thought that it was a group of individuals who had a political goal, who used their religion as a vehicle to mobilize the people.

The deteriorating relations between Pakistan and India might also have played a role in his decision. He could not afford to have problems on two sides of his country at once. Pakistan was engaged in war to the east as a result of the *jihad* which sought to put "Pakistan First" and they were helping Muslims there.

But his attitude towards the *Taliban* quickly changed after he was turned down. First, Musharraf invited *Amir ul-Mu'mineen* to Pakistan, but *Amir ul-Mu'mineen* turned him down; he did not want to travel to Pakistan. Then Musharraf asked to be invited to Kandahar in order to meet *Amir ul-Mu'mineen*. He wanted to discuss a deal with the United States over a possible handover of Osama bin Laden.[28] *Amir ul-Mu'mineen* did not favour the agenda of the talks, and sent a message to Musharraf telling him that he would be welcome to visit as the leader of a neighbouring country to discuss security, the economy or other issues; Bin Laden, though, was a matter that concerned Afghanistan and the USA, not Pakistan. We specifically did not want to discuss it with Pakistan because it could lead to a deterioration of the relationship between the two neighbouring countries. Musharraf cancelled his trip to Afghanistan.

The relationship was again strained when the Interior and Foreign Ministers of Pakistan officially demanded that the Islamic Emirate of Afghanistan hand over certain Pakistani individuals who had allegedly fled to Afghanistan. Moinuddin Haider, the Interior Minister, travelled to Kabul and Kandahar to speak with *Amir ul-Mu'mineen* and other officials about this alleged harbouring of criminals but he returned empty-handed. The problem Pakistan was trying to solve was a domestic one and had nothing to do with Afghanistan. The people they believed were in Afghanistan were actually moving around freely in Pakistan. Some even carried weapons with licenses issued by Moinuddin Haider himself. While Afghanistan did not report this to Pakistan directly, *Amir ul-Mu'mineen* politely said that the individuals that Pakistan sought had been given no refuge in Afghanistan.

Pakistan had submitted a list of twenty-seven individuals whom they suspected to be in hiding in Afghanistan. The Emirate told them that the individuals were not in Afghanistan, and that furthermore the exchange of prisoners or the expatriation of Pakistani nationals who were wanted in Pakistan would have to be regulated on a basis of a bilateral agreement between the two countries. Currently, we told them, Pakistan was harbouring several Afghan nationals who were wanted criminals. Discussions over the repatriation of wanted men should be held in the framework that benefits both sides. Pakistan, however, did not agree that the discussions should be held to reach a legal consensus.

Another issue arose when Musharraf tried to prevent the destruction of the Buddha statues in Bamyan. Discussions were held through Haider, who weakly argued that this was un-Islamic and unprecedented, saying that the pyramids in Egypt had not been destroyed, trying to make a comparison with the statues. By the time Musharraf sent a delegation to Kandahar it was already too late.

At the beginning of 2001, a letter from *Amir ul-Mu'mineen* arrived at the embassy.[29] It was addressed to President Musharraf along with instructions to deliver it to him in person. I contacted the Pakistani Foreign Ministry and informed them that I had a confidential letter from *Amir ul-Mu'mineen* addressed to President Musharraf. I did not know at the time what the letter was about and was only carrying out my orders. I was told that I could hand over the letter at the President's residence. A day after I had delivered the letter it was returned to me by the Foreign Ministry with a request to translate it. The letter had been written in Pashtu and no translation into Urdu or English was supplied. President Musharraf does not speak or read Pashtu, and we translated it into English at the Embassy.

In the letter, *Amir ul-Mu'mineen* called on President Musharraf to implement Islamic law and to give Pakistan an Islamic government. He explained the obligation of Islam and the role of an Islamic government. I still don't know why the letter was sent back to the Embassy to be translated. Pakistan is not a western country and is familiar with the Pashtun language and culture. More than eighteen million Pashtuns live in Pakistan and many of them work in the government and the Foreign Ministry. After I translated the letter, I submitted it along with the original Pashtu version to the Foreign Ministry. The letter had a significant impact; Musharraf made an official statement to the media about this invitation. He mentioned that *Amir ul-Mu'mineen* believed that even Musharraf's wife would support it. Musharraf soon realized that the *Taliban* were not just a group of politically-motivated individuals, but were indeed seeking to implement a real Islamic government. This was anathema to him.

During my time as ambassador I met Musharraf four times. The first occasion was at my inauguration ceremony and the second when I delivered *Amir ul-Mu'mineen*'s letter. The third time we met in Karachi. Pakistan was displaying its military hardware, showing all kinds of different defence systems, weapons and intelligence equipment, including its Ghauri[30] missiles. There were government representatives and diplomats from all over the world present and the event ended with a test launch of one of the rockets, followed by a large celebration in the governor's house. The last time we met in Karachi, Musharraf had changed; he looked tired and worn out, with sunken eyes and pale skin. He had dropped the false façade of brotherhood and showed his real face. His devilish hostility towards the Emirate of Afghanistan would ultimately hurt both countries.

It is Musharraf himself who testifies to his cruel and hypocritical behaviour towards the *Taliban* and other Muslims when he wrote in his book "Pakistan before everything!".[31] He made a business out of his Muslim brothers in Afghanistan, working to sell people for money to the infidels after 11 September. Most of these ended up in Guantánamo. He has left a black stain on Pakistan's history; one can already hear the voices of the true Pakistani people rising up, denouncing his reign for what it was: a betrayal of Islam. His book has angered so many with its self-proclaimed righteousness; it will stand as a testament to his dishonourable rule.

13

GROWING TENSIONS

Pakistan before 11 September 2001 was an empty shell, where a government within the government had become the real force within the country. Musharraf tried to lead the country, but he was deeply involved in this domestic power struggle.

Now, as then, the ISI acts at will, abusing and overruling the elected government whenever they deem it necessary. It is a military intelligence administration that is led by Pakistan's military commanders. It is the combined clandestine services, civil and military. It shackles, detains and releases, and at times it assassinates. Its operations often take place far beyond its own borders, in Afghanistan, India or in Iran. It runs a network of spies in each country and often recruits from among the local population to carry out covert missions. Its personnel are skilled and receive training in various fields, from espionage techniques to explosives.

People are placed in foreign countries in the guise of regular professions—a *Mullah* for a *Mullah*, a *Tablighi*[1] for a *Tablighi*, a tribal man for the tribal man, businessmen for businessmen or a *mujahed* for a *mujahed*. Its reach is far and it has strong roots inside and outside its own country.

The wolf and sheep may drink water from the same stream, but since the start of the *jihad* the ISI extended its roots deep into Afghanistan like a cancer puts down roots in the human body; every ruler of Afghanistan complained about it, but none could get rid of it.

The ISI seeks to find and recruit individuals from all strata of life. It has people in the embassies, ministries and provinces. Throughout my different government positions I always tried to stay away from the net they were spinning in the Afghan government, while avoiding any con-

123

flict so as not to become a target of theirs. While I was working at the embassy, many *Ulema'* and other people came to me with the pretension of being pious and God-fearing; but often they had only come to persuade me to work with the ISI.

I remained loyal to my principles and tried to avoid spending time with people who would try to draw me into the web of the ISI. Many times I received invitations from Generals with the ISI, but I made up excuses and kept away from them. I would pretend that I had a previous engagement or that I was not feeling well. On occasions when I would have to meet due to my responsibility as ambassador, I was still cautious.

Many times I was approached and offered money, but I never accepted a single rupee from them, for if you fall once into their net, you will be stuck there forever. This is the habit of all intelligence agencies across the globe. We have noted that whoever previously fell into the clutches of the CIA, KGB, ISI, SIS and so on is still stuck in those same clutches now, being used by different names and titles. They are still dancing that same *atan*, the one that made them losers in this world and in that world.

Officials from other departments and ministries would also approach me to find out about the current affairs and problems in the Embassy and in Kandahar. The ISI was always very forthright in stressing that they would support me and the Embassy in any issue or problem I had concerning Musharraf or the Pakistani Ministries. Again and again they reassured me that it would be in Afghanistan's best interests—and my own best interests—to work together with them, but I continued to conduct all official business though the Foreign Ministry.

There were ISI officials on most of Pakistan's diplomatic missions to Afghanistan. I accompanied three Pakistani delegations on their trips. The first time I went with Moinuddin Haider to Kandahar he wanted to discuss the criminals Pakistan suspected were hiding in Afghanistan and their expatriation; the case of Osama bin Laden was the main goal of his mission. The second trip concerned the destruction of the Buddhas in Bamyan. Haider wanted to stall the process in order to gain more time for negotiations. For the third diplomatic mission, a delegation of *Ulema'* travelled to Kandahar to meet with *Amir ul-Mu'mineen*. General Mahmud Ahmad was part of the delegation, but he did not take part in the discussions. I don't know if he was involved behind the scenes, but while the talks took place he always sat in silence. I remember the discussion that took place about the destruction of the statues.

Haider had been trying to persuade *Amir ul-Mu'mineen* to delay the destruction, and Mahmud was sitting next to me.

It was clear that while Haider represented Musharraf and the government, Mahmud had his own agenda. When Haider spoke to *Amir ul-Mu'mineen* he seemed to be more eloquent than the others, weighing his words carefully.

He raised his concerns about the plans of the Americans, saying, "You should make a decision. Be aware, though, that I am up to 80 per cent certain that the Americans will attack you. You should think about whether you can defend and save yourselves, and if you know how to. I for one don't know what you can do!"

He was the only one who was worried about the Americans; everyone else seemed not to be concerned about the Osama issue. As Haider talked, Mahmud leaned towards me and whispered. "What is this silly donkey talking about?" I said nothing, but thought to myself what a great difference there was between the two men.

Even though Pakistan and the ISI maintained close relations with the *Taliban*, they also continued to uphold their ties to our opposition. Both before and after 11 September 2001, they assisted various commanders who were operating against us, giving them permission to carry weapons and organize themselves politically. Some of the commanders—like Karzai, Abdul Haq,[2] *Mullah* Malang[3] and Gul Agha Shirzai—were in direct contact with America and were working with the CIA and FBI. They received financial and other assistance through the US embassy. They enjoyed a considerable freedom and privileges in Pakistan. They were—and some still are—important commanders, but without the support of the US they would have had little influence.

A former leading mujahed lived on Street F-10–3, where our own embassy guesthouse was also located. We watched his activities closely from the embassy, and set up surveillance equipment to record the phone calls coming in and out; we also tracked the movements of his associates. There was constant activity at his house, and every two or three days men from the ISI would pay him a visit. At times, even other opposition leaders would gather there. He used to meet Hezb-e Islami commanders and exchange views with the Northern Alliance, the main opposition to the Taliban, led by Ahmad Shah Massoud. From this surveillance we learned that money was being passed to support the Northern Alliance.

The ISI and the Northern Alliance met at least twice, once in Peshawar in the ISI offices and once in their Islamabad guesthouse, no. 8.

I reported all their activities back to the Emirate. When I learned that the ISI had put together a deal between America, Iran, and the Northern Alliance to tackle the *Taliban*, I travelled immediately to Kandahar.

Reporting back to *Mullah Saheb*, I told him that the growing animosities between Afghanistan and Pakistan needed to be brought to an end. "We are not just neighbouring countries", I said, "but share a common sphere and culture. We need to come to an understanding for the sake of the people". I told him that I had strong indications that Pakistan was negotiating with America, Iran and the Northern Alliance in a plot against the Emirate of Afghanistan.

I started to recruit people within the government of Pakistan who would provide information about its plans. Even though I felt we made good progress and managed to extend our network of informants throughout the government and its ministries, we still seemed quite unaware of Pakistan's goals and objectives. At the embassy, I replaced a number of my staff with people who had close relations with the ISI. I hoped to discourage commanders among the *Taliban* and those cooperating with them to seek any direct contact with the ISI or the CIA, who had to fear that my embassy would eventual learn about their betrayal given its close relationship with the ISI. We made sure that people were aware that we knew about their contacts with the foreign intelligence services and monitored their activities.

The ISI was also issuing permits and vehicle licenses to allow vehicles to cross the border into Afghanistan. To gain greater control of who was crossing the border, I made an arrangement with the ISI that every Afghan had to apply through the embassy, giving us the opportunity to copy their documents. The copies were sent to Kandahar.

While the problems with Pakistan grew each day, Afghanistan faced another diplomatic crisis when *Mawlawi* Abdul Wali,[4] the Minister for the Propagation of Virtue and the Prevention of Vice, ordered the destruction of the famous ancient statues of the Buddha in Bamyan, which were turned to rubble under the world's gaze. Somehow the Islamic Emirate's plan to destroy the statues was leaked, and delegations and diplomats from all over the world campaigned against Afghanistan and came to my embassy in Islamabad. Meeting after meeting was requested; we even saw a demonstration by foreign diplomats outside the embassy.

UNESCO, the UN body that is responsible for the preservation of historic monuments, sent us thirty-six letters of objection. Out of all the delegates that became involved, the Chinese, Japanese and Sri

Lankan diplomatic missions were the most active. China requested that the Emirate stop preparations for the destruction of the statues immediately. Sri Lanka proposed that they take the statues out of Afghanistan for repair. The religious leader of the Buddhist sect of Sri Lanka travelled to Pakistan and visited me in Islamabad. He asked to travel to Afghanistan, but his request was turned down.

Japan undertook the greatest effort and suggested two different solutions. The Japanese government sent a delegation led by the Japanese PM and the Minister of Cultural Affairs as well as six other ministers to Pakistan. Their suggestions were similar to those of Sri Lanka. They suggested that they would remove the statues piece by piece, transport them to Japan and re-assemble them there. Another suggestion they had was that they cover the statues from head to toe in a way that no-one would recognize they had ever been there, while preserving them underneath.

The Japanese even offered money; they said that the *Taliban* should consider their suggestion and offered to pay for the statues if the *Taliban* accepted their plan. The meeting with the Japanese delegation lasted for two or three hours. They stressed that Afghans had been the forefathers of their religion and that they had merely followed us by accepting Buddhism. As the forefathers of their religion, they expected us to preserve the historic and religious monuments.

Half joking, I said that they had an interesting point of view, thinking that the Afghans founded Buddhism and still considering us to be the leaders of this religion in some respect. Afghans, I told them, had evolved since then. They had realized that Buddhism was a void religion, without any basis, and had seen the light of Islam.

Since they saw us as their forefathers and had followed us before, why had they not followed our example when we found the true religion, I asked them.

Furthermore, the Buddha statues are made out of stone by the hands of men. They hold no real value for religion, so why were they so anxious to preserve them? They did not like my first question, nor my second one. They argued that the *ka'aba* in Mecca was also made of stone and by the hands of men. God had not built the building. So why, they ask, do millions of Muslims go on pilgrimage each year to circumambulate it? Why did Muslims respect it and still pray in its direction? I did not reason with them for much longer, and promised that I would submit their suggestions to the authorities back in Afghanistan.

The time of the destruction of these monuments was tiresome and particularly hard for me. There was nothing I could do to satisfy the delegations. Detonating the statues put even more strain on Afghanistan's foreign relations. I played no part in the eventual decision that was taken about the statues, and was never consulted on the issue. While I agreed that the destruction was within the boundaries of *shari'a* law, I considered the issue of the statues to be more than just a religious matter, and that the destruction was unnecessary and a case of bad timing.

But soon after the statues were destroyed, the Emirates suffered a far greater loss.

* * *

Al Hajj Mullah Mohammad Rabbani was the second-in-command of the Islamic Emirate of Afghanistan after *Amir ul-Mu'mineen*. During the *jihad*, he was the deputy commander of Abdul Raziq at a *Hizb-e Islami* (Khalis) front. Renowned for his bravery and faith among the *mujahedeen* of Kandahar and Zabul, while fighting the Russians he himself led his men into battle, carrying out many operations over the years. From 1994 onwards, Mohammad Rabbani was involved with the *Taliban* movement and soon became one of its most respected commanders. When the *Taliban* laid siege to Kabul, he commanded the operations and marched his fighters from Wardak province into the city once it had fallen.

He was then appointed the head of the *Sarparasti Shura*,[5] and later he became President of the Ministers' Council. Mohammad Rabbani's health started to deteriorate in 1999 and he had to travel to the UAE to seek treatment. Exploratory surgery confirmed that he was suffering from the early stages of liver cancer. Oncology experts from London were flown to the UAE to operate on him. Even though the surgery was a success, the doctors told him that they had not been able to remove all of the cancerous cells. He never completely recovered from his surgery and needed to weekly injections—each costing 35,000 Pakistani rupees—to manage his pain.

He visited Shawkat Hospital four times a year for treatment. Mohammad Rabbani lived for two and half years after his surgery in Dubai. One day he suddenly became sick again, and his health quickly deteriorated. He hurried back to Islamabad accompanied by his brother

Mawlawi Ahmad Rabbani and *Hajji* Wahidullah, a close friend of his. I received them at the airport along with Pakistani security officials and drove them straight to the Simij Hospital where he had been admitted. I stayed at the hospital for one hour before returning to my office. Immediately I contacted the UAE embassy to assist me in the transfer of Mohammad Rabbani to receive emergency treatment there. I also contacted the embassies of Britain and America to request their assistance.

The UAE embassy responded quickly, stating that they were ready to transfer him to their country and that they would send an ambulance-plane immediately. But the officials had misunderstood, and they thought that the great *Mullah*[6] was ill and not *Mullah* Mohammad Rabbani. When I sent the passports of Mohammad Rabbani, his brother and his friend to the embassy of UAE to obtain visas, they found out that the patient was not the senior *Mullah* but that it was *Mullah* Mohammad Rabbani. The ambassador contacted me again saying that they would send the physicians who had previously operated on *Mullah* Mohammad Rabbani in Dubai to Islamabad. On the second day the physicians arrived and were taken directly from the airport to the hospital. They examined him, went to the Marriott Hotel and called me.

The doctors said that the cancer had spread. After the surgery two and a half years earlier they had informed Mohammad Rabbani that the disease had already progressed too much and could only be managed for a few years. Now they told that the cancer was shutting down his internal organs, his lungs and that others were badly damaged and that his liver had already shut down. They advised me not to move him; they thought he had only a few days to live: seven or eight days at the most. There were no more treatment options, not in the UAE nor in any other country. I told them to inform his brother, since I could not tell him.

Britain and America never responded to my request at all. Even though the doctors had assured us that there was no treatment available, we still looked for new trials in foreign countries and started to prepare *Hajji* Mohammad Rabbani to be transferred for treatment. But he told us, "don't exhaust yourselves. I will not recover from the illness. I know it myself".

General Mahmud, the chief of ISI, Jailani and some other officials visited him. They had been informed about his condition by the doctors of Shawkat Khanum Hospital. He was getting worse each day, and it was clear that he would not recover. Fluid was gathering around his inner organs and the physicians had to drain it daily. He went into multi-organ failure and, as his doctors had predicted, on the 8th day at 8.30 am he passed away.

$$^7\text{ اِنَّاللهِ وانَّا الِيه راجعون.}$$

On his last night he gave me some advice that has been on my mind ever since. It was time for the evening prayer when my phone rang. I left his room to answer the call so as not to bother him. The call took longer than I had expected, and I talked for nearly half an hour. By the time I returned to his room they had already prayed together. Till the very end of his life, *Mullah* Mohammad Rabbani performed all his prayers with others in congregation. Back in the room he signalled me to come over to him. I could hardly hear his voice when he spoke, and it took great strength from him.

"Why did you not pray with us?" he asked me. I told him that I had been on the phone and went out so as not to bother him. The conversation took longer than I had thought and I missed the prayer. Also I did not know that they were praying in congregation.

He looked at me. "When it is the time to worship", he said, "don't get engaged in other affairs. Prefer the right of God over the rights of others!"

Then he said, "لاطاعته المخلوق فى معصيته الخالق" [8].

He never prayed alone, and every time I saw him pray he was doing so with the utmost modesty.

These were his last words to me. When he passed away, I was at home and someone informed me over the phone. By the time I arrived at the hospital, they had already taken his body to the morgue. They had placed the body into one of the refrigerated units but it did not work and his body was warm. I washed the body to fulfil the ablutions and while doing so I looked at *Mullah* Mohammad Rabbani. His entire body was riddled with Russian bullets. There didn't seem to be a single part of his body that did not show the scars of a bullet hole. God had given him life and had kept him alive then, and now he had taken him through the cancer. Later the same day, the body was transferred by a UN plane to Kandahar where *Mullah* Mohammad Rabbani was buried.

14

THE OSAMA ISSUE

The central office of the UN in Pakistan was located in Islamabad and was also responsible for coordinating activities across the border in Afghanistan. At the time it was headed by Francesc Vendrell,[1] the special envoy of UN Secretary General Kofi Annan.

Other UN organizations, such as UNHCR or Humanitarian Aid, were sharing the same offices for their operations. Back then, the UN ran the only flight between Islamabad and Afghanistan. Diplomats from the Islamic Emirate would use it regularly until the imposition of new sanctions put an end to that. The UN worked hard to maintain a good relationship with Afghanistan and the embassy. They would visit regularly and make sure that whenever a senior official from abroad paid a visit to their department, they would include a meeting with our embassy in their schedule. In retrospect, I believe it was as a result of their frequent visits that we came under more and more pressure.

In a meeting with Francesc Vendrell that took place in his office one time, he was talking enthusiastically about handing over Osama bin Laden to America, saying that the *Taliban* should respect the decision of the UN. It was not the UN's decision to discuss handing someone over to America, and also it was not their right, but they were being pressured by America. I told him that I was not in the position to decide about Osama bin Laden. Nevertheless, I was curious and asked him why the Islamic Emirate of Afghanistan should hand him over to America. He was a wanted man in America; but Afghanistan had made no legal agreement with America that would oblige it to hand over individuals. Furthermore, how could he, representing the supposedly impartial UN, support a request without any legal basis? He did not answer my question but said, "Listen! The decision has been taken,

131

and if you don't hand him over soon, America will take him from you by force".

I didn't doubt that America was preparing for a war and that the UN was cooperating. Only when and how she would start her assault was unclear. "America might go to war", I said, "but she will never reach her objectives. A war will ruin her administration and ours, blood will flow, hostility will rise and Afghanistan will fall into war with itself and the world once again".

But they never listened to me. Vendrell travelled many times to Afghanistan and met with *Amir ul-Mu'mineen* in Kandahar. When Kofi Annan came to Pakistan he was staying in the Marriott Hotel and it was there that he met Mutawakil, Afghanistan's Foreign Minister, along with a delegation from the embassy. Annan had also come to focus on the handover of Osama bin Laden to America so that he could be brought before a court. The UN always represented the stance of America and blamed Afghanistan while pretending to be impartial.

A prominent example of the UN's bias is its pronouncements about drugs in Afghanistan. One such report, which was presented to the General Assembly, was filled with baseless accusations and rumours. The *Taliban* had just managed to put an end to the cultivation of poppy and the production of opium throughout Afghanistan, but the report accused them of artificially increasing the world market price by stopping production, while sitting on stockpiles of raw opium. The report influenced public opinion throughout the world and tarnished the *Taliban*'s extraordinary success in putting an end to the production of drugs, which remains unprecedented and unrepeated to this day.

Other matters were often presented out of context, such as retaliation or other Islamic rules that were upheld by the Islamic Emirate and then presented by the UN as brutal killings and murder. In Islam, retaliation for a crime is the right of the heirs of the victim, especially in murder cases. According to these rules, no one can forgive a murderer except the heirs of the person who was killed. Irrespective of whether they are male or female, they should be brought before the *shari'a*.

A prominent example of such misrepresentation concerned the retaliation case of a woman called Zamina. She had killed her husband with her own hands and had confessed to the crime. The punishment was carried out publicly in Kabul Stadium by the relatives of the husband. To this day I don't know how the scene was filmed and the video brought to the UN, but they accused the *Taliban* of killing innocent women without mentioning the court proceedings and crime of which she had been convicted.

On another occasion, the UN released a report accusing the *Taliban* of recruiting under-aged boys to serve in the army and of using children to safeguard and defend the front lines. Eric de Mul, the UN representative in charge, was taken to the front lines and was unable to find a single under-aged child or even young boy there. After his visit, he wrote another paper[2] for the UN explaining his previous report.

Each time the *Taliban* utilized their Air Force, the UN would condemn them for causing civilian casualties. This appears to be quite ironic given the countless civilian losses Afghanistan has sustained in the past years at the hands of ISAF and NATO. And when the *Taliban* detained six foreign nationals who were accused of proselytising Christianity—even though they had signed the visa application forms that clearly obliged them to refrain from any political or religious activities while in Afghanistan—the UN imposed sanctions against Afghanistan, a country of twenty-eight million people, due to six foreigners who had violated a rule they had agreed to uphold. There were two Americans in the group, and the US was quick to say that the *Taliban* had detained them illegally. Many reports were written, and incidents took place in the run-up to the war that often seemed to be provoked by America and that put Afghanistan and the *Taliban* under a bad light.

The UN has changed. It has become a tool that is being used by countries of the world against Muslim nations like Afghanistan and Iraq. What we witness today is unprecedented. America is swallowing the world, brutally bombarding and killing thousands of innocent people in Iraq and Afghanistan, turning hundreds and hundreds of villages into rubble. How can they be allowed to disgrace, kill and detain Muslims around the world in the name of a war against terrorism? How can they hold people for years without telling them their fate or taking them to court?

I was there, and many of my friends still are. We had no rights: there are no human rights at Guantánamo Bay. There are no explanations. There are no visits from friends or family. There is nothing, only the slow deterioration of hope grinding against your spirit, making you believe that it will never end. Yet the very UN organization that imposed the sanctions against Afghanistan stays silent or even supports what America is doing in the eyes of the world.

***

With the unfolding events and growing isolation of Afghanistan, fewer and fewer foreign diplomats asked for personal meetings in Kandahar or Kabul, and the embassy started acting more as the foreign ministry until the two institutions were hardly distinguishable any more. Even though most countries didn't recognize the Islamic Emirate of Afghanistan as a legitimate government, many foreign diplomats would still come to talk with us on a regular basis, or just whenever they had a problem concerning Afghanistan. I learnt a lot from the foreign diplomats when they visited the embassy and talked regularly with many of them.

Apart from the Russian ambassador, I had met all the other ambassadors personally, and I had close relations with most of them. Many of them were polite and knowledgeable. The only ones I do not have fond memories of were the ambassadors to Afghanistan of Germany, Belgium, Kuwait and Saudi Arabia. The Pakistani ambassador was a very kind and intellectual man, however.

The ambassadors of Germany and Belgium were impolite, ruthless and arrogant. Both were tall, broad-shouldered and full of prejudice; they always wanted to discuss the position of women.

The ambassador of Kuwait was an extremely proud person. He had a yellow moustache, and whenever he spoke to me he seemed self-centred, with little regard for the Afghans. The Kuwaitis were always backing America; at times it seemed that they did not even notice that when they uttered the names of America and Bush they did so as if their lives depended on it.

The ambassador of Saudi Arabia looked young; he was eager, and used to making demands. He would often talk about Osama bin Laden. One day I went to his office to discuss the problems of the Afghan *Hajjis*,[3] but when we got down to serious discussions he ignored the reason I had asked him for a meeting. Instead he talked loudly about Osama for a long time. I was astonished by his behaviour; more than once I told him that I was not there to discuss Osama, and that the very subject was far above my level of competence and would be decided by other people. But he would not listen.

The most sympathetic and pitiable ambassador was from war-torn Palestine. All the other ambassadors from the Islamic world were polite and good people, but the ambassador of Palestine was a kind man. Most other ambassadors from non-Islamic countries observed the principles of good diplomacy, however, and took great care to maintain a good relationship with the embassy and despite the limitations caused by the lack of official recognition.

We would hold discussion with the embassies of China, France, Britain and others on specific or current issues. When an Ariana Airlines Airbus was hijacked and landed in Britain, the ambassador came and requested to try the hijackers in Great Britain, but the Emirate rejected their wish. They wanted the pilots of the plane to testify as eye-witnesses, but still the Emirate did not agree. Britain had allied itself with America on the issue of Osama bin Laden and pressure was mounting.

The ambassador of China was the only one to maintain a good relationship with the embassy and with Afghanistan. He asked to travel to Afghanistan and meet with *Amir ul-Mu'mineen* and I made the necessary arrangements to facilitate his trip. First he flew to Kabul where he was welcomed warmly before he travelled on to Kandahar to meet *Mullah* Mohammad Omar. The ambassador explained that the government of China was concerned about rumours that the Islamic Emirate of Afghanistan was allegedly assisting the Muslims in Xinxiang, a former Islamic state that was now part of China and was host to an on-and-off armed struggle for liberty between Muslim resistance groups and the central government.

Mullah Mohammad Omar assured him that Afghanistan never had any interest or wish to interfere in China's domestic issues and affairs, nor would Afghanistan allow any group to use its territory to conduct any such operations or support one to that end. The ambassador seemed to be satisfied following his visit. He was the first foreign non-Islamic ambassador ever to see *Mullah* Mohammad Omar *Saheb*. After the ambassador of China had visited, Francesc Vendrell also met *Mullah* Mohammad Omar. We worked hard in the face of many obstacles to improve Afghanistan's relations with the outside world and overcome the differences.

Contrary to our efforts, however, the situation was deteriorating with each passing day. Sanctions and other impositions were toughened and increased, relations turned from bad to worse and one event after another took place that spoiled each previous effort. This was the downward slope heading to the events of 11 September 2001, when the world was turned upside down.

Our most troubled relationship was with the Americans, with whom we used to have frequent meetings. We had extremely tough discussions over the issue of Osama bin Laden. Their demands caused many problems, and time after time we met in the American embassy or ours. When I first took up my position as envoy of Afghanistan, William Milam[4] was the American ambassador, and a colleague of his, Paula Thedi, the political affairs officer at the embassy.

After President George W. Bush was elected in 2001, he nominated a new ambassador and senior embassy staff to Islamabad. Kabir Mohabat,[5] an Afghan-American national much like Khalilzad,[6] was appointed to a position in Islamabad. Mohabat would facilitate talks and act as a mediator, and at one time was selected as temporary extraordinary envoy. America insisted that Afghanistan hand over Osama bin Laden or drive him from its territory to a country that would be willing to do so.

The *Taliban*, however, argued for a trial—to preserve the dignity of Osama bin Laden. The issue caused a significant rift between our two countries.[7] At one point I discussed the issue with the ambassador at his office late in the evening, long after office hours. The Islamic Emirate of Afghanistan had come up with three possible solutions that they deemed satisfactory for both sides, and I explained all three to him in great detail that night:

Firstly, if America blames Osama bin Laden for the bombings in Nairobi and Tanzania, and can present any evidence for its claim, it should present all its findings to the Supreme Court of Afghanistan, and the Islamic Emirate of Afghanistan will legally summon Osama bin Laden to court. If there is proof, he will be found guilty and will be punished according to the Islamic *shari'a* law.

Secondly, if America finds the first suggestion unpalatable because it does not recognize the Islamic Emirate of Afghanistan or because it does not believe in the independent, unbiased and impartial stance of the Supreme Court of Afghanistan, the Emirate suggests that a new court be formed, chaired by the Attorney Generals of three Islamic countries, proceedings of which would be held in a fourth Islamic country. America would be able to present its evidence in this court and make its case against Osama bin Laden. Afghanistan will be a partner of the court and will ensure that Osama is present at the trial and stands to answer any questions and defend himself against any allegations. If Osama is unable to defend himself and is found guilty, he will be punished for his criminal deeds.

Thirdly, if America does not trust a court that is set up by three Islamic countries and does not accept or recognize the Supreme Court of Afghanistan, we can offer to curb any and all activities of Osama. He will be stripped of all communications equipment so that his outreach will be limited to his immediate refugee life here in Afghanistan, and the Emirate will ensure that he does not use its territory for any activity directed against another country.

America rejected all three of our proposals and insisted that the Emirate hand over Osama bin Laden unconditionally, saying that he would be tried in a fair and impartial court in the US and be punished if found guilty. Afghanistan, however, could not accept America's demand. We explained and reasoned why we could not comply. For one, Afghanistan and America did not have any legal obligations towards each other to hand over criminals. No such contract or agreement was ever signed between the two nations. As is customary in cases like these, any criminal that is not subject to an extradition agreement would be tried in the country where they are imprisoned or found at the time. Bilateral recognition and the sovereignty of each country would be respected.

America insisted on judging Osama in America. No other country was ever discussed; they wouldn't even consider the UN court in The Hague that would at least have had some measure of independence and impartiality, and would have been an option that would have allowed both parties to keep face.

The Islamic Emirate had two principal objections to America's demand that we hand over Osama bin Laden. Firstly, if every country were to hand over any person deemed a criminal by America, then America would *de facto* control the world. This would in turn threaten the independence and sovereignty of all countries. Secondly, America's demands, and its rejection of all suggestions offered by the Emirate, imply that there is no justice in the Islamic world, and with it no legal authority of Islam to implement justice and law among the people. This stands in direct opposition to Islam itself and its system to protect the rights of the people and to punish criminals. This problem remained unresolved till the very end.

There were other solutions that were discussed but never officially acknowledged by the Emirate or America. One suggestion was made to install a joint court comprising America and some Islamic countries. Another was to seek a trial at the International Court at the Hague. None of these suggestions were ever seriously discussed since America would not divert from its demand that Osama bin Laden needed to be handed over to its justice system. The USA made it clear that they were willing to use force should Afghanistan not comply with its demand.

Christina Rocca,[8] the Secretary of State for South Asian affairs, passed through Islamabad on a tour and requested a visit. We met on 2 August 2001 at the American Embassy in Islamabad. She was concerned only with Osama. During the conversation she flouted every diplomatic principle, and every single word she uttered was a threat, hidden or open. Our meeting was a battle of harsh rhetoric.

I held four meetings with the US ambassador over the issue of Osama bin Laden, each without result. Even though we had both tried to improve the relationship between our countries, and had a good personal rapport, nothing came of these encounters as neither of us had the power to take decisions. Other people were responsible for authorising all of our meetings as well as all of our decisions and answers, all of which were negative.

One morning the US ambassador unexpectedly asked for an appointment that very same day. (The Americans occasionally got agitated over small things.) I was tired and on my way home to rest, but they insisted on meeting as soon as possible. After the late afternoon prayer the ambassador came to my house, accompanied by Paula Thedi. He seemed worried and impatient and started to talk as soon as he entered the room. "Our intelligence reports reveal that Osama is planning a major attack on America. This is why we had to come immediately at such a late hour. You need to tell officials in Afghanistan to prevent the attacks!"

I reported their worries directly back to the Emirate, even though I should have communicated this message to the central leadership through the Ministry of Foreign Affairs. But given the urgency of their visit, and remembering the old story of the border commander during Zahir Shah's time[9] it seemed best to break official protocol. Twenty-three hours later I received a letter from Kandahar for the ambassador. "Afghanistan has no intention to harm the United States of America now or in the future. We do not condone attacks of any kind against America and will prevent anyone from using Afghan soil to plan or train for any such attack."

It was a letter of assurance that clearly outlined the Emirate's position. I personally translated it and passed it on to the American ambassador along with the original Pashtu text. But nevertheless, the letter did not rid America of her doubts.

The last time I saw the American ambassador was when he came to say goodbye. He told me that he appreciated the good diplomatic relationship that we had cultivated and expressed his concern about the future and about forthcoming events that were likely to spell disaster. He believed that Osama remained a threat and would continue his fight against America. And nor would the US tolerate any longer his threats and attacks. It was time to find a solution or the problem will get out of hand, he said. Even though America had imposed sanctions on Afghanistan through the UN and had taken diplomatic steps to isolate it further, there were still concerns about Osama bin Laden. The issue was discussed in countless private parties and gatherings; America would drop all its other demands and formally recognize the Emirate if he were handed over.

When the attacks of 11 September 2001 took place on the World Trade Center and the Pentagon, everything came to a standstill and the world was flipped on its back. The negotiation process was derailed by the events and all of us witnessed what happened next.

15

9/11 AND ITS AFTERMATH

It was around seven or eight in the evening and I was at home waiting for dinner to be served when Rahmatullah rushed into the house. He seemed worried, and turned to me with a pale face: "Zaeef *Saheb*, have you seen the news on TV?"

"No. What happened?" I replied.

"Turn on the TV. You need to see what is happening in the United States", he said. "America is on fire".

I didn't own a television at the time; the embassy had a set which was used for media monitoring, but I kept myself personally informed through press clippings and reports about current events happening around the world.

Rahmatullah was the brother of Ahmed Rateb Popal, who lived in the house across from mine, and was Popolzai, the same tribe as Hamid Karzai. He and I went over to Rahmat Faqir's house. Many people had gathered, including colleagues from the embassy, and we watched as one of the towers of the World Trade Center in New York City burned. There was fire and large clouds of black smoke billowing up from the building. A second airplane hit the other tower soon afterwards. It smashed into the building like a bullet, with fire and debris shooting out of the tower on all sides. People who were caught above the fire threw themselves from the sky-high buildings, falling to the ground like stones. The scene was horrific, and I stared at the pictures in disbelief.

My mind raced as I looked at the screen and considered the probable repercussions of the attack. At that very moment, I knew that Afghanistan and its poverty-stricken people would ultimately suffer for what had just taken place in America. The United States would seek revenge, and they would turn to our troubled country.

The thought brought tears to my eyes, but those sitting with me in the room looked at me with genuine surprise and asked me why I was sad. To be honest, some of them were overjoyed, offering congratulations and shaking each other's hands for the events that we had just witnessed.

This happiness and jubilation worried me even more; I was anxious about the future. How could they be so superficial, finding joy in an event for a moment, but oblivious to its impact on the days to come?

I turned to the others, asking them, "who do you think the United States and the world will blame for what has just happened? Who will face their anger?"

They said that they didn't know who would be blamed and that they didn't know why they should care. To them, America was our enemy, a country that had imposed sanctions on our country and one that had attacked us with missiles. The image on their screens—a symbol of that power burning on its own soil—was a reason for celebration.

I didn't talk with them for long time, but I felt the need to share what I believed to be true.

Drying my eyes, I spoke: "I don't want to convince you of anything, or change what you think is right, but I tell you now that you will remember this moment, here in this room with your colleagues, because we will have to pay the price for what has happened today. The United States will blame Osama bin Laden, a guest of Afghanistan as you all know. An American attack on Afghanistan is more than likely given the fear and sorrow of that country today. America might strike soon."

"Bin Laden is America's 'enemy number one' and has been blamed for major and minor incidents in the past. For America, blaming and incriminating a prominent figure of the Islamic world will give them the opportunity to interfere in Muslim countries with the support of the rest of the world. Osama bin Laden is the perfect scapegoat to allow America to pursue its wider agenda. America also needs to cover up its mistakes and failures; it will use individuals like Osama to mislead the world. I fear that he will claim responsibility for the attack and will give Americans the proof they need, whether he was involved or not. Osama's mouth is not easily controlled. And America does not tolerate such events in silence or without taking action."

I reminded them of the Second World War, when the Japanese air force launched a surprise attack on the US Navy at Pearl Harbor. The

Navy suffered greatly in the attack, with heavy casualties, and America was swift to retaliate. Without hesitation, the United States attacked Japan by dropping two nuclear bombs—'Little Boy' and 'Fat Man'—on Hiroshima and Nagasaki, and tens of thousands of civilians burned in the hellfire of the bombs. I told them that I was sure that America would invade our country with equal vigour. The Islamic Emirate of Afghanistan was already a thorn in America's side, and now the world would join her. That, I told them, was the reason for my tears.

Those with me didn't share my worries, though, and insisted that most of what I said was wrong. They quoted a Pashtun proverb back to me: "look where the attacks happened and look where the war now takes place". They thought America was too far away to retaliate. I returned to my house, anxious about what would happen in the coming months.

* * *

Back at home, I called Sohail Shahin,[1] the political affairs chief at the embassy. We discussed what had happened and what position to take with the press, agreeing that we would issue a brief statement to the media in the morning. It was late when I headed up to bed. My worries prevented me from sleeping and a recollection of the meeting with the US ambassador a few months earlier haunted me. They had been talking about a major attack on the United States launched from Afghanistan, and at the time I did not believe them.

I kept recalling that day, and still I couldn't sleep. It was one o'clock and I was staring at the ceiling when my phone suddenly rang. Tayyeb Agha[2] greeted me from the office of the Islamic Emirate in Kandahar and said that *Mullah* Mohammad Omar, the *Amir ul-Mu'mineen*, wanted to speak with me. It seemed that they, too, were unable to sleep on account of what had taken place just a few hours before. Tayyeb Agha put me through to *Mullah Saheb* and after a brief greeting he asked me about the attacks and what I had learnt about them so far. I told him what I had seen and shared my concerns with him. *Mullah* Mohammad Omar explained the official public stance that the Islamic Emirate would take. Our conversation continued for another fifteen minutes, after which I returned to bed.

I went to the embassy early the next morning and advised my monitoring team to follow the news on television closely. *Dawn* and *The*

Nation, Pakistan's main English newspapers, ran a selection of stories presenting media reaction from around the world to the attacks on the United States. I called a press conference for ten o'clock, and just before the press conference Wakil Ahmed Mutawakil, the Foreign Minister, called me to clarify the official stance to be adopted by Afghanistan and its delegates abroad.

We issued a short press release:

Bismillah ar-Rahman ar-Rahim.[3] We strongly condemn the events that happened in the United States at the World Trade Center and the Pentagon. We share the grief of all those who have lost their nearest and dearest in these incidents. All those responsible must be brought to justice. We want them to be brought to justice, and we want America to be patient and careful in their actions.

We sent a copy to the US embassy in Islamabad, but it was already too late. America, in its moment of terror and fear, had become angry and was looking for revenge.

* * *

The situation then changed dramatically, especially when George Bush appeared on television on the second day after the attack, full of anger and hate. He looked terrified, standing in front of the camera in a bulletproof vest like a soldier. Without waiting for investigations to deliver reliable proof, he announced that bin Laden was responsible for the attacks of 11 September. Osama bin Laden, he said, was wanted dead or alive. The Islamic Emirate of Afghanistan was sheltering bin Laden, and was therefore complicit in and responsible for his crime.

Our Foreign Minister, Mutawakil, voiced his disapproval of the statement two days later, but the fear of another attack continued to loom over the United States. President Bush was a refugee in the sky, circling America in Air Force One, unable to land. His plane only touched down for emergency meetings or important press statements. The location of these meetings was undisclosed and heavily guarded by the American security agencies. Each time he made an appearance, however, he seemed to have lost his senses. The situation for Afghanistan deteriorated quickly, especially after the United Nations voiced their support for America and demanded that Afghanistan hand over bin Laden to the USA.

The Muslim world scattered at the wrath of the United States, moving quickly out of her way without looking into the details. It was as if doomsday itself had arrived. The world fell in line with America and in turn Afghanistan became more and more isolated. The Islamic Emirate of Afghanistan, however, did not change its policy, even though it was being condemned for the attacks. It voiced the same doubts and pointed to the lack of evidence and proof, just as it had done after the Nairobi and Dar as-Salaam bombings.[4]

Sanctions on Afghanistan were tightened and the rumours of a possible war gained momentum each day; America was sending delegations to countries around the world to ask for their backing. Officials arrived in Islamabad more than once to ask for Pakistan's support, but they chose not to seek the cooperation of Afghanistan, isolating it throughout the months leading up to the war. America's list of demands grew day by day. They started with a call for the handing over of Osama bin Laden, but soon included provision for the formation of a broad-based democratic government, human rights and women's rights, as well as for full access to any location in the country for search operations by American troops.

I tried my best to resolve the dispute through political means, hoping to avoid a war through talks and negotiations. I had the personal email address of President Bush and the White House, as I had written to him in the past. Back then, I had congratulated him on winning the presidential elections. This did not mean that I was glad that he had won. I remember asking myself what need there was to congratulate a man whose personality was questionable, both from an Islamic and political point of view.

However, after 11 September I tried to initiate a dialogue with the White House and President Bush, hoping to be able to open up lines of communication and avoid what we all by now know actually happened. President Clinton had set the tone for America's behaviour in Afghanistan: he sent cruise missiles and imposed international sanctions.

Once again, I wrote a long letter to President Bush and the White House on behalf of the Afghan people, depicting the problems we faced: the hunger, the drought, the refugees… I went into great detail about the severe impact that continuous warfare had had on Afghan society, the many domestic enemies, the fractionalisation and the many casualties of war and lawlessness. I asked him to be cautious, to take into account the disastrous effects of war, and to avoid repeating the mistakes of the past. If they continued further down the same path, America would be solely responsible for what would follow.

"There is no doubt", I wrote, "that America is the only superpower in the world, just as there is no doubt that Afghanistan has already lost everything in the previous two decades of war. We don't have any power—economic or political—and even our military is stretched to hold on to the lawless provinces in the east, let alone stand up to America. Afghanistan grew tired of fighting during the *jihad* and civil war ten years ago. We don't want to fight anymore, nor do we have the power to do so".

With all this in mind, I advised him to choose dialogue and talks instead of war. A copy of my letter was sent to the US embassy in Islamabad and to members of the US parliament and Congress as well. I was trying to draw their attention to the terrible outcome that a military solution would have for both Afghanistan and the United States.

At the same time, I contacted the Afghan-born advisor to President Bush, Zalmai Khalilzad. I told him that as an Afghan he should help and make every possible effort to try to prevent the dispute from turning into a war. I always spoke with Khalilzad on the phone from Jalalabad, where I travelled from Islamabad so that Pakistan wouldn't eavesdrop on our conversations. I told him that America should be talking to Afghanistan directly and that they shouldn't focus on Pakistan. The *Taliban*, I said, do not listen to Pakistan, nor do they accept its decisions. As a mediator, I reasoned, Pakistan wouldn't serve the interest of Afghanistan or America. Bush remained arrogant, though, and refused to listen to reason.

Despite the total obedience of Pakistan's autocratic ruler to Bush, our embassy in Islamabad was not immediately closed. Musharraf could have closed it on the day of the attacks, but the United Nations and even the United States did not want to close the only open channel to Afghanistan straight away. In any case, Pakistan had also demanded that Afghanistan hand over Osama to the United States.

I recently read Musharraf's autobiography,[5] in which he portrays himself as a heroic figure, a courageous military commander. He writes that he isn't afraid of anyone but God, and that he cannot be killed by anyone except Almighty *Allah*. There is little to criticise here: a Muslim should have faith in God the Almighty and know that only He can give life and take it away. Elsewhere in his book he wrote that he was threatened by President Bush in the period after the attacks. If Pakistan didn't cooperate, so his narration of Bush's threat goes, it would be sent back to the Stone Age. Musharraf should be clear: either he is with us or against us. The threat, Musharraf writes, forced him to give access to military bases inside Pakistan to America, from which they were able to bomb the sacred soil of Afghanistan and turn the homes of our people to rubble.

How can someone who claims only to be afraid of God bow down to the threat of Bush when he is faced with an attempt to overthrow the Afghan government and target the people of Afghanistan—women, children and the elderly—with bombs and missiles?

During the months preceding the American attack the ISI contacted me several times. On one occasion two ISI officers came to the embassy. They wanted information about the different political positions within the government of the Islamic Emirate of Afghanistan, and who filled them at the time. Being aware of what they were actually looking for, I handed them an organizational chart of Afghanistan's administration, pretending that I was not ignorant of the structure or system of the military. The officers were suspicious and continued to question me about the military but I assured them that I really was not the person to talk to on the subject.

Another time the ISI asked me to visit their central office. I replied that I could not come, but would be glad to meet them if necessary in the foreign ministry. There, I said, we could discuss any issue at hand. Their request was soon followed by a demand: I should come to their guesthouse. Again I declined. Finally General Mahmud, General Jailani and Brigadier Farooq, accompanied by Mahmud, came to my house, where I welcomed them.

They were not in the mood for pleasantries: "We know that you are aware of what will happen in the near future", General Mahmud said, "and we also know that you believe that Pakistan will join the international community and America against Afghanistan. Maybe you think that this would be an action against Islam and neighbourly principles. Maybe that's why you are suspicious and didn't want to come to the central office. We have come today to tell you two things: firstly, we have received reports that you are planning to assassinate President Musharraf. Any plan for an assassination will fail and I must strongly advise you to immediately cease work on these plans, if indeed they exist. Secondly, we both know that an attack on Afghanistan from the United States of America seems more and more likely. We want to assure you that you will not be alone in this *jihad* against America. We will be with you".

I listened to them patiently and when they had finished spoke to them calmly. "If someone plans to assassinate Musharraf", I said, "then that's an internal affair of Pakistan and none of my business. I for one have neither the possibilities nor the facilities to assassinate him". In a sarcastic tone I said that they should not involve the Emirate in such plans of theirs.

"Secondly", I said, "if America is going to attack Afghanistan, then you know better than me from which airports and territories it will attack us. We will see later how many Afghans will be martyred in this war. But, General, you will be responsible for the bloodshed and the killing when you cooperate with America, in this world and the next. You will be Afghanistan's enemy number one".

I was still in the middle of my sentence when General Jailani cut me off and started screaming. But even though he was already upset I continued talking, turning towards Mahmud. "Wait, General!" I said. "You speak of *jihad* while the Americans are stationed in your airbases and flying through your airspace, even attacking Afghanistan based on your intelligence reports. You should be ashamed even to utter the word *jihad*. Have you no fear of God that you talk to me of *jihad*? Why do you want Afghans to fight the *jihad*? Why don't you start it in your own country? Is *jihad* only an obligation for Afghans? General! Please don't speak to me about supporting something you are actually against!" I had become emotional and had talked myself into a rage. When I looked at General Mahmud, tears were running down his face. Jailani was crying out loud, with his arms around my neck like a woman. I was puzzled by their reaction. A few moments later they excused themselves and left.

Pakistan was sending out mixed signals. At the same time as General Mahmud was telling me that an attack was imminent, the Pakistani Consulate in Kandahar continued to assure us that America would never launch an attack on Afghanistan. They said that the rumours of war and Bush's ongoing bellicose rhetoric were just to calm the widespread anger of the American people. A number of high-ranking Muslim officers in the Pakistani army, though, also served as advisors to President Musharraf and they kept us supplied with information that seemed far more realistic. We also had ties to staff from the Pakistani Ministries of Interior and Foreign Affairs.

During those days I did everything I could to keep myself informed about the various plans and programmes that were being put into motion. I even once asked for a meeting with Musharraf himself through one of my contacts in the Foreign Ministry. He declined the request.

I learnt of some of the war plans and America's efforts to form an alliance. This worried *Mullah* Mohammad Omar. America, together with the Pakistani intelligence agencies, had apparently prepared a plan to launch a cruise missile attack on the residences of *Mullah* Mohammad Omar and Osama bin Laden in order to eliminate them in the first phase of their campaign. This would, I had heard, eventually become part of a vast military operation including heavy air strikes by the US Navy and Air Force. The ground offensive, according to that plan, would be carried out by Afghan allies who would receive financial and material assistance—as well as guidance—from America. Most of the commanders who joined America were from the northern provinces.

Our enemies were known to us, and the implementation of America's attack on Afghanistan would rely on such commanders. Abdul Haq and Malik Zarin[6] were the American allies in the east. The former was a prominent *mujahed* and anti-*Taliban* leader from Nangarhar, while the latter, a prominent commander in Kunar province, was from the Meshwani tribe. Padshah Khan Zadran[7]—the Pashtun leader from Paktya province—operated in the southeast along with a number of smaller commanders. Hamid Karzai, Gul Agha Shirzai, Hamid Agha[8] and some others would be in the south. Only in the south-west were America and Pakistan unable to find allies.

I travelled to Kandahar to meet *Mullah* Mohammad Omar, the *Amir ul-Mu'mineen*, at his new house. I presented him with all the information I had gathered over the past few weeks about the operation America was planning. *Mullah* Mohammad Omar was unwilling to believe the details of what I had told him; he reasoned that America couldn't launch an offensive without a valid reason, and that since he had demanded that Washington conduct an official investigation, and deliver incontrovertible proof incriminating bin Laden and others in the 11 September attacks, the government of Afghanistan would take no further steps regarding the matter till they were presented with such hard evidence.

In *Mullah* Mohammad Omar's mind there was less than a 10 per cent chance that America would resort to anything beyond threats, and so an attack was unlikely. From the information I had seen, I told him, America would definitely attack Afghanistan. I told him that I was almost completely convinced that war was imminent. Pakistan and America were on the verge of reaching an agreement that would seal Afghanistan's fate.

Pakistan was making every effort to meet with Communist generals and former *mujahedeen* commanders while the ISI facilitated contacts for the United States, introducing them to potential allies in a war against the Islamic Emirate. America was willing to pay for the cooperation of commanders; they spent millions of dollars, providing free satellite phones and other resources in unimaginable quantities. Even staff from the Afghan embassy in Islamabad received money to gather information for America. America's efforts were a blessing for Pakistan, which grasped at the generous provisions of money and resources with outstretched hands. Pakistan provided military bases in Sindh and Baluchistan province to the US and these were soon overflowing with stockpiled arms and munitions for the war against Afghanistan. The Pakistani and American intelligence agencies shared information on various issues, including details about the leaders of the Afghan forces who commanded the Afghan military and air bases.

The ISI, however, had their own secret agenda in order to gain a strategic advantage in Afghanistan. They sought to regroup and organize the *jihadi* commanders who were living in the frontier regions—as well as throughout Pakistan—who hadn't been involved in operations inside our country since the end of the wars of the 1980s. In a parallel move, they secretly planted commanders among the military forces of the Islamic Emirate of Afghanistan who would be used to bring down our government. And finally, Pakistan held its own secret talks with the Northern Alliance to discuss the military and political future of the country. Pakistan saw the Northern Alliance as the future leaders of Afghanistan, who would have not only a considerable stake in any new government, but also continue to be important to the United States, which would have to rely on them for a long while yet.

All the signs were pointing towards war, and the more I learnt the clearer it became to me that a war could not be avoided. Pakistan, once our brother, had turned its back on us and the world was rallying behind President Bush and his call for action. I knew that the calm days would soon come to an end, and that the Islamic Emirate of Afghanistan would have to face a mighty enemy in a battle for its very survival.

* * *

It was an October morning when I was told by high-ranking Pakistani authorities that the coming night would herald the start of the invasion. Americans troops had already been deployed in Pakistan's military air bases, their aircraft were patrolling our airspace. A US aircraft carrier with hundreds of jets and cruise missiles had dropped anchor in the Persian Gulf. Their computer-guided intelligence drones were already spying over Afghanistan; one had already crashed in Mazar-e Sharif.

The US ambassador to Pakistan[9] had also handed over a secret file to Pervez Musharraf containing evidence about the 11 September attacks and the alleged complicity of the *Taliban* regime with *Al Qaeda*, thereby providing the General with a pretext to explain his government's cooperation with the Americans in the invasion of Afghanistan. It remains a mystery why the United States would give such proof to Pakistan rather than to Afghanistan, when our government had specifically asked for these documents. In reality, these were only the old confessions of an Arab called Ali who had been captured. The Americans claimed he had been involved in the Dar es Salaam attacks, and Ali disappeared, going crazy after he was injected with chemicals that meant he would never return to reality. This was a serious embarrassment for Musharraf, and his reputation was further tarnished.

I relayed all this information to my headquarters, saying that they should be prepared for an attack during the night.

As the next day passed into evening, I was tense and alert, trying to find out what was happening. It was 10 p.m. when I received a phone call from the commander-in-chief of Kandahar Corps, *Mullah* Akhtar Mohammad Osmani,[10] now deceased. He told me that Kandahar airbase was being hit by missiles at that very moment. "Has *Amir ul-Mu'mineen* been informed?" I asked. The commander replied that, yes, they had told him. "Wait", he said. "More missiles are coming down on *Amir ul-Mu'mineen*'s house!" He wanted to say more but the phone line went dead.

I became agitated. The thing that worried me more than anything else was the possibility that *Mullah* Mohammad Omar might be killed. He had been assured by some Pakistani authorities that there would no attack, so he might not have paid close attention to our information. In reality this wasn't a real assurance, but was intended to keep him in the dark about America's intentions and the secret conspiracy to kill him.

I was still thinking about this when the phone rang again, this time from Kabul. It was *Mullah* Abdul Ghaffar,[11] the head of the communications department at the Defence Ministry. "Kabul air base is being hit by missiles", he told me. Then he connected me with the minister, *Mullah* Obaidullah. I had given him the war plan, and he had been listening to my advice. I spoke to him using just a few short words: "This is not the time for soft beds and luxurious palaces. Get yourself somewhere safe. We will see what God wills". Then I hung up.

For a time I just sat there, head in my hands, wondering what would happen. How long would Afghanistan burn in this fire again? But I consoled myself with the old proverb about the man and his saddle-bags—if you worry too much, you may lose everything. I told myself that this was no time to sit and worry; it would not do me any good. Better that I should work.

The telephone was ringing off the hook. People wanted answers, journalists wanted answers, but I did not pick up the phone. Instead I called Shahin and said, "It has begun. Call the journalists together. We can take care of them all at once". On that first night, I gave a press conference at midnight in my garden.

This was the beginning of the war.

* * *

Prior to the attacks, the ISI officers who had visited me earlier were all dismissed from their duties. General Jailani was transferred to Maiwali,[12] and General Omar took General Mahmud's position as head of ISI. I never learnt what happened to General Mahmud after that.

According to a classified report, the ISI had burned documents regarding Afghanistan that the Americans had requested and had also informed *Mullah Saheb* that the American's primary goal was to kill him and the senior leadership of the *Taliban*. The ISI had even advised *Mullah Saheb* to find a safe haven.

Other Pakistani officials had dismissed the information, suggesting that America would continue to raise pressure through military measures but that no real attack or invasion was planned. *Mullah* Mohammad Omar stayed in his house and disregarded the growing danger. I had personally informed him of America's intention to go to war, sometimes showing maps and other evidence I had gathered, but Kandahar thought our reports to be wrong. *Mullah Saheb* believed that there was no logical reason for America to attack Afghanistan and therefore considered the possibility of an attack rather unlikely.

Two days after the hostilities began, General Omar visited me. He had two demands: he said that as a senior leader and representative of the *Taliban* I should assist in separating the "fundamentalist" from the "moderate" *Taliban*. This, he said, would ultimately help the *Taliban* and would keep the movement alive. In reality, his intention was to split the *Taliban* into factions in order to weaken them. I was supposed to lead moderate *Taliban* against *Amir ul-Mu'mineen*. He assured me that they would support me financially and logistically.

This is the suggestion that the new administration of the United States under President Obama is working on. Bush, while he was still in power, and together with Britain and Karzai, also tried to do this during his seven years. They think that the *Taliban* exist for the sake of money or power, so logically it would seem that they can be destroyed with money and power. In reality, the *Taliban* movement is one based on Islamic ideology, struggling for holy *jihad* under the principles of *itta'at* or obedience and *samar* or listening, as well as that of dialogue. The thought of dividing them into moderates and hardliners is a useless and reckless aim.

Secondly, he told me to refrain from talking to the media and to cease all press conferences at the embassy.

If I needed to make a public statement, I was to hand over the press release to the Pakistani government before issuing it so that it could be censored and tailored to their needs. General Omar and the men that accompanied him left after he finished talking. I didn't respond to him, and continued my work. I understood what they had advised me to do, but I could not see how they expected to benefit from my forming a faction of *Taliban* or what the result would be for the *Taliban* and *Mullah Saheb*. I kept the information to myself.

* * *

Every day at 4 p.m. I held a press conference to tell the world what was happening in Afghanistan. I would present information about the general situation or on specific events as well as answer the journalists' questions. I received frequent calls from Aziz Khan at the Foreign Ministry to keep quiet.

At 3 p.m. I would gather information from all over Afghanistan, and at 3:30 p.m. I would print it out. I then gave a copy to the ISI agent, but before he even got back to his office I was already holding the press conference. In this way, I managed to get the news out before they had a chance to do anything.

The ISI formally warned me three times, saying that they were receiving the information at the same time as I was holding the press conference. I made excuses; I told them that I had only received the report from Afghanistan at three in the afternoon, and that I would correct it and send them a copy thirty minutes later. I would make excuses for the time delay, saying that my information was incomplete, that my translator was absent, that my typist was late. Using such methods I thwarted their every attempt to censor me.

Even while under constant threat, I continued my work. When Mazar-e Sharif fell to the Northern Alliance on 9 November, the ISI urged me to contact *Mullah* Obaidullah, the Defence Minister, and *Mullah* Mohammad Hassan Akhund, the governor of Kandahar, to tell them to come to Pakistan. I told the ISI representative that I could not simply call them and ask them to come to Pakistan since they were higher in rank than me. Furthermore, I told the ISI that I did not want them to come to Pakistan as I believed the ISI wanted to arrest them.

Every few minutes they called to ask if I had talked to *Mullah* Obaidullah Akhund or *Mullah* Mohammad Hassan Akhund. I replied that I had talked to them and advised them that they would be arrested as soon as they set foot on Pakistani soil. I did not trust anything Pakistan promised. It was difficult to navigate in Islamabad those days, doing my work while trying to prevent being banned and keep from losing my credentials.

I spent most of my time tracking events and following the international situation as well as that in Afghanistan. The last person I met from ISI was Colonel Imam.[13] He was well-known among Afghans from the early years of the anti-Russian *jihad* and was now the Consul at Pakistan's Consulate in Herat. He was expelled from Afghanistan after America started its attack. The *Taliban* did not trust him and even though he tried to stay in Kandahar, he had to leave the country.

He asked for an appointment and we met in the embassy. After we exchanged greetings he started to cry. Tears were running down his face and white beard and when finally he composed himself he could not speak. Then he blurted out "Almighty *Allah* might have decided what is to take place in Afghanistan, but Pakistan is to blame. How much cruelty it has done to its neighbour! And how much more will come!" He blamed Musharraf, who had erased and stamped out the achievements of the past two decades of cooperation, suffering and friendship, and had stripped the *jihad* of its glory. Pakistan would be forced to bear the shame, not Musharraf. He started to cry again, saying that they would never be able to repent for what Musharraf had done, and that they would bear the blame not only in this world, but in the next. He left straightaway, and I did not meet another officer from the ISI until they came to arrest me. I was watched closely, though. Three motorbikes and one car would follow me and stand outside the embassy and my house day and night.

This was the government of Pakistan; the public was quite different. All over the country violent anti-American demonstrations took place and there were daily clashes between the police and protestors; every day people died. The Pakistani government was trying very hard to suppress the protests. They put many people—including religious leaders—in jail, but still the demonstrations kept growing.

Thousands of volunteers were coming to our embassy in Pakistan to take part in the war. Thousands of others travelled into Afghanistan through Baluchistan and the NWFP in order to join a volunteer brigade, some ten thousand–strong, that crossed the Durand line at Miram Shah.

The government in Islamabad tried to discourage its people from going, but Pakistan itself was rocking on its foundations. The situation was now beyond the capability of the government to control. When I too became tired of the flood of volunteers, I spoke on television, saying that people should no longer come to us in order to get to Afghanistan. I said that we needed a financial *jihad* rather than a physical one. It did not work; still the people kept coming, motivated by their Islamic zeal.

16

A HARD REALISATION

During the first two months of the war I spoke four times on television. On each occasion I delivered the same basic message:

My dear Muslim brothers and sisters! As you well know, the Americans are attacking us, using bombs and missiles from far away. It doesn't help to bunch together as big groups. This just makes you a better target for the airplanes, and results in more casualties. This does more harm than good. More deaths mean more harm. So, for now, we don't want to send large numbers of people into Afghanistan in order to prevent unnecessary harm. Instead, we need financial support.

In the Arab world and other Islamic countries, emotions were running high. Many people came to the embassy, volunteering to go to Afghanistan. Even though we discouraged everyone from making the journey, thousands still made their way across our borders. There was such a flood that I could have sent five thousand people a day into Afghanistan. Hundreds of thousands were ready to sacrifice their lives.

When a fellow Muslim came to me seeking help to make the journey, I would look him over from head to toe and ask about his life, his behaviour, his career. Strong, handsome young people were coming. They wanted my assistance, but what feelings were in their hearts? What emotions had brought them to me?

It was difficult for me to persuade them to take a different path without insulting their convictions. I wish there was an army of these holy young people to defend Islam and Islamic beliefs, an entity that allows their emotions to be satisfied and hopes to be fulfilled, and which serves the proper purpose. It is sad to see the armies of the Islamic world being deployed against Islam itself these days.

Soon after the first attacks, people started to raise money to support the Emirate. All the cities in Pakistan were collecting donations; some

157

were bringing them directly to Afghanistan, while others went to our offices in Karachi, Quetta, Lahore, and Peshawar. A large amount was flowing into the coffers. We were giving out receipts for donations that stated what the money was intended for: education, refugees or orphans. Whatever was donated was used for a specific purpose. Some people gave us a hundred Pakistani rupees, while others brought a million. For us it made no difference. Everyone gave what they could, freely and out of solidarity. Many Muslim sisters were giving us their jewellery and other possessions. We collected gold by the kilo. Soon we also started to accumulate blankets, shoes and other much needed goods in the embassy. I still remember the passion of our Muslim brothers, and how much they wanted to help.

One morning, a young man wanted to see me and I invited him to my office. He was a young Pashtun from the NWFP.[1] I invited him to take a seat, but he told me that his wife was with him and that she too wanted to speak with me. I agreed, and a few minutes later he brought her in, covered by her *burqa*.[2] She said "hello" very politely. Although I could not see her face, I could tell by her voice that she was in tears. "Ambassador", she said. "I have many possessions in my house that I could offer for God's work. But I have heard from the *mullah*s that the best charity you can give are your most precious possessions. The jewellery that my father and my husband gave me for my wedding is my most beloved possession. I want to offer this gold necklace for God's work. I am giving it directly into your hands, so that you can bear witness to this act of charity on the Day of Judgment. You are now responsible for spending this on the *mujahedeen*".

She handed me a beautiful golden necklace. Her husband unfastened his gold Rolex watch and put it on top of the necklace. I was so touched by the sacrifice of this Pashtun sister that I could barely speak. I kept their donation separate from the other donations, and gave it to *mujahedeen* whom I considered the most trustworthy. I knew that I would be required to bear witness on Judgment Day. I often think about the next world, and I know that if I am faithful to God then everything will be easy for me. May *Allah* grant that I meet this Pashtun sister and her husband in paradise. *Ameen*.[3]

Another day, when I was on the way to the office in my car, I saw a young man and woman waving to me. I told my driver to stop and rolled down my window to ask them what they wanted. "This is the third day that we have tried to visit you", the young man said. "We come and we wait in front of your office. But there are too many people and we cannot get in".

I told them to come in. The moment they arrived, the woman started crying. Then her husband started crying, too. There was so much sorrow that I also began to cry. My heart was so heavy that all I needed was an excuse.

We cried a lot.

"The Pakistani government and Musharraf have made a stain that can never be washed from Pakistan's name", the man said. "He has destroyed the brotherhood that we built with the Afghans during the Soviet *jihad*, when we helped the *mujahedeen* and hosted Afghan refugees. I do not know how I, as a Pakistani, can even look into your eyes now. We apologise. It was not our decision. We are Muslims".

They told me that they lived in Lahore and had sold all of their possessions. His wife had sold all of her jewellery. "We have 250,000 rupees,"[4] the man said. "This is why we are here. We want to give it to you. It is all we can afford".

Then his wife spoke up. "I have a ten-year-old daughter, and I had ordered her custom-made earrings from a goldsmith. When I was selling my jewellery, I forgot about them. But when we were heading here to you, I saw the gold glinting in her ears. So I took them, and I have brought them to offer them to you for God's work". I insisted that they take back their child's earrings; I really tried. But the woman demurred, and with that they left.

* * *

When Kabul fell on 11 November 2001 I decided to go to Kandahar. There was no flight from Islamabad to Quetta that day, so I went to Peshawar, from there I boarded a plane for Quetta. The flight crew and all the passengers kept coming up to me, one by one, and greeting me.

One woman, who had held back, waiting for the other passengers, finally came forward. She begged my neighbour to give her his seat, and sat down next to me. Then she started crying. She apologized, and told me that she needed to ask me some questions. I remember she told me her name, but I have long since forgotten it.

"Mr Zaeef", she began, "I am a doctor. I have two private clinics. One is in Peshawar and one is in Quetta. I divide my time between them. I have a husband and a daughter. Whatever my income is, I divide it into three parts".

I made a mental calculation to myself that her income would be in the region of hundreds of thousands of rupees.

"I gave half of my income to the *Taliban* to promote God's work", she continued. "The other half I also divided into two—one part for my living expenses, and one part for my patients. I gave money to the most deserving. Since I was a young woman I have not missed daily prayers, not once, and I recite the *Qur'an* every morning. In spite of all this, I have a terrible sickness. Can you help me?"

"Why not? I will help if I can", I said.

"I used to think", she said, "that the *Taliban* were the only group in these times who serve God's religion and implement His law on earth. They were the ones who brought *shari'a* law to Afghanistan. But when the Americans began to attack Afghanistan, I thought at first it might even be helpful to the *Taliban*, but now I see that they are about to be defeated. Many *Taliban* have been martyred. The Afghan capital has fallen. So I have been wondering to myself, 'where is God? Why does he not help the *Taliban*? Why has he done this to them?' And now I cannot pray. I just do not want to. I am afraid that my faith is gone. All sorts of thoughts sneak up on me, and I do not know what to do".

I listened to her story, trying to think how to answer her. I felt sorry for her, but it made me think that perhaps many people were feeling this way. God was testing us. I tried to comfort her as best I could before the plane landed. There were many people and tales like this that deserved to be written down, but most have been wiped from my memory by the passage of time.

This was Pakistan. But all over the Islamic world, the situation was the same. Muslims everywhere were worried, and they supported us both financially and in person.

At the time I received many phone calls, but instead of talking to me, people just cried.

One day an Arab-speaking Muslim called me many times, but after saying "hello" he always started crying, so eventually I hung up. Finally he managed to speak, asking me not to put down the phone. I promised to hear him out. In the background, I could hear his wife crying and it took him several minutes to speak clearly.

He told me that his wife had become agitated and emotional. She would not eat or drink and would cry all day. They were Palestinians. He asked me to speak to his wife and gave her the receiver. Even though she could not talk and all I could hear was her weeping, I tried my best to console her. I recited verses from the holy *Qur'an* and the *hadith* of the Prophet Mohammad (PBUH). Two or three days after this conversation, the man called me again. He wanted to thank me. "My wife is well now, since you spoke with her", he said.

The war in Afghanistan continued through the second week of October, and I was still meeting with many ambassadors. Saudi Arabia and the UAE had withdrawn their recognition of the *Taliban* government and had expelled our diplomats from their soil. Only Pakistan still recognized the Islamic Emirate of Afghanistan.

***

Two days before *Ramazan* on 15 November, I went to Kandahar again to discuss with *Amir ul-Mu'mineen* the possibilities of talks between Afghanistan and America. Qatar had offered to mediate between the *Taliban* and the USA in order to stop the fighting. I left Islamabad in my Land Cruiser, followed all the way by Pakistani intelligence. As I crossed the border at Chaman, I was worried that Pakistan might not allow me to return.

When I reached Kandahar, the city was in chaos. Kabul had fallen only two days previously, and a cloud of sorrow hung over those left in Kandahar. I went straight to the headquarters that had been set up in a new building inside the city. I wanted to meet *Mullah* Mohammad Omar.

He was not at the office and I waited for a while. An hour after I left, the headquarters was attacked by the US air force. The airstrike destroyed the building, but luckily no one was killed. Since the attack and my departure had happened in such quick succession, *Mullah* Mohammad Omar suspected that I was under surveillance and that meeting me would endanger him.

I was on my way to *Mullah* Mohammad Omar's old house, which stood empty behind a *jihadi madrassa*, when another airstrike hit close to my car. The shock wave of the cruise missile destroyed my Thuraya satellite phone. After the second attack *Mullah* Mohammad Omar was certain that my position was being tracked. Perhaps it was true, and perhaps it was connected to my satellite phone; only God knows, but after my phone was destroyed I had no more near misses. Some minutes later, the Russian state news agency, ITAR-TASS, announced that the *Taliban* ambassador to Pakistan had been killed in a cruise missile attack in Kandahar. It was only a short news bulletin, but I knew why the Russians had said this.

Even though I didn't get a chance to meet *Mullah* Mohammad Omar, I managed to pass on a message through Tayyeb Agha.

On the third day of *Ramazan*, I left Kandahar and headed back to Quetta. Some *Talib* brothers accompanied me as far as Arghestan Bridge. I stopped the car there and bid goodbye to all of my friends.

I turned towards Kandahar and began a prayer:

Oh beautiful city that contains the soil in which we crawled as infants. Only God knows when we will see each other again. Only God knows what will happen to you, or to me. But I know that this separation will be for a long time. I am frightened that I may not pass this way again for quite some time, and I fear that this beautiful land, these houses and gardens, will burn in the flames of war.

The *Taliban* were laughing at me, asking me why I was being so serious and acting so strangely, but I said nothing. They returned to Kandahar, and I went on towards the border at Spin Boldak.

On the Pakistani border in Wesh, I was delayed and did not receive my entry visa until 9 p.m. It was late by the time I arrived in Quetta and I spent the night at our consulate there. The next morning I went to the airport and flew back to Islamabad.

Arghestan Bridge, Kandahar province

Upon my arrival at the airport, a swarm of journalists surrounded me, and I took the time to answer their questions. Even though I was travelling on my diplomatic passport, the police insisted on searching me. They had been instructed to search everyone without exception. The situation in Pakistan was bad, they said.

I had returned to Islamabad on 20 November, only to be given a formal letter from the Foreign Ministry of Pakistan. They "no longer recognized the Islamic Emirate of Afghanistan" but allowed me, its ambassador, to "remain in Pakistan until the emergency situation in Afghanistan comes to an end". I remember they used the phrase "until a more reasonable time".

I was given strict orders by the Pakistani government to stop talking to the media. I was also shadowed by the intelligence services everywhere I went. A Land Cruiser and a motorbike were parked in front of my house at all times, and when I went out they followed me. Still, many visitors came to see me.

* * *

A day after the bombing had started, a Pashtun doctor came to the house, telling the guards at the door that he had been summoned because I was ill. He told me that it was time for me to leave, and that I should quietly disappear.

"I have a garden in the border agencies and have built a villa", he said. "I will take you there. You can stay there for a while". He said that I could not trust the government of Pakistan. "They may just hand you over to the Americans. Pakistan is indebted to the United States".

I thanked him for his generous, kind-hearted offer, but turned it down.

I was worried. I had sent requests for political asylum to the embassies of four countries: Saudi Arabia, the UAE, Qatar, and Pakistan, but none of them had given me an answer. I also approached the British and French ambassadors, but they didn't bother to reply either.

I even went to register myself with UNHCR. They gave me a document that was valid for a month and promised to help me through any difficulties I would have. Despite this suggestion, I knew well that I would face bigger dangers than being captured, namely that of being killed. But I thought little about being arrested, since it would have been easier for Pakistan to assassinate me and blame someone else than to hand me over. That's an everyday matter in Pakistan, and I doubted that the authorities there would throw me, like a bone, to the Americans. I could have gone somewhere, but my presence in Pakistan was important for the talks about the *Taliban* prisoners being held and captured in the north by the Northern Alliance.

My situation in Pakistan deteriorated with every passing day. When the embassy of Libya held a ceremony in celebration of their national Independence Day on 24 December, I received an invitation and joined the festivities at the Marriott Hotel. President Musharraf was also present. I saw him when I arrived at the hotel, surrounded by many diplomats and ambassadors, but did not greet him and walked past the crowd to sit elsewhere.

Most of the ambassadors from Islamic countries came and greeted me; the Iranian ambassador even sat down beside me. They asked me lots of questions about the situation in Afghanistan and my opinions. I ate my dinner quickly and took my leave.

In those days almost all of Islamabad's hotels were full of reporters, especially the Marriott. When I reached the doors, there were hundreds of journalists waiting, and they swarmed towards me like bees. I turned and went back into the hotel but they followed me in, flooding into the lobby and onward into the main hall where the celebration was being held. Seeing the crowd of journalists and onlookers entering, the diplomats were terrified. Musharraf got up and ran to a different room shielded by his bodyguards. It didn't take long for the police to arrive and they guided me through the hotel towards the back entrance where I got into my car and drove home.

The next day, a man from the Pakistani Foreign Ministry who had been with Musharraf at the ceremony told me that it was possible that the Pakistani government was plotting against me.

"They could assassinate you or throw you in jail", he said. "The possibility of assassination is quite high, because when Musharraf saw that rush of people at the Marriott last night, he said 'this is not acceptable.'"

I had no idea what he meant by that, as, even before the incident at the Marriott, I had been accused of planning to kill Musharraf. The ISI had told me that they had evidence of my intentions; I had been discussing it with someone, they said. This was news to me: I had never spoken to anyone about an assassination plot because I have never planned an assassination in my life!

Ever since I announced the *fatwa*[5] of seven hundred *Ulema'* to the international media and Pakistan, I had been a thorn in Musharraf's side. Part of their statement read as follows: "Whoever helps the Americans invade Afghanistan, or fight against Muslims, or assists in any other way, is committing a sin. He becomes *mubahu d-dam*,[6] meaning that it is not wrong to kill such person".

A Pakistani journalist at the press conference asked me: "Pervez Musharraf is the most important person in Pakistan, and he has given the Americans military bases, and has ordered the intelligence services to help the Americans with information. So does he fall under this article?"

"The *fatwa* is general" I said. "It does not target anybody specific, nor does it exempt anyone". I added that you cannot tailor *shari'a* to fit the wishes of certain individuals. People have to adjust to the fatwa, not the other way around".

I felt that each day I spent in Pakistan after the announcement became more dangerous for me.

* * *

When Kandahar fell and the last resistance of the Emirate crumbled away, I was still in Islamabad. I did not know what had happened to the *Taliban* leadership and my friends, and had no way of contacting them. I tried to find out about their fate. Who had been killed? Who was in the hands of Dostum and other commanders from the Northern Alliance?

I was isolated, and consulted a few friends about what to do. They advised me to contact UNOCHA[7] in order to seek refuge. I went to their offices but before I was able to register a man and a woman started to ask me all sorts of questions. The man was short and brown-skinned, and when I asked him what his position was and where he was born, he said that he was in charge of intelligence for the UN and was born in America. I told the women that all their questions did not make me feel like I was being registered for refuge; it felt like an interrogation.

She said that I only needed to wait; there would be many more questions for me to answer. At the time, I did not understand what she meant. Only after I fell into the hands of the American beasts did I remember her words and understand their meaning. While all this was going on, I went to Quetta for a short while. A message reached me from UNOCHA telling me that I needed to return to Islamabad or they would not grant me refuge.

Back at home, even my wife was telling me that I should leave. She was worried that the Pakistani government might arrest me. Many other friends were telling me to flee, but it was difficult for me to just leave. It felt like an act of betrayal to abandon those *Taliban* prisoners who had been captured in the North. I also thought about the twenty-five thousand Afghans who were killed in the American bombings and about the thousands more who were thrown in jail. What difference did it make if I shared their fate? I could not leave them behind. I could not be disloyal.

I had been trying to help the prisoners, talking to the members of the Northern Alliance in Pakistan, and giving money to get information about them. I was using any influence I had with the commanders, supplying them with money just to keep the prisoners alive. To this end, I was trying to enlist the support of the Red Cross and human rights institutions to help protect them. I contacted the leaders of the Northern Alliance in Afghanistan, speaking to them on the phone. I also spoke with Dostum and Ismael Khan many times, asking them to release the prisoners. In only a few days I spent more than $180,000, trying my best, but achieving little.

I feared my arrest at every moment, but still I could not leave.

At the same time I continued to call the Pakistani Foreign Ministry to ask about the status of my asylum request. "We're working on it", they would tell me. "Don't worry. No one is going to bother you". Maybe they were already negotiating over my price with the Americans.

After *Eid*, the ISI intensified its surveillance. The house was surrounded on all sides, and when a car left the house it was searched, making sure I was not trying to flee. They wanted to make sure that I did not escape. At least I was still allowed to receive visitors.

* * *

To this very day I remember a dream that haunted me a few days before I was arrested at my home in Islamabad. In this dream, my elder brother came to me with a knife in his hand. His face was filled with rage all the while he fastened his grip around the knife's handle, moving closer. He stopped in front of me, so close that I could feel his breath on my face, and said in a cold voice, "My brother! I have come here to behead you with this knife".

He was standing in front of me with his sleeves rolled up. I was shocked, unable to believe what I had just heard. How could my own brother—my own blood—come to me hoping to commit this vile act? I had never mistreated him or given him cause for grief. I thought he could have been playing a practical joke on me, but I saw in his face that he had every intention to do what he had just said. In my dream, I thought to myself: "If this is what will bring him happiness, then I should let him have his way without a struggle, especially if I fail to reason with him". So I spoke with him, "Brother! I have never done you wrong, nor have I brought harm or grief to you. But you still want to take such unlawful revenge on me now". But my words failed to convince him.

So I prepared myself, still filled with hope that he would come to his senses and show me mercy. I lay down on the floor and my brother took the knife to my neck, as a slaughterer does, and cruelly beheaded me with a swift motion.

This was the dream I had only days before the Pakistani security forces surrounded my house. Only then did I start to understand the dream of my brother's betrayal.

It was the second day of the New Year; Pakistan had just celebrated the beginning of 2002, and I was at home with my family. I was still trying to secure the release of the prisoners from Dostum and the Northern Alliance. The events in the north made me forget everything else that was happening, and I was desperately trying to find a safe way home for our remaining fighters, along with their wounded. The situation kept me deep in thought. How would our brothers make it home? What would happen to those captured by Dostum? How could I find a safe way out for them? How could I find out about their situation and where they were?

I was turning these questions over in my mind when all of a sudden my guard appeared and told me that Pakistani officials were at the gate asking to see me. It was eight o'clock at night, a highly unusual time for meetings to take place at my home. I went to the smaller guest room. Three men were in the room. They introduced themselves when I entered: one was a Pashtun called Gulzar; the two others spoke Urdu.

After exchanging greetings we sat down together and I served tea while I waited to hear why they had come at such a late hour. The Pashtun man seemed angry; his face was black and intimidating, his lips swollen, and his nose and belly were large. He looked as if he had been dragged out of hell itself. He showed little respect for me or my home, and behaved rudely.

He said, "Your Excellency, you are no longer an Excellency! America is a superpower, did you not know that? No one can defeat it, nor can they negotiate with it. America wants to question you and we are here to hand you over to the USA".

Pakistan wanted to save itself from any harm. I replied by saying that I knew that America was a superpower, the only one in the world, but that the world had rules and restrictions.

"On account of those laws", I said, "be they Islamic or not, how can you deliver me to the United States? I have yet to hear of a constitution that gives you the right to do so. You can give me an ultimatum to leave your country, but you can't arrest me".

The man from hell replied abruptly. "Neither Islam nor any other rules or laws have any bearing on the current situation. Only our profit and Pakistan are important right now".

I realized than that the discussion had taken a turn for the worse. I calmed myself and said that they could do as they wish. "I am at your mercy. I have no shelter here, and Almighty *Allah* will judge when the final day comes".

They ordered me to stay at my house until midnight, at which time I would be transferred to Peshawar. Their men surrounded my house, leaving no way for me or my family to leave.

The officials had told me that I would be interviewed and questioned for ten days after I arrived in Peshawar. The Americans were carrying out an investigation, after which I would be released and could return home. At that time I held a ten-month visa for Pakistan. I had an official letter which had been sent to the Pakistani government and the foreign ministry to recognize my status as a representative of the Islamic Emirate of Afghanistan in Pakistan, until such time as the difficult situation in Afghanistan would be resolved.

Despite all my documents—the protection I should have had under international law, even the letter from the United Nations stated that "the bearer of this letter should not be harmed due to his status of representation"—three vehicles pulled up at my door at midnight. All the roads were blocked and guards posted. Even journalists who were there at the time were denied access. I wasn't allowed to speak to them to let people know what had taken place. They ordered me to leave my house. My children were crying as I walked out through the garden into the street.

If it hadn't happened to me, it would be hard to imagine that the Pakistani soldiers—trained to defend Islam—would turn on their Muslim brothers even when they had committed no crime. In fact, no law offered justification for what they were doing, but American pressure, the anger of its people and the hope of a lucky break turned them against us. I find it difficult to understand how they could abandon their honour and self-respect; how they could turn against the word of the Holy *Qur'an* and its customs of bravery and hospitality; how they could ignore international laws and even the humblest notions of brotherhood and sympathy.

As I walked into the street and out into the thick dark night, it struck me that there was no one who could rescue me, nobody to prevent them from doing whatever they wanted.

I was put in one of their cars. Even at this point, I was still unable to comprehend this treatment that the Pakistani government was subjecting me to. After all, I was a brother of the same faith, which should at the very least have meant something to their rhetoric of religious piety. It was a hard realisation for me, especially when the men who took me dared to utter the name of the holy *Qur'an* or discuss what the idea of *jihad* meant amongst themselves. They squeezed me into the middle of the back seat. Men who appeared to be ISI officers sat on either side of me. They did not carry any weapons that I could see, but our car was in the middle of a three-car convoy that raced to Peshawar. The other cars were packed with armed men. The driver put on a tape of a female Urdu singer for the entire journey; it was clear that the sole purpose of the music was to irritate me.

On the way to Peshawar I asked them to stop the car so that I could conduct the morning prayer, but they told me to wait until we arrived in Peshawar. I kept on asking them, but they didn't care about prayer and ignored my requests.

17

PRISONER 306

When we arrived in Peshawar I was taken to a lavishly-fitted office. A Pakistani flag stood on the desk, and a picture of Mohammad Ali Jinnah[1] hung at the back of the room. A Pashtun man was sitting behind the desk. He got up, introduced himself and welcomed me. His head was shaved—seemingly his only feature of note—and he was of an average size and weight. He walked over to me and said that he was the head of the bureau. I was in the devil's workshop, the regional head office of the ISI.

He told me I was a close friend—a guest—and one that they cared about a great deal. I wasn't really sure what he meant, since it was pretty clear that I was dear to them only because they could get a good sum of money for me when they sold me. Their trade was people; just as with goats, the higher the price for the goat, the happier the owner. In the twenty-first century there aren't many places left where you can still buy and sell people, but Pakistan remains a hub for this trade.

I prayed after dinner with the ISI officer, and then was brought to a holding-cell for detainees. The room was decent, with a gas heater, electricity and a toilet. I was given food and drink—even a copy of the holy *Qur'an* for recitation—as well as a notebook and pen. The guard posted at the door was very helpful, and he gave me whatever I requested during the night.

I wasn't questioned or interviewed while being held in Peshawar. Only one man, who didn't speak Pashtu and whose Urdu I couldn't understand came every day to ask the same question over and over again: what is going to happen? My answer was the same each time he asked me. "Almighty God knows, and he will decide my fate. Everything that happens is bound to his will".

171

All of the officials who visited me while I was detained in Peshawar treated me with respect. But none of them really spoke to me. They would look at me in silence but their faces spoke clearer than words could, humbled by pity and with tears gathering in their eyes.

Finally, after days in my cell, a man came, tears flowing down his cheeks. He fainted as his grief and shame overcame him. He was the last person I saw in that room. I never learnt his name, but soon after—perhaps four hours after he left—I was handed over to the Americans.

It was eleven o'clock at night and I was getting ready to go to bed when the door to my cell suddenly opened. A man (also with a shaved head) entered; he was polite and we exchanged greetings. He asked me whether I was aware of what was going to happen to me. When I said that I knew nothing, he said that I was being transferred, and that it would happen soon. So soon, in fact, that he recommended that I should prepare straight away by taking ablutions and by using the toilet. Without asking for any further details, I got up and took my ablutions.

Barely five minutes had passed when other men arrived with handcuffs and a piece of black cloth. They shackled my hands and the cloth was tied around my head covering my eyes. This was the first time in my life that I had been treated in this way. They searched my belongings and took the holy *Qur'an*, a digital recorder and some money I still had with me. As they led me out of the building, they kicked and pushed me into a car. None of them had said a word so far. We drove for almost an hour before they stopped the car. I could hear the sounds of the rotating blades of a helicopter nearby. I guessed that we were at an airport where I would be handed over to the Americans. Someone grabbed me and pulled an expensive watch that I was wearing from my wrist as the car drove closer to the helicopters. The car stopped again, but this time two people grabbed me on each side and took me out of the car. As they brought me towards the helicopter, one of the guards whispered into my ear. *Khuda hafiz.* Farewell. But the way he said it, it sounded like I was going on a fantastic journey.

Even before I reached the helicopter, I was suddenly attacked from all sides. People kicked me, shouted at me, and my clothes were cut with knives. They ripped the black cloth from my face and for the first time I could see where I was. Pakistani and American soldiers stood around me. Behind these soldiers, I could see military vehicles in the distance, one of which had a general's number plate.

The Pakistani soldiers were all staring as the Americans hit me and tore the remaining clothes off from my body. Eventually I was completely naked, and the Pakistani soldiers—the defenders of the Holy *Qur'an*—shamelessly watched me with smiles on their faces, saluting this disgraceful action of the Americans. They held a handover ceremony with the Americans right in front of my eyes.

That moment is written in my memory like a stain on my soul. Even if Pakistan was unable to stand up to the godless Americans I would at least have expected them to insist that treatment like this would never take place under their eyes or on their own sovereign territory.

I was still naked when a callous American soldier gripped my arm and dragged me onto the helicopter. They tied my hands and feet, sealed my mouth with duct tape and put a black cloth over my head. That was in turn taped to my neck, and then I was shackled to the floor of the helicopter.

All this time I could neither shout nor breathe. When I tried to catch my breath or move a little to one side, I was kicked hard by a soldier. On board the helicopter, I stopped fearing the kicking and beating; I was sure that my soul would soon leave my body behind. I assured myself that I would soon die from the beatings. My wish, however, wasn't granted.

The soldiers continued to shout at me, hit and kick me throughout the journey, until the helicopter finally landed. By then I had lost track of time. Only *Allah* knows the time I had spent between cars, helicopters and the place where I now found myself. I was glad when the helicopter landed, and allowed me to hope that the torment had come to an end, but a rough soldier took me and dragged me out of the helicopter. Outside, a number of soldiers beat and kicked me. They behaved like animals for what seemed like hours. Afterwards, the soldiers sat on top of me and proceeded to have a conversation, as if they were merely sitting on a park bench. I abandoned all hope; the ordeal had been long and I was convinced I would die soon.

Still I saw the faces of the Pakistani soldiers in my mind. What had we done to deserve such a punishment? How could our Muslim brothers betray us like this?

I lay curled up for two hours on the ground and then they dragged me to another helicopter. It appeared to be more modern than the last one. The guards tied me to a metal chair, and throughout the flight I was not touched. No one told me where I was being taken, and the helicopter landed some twenty minutes later. Again, the soldiers grabbed me and led me away. It seemed like a long way; I was still blind-folded, but I could hear that there were many people in the vicinity. They pulled me up to my feet and an interpreter told me to walk down the staircase in front of me. The stairs led inside and the noise of the people above slowly faded. There must have been six flights of stairs before we stopped and the black bag was pulled from my head. The duct tape was ripped off my face, and my hands were untied.

* * *

Four American soldiers stood around me and to my left I could see cells—they looked more like cages—with people inside. The soldiers brought me to a small bathroom, but I couldn't shower. My limbs and body throbbed with the pain of the beating I had received earlier in the day during the torment of the helicopter flight. I felt paralysed and had little sensation in my arms or legs. I was given a uniform and led into one of the cages. It was small, perhaps two metres long and a metre wide, with a tap and a toilet. The walls were made out of metal bars with no seals. Before they left, the guards told me to go to sleep and locked the door behind me. Alone in the cage, I reflected on the last few days. How did I end up in this cage? Everything was like a dark dream, and when I lay down and tried to get some sleep amid the aching of my bruised body, I realised that I no longer knew whether I was awake or asleep.

The next morning I looked out from my cage and saw a soldier guarding the door. There were three other cages around mine, all covered in rubber. It dawned on me that I was in a big ship, one of the ships used in the war against Afghanistan off the Pakistani coast. I could hear the loud rumble of the ship's engines throughout the night and morning, and I was sure that this was one of the ships that had launched missiles at Afghanistan.

I barely moved my eyes—not daring to look around—out of fear. My tongue was dry and stuck to the top of my mouth. On the left side I could see a few other prisoners who were together in one cell. A soldier came with some food and another prisoner was brought onto the ship.

The men ate their breakfast and stood together. We were not permitted to talk to each other, but could see one another while the food was handed to us. I eventually saw that *Mullah*s Fazal,[2] Noori,[3] Burhan,[4] Wasseeq Sahib[5] and Rohani[6] were all among the other prisoners, but still we could not talk to each other.

A soldier entered my room and handcuffed me to the bars of the cage. They searched my room and afterwards I was interrogated for the first time; fingerprints were taken and I was photographed from all sides. They wrote up a brief biography before bringing me back to my cage. I found that I had received some basic items in my absence: a blanket, a plastic sheet and a plate of food—rice and a boiled egg. I had not eaten for a long time, and returned the empty plate to the guard who stood in front of my cage.

I had just lain down to rest when I heard another soldier coming with handcuffs. Shackled once more, I was brought to the interrogation room. This time I was asked about *Sheikh* Osama bin Laden and *Mullah* Mohammad Omar. They asked me where they were, what their current condition was, and then about some key commanders of the *Taliban* forces—where they were hiding, what had happened to them and what they were planning. 11 September came up only once, and then only in a very brief question. They wanted to know if I had known anything about the attack before it happened. These were the main things I was asked in the dark and small interrogation room on the ship.

The Americans knew—I was sure—that I had little to do with the things that they asked me about. I had not been informed, nor did I have any previous knowledge, of the attacks on the United States or who was responsible for them. But just as these things happened to me, thousands of others were defamed, arrested and killed without a trial or proof that they had been complicit or responsible.

On the ship I thought that I would never see my friends and family again. I thought they would never know what had happened to me. No one should be in such despair, especially a Muslim, but I had to remember the Soviet invasion, and the behaviour of the Russians in Afghanistan. I thought of the destiny of those sixty thousand Afghans who were just devoured by the Soviet monster.[7] They were gone forever; no one returned alive, and no one knew anything about them.

For the first time, I could feel what those people must have felt, deep in my bones. I wanted my spirit to join them and to be finished with this anguish. I wanted to escape the cruelties of those vicious animals, those barbarous American invaders.

After five or six days on the ship I was given a grey overall, my hands and feet were tied with plastic restraints and a white bag was put over my head. I was brought onto the deck of the ship along with the other prisoners. We were made to kneel and wait. The restraints cut off blood to our hands and feet. Some of the other prisoners were moaning because of the pain but the soldiers only shouted and told them to shut up. After several hours we were put into a helicopter and we landed three times before we reached our final destination. Each time we landed the soldiers would throw us out of the helicopter.

We were forced to lie or kneel on the ground and they kicked and hit us when we complained or even moved. In the helicopter we were tied to the walls or the floor, most of the time in a position that was neither kneeling nor standing. It was torment, and with each passing minute the agony grew. On our penultimate stop when I was thrown to the ground, one of the soldiers said, "this one, this is the big one". And while I could not see them, they attacked me from all sides, hitting and kicking me on the ground. Some used their rifles and others just stomped on me with their army boots.

My clothes were torn to pieces and soon I was lying naked in the fresh snow. I lost all feeling in my hands and feet from the restraints and the cold. The soldiers were singing and mocking me. The USA is the home of Justice and Peace and she wants Peace and Justice for everyone else on the globe, they said over and over again. It was too cold to breathe and my body was shaking violently, but the soldiers just shouted at me telling me to stop moving. I lay in the snow for a long time before I finally lost consciousness.

* * *

I woke up in a big room. I could see two guards wearing balaclavas and holding large sticks in their hands in front of me. My body ached all over. When I turned my head I saw two more guards behind me in each corner of the room, both pointing pistols at my head. They were all shouting at me. "Where is Osama? Where is *Mullah* Omar? What role did you play in the attacks on New York and Washington?"

I could not even move my tongue. It had swollen and seemed to be glued to my upper palate. Lying in that room, in pain and being screamed at, I wanted to die. May *Allah* forgive me for my impatience! They left when they noticed that I could not answer; then other soldiers came and dragged me into a run-down room without a door or a window. They had given me some sort of clothes but still it was too cold and once again I lost consciousness. I woke up in the same room.

A female soldier was guarding the entrance and came over to me. She was the first soldier that was nice and behaved decently, asking me how I was and if I needed anything. Still I could not talk. I thought I was in Cuba at first, having lost all sense of time, but when I saw that the walls were covered in names and dates of *Taliban* I realized that I was still in Afghanistan.

I could hardly move. My shoulder and head seemed broken and the pain rushed through me with each heartbeat. Silently I prayed that *Allah* would be pleased with me and that he protect other brothers from the ordeal I was going through. When it became dark I called for the female soldier to help me. I asked her if I was allowed to pray. She said that I was.

My hands were still tied so that could hardly perform *tayammum*.[8] I was still praying when two soldiers entered the room. They let me finish my prayer before they asked me if I felt better, if I was cold or needed anything. All I said was *alhamdulillah*.[9] I dared not complain, and I knew they could see the bloody bruises on my face, my swollen hands and my shaking body. They asked me about *Sheikh* Osama and *Mullah* Mohammad Omar but I had nothing to tell them. My answer did not please them, and I could see the anger in their faces. But even though they threatened me and tried to intimidate me, my answer stayed the same and they left.

I had not eaten for six days because I was not sure if the military food rations they gave me were *halal*. For nearly one month they kept me in that small run-down room, and all I had for food was a cup of tea and a piece of bread. The soldiers would not let me sleep. For twenty days I lay in the room with my hands and feet tied. I was interrogated every day.

On 24 January 2002, six other prisoners were brought into my room, most of whom were Arabs. They stayed for a few hours before they were taken away again. They returned the next day and I asked them what had happened. They told me that Red Cross[10] representatives had come to to inspect the camp, register prisoners and collect letters for their families. They said that they did not know why they were being hidden away. We talked some more, and food was brought, the first time I had had enough to eat.

In the following days we were moved several times. Each time we would be blindfolded, made to kneel and sit in uncomfortable positions for hours. On 9 February we were transferred out of Bagram and flown down to Kandahar. Once again we were tied up, kicked and beaten, dragged through the mud and made to wait outside in the cold. Many of the prisoners screamed and cried while they were abused. The same happened when we arrived after the brief flight. I was hit with sticks, trampled on and beaten. Five soldiers sat down on me while I lay in the cold mud.

They ripped my clothes to shreds with their knives. I thought I would be slaughtered soon. Afterwards they made me stand outside; even though it was extremely cold I felt nothing but pain. They dragged me into a big tent for interrogation. There were male and female soldiers who mocked me, while another took a picture of me naked.

After a medical check up I was blindfolded again and dragged out of the tent. The soldiers rested on the way, sitting on me before bringing me to another big prisoner tent that was fenced off with barbed wire. Every prisoner was given a vest, a pair of socks, a hat and a blanket. I put the clothes on and covered myself with the blanket. It was cold in the tent and other prisoners were brought in one after another.

Interrogations went on all day and night. The soldiers would come into the tent and call up a prisoner. The rest of us would be ordered to move to the back of the tent while they handcuffed the prisoner and led him out. The soldiers would abuse prisoners on the way, run their heads into walls—they could not see—and drag them over rough ground.

A delegation of the Red Cross came to the camp to register us and gave each prisoner an ID card. We were all suspicious of the delegates and believed that they were CIA agents. The Red Cross was trying to connect the prisoners with their families, arranging for letters to be exchanged and providing some books. They also arranged showers for us. Each prisoner got a bucket of water and was forced to take his shower naked in front of the other prisoners. We were allowed to shower once a month.

No water was provided for ablutions. We received bottled drinking water from Kuwait and sometimes prisoners would use it to wash their hands and face, but as soon as the guards noticed the prisoner would get punished.

I was held in Kandahar from 10 February till 1 July 2002. We were repeatedly called for interrogation. The tactics of the Americans changed from time to time; they would alternate between threats and decent treatment or they would try to cut deals with us. I was asked about my life, my biography, my involvement in the *Taliban* movement and so on. But the discussion always returned to *Sheikh* Osama and *Mullah* Mohammad Omar. Often an interrogation that began in a humane and decent way would end up with me being grabbed and roughly dragged out of the room because I did not have any information about the life of *Sheikh* Osama or the whereabouts of *Mullah* Mohammad Omar.

There were twenty people in each prison tent. The camp in Kandahar was better than Bagram. We were allowed to sit in groups of three and talk to each other; there were more facilities in general. All in all I believe there were about six hundred prisoners in the Kandahar camp. They conducted night-time searches, rushing into each prison tent and ordering all prisoners to lie face-down on the floor while they searched us and every inch of the tent. They brought in dogs to go through the few belongings we had, and to sniff up and down our bodies. There was no real food; all we were given was army rations, some of which dated back to the Second World War. Many were expired and no one could tell if we were allowed to eat the meat that was in the rations, but we had no choice: we had to eat the food or we would starve. The situation improved in June when we were given rations that were labelled *halal*. The new rations tasted better, and they weren't out of date any more. We were also given some Afghan bread and sweets, a real luxury.

Helicopters and airplanes landed day and night close by and the constant noise kept us awake. Many of the soldiers would also patrol during the nights, shouting and waking us. Three times each day all the prisoners would be counted. We were all given a number; I was 306. Until the time I was released I was called 306.

* * *

When I was taken to Bagram, every day I hoped that it would be my last. I only had to look at my shackled hands and feet, my broken head and shoulders, and then I would look at the inhuman, insulting behaviour of these American soldiers; I had no hope of ever being free again.

When I met the six prisoners[11] who were being hidden from the Red Cross in Bagram, I understood that there was something going on outside. I did not see any representatives of the Red Cross at Bagram because the Americans had also hidden me from them, but when I was transferred from Bagram to Kandahar, I saw the Red Cross on the second day after I arrived.

They did not have a Pashtu translator with them, just an Urdu speaker whom they had taken from their Islamabad office. He was not Pakistani himself, but he could speak fluent Urdu. They had Arabic-speaking staff as well. For Pashtu they had three people who hardly could speak the language at all: Julian, Patrick, and a German who had spent a lot of time in the Peshawar area.

It was the first time that I had been able to tell my family that I was alive. I was given a pencil and paper, and a soldier sat in front of me while I wrote. When I was finished I gave the pencil and the paper back to the soldier. I did not receive any letters from home when I was in Kandahar, and nobody gave me any information about my family, about what had happened to them after I was arrested.

There were lots of Red Cross representatives going back and forth, talking to us through barbed wire. They were asking questions about our health and other problems. They told us that whatever we said would stay safe with them, and that they would not tell the Americans. But we were suspicious. We thought they might be lying; we could not trust them and we were not open with them. We did not tell them what was in our hearts. We could not complain about the situation, because right in front of their eyes the Americans were taking us to interrogation, they were dragging us along the ground, sometimes with two or three soldiers sitting on top of us. The Red Cross delegates saw this, but they were unable to help.

The Arab detainees told all of the brothers to be careful in what they said. According to them, there were many American spies masquerading as Red Cross delegates, tricking us while pretending to help. But in any case we had nothing useful for the Americans. We had nothing to do with any spying. The only sensitive issue was complaints, and the fact that many of the brothers had given false names and addresses when they were captured. So now they could not give new names and addresses to the Red Cross, so their letters were being sent to the wrong places.

It was hard for them to tell the truth to the Red Cross, because they were afraid the information would get back to the Americans. I had the same suspicions when I was in Guantánamo.

We did not understand the level of assistance we were getting from the Red Cross while we were in Kandahar. But I did know three things they were doing: first, they were connecting us to our families with those letters, which was very important. Second, they gave us four *Qur'an*s per each set of twenty people. Third, they arranged for us to take our first shower in four months, even if it was a communal, naked, and very embarrassing shower. They also gave us clean overalls.

According to the Red Cross, all of these things were done at their suggestion.

Our guards changed shifts twice a day and many of the low-ranking soldiers misbehaved, bearing ill-will towards Muslims. Every time they would appear, we had to stand in a row looking at the ground, and if the number of a prisoner was called he had to say 'welcome'. Any prisoner who disobeyed these orders was punished.

Every day all prisoners were lined up outside and made to stand in the sun. There were about twenty tents that held eight hundred prisoners. Not all soldiers were the same, but some would command us to stand there for half-an-hour before they took the attendance register and almost two hours afterwards. No one was allowed to sit down or stand in the shade, no matter what his condition. May *Allah* punish those soldiers!

The guards inspected the tents inside and outside along the barbed wire every day. One time a soldier found a piece of broken glass outside on the ground. He was one of the meanest soldiers, and upon discovering the piece of glass he gave it to me and asked where it had come from. I tossed it back to him and said that I did not know; we had brought nothing with us. The glass must have been here before, I told him.

The soldier kept repeating his question. "Don't talk. I will fuck you up", he screamed at me. I was forced to kneel with my hands behind my head for several hours; from time to time he would kick or push me to the ground. There was no point in complaining about the behaviour of the soldiers; it would only make the punishment even worse.

I will never forget the treatment I suffered at the hands of these slave rulers.

* * *

Kandahar prison camp had several sections. Next to the ordinary prison tents, one of the old hangars—previously a workshop for airplanes—was now being used for the prisoners. Most prisoners feared it as a place of extreme punishment. Several times I saw prisoners being transported to the hangar bound with metal chains. In another separate location they deprived prisoners of sleep, holding them for months on end. The camp was guarded by six watchtowers and patrols, on foot and with vehicles, which took place all day and night.

There are too many stories from the time when I was a prisoner in Kandahar. One day a new prisoner was brought to the prison tent where I was detained. He was a very old man. Two soldiers harshly dragged him into the tent and dropped him on the floor. He was ordered to stand but neither could he stand nor was he able to understand the men. He seemed to be confused; other prisoners told him to stand up but it was as if he could not distinguish the soldiers from the prisoners.

On the second day when he was called for interrogation and had to lie down to be tied up, he did not understand again. None of the other prisoners were allowed to help him; we were told to move towards the far end of the tent. Soon the soldiers let their passions loose and kicked him to the ground. One of them sat on his back while the others tied his hands together. All the while the old man was shouting. He thought he was going to be slaughtered and screamed, "Infidels! Let me pray before you slaughter me!"

We were shouting from the back of the tent that he was just going to be interrogated and that he soon would be back at the tent, but it was as if he was in a trance. I cried and I laughed at the same time. There was so much anger in me as I watched the old man being dragged outside.

When he came back I sat down to talk to him. He said he was from Uruzgan province and that he lived in Char Chino district. He told me he was 105 years old, and eventually he was the first man to be released from the Hell of Guantánamo.

In the camp we would pray together in congregation. One morning while I was leading the morning prayer, we had just started performing the first *raqqat* when a group of soldiers entered our tent and called the number of an Arab brother to take him for interrogation. The brother did not move, but continued with his prayer as is commanded by *Allah*. He was called a second time. By the third time, the soldiers rushed in, threw me to the ground, pressing my head into the floor, sitting on me while two others grabbed Mr Adil,[12] the Arab brother from Tunis, and dragged him out. There was no respect for Islam.

Every day prisoners were mistreated in the camp. A Pakistani brother who had a bad toothache had only been given Tylenol by the medic in the camp. Eating was painful and difficult for him, and he could not manage to finish his food in the thirty minutes allocated for each meal. When the soldier came to collect his plate, he asked to be given more time because of his teeth. The soldier took him to the entrance and hit him in the mouth while the rest of us watched helplessly.

After we saw how they treated the Pakistani brother, we decided to go on hunger strike. Word spread quickly and soon the entire camp had stopped eating. When the camp authorities came to find out what the reason for the strike was, we informed them about the abuses of the soldier and that we would no longer tolerate them. We were promised that incidents like this would be prevented in the future and we stopped the hunger strike. Even though we were subject to harsh conditions, this was the first hunger strike to have taken place under the American invaders' custody.

The next day Mohammad Nawab,[13] who was very ill and could not stand up, was beaten and kicked. The soldiers had come to inspect the tent and ordered the prisoners to move to the back. Mohammad Nawab had not moved; he had remained in bed. When the soldiers saw him, a group of them started to beat and kick him before they dragged him to the end of the tent and dropped him at our feet.

I should mention that not all American soldiers behaved in this way; some were decent and respectful and did not join their comrades in the abuses.

Some abuses were worse than others and affected everyone in the camp. One afternoon I woke up to the sound of the men crying. All over the camp you could hear the men weep. I asked Mohammad Nawab what had happened. He said that a soldier had taken the holy *Qur'an* and had urinated on it and then dumped it into the trash. We had been given a few copies of the *Qur'an* by the Red Cross, but now we asked them to take them back. We could not protect them from the soldiers who often used them to punish us. The Red Cross promised that incidents like this would not be repeated, but the abuses carried on. The search dogs would come and sniff the *Qur'an* and the soldier would toss copies to the ground. This continued throughout my time in Kandahar. It was always the same soldier who acted without any respect towards the *Qur'an* and Islam.

There were many other incidences of abuse and humiliation. Soldiers were conducting training with the prisoners as guinea-pigs: they would practise arrest techniques—all of which were filmed—and prisoners were beaten, told to sit for hours in painful positions. The number of such stories is endless.

All the while the interrogations continued. One night, when I had already been in Kandahar for several months, I was called for interrogation. I was asked if I wanted to go home, told that they had not benefited from my detention and had found no proof that I was involved beyond my dealings as Ambassador. They were planning to release me, they said. They would arrange for money, a phone and anything else I needed. After all this they told me the condition for my release: all I had to do was help them find *Sheikh* Osama and *Mullah* Mohammad Omar. Any time I would choose detention over this kind of release. I would not dare to put a price on the life of a fellow Muslim and brother ever!

I interrupted them and asked them what the reason for my detention was. They said that they believed I know about *Al Qaeda*, the *Taliban*, their financial branches, and about the attacks on New York and Washington. I had been arrested to investigate all these allegations. Given that they had not found any proof of what they had accused me of, they must see that I was innocent, I said. I had been arrested by the Pakistani government, and should be released without any conditions.

For three days they talked about financial aid and a possible deal if I would agree to their terms, but I turned all their offers down. Once again their behaviour changed. They threatened me and my life, again.

The next day a group of soldiers came to our tent throwing a bunch of handcuffs towards a group of prisoners. After they put on the handcuffs, they were tied together and led away. We all wondered what was happening. Some believed that we were being released; others speculated that they might get transferred. But they all were brought back a few hours later. Each and every one was shaved—their beards, hair and eyebrows. Every single hair was gone.

This was the worst form of punishment. In Islam it is forbidden to shave one's beard. It is considered a sin in the *Hanafi*[14] faith. It is better to be killed than to have one's beard shaved. I was in the next group that was led away to the barber. I asked the barber not to shave my beard; he replied with a hard slap to my head. I did not open my eyes for several minutes while the pain rushed through me. Later, when a doctor asked me what had happened to my face and I complained about the barber, I received another slap from the doctor, telling me I should not complain about the American invaders.

During one interrogation session, I was asked if I knew Mr Muta-wakil and there were several other questions relating to him. Finally I was asked if I wanted to meet him. I doubted that he had been arrested and asked where he was and how I could meet him. A few moments later he entered the room. He had brought me a packet of Pakistani biscuits, but my hands were tied and I was unable to eat them. Nor was I allowed to take them with me. We talked for ten or fifteen min-utes and then he left again. In the short meeting I learnt that I would soon be transferred to Cuba. Mr Mutawakil did not say much more about that. He knew that *Allah* knew best what would happen to me.

The next day I was interrogated again. I was told that I would be transferred to Cuba on 1 July. The interrogator added that those going to Cuba would spend the rest of their lives there and that even their bodies might never find their way back to Afghanistan. This was my last chance, he said; I had to make a decision to go home or to be transferred to Cuba. Once again he stated the conditions for my release. If I were to go home, I would have to work with and help the American intelligence agencies in their search for *Al Qaeda* and *Tali-ban* leaders, remaining their slave for the rest of my days. May *Allah* save us from committing such a sin!

Even though I was given a day to think about it, I replied immedi-ately: "I am not more talented or important than any of the brothers detained here. I accept the decision made for me by Almighty *Allah*. I have not committed any crime, and so will not admit to any crime. It is now up to you to decide what to do with me and where I shall be transferred". After this interrogation I hoped that the transfer would come soon.

18

GUANTÁNAMO BAY

On 1 July 2002 I was taken to the barber and shaved once again. Afterwards a group of soldiers came and threw chains at the entrance of the tent. One after another we were chained together to be transferred to Cuba. I was the fourth person in the row. Our hands and feet were bound and our heads covered by black bags, chained together in groups of seven or eight people.

We were brought to another waiting area; the black bags were replaced with black goggles and plugs were put into our ears. Before we were brought to the plane, we were photographed again, and given a set of red clothes and red shoes. Our mouths were covered with a mask and hands and feet bound with two different kinds of chains. Once in the plane, our feet were locked to a chain on the ground, and our hands were bound behind our backs and locked to the metal chairs. It was impossible to move, not even an inch. It was a painful position and soon after the plane took off some of the prisoners started to struggle with their chains, screaming and moaning in pain. They remained chained in this position for the entire journey, and weren't allowed to use the bathroom.

We were locked into these positions four hours before the plane even took off and we still remained there three hours after it had landed. We spent close to thirty hours locked in those chairs. The chains cut off the blood supply to our hands and feet. After ten hours I lost all feeling in them. Our hands were so swollen that it was difficult for the American soldiers to open the handcuffs, which had sunk deep into the flesh. The airplane landed once during the flight before arriving in Cuba.

Once off the plane we were ordered into rows while being screamed at in Arabic and English: "Don't move. Stick to your place!" But after thirty hours in chains, with hands and feet hurting, some moved and stretched. Seeing this one of the soldiers kicked and beat them. I myself was kicked three times.

We were moved to the base and I was brought for a medical check-up. Then they took me to an interrogation room and chained me to a chair. A few moments later an interrogator came in—accompanied by a Persian translator. He introduced himself as Tom. He was assigned to probe me, he said. I was too tired from the long and painful journey to talk and told him that I just wanted to be transferred to wherever I would stay from now on and that we could talk tomorrow if he wanted, but Tom insisted that we talk straight away.

My mouth was dry, and I could hardly stay awake. Up until then everyone had been advising me to try to avoid being transferred to Cuba, but now that I had arrived I had nothing left to fear. I did not even care about the punishment anymore. Now in Guantánamo, we preferred death over life. Even though Tom insisted, I barely responded to any of his questions and so he finally left the room. I was brought to a small cage made out of a shipping crate. My hands and feet were unfastened and I was left alone. A food ration had been left for me in the cage but it was having water that made me most happy. It was the first time in months that I had the amount of water necessary to perform my ablutions. I washed, prayed and went to sleep. I slept well, missing the night prayer, and woke up just before the morning.

* * *

My cage was in the Gold block of the Guantánamo prison camp. The soldiers treated us better than in Bagram or Kandahar, and we were allowed to talk to each other. Even though it was lonely in the cage, there still was a sense of freedom after the months imprisoned in Afghanistan.

The cages were four feet wide, six feet in length and were lined up next to each other. Each cage had a metal board to sleep on, a water tap and a toilet. There were no real walls, just metal mesh which separated the cages from each other. It was very uncomfortable having to wash and use the toilet in front of the other prisoners. There was a lot of confusion among us. Some believed we were not in Cuba but on an island somewhere in the Persian Gulf, and others thought that it was just a temporary camp on the way to Guantánamo. We prayed in different directions since no one knew where Mecca was located.

We were visited by Red Cross representatives at the camp who said that they had been at the airport to ensure that we were not mistreated by the soldiers.

"But in the bus they beat us like a drum", I told them.

"We were at the airport, but we were not on the bus", said one of the representatives.

In those early days in Guantánamo, we got used to the Red Cross. They visited the prisoners individually, and spoke to them semi-freely, but still the prisoners were afraid of American intelligence equipment, and were very cautious when they were speaking.

When a prisoner was to be taken to a Red Cross representative, the soldiers used a special rope to tie his hands. When we got there, they untied one hand, and there was usually tea, biscuits and juice on the table. They would interview us, and if a prisoner wanted to write home or to friends he could do so.

The process changed as time passed. For one thing, the rope changed into steel chains, but the Red Cross still interviewed prisoners. They also brought the prisoners letters from home and sometimes they interviewed prisoners in their cells.

But for a long time there was no Pashtun translator. There were some Europeans who spoke some Pashtu, but mostly they could not understand us, and we could not understand them. There was a widely-believed rumour that there were spies among the Red Cross representatives, and we remained wary of them. I myself was suspicious and wondered whether they were spies.

One day the translator from Germany came to me and looked at me as if he had seen me before. "What's the matter? Why are you looking at me like that?" I asked him.

"You seem so familiar, as if I have seen you before somewhere", he replied.

"Of course. You may have seen me; I have seen you many times while I was in the prison camp in Kandahar before I was brought here", I told him. But he said that he didn't think he had seen me in Kandahar. "Maybe I have seen you on television. Your face and figure are so familiar".

He asked me what my name was, and I told him that I was *Mullah* Abdul Salam Zaeef, the *Taliban* ambassador to Pakistan. He looked surprised. "Oh, how are you?" he replied. Then without any real connection he asked: "*Mullah* Dadullah? Do you know which block he is in?"

I was taken aback by his question. I had not heard or seen of *Mullah* Dadullah since I had been taken captive. I now thought he might have been captured and brought to Cuba.

"Is he arrested?" I asked him. "When did that happen? I did not know that he had been captured".

"Oh, he is not here?" he replied.

"I don't know", I said.

The Red Cross had a complete list of all the prisoners in Guantánamo; they knew who was here and who wasn't, so his casual evasiveness in asking me about *Mullah* Dadullah made me suspicious.

Among the prisoners in Guantánamo there were two men who had lost one of their legs. One was Abdul Rauf,[1] the other was Suleiman.[2] The Americans thought that one of them might be Dadullah, but neither of them was.

The prisoners did not really think that all the Red Cross representatives were spies, but they thought that maybe the American intelligence agencies had infiltrated the Red Cross and planted spies among the representatives. Even with all this suspicion, the best thing by far was the letters they sent and brought to us.

They also brought books to Guantánamo, but the Americans took them away. If we complained about our treatment, about the food, or about being ill, it only made things worse for us and caused more problems. For example, when we complained to the Red Cross delegates that we were not being given enough food, they passed our complaints to the Americans, who got angry. The following week the menu would be even worse.

I remember I had a pain in my left lung and an earache. I was really suffering, and I asked the Red Cross to help me. Once the Red Cross representative examined me, and told the American doctors about my problems. But the doctors did not treat me; I didn't get any medicine, nor was I examined. Every week I would complain about the pain and my health but no one helped me.

On one occasion Badrozaman Badr[3] was being interviewed by the Red Cross in his cell. He was complaining about the situation and spoke in English. The soldiers outside the cell understood what he was talking about and even before he was finished, the NCO of the cell block came and commanded Badr to hand over all his clothes and possessions.

Badrozaman said, "But I haven't done anything. Why are you punishing me?"

He said, "Don't talk. Just give me the stuff".

He had to hand over all his clothes and other things in his cell in front of the Red Cross representative. The representative just stood and looked at the scene; there was nothing he could have said or done. Once the interview was over and Badr was alone in his cell again, the sergeant returned.

"Hey, crazy man! Who are you complaining to?" he said. "What do you think he can do for you?"

Then he gave him back his things.

We did not complain to the Red Cross much after that. But everybody was still keen to go to their meetings. For one, it was a break, a different environment. We also all really enjoyed the biscuits and the juice.

By the last two years of my stay in Guantánamo they had found two Pashtun translators. One was called Habib Kabir, and the other was called Arman. Both of them were Afghan. One of them had been living in Germany, the other in France. They were both good people, who showed a lot of compassion for the prisoners.

You could tell from their faces that they were suffering from our experiences. Habib came to us only once, and then we didn't see him again for a while.

"I cannot stand seeing you like this", he said. "When I enter the camp I am afraid I will have a heart attack".

He would help the illiterate. All day he would write letters for them to their families. Lots of the prisoners had no idea where their families were, and he would try to find this out and pass a message to them.

Arman also helped to connect the prisoners with their families. He understood our problems, our language and culture, and we trusted him.

While I was in Guantánamo I did not know how much work the Red Cross was doing on behalf of the prisoners. Only when I was released did I start to look into their activities; I realized how involved they were. The Red Cross tried to help us while we were being tortured by America, the land of the free that trod all over the law and human rights with her boots.

I wish to thank the Red Cross and wish it every success for the future.

* * *

There were various different groups of soldiers working in the camp. Each group wore a badge with a different symbol. The three main groups at the beginning had either a tree, a cross or a moon on their badges. The group with the tree sign treated us the best. They did not discriminate between us, and treated us well. They served us enough food and at times they even brought us fruit. We were not disturbed during our sleep by them, and if a prisoner needed to see a doctor they would take care to relay the information as soon as possible. In turn we tried to cooperate as best we could with them. Sometimes when a brother was very tired or disappointed, we would persuade him not to complain about the soldiers, because they were good people and we made sure to treat them with sympathy and respect as is written in the holy *Qur'an*.

The soldiers with the cross sign were very strict, and made sure to enforce every rule and law of the camp. At times they were discriminating and abusive and we would often not get enough food to eat. Nevertheless, a few soldiers among them were good and decent people.

The group with the moon-like sign, in contrast, was rude and discriminating. They never gave us enough food or even adequate clothes. During the night they would make sure to disturb our sleep. They were quick to anger and to punish prisoners.

There were three more groups, the key sign, the number 94 and the Spanish. The soldiers with the Spanish sign were the most polite and respectful of all soldiers I met in Guantánamo; they showed great sympathy and compassion for us. We often talked and they would tell us the story of their ancestors who used to be Muslims. We would get additional food, soap and shampoo. They respected Islam, took care not do disturb us while praying and never mistreated the holy *Qur'an*. At times they would tell us about what was happening in the world outside the prison. But they all disappeared and were replaced by red Americans.

The soldiers with the key sign were wild animals. They were still stationed at the camp when I was released. They were rude, had no respect for Islam and would go out of their way to make our lives as difficult as possible. They conducted night searches, disturbed us whenever we slept. They falsely reported prisoners to the authorities and would abuse us and the holy *Qur'an* at times.

The worst group of all, however, was the one with the number 94 on their badge. They abused the prisoners and the *Qur'an*; prisoners were punished for no reason by them. The animosities between group number 94 and the prisoners grew, and the prisoners in turn started to disobey them whenever they could. They would throw water at them, not answer their questions and be as uncooperative as possible. Finally, the prisoners decided that group #94 needed to be removed and announced that they would create more and more disturbances until they left. The authorities reacted by dismembering their group and putting the individual soldiers into different groups throughout the camp.

Every six months, soldiers would be transferred from Guantánamo, and bad soldiers would usually arrive in the new groups and good ones would leave. Some of the soldiers expressed their sadness about what was happening in the camp. They said that once they left they would talk to the international media and, with it, the rest of the world about what was happening to us in Cuba.

There was also a difference between the different soldiers and their ethnic heritage. There were red, white/Latino, black and Indian soldiers serving at Guantánamo. The white/Latino soldiers were mostly polite and showed sympathy with the prisoners and most of them did not discriminate.

The African American soldiers seemed to be always tired; mostly they slept or were eating. They seemed to have less education and many came from poor countries. Only a few of the African American soldiers discriminated against us, but the ones who did so were the harshest and toughest. They sometimes scolded the white and red Americans, saying that they were selfish and cruel and that they were being insulted by them. There was mistrust between them and every time a African American soldier was talking to a prisoner or giving him something, he would look around.

The red Americans, who hold all key positions within the government, are tricky and best known for their lies and frauds. The majority of senior soldiers were red, and they seemed to be better educated and have better financial circumstances than the African American and Latino soldiers.

The fourth group was the Indian soldiers; there were only a few of them. They are native to America and the real owners of the United States of America, living there long before it was discovered. Most of them now live in very remote rural areas of America and illiteracy is high amongst them; many are addicted to alcohol and drugs. They were killed and persecuted by the first Americans, their land was taken from them and they were driven into the mountains. Even now they have little representation within the government and many of the soldiers still regard the other Americans as invaders and don't agree with what the USA is doing. They consoled us about what was happening.

* * *

When I first arrived in Guantánamo there was only one camp consisting of eight blocks and a separate confinement ward. There were forty-eight cells, two walking sites, four simple bathrooms and twenty-four cells in the confinement ward. We were issued with red coloured cloth made out of thick material that gave some prisoners a rash. Every prisoner was given two blankets, two water bottles, two towels, a small plastic carpet, a toothbrush and toothpaste, one holy *Qur'an* and a mask. A common punishment was for all these items except the plastic carpet to be taken away.

When the second camp was built and the general who had been in charge was replaced, the conditions for us changed. We were divided into categories and the punishments got worse. The number of cells increased to three hundred, the *Qur'an*s were taken away, we were shaved again and prisoners were increasingly abused during interrogations.

The name of the new general was Miller;[4] he was later transferred to Iraq and took over Abu Ghraib prison there. He established Camp Echo,[5] a very dark and lonely place. There were different places for detention within Camp Echo, one of which was a cage inside an average room with a bathroom in front of it. The room and doors were operated by remote-control and prisoners were monitored 24/7 with video cameras. Inside the room you could not tell whether it was night or day, and several brothers who were detained in these cells suffered from psychiatric disorders afterwards.

No one could hear you when you were screaming inside and were waving a hand in front of the cameras to get the attention of the guards. No books, notebooks or any other items were allowed and the prisoner was left alone living with the four walls that surrounded him.

Many prisoners suffered from psychiatric disorders after a few years in Guantánamo. Ahmad,[6] who was from the west and had migrated to Britain, had been in Pakistan for religious studies when he was detained. He had been my neighbour in the Kandahar prison, where he was among the group of people who were wearing heavy metal chains all the time. Finally he broke down and started to suffer from some psychiatric disorders because of the difficult situation in detention. But instead of being helped he was punished over and over again and I remember him fainting several times. His condition got worse when he came to Guantánamo. At some point he was brought to the cage next to mine; all night long he would recite the holy *Qur'an* and poems. He would proclaim over and over again that the *Mehdi* (PBUH) would return this year. He was consoling himself. One day he hit a soldier with his food plate. He was transferred to Camp Echo and spent three years there.

Ahmad was well-educated but the detention made him lose his mind. The soldiers were well aware that he was suffering from the very final stages of depression, but he was still abused and not helped. There were numerous people who suffered from psychiatric disorders, like Dr. Ayman,[7] Tariq or Abdul Rahman.[8] The mad and psychotic are forgiven in front of almighty *Allah*, but not by the American soldiers.

I was detained in cage fifteen of Delta block and cage eight of Gold block in Camp Delta[9] till the beginning of 2003. I was later moved to cage 37 in Cube block. From my cage there I could see the ocean and ships passing by, but after a short while I was brought to a separate set of cages for detention where I spent a lot of time.

In the beginning we were allowed to shower once a week and could walk in one of the exercise courts for fifteen minutes with hands bound. The time was later extended to thirty minutes, twice a week. Our clothes were changed weekly. For a long time we could not trim our beard or clip our nails. Later this too also changed and we could use nail clippers and razors once a week.

Military food rations were replaced by freshly cooked food for breakfast and dinner, and the following year lunch was also provided fresh. The soldiers who handed out the food decided how much each prisoner would get served but it was cooked in a manner that made it tasteless. It was served in small quantities and we were often hungry. Fresh fruit was served three times a day, which felt like a big privilege.

We were allowed to pray five times a day and even the night prayer was announced. The soldiers played a tape for the *Azzan* and would imitate it themselves, but still we relied on the sun for the proper time. Later we were even permitted to pray in congregation. Praying in separate detention rooms was more difficult. Often there was no way to judge what time it was, and prisoners had to pray whenever they thought was appropriate.

When the third camp was built, our circumstances deteriorated. We were served less food, the quality worsened and punishment increased. Cube block was an example: newly made, the living conditions were very hard. Prisoners were left to live in open cages in their underwear no matter what the season, not being able to cover themselves even for prayers. Very little food was served and the soldiers would abuse the prisoners. The toilet was visible to all and the cages weren't big enough for prisoners to lie down to sleep.

In the winter it was very cold; prisoners would jump up and down just to get warm. One of the worst things was when the toilets became blocked. The smell of dirty water and faecal matter would blanket the whole block. We were not given toilet paper or water to clean ourselves after using the toilet; only our hands could be used, but could not be washed afterwards. The prisoner had to use those same hands to eat his food with afterwards. This is how those who claim to defend human rights made us live.

Prisoners were made to live in Cube block for one to five months at a time. Those who could not control themselves stayed for longer. A separate block was built for psychiatric patients; most of the prisoners detained there were suffering from severe depression and wanted to kill themselves. At the time I was there, there would be suicide attempts even on a daily basis. They were chained afterwards and given injections of barbiturates to calm them down; many of them became addicted to the injections.

But there was also violence among the prisoners. Some of the prisoners were believed by others to be spies and to be cooperating with the Americans; they were scolded and at times abused. Other prisoners would spit on them and they would ask to be transferred somewhere else. Many of them tried to hang themselves in their cell and then got transferred to the psychiatric ward, which itself made things worse for them.

Some of the spies were Afghan, and a number of them changed their religion and abandoned Islam. They would abuse the name of *Allah* and the holy *Qur'an* that was then taken away from them. There were people from Iraq and Yemen among them. Prisoners would be careful and suspicious when one of those people was placed in the cage next to them and would thank *Allah* when they were transferred elsewhere.

All this happened in Camp Delta; the group of disbelievers even wore crosses around their neck and they grew in number each day. Many believed that this was a plot of the Americans to change our minds to abandon Islam.

Two more camps were built; one was a good place with facilities and better living conditions. The other was another place for punishment. Camp Five[10] was far away from the other camps, but word about this place soon spread, and even the interrogators told us that it was the worst place to live.

In reality, the conditions in Camp Five were not good, but the brothers could tolerate them. The rooms had no fresh air and no window, so there was no sunlight coming in. Each room was monitored with a video camera; there was a kind of cement-made bed, toilet and tap. The walls were made of concrete and the doors were remote-controlled. Only a *Qur'an* was allowed in these cells. Food was served through a small window in the door, but we were not allowed to face the window while the food was handed over. Often during the process food would be spilled on the floor, but no new food was provided. Walking outside in the sunshine once a week was a privilege. Medical treatment was only provided in severe cases and never seemed to cure their illnesses.

Mullah Fazl was detained in Camp Five; he was suffering from a gastric disease and so asked for treatment for over one year but was only transferred to the hospital after he went on hunger strike and lost consciousness.

The conditions were extremely severe. The American soldiers often lied and deceived us, and there were many cases of abuse. Each brother who spent time in Camp Five looked like a skeleton when he was released; it was painful to look at their thin bodies. When Abu Haris[11] returned from the camp, I did not recognize him; there was no resemblance between the man who had been taken away and the body that was returned. I was so scared by his appearance that sometimes I would even dream of him and would wake up screaming. May Almighty *Allah* release all Muslim brothers in good health and save them from the hands of the pagans and cruel people. Camp Five was often called Grave Five; it was like a grave for the living.

Camp Four was made to hold prisoners who would soon be released from Guantánamo. Prisoners were well treated and adequately fed; the idea was that they could regain their weight and strength and get back to normal again.

Prisoners lived communally at Camp Four; they ate together and prayed in congregation. Games and sports were allowed, prisoners could shower several times a day if they liked, and once a week a film was shown. Some elders had received school lessons. In addition to the normal meals, we were given dates, honey, cake, tomato ketchup and other things, while prisoners in other camps were dying just to get a loaf of bread. There was a football field, a volleyball court and a ping-pong table, and we were permitted to exercise. Many journalists, senators and other visitors came to Camp Four; videos were made and pictures were taken, but we were not allowed to talk with them. We were given white uniforms, and soap with which to wash them.

At the beginning, when a prisoner was transferred to Camp Four, he and others thought that he would be released soon. Even the Americans would tell us that no prisoner would spend more than one month in Camp Four before being released, but the months turned into years for many in Camp Four. In the end not many of us were surprised; the Americans had often promised or said something that was soon after forgotten.

Once, after I had been moved from Cube block into different cages, a soldier came and told me to prepare myself to be interrogated. I was brought to a place I had not seen before and tied to some metal rings in the middle of the room. A group of Afghans entered and greeted me, sitting down in chairs around me. They introduced themselves and said that they were a delegation from the government of Afghanistan. They started to ask the same questions as the Americans, and from time to time an American woman came in and gave them a note or whispered something in their ears. I doubted that they really were sent by the Afghan government, and thought that they might be part of a plot by the Americans to trick us.

When I asked them what they had come for, they said that they were here to secure my release. I told them that this was nice to hear but that their questions felt more like being probed than anything else. They did not reply and left soon after. Most prisoners did not believe that these people were a delegation from Afghanistan, and abused them.

Later I was shifted to Camp One, and then to Camp Four in June 2004, where I stayed until my release one year and three months later.

19

GRAVEYARD OF THE LIVING

During my four years in Guantánamo I witnessed and heard of many unbelievable events that took place in Camps One, Two and Three. The detainees faced many difficult situations that violated every international, constitutional, civil, Islamic and non-Islamic law.

In 2003, at the beginning of the month of *Ramazan*, the month of fasting for Muslims, we were told that we would get some dates, honey and special bread. Even though these are small things, we still felt happy. On the second day of *Ramazan*, however, one of the soldiers mistreated us. There were forty-eight prisoners and three of us reacted, one person throwing water at the soldiers. The prisoner was immediately taken away and brought to a different cell for punishment. The day after it was announced that we would all be punished, that there would be no fresh food for thirty-four days and that water would not be served. We approached the senior officer, telling him that they should respect the month of *Ramazan* and that only one prisoner had misbehaved while now they were punishing all of us. His answer was negative: "this is the way of the military", he said. "The group gets punished for the mistakes of any one member".

Another time a female soldier mistreated the holy *Qur'an* while searching a cell, throwing it deliberately onto the ground. The event triggered a strike among the prisoners; they would not change their clothes, take a shower, help the soldiers in any way or even walk outside. The strike quickly spread, but instead of meeting the prisoners' demand to punish the soldier for her actions, they reacted with force. Gas was fired into the cells knocking the prisoners unconscious. Soldiers rushed in and took each prisoner out. All items were taken from them and they were shaved. The entire building was full of noise, preventing anybody from sleeping.

Another time the prisoners detained in a separate block called Indiana started to shout *Allahu Akbar* and banged on their cages. At the time no one knew what had happened in Indiana block, but soon after I learnt that soldiers had beaten an Arab brother called Mashaal[1] so severely that many believed he had died. All the prisoners were demanding information about brother Mashaal and threatened to create a crisis in the camp. The Americans first reacted by increasing security measures, but then announced that Mashaal was still alive but in a critical condition. Two months later, we found out that he had been completely paralysed. He could not sit or walk or move himself in any way. He could not even talk. He stayed in the hospital ward of Guantánamo for two and a half years. His condition did not improve and he was finally handed over to the government of Saudi Arabia.

In Guantánamo, everything happened in reverse. Even though the conditions were difficult when I first arrived, everything seemed to get worse with time. Food was a constant issue and it took the authorities a long time to arrange for adequate and sufficient amounts of food. Even then, in Guantánamo everything was a business. Privileges and treatment were solely dependent on the interrogators. If a prisoner was answering the questions of interrogators—satisfying their expectations, that is—then everything was possible: toilet paper, bottled water or even a transfer to Camp Four. Brothers who did not cooperate, on the other hand, were punished.

Mullah Fazal was punished for forty-one days because he did not answer the questions during an interrogation. During the nights he remained chained up in the interrogation room with the air-conditioning unit on full blast. The soldiers made sure to keep him awake. During the day they forced him to walk around so he wouldn't fall asleep.

Visitors were always brought to Camp Four, and never saw the real Guantánamo, just a few metres away.

Many times the holy *Qur'an* was abused; the soldiers deliberately used it as a tool to punish us. More than once we collected all the *Qur'an*s and handed them back to the authorities because we could not protect them. But instead of taking them back, we were punished.

Prisoners are the weakest people in the world. A detainee in Guantánamo, however, is not even a person anymore. He is stripped of his humanity as each day passes.

* * *

Many recounted their experiences to me while we were locked up in adjacent cages. Mukhtar[2] from Yemen and Yousuf[3] from Tajikistan had been in Qala-ye Jangi,[4] in Kunduz, among a large group of *Taliban* fighters who surrendered to the Uzbek militia. They thought that they had negotiated the surrender terms, and that they would not be harmed. But the Uzbek fighters ignored their promises. The *Taliban* were beaten, and many were killed or tortured. Then they were pressed into metal containers, hundreds at a time, many in a severely injured state. At Qala-ye Jangi they were thrown onto each other, beaten once again and even forced by the guards to fight among themselves. They weren't given anything to eat or drink. At the time they wished that they had been killed.

Yousuf Tajiki[5] told me that while one soldier rummaged through his clothes, robbing him of anything of value, another noticed a gold-capped tooth at the back of his mouth. Yousuf pleaded with the man, and explained that the tooth was not made of gold, but he tried to rip it out. It was stuck deep in the jaw and the soldier got a piece of metal and tried again. He only let go of Yousuf when some other soldiers said that they also thought the tooth was worthless.

Mukhtar was very young at the time, and started to cry when he talked about what had happened in Qala-ye Jangi. He said that they wanted to die, and had made a plan to attack Dostum's soldiers. When their hands were unfastened they seized a few weapons and started to fight. Many were martyred in the six days they managed to hold out, and then they were arrested once again.

Mohammad Yousuf Afghan said that the *Taliban* had recruited him from his village. When they were captured by Dostum's militia, he thought that he would be sent back home. Instead he and others were lined up and beaten. The wounded and injured were shot or were drowned in pools of rainwater. The militia took everything they had with them: their money, sweaters, boots and even toothpaste. Some of his friends were beaten to death. They were forced into shipping containers. He said that there were about three hundred people in the container when it was sealed up. They were transported for four days; from time to time they stopped and the doors were opened. People would be pulled out and beaten without any reason and then forced back again. Finally the container was set down. The militiamen closed the doors for the last time and left. For three more days they were locked inside. People were screaming for help. Some said that they saw the Prophet Mohammad (PBUH). When the doors were opened again most of the prisoners had died and he had to climb over their bodies. A representative of the Red Cross was the first person he saw, but then he was blindfolded and brought to a prison in Jawzjan.[6]

Some 8,000 or so *Taliban* fighters surrendered, but of these only 3,000 were to survive captivity. I had been in Islamabad trying to secure their release, and talked to Dostum several times, and he had assured me that the prisoners would be well treated. I even went to the United Nations to inform them about the prisoners, as well as the Human Rights Commission and the Red Cross.

Abdul Ghani[7] from Khushab in Kandahar province said that he was taken from his house and that he was accused of having launched rockets at the airport by the governor of Kandahar. He said that he had not launched any rockets, but, even so, was handed over to Allah Noor,[8] a commander with a fearsome reputation who had been with the Communist regime. He was responsible for communications at the military base in Lashkar Gah, but at this time he was in charge of Kandahar Airport security. Abdul Ghani was brought to Kandahar Airport, then beaten in a dark room with steel wires, but still he did not confess. Then they hung him upside-down from the ceiling, and beat him throughout the day. He could not bear the pain and finally confessed to the accusations.

He was given to the Americans.

Many of the brothers who had been arrested in Pakistan told similar stories. The ISI or the police had captured them and if they could not pay a bribe, they were interrogated, beaten and abused. The interrogators would ask questions about Afghanistan, about which they did not know the answers themselves. In the end, they were all sold to the Americans. Many had never been to Afghanistan or had any involvement with *Al Qaeda* or the *Taliban*. There were journalists and teachers, shoemakers and merchants in Guantánamo. Many are still there.

Pakistan was known among the prisoners as *Majbooristan*, the land that is obliged to fulfil each of America's demands.

* * *

On one occasion I was taken from my cell for interrogation and brought to a room I had not seen before. There was a white chair in the middle of the room for me to sit on, next to a desk with some sort of machine. The guards unfastened my hands, which was unusual for an interrogation. An American came in accompanied by a Persian translator. They told me that the device on the desk was a lie detector machine. I was asked if I would agree to be questioned while being monitored by the machine; this way, they said, they would be able to tell whether I was telling the truth or not. I replied that they should have brought me to the machine a long time ago, as it would have saved me from hours and hours of painful interrogations.

The first question asked by the interrogator was, "who knows everything about you?" I said *Allah*, my creator. Then they asked me who else knows everything about me. I replied that I myself know everything about myself. Again they asked who else.

"No one besides *Allah* knows everything about me", I said. The American looked at me and said that he himself would discover every secret in my heart using the lie detector. I told him that he should not claim to be *Allah*. "Not even a father knows the heart of his son", I said.

Then they placed the various wires on my body. The machine shows the temperature, blood pressure, heart rate, the amount of sweat on your fingers and other signs of excitement which then is used by the interrogator to determine whether a person is lying or not. I was asked a number of very simple questions. The machine itself often creates excitement and fear for prisoners, and in reality it only shows how strong the heart of a person is. The strong heart wins, answers the questions quickly and doesn't think for too long or you and the interrogator will start to have doubts. Most courts of law do not accept the findings of a lie detection machine as proof. It is merely a tool to scare the prisoners.

In a different interrogation session, without the lie detector, a map of the world centred around Afghanistan was placed before me. It had various lines and arrows on it, and the interrogators told me that it was a map showing the illegal trade in gold. They accused me of having taken part in the trade myself. Not only was I surprised, but it really made me wonder; how foolish are these people, I thought, wasting their time on meaningless issues like this.

I noted that the map indicated that the gold route originates in Afghanistan. "So according to your map", I said, "the gold is mined in Afghanistan and then sold throughout the world". They said that I was correct; that was what the map showed.

I told them that, "if you can prove that Afghanistan is producing gold, then I will be happy to accept any accusation you have against me".

They did not reply but started to ask me some other questions instead. They gave me a questionnaire, the first question of which asked if I travelled to Peshawar each week. I told them that I didn't. The second question asked for a reason why I went to Peshawar each week. Often the interrogators' questions made no sense like this.

The interrogations often appeared to be all over the place; there were questions about other prisoners, crimes, trips we had made, life experiences, parts of our careers, school time, *madrassas*, locations of people, educational institutes, political figures, businessmen, mines and natural resources, religious and political conferences, political parties, social organization and culture, rural people, the tribes, regional differences, geography and so on.

At the beginning all questions were related to the current situation in Afghanistan, but later this changed completely. Questions were of a general nature or concerned with the country's economy. Many questions were asked about natural resources or mines and their location. In particular I was asked many questions about oil, gas, chrome, mercury, gold, jade, ruby, iron and other precious stones. I was asked several times about uranium, even though I had previously not heard that there was any in Afghanistan. Often when I said that I did not know or when I had no information, I was punished and put into an isolation cage. There were countless questions about Islam, *madrassas*, religious institutions, famous scholars and religious conferences.

Once an interrogator accused me of being guilty of an attack[9] on a ship in Yemen, in which eleven Americans died. They said I had been in Yemen at the time. I was surprised, and asked them how I had reached Yemen. They said I had travelled to Iran, then onwards to Qatar, and from Qatar to Yemen. I asked if they thought I knew about the attack on the ship before I went there. They said that they thought I hadn't known. I asked if I had taken the explosives for the attack with me. They said that they had no information about that. I asked them: "I did not know about the ship, where it was, or where it was going, so how could I have attacked it? How could I have travelled through Iran, Qatar and Yemen to an unknown location on an unknown mission?"

"Furthermore", I said, "I have never been to Iran, Qatar or Yemen. If you can prove that I have been to any of these countries, then I will accept your accusations". The interrogations were depressing, questions were repetitive and often these false accusations came from nowhere without any proof or any truth to them.

They were trying to wear us down. Punishment was followed by offers, promises of cooperation and then more punishment. A group of interrogators once came led by a man who looked like a magician with a French style of beard. He said that I had not been treated well so far and that he had come with good news for me. He said he would make me a rich man. He would give me five million US dollars, a nice house and a car. I would be the richest person in Afghanistan, he said. I asked him why he would do all that for me. He said that I would be their very close friend. I would help them find the answers to their questions.

I smiled at the interrogators and told them that I was already a very rich man, unimaginably rich.

"*Alhamdulillah* I have no need for your money. I have spoken the truth and have answered all your questions, and I will continue to speak the truth in the future. I do not know about this business of yours, and I will not be involved in it. All I need", I said, "is my freedom".

He said that I didn't trust them and that I couldn't understand what they were saying. I told him that there was nothing to be trusted. "So thank you for everything you came here to offer today", I said, "but all I need from you is to help me get released from here".

The discussion lasted four hours and then they left. A few stayed behind. A short woman who called herself Angel came forward and asked me if I knew who she was. I said I knew that she was an American. She said that I had not understood much about her. She said she was in charge and that she held the real authority over me: my release, my life, and my punishment. Even though other people had already interrogated me, she did not trust or accept what they had found out so far.

She would start all over again, and I would have to tell her the truth and behave with her. I asked what would happen when the next interrogator came. "Will he accept your information", I said, "or will he again start from the beginning? How will we ever know our destiny here?" She cut me off and told me to be quiet.

"Don't speak unless you're told otherwise", she said. "I will teach you. I will strip you of all your pride". At this point I lost my temper with her, and I said every word that came to mind. The discussion was over. They left, and I never saw them again.

There was no rule in the camps. The interrogators that came and went behaved however they wanted, just like the other camp authorities and even the soldiers in the individual blocks. There was no rule-book; no way to know how one soldier would act. They did whatever they pleased, punishing us and abusing prisoners as they felt was appropriate. In the end, even when a prisoner complained or an investigation was conducted, only the soldiers would be consulted with the general idea being that they would not lie. Prisoners, even those involved, were hardly ever consulted, and whatever they said was presumed to be a lie if they were asked.

I can't even remember how many different interrogators I had over the years that I was detained in Afghanistan and Guantánamo. Most of them wronged me, punished me in different ways and harmed me. May *Allah* take revenge for what they did to me in this world and the next.

***

In the outside world there was mounting pressure on America because of Guantánamo. After three years they introduced the Enemy Combatant Status Tribunal Review Board[10] to deceive the world and the prisoners alike. Many of the prisoners were hopeful when they heard of it, even though in reality it was unlawful and unconstitutional. The board had been convened to determine which prisoners were "enemies" and who, when accused, could approach Columbia district court for a trial.

The tribunal was made up of our interrogators. One would be judge, another the defender, and the third the prosecutor. All worked for the CIA, FBI and other intelligence agencies. All were trained interrogators; none of them had studied law, or understood it. It was only one of the games they played. I was brought to an interrogator who said that he was my personal representative. He was more rude than most of my previous interrogators, and demanded that I tell him all the facts about my detention so that he could defend me in front of the tribunal.

I was suspicious about him and the tribunal and told him that I had a few questions. I asked if he had studied any kind of law at school or university. He said no. I asked him about the tribunal board that was going to judge me: did they have any previous experience with law or tribunals? Again he said no. Then I asked him under which law—national or international—I would be judged. He said that there was no such law because none of the laws applied to the prisoners. The board would just announce its findings. Finally I asked him about the notice that we had all been given, that all prisoners had been proven "enemy combatants". What law did that relate to, I asked. He said that he did not know.

Then I spoke.

"It is good that you do not know the law, that the judge does not know the law, that there is no law under which I will be judged. There is no law here at all, and given three years ago they ruled without any law that we are enemy combatants, what is the need to ask me now, all of a sudden? You say you are my representative but I would have to agree to that, no? You are my enemy. I do not accept, nor agree, with any tribunal of this kind or visits made by you. I do not accept you as my representative. Do as you please now—punish me or not—but do not come here to meet me again!"

He said that it would be wise to cooperate with him because he would represent me in my absence anyway. I told him that I did not trust him, that I did not trust his tribunal and that he should do whatever he wanted. I for one would not allow anyone to make decisions on my behalf. In the end, I had to scold him to get rid of him.

The tribunal came and went. Another board, the Administration Review Board[11] was put in place but I turned it down as well. I did not go before them, and they did not issue anything about me. We were all accused of being enemy combatants, be it *Al Qaeda* or *Taliban*. We never really heard the reasons or saw the proof of these accusations. People in Guantánamo were detained for all sorts of reasons; often prisoners had no links to *Al Qaeda* or the *Taliban* whatsoever. They would be accused of sheltering a *Talib* or offering food to them, or accused of knowing a famous *mujahedeen* or *Talib* commander. People were accused of having carried out attacks and explosions. Some had been captured because of false information; others had been wearing "the clothes of a *mujahed*". One man was arrested because he was carrying a mirror, another for having a phone, and a third for watching his cattle with binoculars. One of the prisoners said that they had taken him because his only form of identification was a 25–year old ID card from the time he had been a refugee. These were the facts and the proof of America.

I heard many stories like these. There were former *Taliban*, a member of the present government, a shoe maker, a smith, a shepherd, a journalist, a money changer, a shop-keeper and an *Imam* of a mosque. Many old *mujahedeen*, and even their own interpreters, were detained in Cuba. Some Pashtun brothers had been brought to Guantánamo because they had been in an Arab country and their visas had expired. Many of them spent three years in the prison before they were found innocent and released. They received nothing; no compensation for the time they had been robbed of, and nothing for the hardship they had been put through.

In the summer of 2005, the disillusionment and hardship cumulated in a widespread hunger strike.[12] Prisoners stopped eating or drinking, and at its peak 275 people were on strike, with some Arab brothers intending to continue till their deaths. The prisoners demanded a free and just tribunal and that their human rights be respected.

The strike continued for twenty-six days, and about two-thirds of the prisoners participated in it to some extent. The commander in charge of the camp, Colonel Bumgarner,[13] announced that some points of the Geneva Convention would be applied to the prisoners' rights and called for the strike to be stopped. Sheikh Shakir[14] from Saudi Arabia, who himself was on hunger strike and was well respected among the prisoners, was taken round to each individual to ask them to break the hunger strike.

Finally the strike ended. A body of six representatives was formed from among the prisoners to discuss the situation, and to offer suggestions on behalf of the prisoners to the American authorities. The group was made up of Sheikh Shakir, Sheikh Abdul Rahman,[15] Sheikh Ghassan,[16] Sheikh Sabir,[17] Sheikh Abu Ali[18] and me. We tried our best to find a quick solution in order to avoid arousing the suspicions of the other prisoners. We took great care not to fall into the traps of the Americans. Three meetings were held between the body of representatives and the camp authorities. The first took place on 7 August 2005. Colonel Michael Bumgarner, the senior official responsible for the camp, the camp commander and one other person participated in the meeting.

Bumgarner, a man of short stature, opened the meeting by saying that he respected the body of prison representatives; he wanted a secure prison and said that for that he needed us, since the other prisoners listened to what we said. He added that he would respect our decisions and that he had contacted the Secretary of State for Defense, Mr Donald Rumsfeld, requesting that some of the agreements of the Geneva Conventions would be applied in the camp, the selection of which would be up to us.

We told them that they should immediately stop threatening and abusing the prisoners. For four years they had tricked the world into believing that they had detained terrorists without any proof, any law or any formal accusations being made, throwing us into cages. They accepted what they heard, and said that they would start treating us like human beings. But their words were lies: empty promises that never materialized. The representatives were taken away from the other prisoners and badly punished. No one knew where they were, and the difficult situation continued. The strike started again with almost three hundred prisoners refusing to eat. Twenty pledged not to eat until they died.

Several hunger strikes took place in the camp, and were ended only after receiving promises from the Americans, but the one that started at this time lasted until the day of my release on 11 September 2005. Each day the number of participants increased; several became extremely weak and were close to death, fainting in their cages and cells, and being taking to the hospital for treatment. They were force-fed intravenously, but even while in the hospital they still tried to prevent the doctors from feeding them. They could no longer tolerate what was being done to them and chose death over life. The hospital was filled with starving patients. The doctors were so busy with the emergency cases that other patients had to wait to be treated. The doctor-in-charge refused to force-feed the prisoners, so five other doctors were brought. The problem continued until 19 January 2006.

Where now is the United Nations, which so readily supported sanctions against twenty million Afghans, while now thousands of Muslims are detained, clamouring for justice, law and human rights? And for what?

20

GETTING OUT

On 11 May 2004, the sixteenth day of *Ramazan* that year, I was transferred for what I thought would be another interrogation. The room that I was brought to looked like an office, nicely furnished with a desk and a television set, and after I was guided into the room my hands and feet were untied–the first time they had been untied outside my cell since I had arrived in Guantánamo. After a short while an Afghan man came into the room accompanied by three Americans. I knew two of the Americans, both interrogators who had treated me very well in the past. The third American introduced himself as an officer in the new American Embassy in Afghanistan.

The Afghan man said that he was a representative of the Afghan government; he seemed very kind but I was suspicious if he really was who he said he was. We talked for a while. He expressed his grief and sympathy for the prisoners and myself, and acted very differently from the first group of Afghans who had claimed to be a delegation.

I met the man twice. For our second meeting he invited me for lunch. The food was delicious, with fresh fruit and Pepsi, and I felt respected. He promised me that he would try his best to secure my release from Cuba; in the event, it took another year before I was freed. I was eager to leave this graveyard of the living which the Americans had built.

After meeting with the delegate, I was visited once or twice a week by some other interrogators. For the first time I was treated like a human being; they asked me if I needed anything and would bring me anything I wished to eat. My life in the camp improved while that of others got worse. The little I got from the interrogators–perfume, shampoo and very good olive oil–I would share with the other prisoners.

211

The Afghan delegate had promised to return in a month, and I was waiting for him. The month turned into two and I began to have more and more doubts. I was disappointed. The interrogators just told me to wait for the delegate. He would come and I would be released, they said. Some months later, I was told by an interrogator that the Afghan delegate would return the following week and that I would be released; he would take me back to my homeland. Before that, I would be transferred again. I did not trust them; the Americans had lied to me too often, and by then I could no longer tell if what they were saying was the truth or not. Many of the other prisoners laughed at me for even considering that I would be released, and some even swore that it was just another plot by the Americans.

The following week I was transferred to another place. It was a nice room, well furnished, with air-conditioning, a refrigerator, a TV set, and a separate bathroom. There was a tea and a coffee maker, shampoo and soap. For the first time in years I made myself a cup of green tea, which had been one of my biggest wishes while in the cages.

Another interrogator came and told me that I had been released. He congratulated me and said that the General responsible for the region had come to see me, and he also offered his congratulations. Tomorrow, he said, the Afghan delegate will return and give me more information. Even though I was happy that I would be leaving, I had to think about my friends that I would have to leave behind, without any law and rule, without any respect for human beings.

The delegate came and told me about my family and the current situation of Afghanistan; in turn I told him about the camp, the living conditions of the prisoners and what was happening all around us. I advised him to talk with the Americans and address these issues. I was transferred back to my previous cage the following morning. I was waiting for the Red Crescent delegation that visited all prisoners before they were released.

Suddenly, a group of Americans came to the cage. They had a video camera and a Pashtu interpreter, and presented me with a note. I was told to sign the paper in front of me, accepting everything written on it in order to be released.

- The criminal confesses to his crime and thanks the government of the United States of America for forgiving him and releasing him from the prison.

- The prisoner was a member of *Al Qaeda* and the *Taliban* movement. He will eliminate any links he may have with them.
- The prisoner promises that he will not participate in any kind of terrorist activities.
- The prisoner promises never to participate in any kind of anti-coalition or anti-American activities.
- If the prisoner violates the aforementioned terms, he will be re–arrested and detained for the rest of his life.

Signature of the prisoner:

I was astonished to read the terms listed on this piece of paper. The group of soldiers and some senior officials were recording everything with their video camera as I listened to the translator. They handed me the paper to sign it, but I threw it back at them in anger.

"I am innocent, and not a criminal," I said. "I never have, nor will I, accept any kind of accusations. And never will I excuse or thank the Americans for releasing me. If I have committed any crime, which tribunal or court has proved me a criminal!?

"Secondly, I was a *Talib*, I am a *Talib* and I will always be a *Talib*, but I have never been a part of *Al Qaeda*!

"Third, I was accused of terrorist activities, which I have never done. So how could I admit to doing something that I never did to start with? Tell me!

"Fourth, Afghanistan is my home. No one has the right to tell me what to do in my homeland. If I am the owner of my house, how can someone else come and tell me what to do in it?

"Fifth, I am still detained here, innocently detained. I can be arrested again, accused of any crime, so I am not going to sign any kind of paper."

They insisted that I sign the paper. They told me that I would not be released if I refused, but still I did not sign it. Even if it would have meant that I spend the rest of my life in prison, I could never accept to confess to being a criminal. Many times they left and came back, but I still did not sign.

Finally, they told me to write something myself instead of what was written on the paper. I was obliged to write something, so I took the pen and wrote the following:

I am not a criminal. I am an innocent person. Pakistan and the United States of America have betrayed me. I was detained for four years without specific accusations. I am writing this out of obligation and stating that I am not going to participate in any kind of anti-American activities or military actions. *Wasalam*.[1]

After that, I signed what I had written and they left me alone. I wondered if they would accept what I had written. After a short while a Red Crescent delegation came and congratulated me on being released. Soon, they said, I would be brought back to Afghanistan if I agreed.

This was a strange question, I thought, and asked them what they could do to help me if I did not want to go back. Would I have to stay here in prison for the rest of my life? They said that they could not do anything. It was all up to the Americans.

Indeed, they had no authority to help me, so I had no other option. Return to Afghanistan, or prison for the rest of my life... Afghanistan is my homeland; I love Afghanistan, but I just wanted to find out why they were asking me those questions about going somewhere else which was not in their authority. They were giving a legal framework to what the Americans were doing to prisoners. The Red Crescent delegation left.

I was moved to Camp Five to say goodbye to the prisoners. The brothers were taken out of their graves and all put in a big cage. I talked to them for one and a half hours, and then I left them. It was very shameful to be released. My religious brothers remained in the worst conditions of their lives, but they were all happy about my freedom. I only met the Afghans who were detained in Camp Five; I was not permitted to meet the Arab brothers. Later, I was moved to Camp One to say goodbye to the Afghan prisoners there, and then to Camp Four where I said goodbye to all the brothers, Arabs and Afghans.

I went back to the previous place to relax and eat. It was eleven o'clock so I prayed and slept. At one o'clock that night they came and brought me to the airport. My hands and feet were shackled the same way as when I had arrived in Cuba some four years before. When we reached the airport, a General told the soldier to unfasten me.

All the lights in the airport were off. I saw an airplane getting ready to fly, and I went closer to the airplane where some Americans accompanied by some Afghans were waiting to receive me and officially hand me over to the Afghan authorities. The representatives congratulated me on being released, and told me to get on to the plane. This was the first time I had walked by myself, without American hands on my shoulders.

The small jet airplane had been chartered by the Afghan delegation. The General came inside the airplane and said goodbye. We were accompanied by four other Americans who looked like security officers. It was almost three o'clock when the airplane took off. The Afghan representative had brought Afghan traditional clothes and a turban for me. I could freely walk in the airplane and could use the toilet. I was eating food, fruit, and could sleep without any problem.

The airplane landed in England after a ten-hour flight for refuelling; then after another seven hours in the air we landed at Kabul International Airport.

* * *

Kabul had changed in the four years I was away, especially the airport; the Americans had built roads and security fences and a camp that looked like a small city itself. I gave thanks and praise to *Allah* when I got off the plane by performing a *sujdaah*.[2]

I was freed on 11 September 2005 from Guantánamo. I landed at Kabul International Airport the next day and was taken to the National Directorate of Security by the Americans. From there I went to *Mullah* Mutawakil's house, where my family was, and then I went on to Mujaddidi's place for the formalities.[3]

Two days later I was taken to a house which the government had rented for me in Khushhal Mina. Then something happened which made me very emotional and upset. When I was leaving Guantánamo, I was promised that I would never be interrogated by Americans in Afghanistan. I had told the Afghan delegation in Guantánamo that the questioning should not continue on Afghan soil.

I was sure that America would face more and more problems every day in Afghanistan. If they wanted to talk to me about those problems, it would mean interrogation. It would be very hard for me to answer their questions every day, or to help them. So I made them promise me that the interrogations would end. Americans should never enter my house, I said, with the purpose of asking questions. They accepted that, and they even said that they would pay for my expenses for the next year.

For four months it all went according to plan. I didn't see any Americans, but in the fifth month I got a phone call from the Afghan National Security Council. They asked if they could come for a visit. I said, "you are most welcome," thinking that they would be Afghans.

At 2 p.m. I saw armed American soldiers with bullet-proof vests outside my house. I did not like what I saw. I never wanted to see armed American invaders near my house. Even so, I tried to stay out of trouble and to control myself. I refused to answer their questions, saying that I was sick, because silence was better than a reply. They left, but two days later the same man who had called me before told me that he would return the same day at 2 p.m.

This time I asked him who would come. "The same people as last time," he said. I explained that I had been promised in Guantánamo that these people would not come to my house. I told him that if I was free to make a choice, then that I would request them not to come to my house. "If I am not free," I said, "then come with handcuffs and chains and take me wherever you will for interrogation."

A short while later, one of the men who had helped me to get out of Guantánamo called me. After greeting me, he asked that I let those people come to my house. "They have some questions. Just get it over with and get rid of them," he said.

I could not turn him down; he had done a lot for me and I could not refuse. I agreed and said that they could come. Under the surface, though, I just wanted all of this to stop once and for all. Nevertheless, it was not in my hands. I would see what would happen.

They came at 2 p.m. with a long scroll of questions. But instead of answering them, I asked questions of my own. "Okay," I said, "I understand that you face problems in Afghanistan. You will have new questions every day, and you will come to me to find the answers. If I answer you now, this will never stop. So I will not answer you."

I shouldn't be afraid, they said. "Your security is tight. There will be no danger to you or your family. Your information will be safe with us, and we will give you more assistance".

I told them that giving privileges and guaranteeing security was one thing. "But," I said, "I cannot cooperate with you. I do not want to. I cannot make these deals, so please leave me alone. I was in Guantánamo for four years and I was constantly being interrogated. Wasn't that enough for you?"

Still they tried, sometimes with threats, and sometimes with words of encouragement. "You have a future. You have a home and children," they would say.

It was harder for me than Guantánamo, to be honest. They were trying to take away my beliefs. But I thank *Allah*, who gave me the strength to avoid their trap. Finally I spoke frankly with them. "This is my last word. I will never be ready. I ask you not to come to my home again. If I am free, if my country is, as you say, independent, and if I have the authority over my home, then do not come. I do not want to see you here again."

They became angry. "Why do you hate us?" they asked.

"I do not like you," I told them. "Just look at what you are doing, and what you did to me and other Muslims. What do you expect?"

They looked at me with bulging eyes and mottled faces.

"Do you want to go back to Guantánamo?" they asked.

"Whatever you do is your business," I answered. "You kept me in Guantánamo for four years when I had done nothing. If you want to do it again, there is nobody to stop you. But if it's a question of freedom, then I have the right to tell you to leave me alone. But if it's a question of power, then do as you wish, for you have all the power. But I don't want to see you. So throw me in jail or leave me alone, it's up to you."

They left.

I thank *Allah* a billion times that I never saw them again. Even so, my situation became more difficult since they stopped paying my expenses. They had paid the lease of the house for one year, and I found support from other friends and Muslims. The government posted soldiers outside my door from the security services. Still today, 24 hours a day, 7 days a week, my life is restricted in many ways. Only *Allah* knows what the future holds.

21

NO WAR TO WIN

Afghanistan's story and my story are not over. On 11 June 2006 news reached me about three prisoners in Guantánamo who were martyred.[1] It is heartbreaking to hear of events like this. Every day I still pray for my brothers who I had to leave behind. I pray that *Allah* will guide them and will save them in this life and the next, that he will give them and their relatives the tolerance and patience to endure.

This was not the first time a Muslim brother died in an American prison, but it was the first time that it happened in Guantánamo. The circumstances of their deaths are not clear, and the only source of information is the American government or the soldiers who work in Guantánamo. They claim that the prisoners killed themselves. I, for one, cannot trust a single thing coming out of the mouth of America. It is a lesson I learnt while I was in their hands for over four years. In Guantánamo, they lied to us. Nothing they said could be trusted, not even the time of day.

But even if what they say about the death of the Muslim prisoners in Guantánamo is true, we should still ask ourselves who is responsible. The conditions in the camp and the treatment by the American soldiers caused the deaths of the prisoners, who after years and years could no longer tolerate and sustain the pressure, the hopelessness and the constant threats. Time ground away at all that they held dear, debasing them. Every prisoner I knew suffered from psychiatric illnesses in Guantánamo. The system of the camp itself systematically wears prisoners down to the point where they lose their sanity.

There are many rules, regulations, systems and processes that are responsible. There is no rule of law in the camp; the treatment and punishment of the prisoners are illegal and strip them of any basic human rights; and the soldiers often misbehave and abuse their power and the prisoners alike. Even after years in Guantánamo, no prisoner knows his fate or when or to where he will be transferred, or if he will be released. Many prisoners are isolated with no contact to the outside world for years at a time. The holy *Qur'an* and Islam are insulted and used as a tool to punish and further degrade prisoners. In Guantánamo, you have no access to information, books or other means to study or pass the time. Sleep deprivation is widely used as a tool, often over weeks and months, which seems directly responsible for mental breakdown in many prisoners. Every prisoner is subject to degrading behaviour, like being left naked in front of others. Interrogators often use information as a weapon, telling prisoners that they have arrested their relatives, their father or son, or that their relatives have been killed. Many prisoners do not receive adequate health treatment, and letters to and from family members are steamed open and altered.

These are some of the things that all prisoners in Guantánamo have to endure; everything seems to be a lie, and there is nothing and no one to be trusted, with no end to it. Prisoners do not even know what to say or do to stop what is happening to them. No human can endure a situation like this forever.

So even if the prisoners really killed themselves, as the Americans would have us believe, there can be no doubt that the responsibility still lies with them. It is the camp—Guantánamo itself—that killed them. The Bush administration is responsible for their deaths, even though they might have died by their own hands. And the American people are responsible for what is happening in Guantánamo, for allowing their government and leaders to break international and even national laws, and even for electing Mr Bush for a second term.

* * *

Afghanistan is the home of each Afghan, a family home in which we all have the right to live. We have the right to live in our country without discrimination and while keeping our values. No one has the right to take this away from us. Each Afghan has the right to help his or her country, be it in cultural issues, national security, protection, their own well-being, religious traditions, economic well being, or in terms of cultural values. National unity, tribal agreements and religious traditions form the basis for any development and progress in Afghanistan and need to be supported by its people. May Almighty *Allah* help us create a free Afghanistan!

The most important matter is to protect the honour of Afghanistan and its Islamic framework, including national Afghan traditions. These are the values which have protected Afghans, and for which Afghans have shed their blood and which have fuelled their bravery, defeating every foreign invader and superpower in the world with the help of *Allah*. Afghanistan never was and never will be a captive: it has always been a free country throughout its history. The Afghan nation has stood against all invaders in unity.

Throughout our history, every invader has been defeated by the Afghan nation. To be specific, it was national movements fuelled by the people who came to the streets to demonstrate and fight that have saved Afghanistan over and over again, not just from problems brought from the outside but even from their own governments at times.

The Afghan youth have answered all those problems with arms wide open. The main dispute is trust—trust is an invisible force, and the lack of trust is the reason for the current weakness in Afghanistan. All Afghans need to come together and help each other. Naturally, all Afghans have a great respect for the way of Islam, and through Islam we can find a solution for the current problems and possible conflicts on the road ahead. The political vacuum that has ensnared our nation must be filled. Islam can guide us.

The only way to find a solution for the problems is to respect Islamic values. Poor Afghans are killed in many ways: they have been ambushed, kidnapped, and detained; foreigners are attacking their homes, killing and injuring their wives and children; they have been made to leave their country. All these issues need to be addressed. Anyone who wants to solve the current crisis needs to do so from a position of unity and by offering solutions that address all parts of the problem.

It is very difficult to find any hope in the current situation, which has addled the brains of our domestic politicians and turned the dreams of the foreigners inside out. Everybody thinks that a solution must be found for this stalemate. Some people are trying really hard, but they are mostly working for their own benefit.

I have met Hamid Karzai three or four times, at his invitation, since I returned to Afghanistan. We sparred verbally, but tried to find a solution together. It is quite an enigma, and it is hard to see who can cut this knot. But one truth is that Afghans and Afghanistan are victims of these problems. Sometimes they understand this, sometimes they do not.

Even though Karzai talks incessantly about peace and stability, he is a very long way away from bringing them into being. He has damaged his own standing with the people through false propaganda and empty promises. I do not know whether or not he understands this. He is imprisoned within a circle of people that keeps him far from the truth, and the information he seems to get is very weak and often has nothing to do with reality. But he relies on this information, and it results in inappropriate action. Karzai has very few friends who can help him to shoulder the burden. There is no one to help him keep his good name, to accept his ways as their own. He has no one with whom to share the good and the bad. The way he came into power at the hands of foreign sponsors weakened his position from the very beginning. He has very few smart advisers who can give him clear, tough direction, in the light of Afghan culture. He also finds himself between the tiger and the precipice—he wakes up every day not knowing which way to go. And finally, he cannot differentiate between friend and enemy, because he did not come to power in the way he should have, through slow, difficult steps. That way he would have made true friends, honest friends. But when you are in power, everyone is your friend, and it is difficult to tell the difference between real friends and false ones.

There are other reasons too, and they will not have a positive impact on Afghanistan's future.

When I talked with Karzai for a long time, and studied him, I began to compare him with *Mullah* Mohammad Omar Akhund. First, *Mullah Saheb* gave everybody who visited him enough time to empty their hearts. He listened, he was patient, and he did not react in anger. Any visitor could tell that he was thinking very deeply about what he was saying. Karzai is the opposite. He does all the talking, and gives little time to his visitor. The truth is that by listening you can understand an issue, while if you talk a lot you might say something that you will later regret.

Second, if *Amir ul-Mu'mineen* promised something, he did it. Third, Karzai likes to show off and pretend that he knows a lot, while you never felt that with *Amir ul-Mu'mineen*. There were many of these similarities and differences between the two men.

Karzai is trying to find a solution, and one can feel that he is not a cruel man. He would not consider killing someone or throwing him in jail. But he is responsible for the cruelties of his guests. He could condemn those actions, but he is caught up in politics. He loves power, and wants to stay where he is. He also wants peace.

But those who helped him get that power are also very important to him. It is very hard to maintain a balance between two opposites. I do not know how aware he is of his deficiencies, but I can see that he is important in his job right now. He can play a crucial role. But Afghanistan's problems are going on above his head. He is just a pawn in the hands of the main player.

But we can be sure that his time will end. I remember, at the beginning of the American invasion, how sure they were that no one would ever be able to raise a hand against them. They told me very smugly that "we will be in Afghanistan for a long time. We will root out the *Taliban* and *Al Qaeda*, and we will bring democracy and freedom".

I could only laugh at them. "That may be your opinion, but I do not agree".

Then, patronizingly, they would ask: "So, what is your opinion? What will happen?"

In reply I would hold out an outstretched hand, all five fingers spread.

"Here is where you are right now", I told them. "But in three years it will be like this". I contracted my hand into a claw. "If you are not complete idiots you will understand. Otherwise, in six years it will be like this". And I made my hand into a very tight fist. "It would be good if you use your brain at this point. Otherwise, in ten years everything will be out of your control. You will have an embarrassing failure, and we will have a disaster".

But they treated my words like those of a child. They told me that I did not understand. But I told them, "I am an Afghan. I know this".

* * *

Afghanistan's political situation is tied to the international scene, a political game in which the most disparate nations are tied together in one dishonest chain. Things are so confused you cannot tell back from front. Why don't these people get themselves out of Afghanistan? It is all temporary anyway. Maybe they will leave sooner; maybe they will stay a bit longer. But one thing is clear: Afghanistan has the right to resist invasion. We have the right to save our honour. We have the right to take revenge on those who have spilled our blood.

Afghanistan and America are now bitter enemies; even the liberal use of the term "terrorists" does not conceal this fact. But Europe made a big mistake when it took America's side. Those countries are now tarred with the same brush as America. They are trying to put both their feet into one trouser leg; this brings back old memories, and it makes us even more determined.

The world cannot be run by a select few; this does not make sense. If we look at each century we see examples of bloody disasters that caused enormous destruction of life and property.

All of this is because countries in the world lose their sense of balance and take sides. There have to be neutral countries that can stand between those who are in conflict. There must be countries that can be trusted when mediation is called for. Not like today, when the whole world is on one side. If this is not controlled the results will be catastrophic. We can see the deterioration right now in Afghanistan and Iraq; in other countries too, problems are becoming more and more serious. It is very difficult to say who benefits from all of this misery, or where it might spread next.

Why is America continuing to spill blood? Why do they continue to play this game, destroying buildings in the name of fundamentalism and terrorism? What other human rights will disappear into the greedy maw of America? Will this monster finally devour itself? Will it consume the whole world? Is it going to bring security or will it start World War Three? Will it accomplish its stated goal, which is to eliminate terrorism, or will it instead cause it to double or triple?

No one answers the sword with *salaam*.[2] And you cannot wash out blood with water. The sword is answered with the sword, and *salaam* with *salaam*. But it seems clear these days that America cannot tolerate anyone but itself, and this may lead to its collapse. Tolerance is the most necessary quality on earth; it can make the world into one home. But it is impossible that one person's wish should dictate everything, no matter how much money or power is used.

It is a fact that America has lost its reputation as a peaceful and humanitarian country. Throughout the world American is now regarded as selfish, reckless and cruel. If a country is despotic, they help those who are cruel. It does not matter whom they are fighting against; that is a different issue altogether.

It makes no sense to repeat history. Afghanistan is now facing the direst consequences of the mistakes of the past. It is clear that the world is heading for a major change when one looks at the fast pace of recent years. We cannot know whether this will be a peaceful change or a bloody one. Peace seems unlikely. It is what we all pray and wish for. If more violence is to come, then we Afghans will once again be the victims. Our soil and that of our neighbours will bear much of the sorrow.

But before looking to the world and judging its direction, we have to ensure that we are not just being swept along, or crushed underfoot, like ants. In this crucial time, talking about our internal differences is extremely ill-advised. The *Taliban*, as well as Gulbuddin Hekmatyar and other elements of the resistance, should pay close attention to this. The Northern Alliance and other figures in the Karzai administration who hope to live in this country for a long time should also consider this quite seriously. Some people whose brains are steeped in the murky water of bias see some personal benefit in creating divisions. But they should know that in Afghanistan each ethnic group may only prosper if there is unity. No one can protect their national honour with selfishness.

Then there is the issue of foreign forces who have been placed over Afghans. These forces need to learn the truth. They must understand that Afghanistan can never be conquered by force. This is a society of tolerance, respect, and *jirga*s. Cluster bombs, B-52s, cruise missiles, disrespect, and throwing people in jail can only bring enmity. This is not the way to peace. It has no benefit at all except to thicken the walls of hatred and bias.

The American interrogators used to tell me that there were only a thousand *Taliban* fighters, and that once they were killed the resistance would be finished. Since I have been released from Guantánamo I have been following the reports of the Americans and their Afghan allies, who by 2006 had claimed to have martyred 12,700 *Taliban* since they arrived in 2001. But the resistance is getting stronger and stronger with every passing day. This clearly shows that killing people, or throwing them in prison, cannot eliminate the enemy. Instead, it just creates more enemies, more people with hatred in their hearts.

Some of the countries involved have tried to get their feet out of this quicksand. But they do not know how. Other countries are looking for alternative strategies to stave off defeat. But they have no idea how to proceed.

It is all just empty words. Every country holds its own interests above all, secret from the others. There is no honesty in their promises and actions. It is just fear that brings them together in their devil's pact.

225

Maybe it is fear of the future that motivates them. This is a paper tiger conceived of by the CIA and the FBI. I agree with those countries who look for an alternative strategy. But they should be aware that, while they are working on this alternative strategy, they have already taken sides. They have chosen the side that took the lives of thousands of Afghans. They have chosen the side that has displaced thousands of families, that has made thousands of children orphans, and thousands of Muslim women widows.

It is the eighth winter since the invasion, but still the cruelty and dishonour continue. The series of killings, of funerals, of bloodletting, is getting stronger by the day. So what strategy are they working on? Their brains have atrophied in their skulls. And what empty-headed, selfish Afghans are they listening to?

It would be good if these countries would leave the alternative strategies to the Afghans. We should decide our future by ourselves. We should be making the decisions, the compromises, and the system. These countries should abandon the idea that all of these things can be under the prerogative of just one empty president, who dances according to their tune. The law of the country is disregarded, the ministers are appointed according to their wishes. The judiciary forgets its own decisions, or even takes actions that violate previous decisions. They cannot have an economic monopoly, or try to manipulate Afghan honour for their own ends.

They process governors and parliamentarians through their own filter. And for them killing an Afghan is just like killing a bird. If they kill or injure an Afghan, no one can take them to court; no one can make them answer.

The diabolical United Kingdom and stubborn America will widen the gap between Muslims and other religions. They will create an atmosphere of distrust and suspicion.

This satanic policy has gone on for long enough. Afghans should forget their fear of this paper tiger. They should take back their independence, in such a way that the foreign invaders have no more excuses. Is this possible or not? Perhaps it is too early to say. But if the situation continues as it is now, after this unholy alliance came together for the Afghan elections, it will not benefit either the Afghans or their neighbours. Afghanistan will survive. It was here long before America was born and will still be here long after the Americans have left. Now our nation is caught in a web woven by our neighbours and the foreigners with the help of a few. But the time will come when the Afghan people find their voice and come together to once again move forward at their own pace and along their own path.

EPILOGUE

AFGHANISTAN TODAY

It is unclear in what direction the political situation in Afghanistan is developing. The general perception is that it is part of a wider regional crisis, one that becomes more complicated every day on account of the imbalance of power and the atmosphere of suspicion and political mistrust.

Afghanistan has once again been transformed into an arena in which the powers of the world lock horns. Given the political and military vacuum in the country, it serves as a superpower laboratory for the development of influence and alliances.

The departure of George Bush and the arrival of Barack Obama has raised hopes among some Afghans, but the situation is getting more and more complicated on the regional level. America no longer occupies the position it did in 2001, when it invaded Afghanistan for no other reason than a vague notion of revenge. It is also not where it was in 2003 when it invaded Iraq, using weapons of mass destruction as an excuse to grab the country's oil reserves. America's reputation has changed. It is now known all over the world as a breaker of laws, a violator of human rights, and a provoker of hatred. Matters have reached the stage where American citizens are reluctant to show their passports in certain countries out of fear or embarrassment for the deeds of their own nation.

In economic terms, America is in crisis: unemployment is rising by the day, prices are soaring and major companies are going bust, one after the other. As America seeks new supply routes through Russia or the former Soviet Central Asian republics, its central problem with Pakistan is becoming more and more obvious. Pakistan under Pervez Musharraf was a good ally for America. It oppressed Muslims, allowed

229

its soil to be used for the destruction of another Muslim country, helped in the killing of innocent Afghan civilians, suppressed Islamic parties within Pakistan and cultivated the seeds of hatred between the government and the people.

It now seems as if the udders of the American cash cow are drying up.

The Arab world also appears to be turning away from America because of its enmity with the Muslim world. This are many reasons for this, but the strong support that America gives the Israelis against the Palestinians plays an especially important role. Arab leaders cannot overlook this.

In addition, no one can fail to grasp the significance of American defense installations in Georgia, Ukraine and the Czech Republic. But the growing strength of Russia, the dramatic development of China, and Iran's readiness to obtain nuclear weapons is further challenging America's power.

In spite of all these challenges, President Obama's political strategy is still based on the assumption that America is the sole world leader. This is, in itself, a confusing problem and an incurable disease. America is now working on a new Afghan strategy, and is planning to replace Hamid Karzai with another president. It has to show Afghans how much America has usurped their independence by putting another puppet in power. In this respect Obama could be even more dangerous than Bush. He may be willing to bring change and peace, but he will come under pressure from the intelligence agencies, who will have a strong influence on his decisions.

There are many signs that the Americans intend to stay in Afghanistan for a long time. They want to cover up their failure and improve their image. They are leaving Iraq because of the growing resistance in the Arab world. Economically, the Arab countries are very important for America.

America does not want to be defeated by the Arabs, and nor does it want to further harm its relations with the Arab world. Afghanistan, however, is easy for America; they are fighting an ethnic group that does not have extensive roots anywhere else in the world. They can continue to fight and ignore civilian casualties and the suffering of the Afghan people without facing a strong reaction throughout the world. This would be a problem for them if they were fighting in Palestine or continued to fight in Iraq.

The gap is widening between the Afghans and the foreign invaders, and the problems are getting worse and worse. The oppressed Afghans have a great deal of patience; unfortunately the world also has a lot of patience with their suffering and cares nothing for their blood.

Afghanistan is the most oppressed country in the world. Afghans take their revenge in silence, even if they have to sacrifice themselves in the process. No Afghan, least of all a Pashtun, believes that America is doing anything other than killing people and sowing hatred. The primary goal of the invasion was to render Afghanistan powerless; even those Afghans who at first marched to the American tune are starting to feel this way.

The security situation in Afghanistan is getting worse by the day. The foreign invaders and the Afghan authorities have even less control than before. In villages and districts life is getting harder and harder for the people, especially for businessmen and those who have livestock or other possessions. People feel insecure and are trying to get their investments out of the country.

There is a direct relation between security and the economy. As the security situation deteriorates, the economy and the political situation follow suit. Obama now thinks he should increase the number of troops and send thirty thousand more soldiers. He is also encouraging other countries to increase their troop numbers. They think it will help the security situation. They do not know that more troops mean more blood. What's more, it will lead to further tension with our neighbours. The more troops there are, the harder it will be to get them out. Obama's new strategy might turn the problems of Afghanistan into problems for the entire region far beyond what we are seeing right now.

The solution, in my opinion, is for Americans to revise the war policy they developed under their insufferable last president Bush and put an end to the conflict. They should begin a campaign of peace instead of war. Only a major revision of their strategy can help both Afghanistan and America alike.

The entire southern region—Kandahar, Helmand, Zabul, Uruzgan, Farah and Nimroz—is interconnected economically and in terms of security. One province can directly influence others, especially in the southwest, southeast, and central region. But the political impact of the southern provinces also has a direct bearing on the north and the west as well, and on the tribal areas reaching far into Pakistan.

Some people, however, just want to oppress the Pashtuns and the South. They either do it directly, or by encouraging the foreigners. They know that oppressing one of their fellow Afghans is only to oppress themselves, but they do it for the money.

In 2007, the political, economic and security situation in the southern provinces was very complicated. Lots of foreigners and many more Afghans lost their lives. In many rural areas in the south the relationship between the foreign troops and the local population shifted from mere hatred to outright enmity. If you went out onto the streets and were to ask every single Afghan how he thought the Americans were treating the people, 95 per cent would tell you that they are the enemies of the Afghan people. The only people who would answer differently are those who work with the Americans, but they are hated even more than the Americans themselves. As for the British, I think everyone agrees that they have come to Afghanistan to avenge their fathers and grandfathers.

Too often it is forgotten that it is the Afghan people who suffer; it is they—the farmer and the shopkeeper—who pay the price for bad policy and uninformed decisions. Our men and women, friends and brothers are losing their lives and their independence while our country is turned to ruins in the name of reconstruction. Why are our hands and feet shackled? What is it that the foreigners want from us?

Everybody lost under the Bush administration. Only the enemies of Afghans and Americans benefited under his rule. But is President Obama any different, you might ask? It is all too obvious that his hands will also be stained by the blood of Afghans. He has already announced that he will send more troops. Obama was elected by a wide margin, but his campaign slogan, 'change we can believe in', was vague and unclear. Obama is also from a minority—the minority that once were slaves—who were deprived of their rights for centuries in America. A minority that was neglected economically and politically. But in the end, President Obama may be manipulated even more than Bush was.

We see the beginning of this process in the increase of the number of American soldiers in Afghanistan, and in the threats issued to other countries. If Obama truly wants to save America from collapse and end the enmity towards the Islamic world and Muslims in general, he should be more cautious.

We all know that increasing troop numbers in Afghanistan was not Obama's plan or suggestion. It was decided before he even got elected.

Senior American advisers say that a troop surge will bring the situation under control. America should take a look at Afghanistan's history: we have been invaded many times before. How many troops did their predecessors bring? And why did they fail? They should look at Iraq. A million lives were lost while 300,000 US soldiers were there, and the killing continues to this day.

Americans should know that they are no longer thought of as a people of freedom and democracy. They have sown the seeds of hatred throughout the world. Under their new banner they have declared a war on terrorism and terrorists, but the very term "terrorist" is of their own making. The *jihad* against them will never stop as long as America doesn't take steps to correct its mistakes.

Be warned, you are not prepared for Afghanistan! Yes, there is hunger and poverty; our country lies in ruins and our economy is destroyed. Be this as it may, it is not the issue. In Afghanistan, our ideology is not for sale. There is no easy solution in Afghanistan, and America will never solve the problems through tribal militias or *arbakai*s. Turning brothers against each other can only create more conflict. These militias will be an uncontrollable force, outside the army and police. America will awaken a sleeping monster. All of this has happened before. We have seen it before and we can still see its effect even now.

Some Americans and pro-Western Afghans believe that America should first strengthen its military and political position, and then pave the way for peace talks. Perhaps that is the reasoning behind the increase in troops. It may have worked for them in Iraq, but Afghanistan is very different from Iraq or the West. Afghans do not back down. If they are in a weak position their thoughts will be consumed with fighting for their rights and plotting their revenge. America is in a strong position; any attempt to increase its power will only push more people to fight.

America invaded Afghanistan, she violated Afghanistan's sovereignty, threw thousands in prison, tortured and humiliated them and killed tens of thousands of Afghan citizens. Obama and America should apologize for this instead of continuing the violence. They should seek a real peace. This is important for everybody. We all talk about peace, but the approaches are very different. Perhaps it is true that the Americans want peace as well. But it is their own peace, on their own terms. That is not peace; it is war by the name of peace.

America needs to treat Afghanistan as a sovereign country and realize what rights she has here. Only if America is publicly recognized and if the Afghan government independently grants them rights, only then will the Afghan people accept her presence here.

As for now, America's goal in the region is unclear. What do they want? How much longer are they going to kill and oppress people and call it "the war on terrorism"? When the Americans first came to Afghanistan, there were only a few of them. Then it reached 6,000, then 18,000, after that, 30,000. Now we see that it will soon be twice that— 64,000. Perhaps next year it will be 100,000. What does this mean?

Who will control them? Who will still be able to claim that Afghanistan is an independent country? We are very far from a timetable for withdrawal. If the Americans continue to be stubborn instead of working towards a realistic timeline for withdrawal, they will strengthen their bases, construct more airports and ammunition depots, and amass supplies for dozens of years. They will try to profit from the poor conditions that Afghans find themselves in, and will buy Afghans with the money that will then be used against them.

Afghans need to unite. They must not let themselves and their children serve the Americans, killing other Afghans and being killed themselves. They should wait and see what happens. Afghans need to know that their deaths will harm only themselves. No one will cry for them—indeed, others may even be happy that they have been killed.

Pakistani Jails

The inhuman American jails have provoked criticism and objections from human rights organizations around the world. They are famous for their illegal oppression of Muslims. But they are a reality in this world. They torture people and they deprive them of their human rights; they perpetrate injustice. They have violated international and US law, as well as the 1946 Geneva Conventions. This has happened, and still is happening, in Afghanistan, Iraq, Guantánamo and other places far from the public eye.

But other countries that have done even worse than the Americans have escaped notice. Countries like Egypt, Jordan and Pakistan, supported by the United States, are committing acts that cannot be justified by any law, Islamic or otherwise. Look at Pakistan, our neighbour. How does it treat Afghans?

Pakistan, which plays a key role in Asia, is so famous for treachery that it is said they can get milk from a bull. They have two tongues in one mouth, and two faces on one head so they can speak everybody's language; they use everybody, deceive everybody. They deceive the Arabs under the guise of Islamic nuclear power, saying that they are defending Islam and Islamic countries. They milk America and Europe in the alliance against terrorism, and they have been deceiving Pakistani and other Muslims around the world in the name of the Kashmiri *jihad*. But behind the curtain, they have been betraying everyone.

Their Islam and their *jihad* were to destroy their neighbouring Islamic country together with the infidels. They handed over their airports to the Americans so they could kill Muslims and destroy an Islamic country. Their loyalty to the Arabs is so great that they sold diplomats, journalists and *mujahedeen* for dollars. Like animals. God knows whether they will ever use their nuclear bomb to defend Muslims and Islam. They might use their weapons—as they have used everything else—against Muslims.

Afghans are imprisoned around the world. Governments come up with new excuses to torture and imprison us every day. Much is known about how Afghans are tortured in Afghanistan, Iran, Guantánamo and American prisons, but little is known about the situation in Pakistan.

Pakistan manufactures the charges, political or criminal, often extorting money from Afghans. Criminals tend to get off lightly compared to political prisoners in Pakistan. People imprisoned on criminal charges at least have the chance of a trial and often manage to bribe officials to be released. In the prison they also have a certain degree of freedom unknown to the political prisoner. In Pakistani jails, criminals can meet with their relatives by bribing officials, even though they too can remain in prison for many years without being charged; they may not be given the right to hire a lawyer; they can be beaten or tortured into confessing, and their voices can be silenced.

But the life of political prisoners is much harder, especially with the treacherous game of "terrorism" being played these days. Most of the victims of this deadly game are Afghans. The status of Afghan prisoners is very different from that of Pakistanis. For one thing, Pakistani prisoners can communicate easily. Also, politicians in Pakistan can help Pakistani prisoners. Afghans are treated as second-class citizens by the Pakistani police. Once they have Afghans in their claws, they can do whatever they want with them. Most of the political prisoners are held by the ISI. They are isolated; there is no law in the places they are being held.

There are many Afghans who have been imprisoned for the past five or six years in Pakistani intelligence prisons. There are many more who have been imprisoned for the past two or three years, with no future and no hope. Their relatives cannot find out what has happened to them, they cannot ascertain what the charges are, or what lies in store for them. They cannot even find out whether their son, brother or father is imprisoned, or whether they are sick or in good health. They have no connection to the outside world at all, not through the Red Cross, not by letters, not by telephone or video.

They remain in their cells as dead men, waiting for the Day of Judgement.

May God save these prisoners from the Pakistani jails. For the relatives, life is hard, but it is much worse for the prisoners themselves. Their time in prison is a tragedy. They are stripped of all dignity. When the Pakistani ISI comes to arrest somebody, they raid his house just like the Americans do in Afghanistan. They turn the whole house upside down. They tie up the rest of the family members and put black sacks on their heads. Sometimes they even arrest other members of the family, or even guests that just happen to be there. They curse the prisoners all the way to the detention centres. They treat them in an inhumane and un-Islamic way.

During interrogation, they are tortured and often deprived of sleep. They can only go to the toilet once every 24 hours. They are not allowed to speak to each other. They can only communicate by gesture. If they are caught talking to each other, they face severe punishment.

One prisoner told me his story: "When I was arrested by Pakistani spies", he said, "they took me to a very frightening place. It was a small, narrow room, and everything—ceiling, floor, walls, door—was painted black. You could not tell the difference between night and day. Only when they were taking us to the interrogation room did we see a small lamp switched on.

"That was it. The first time they took me to that room, I became short of breath, my blood pressure skyrocketed. I felt as if I had been thrown into a grave. I screamed and shouted, but was cursed in response. After shouting for a while, a soft voice touched my ears, speaking. 'Hey, new prisoner. You won't find anybody to be kind to you even if you scream until the morning. So better to wait instead of screaming and shouting. Ask God for help.' I calmed down a little bit after that.

"When Pakistani soldiers came to my cell and turned on the light, I realized how black the walls and ceiling were. It was very frightening. I had never seen such a place. There were pegs on the walls and they would tie the prisoners to them. The pegs had rings, two rings for the hands and two for the feet. There was a fifth ring as well that they used to tie the prisoners' necks with a rope. When they tortured the prisoners, their blood stained the walls. When I looked at the Pakistani soldiers, wearing their black clothes and black hats, the only thing I could see were their evil eyes moving. Then I fainted. They woke me up and put a black sack on my head, then took me to another place. I could only hear the voice of the interrogators there, speaking English with an American accent. One of them would ask me questions and the other would translate his questions and translate my answers back.

"This continued for a month. Once a week I was interrogated by the Americans, and two or three times I was interrogated by the Pakistani officers. Then the situation changed. I was thrown into another small room with three other Afghan prisoners. The new cell had a light and we had a chance to go to the bathroom twice every 24 hours".

This prisoner, who spent a year and three months in that secret prison, never heard from his family the whole time. They did not know where he was.

"When the Pakistani intelligence officers and the American interrogators understood that I was just an ordinary Afghan, not connected to any political party, and that I had no information about *Al Qaeda* or the *Taliban*, they decided to release me. They came to me in the middle of the night, handcuffed me and shackled my legs, put a black sack over my head, and threw me in a car. After a three-hour drive they stopped somewhere and in complete silence they took me out of the car, threw me on the ground, released the handcuffs and removed the sack from my head. It was very cold. The Pakistani soldiers told me: 'You are free now, but you have to do two things. First, you should not move for fifteen minutes, until we get far away. Second, you should never tell anyone what happened to you. If you do, then you will face worse consequences than this. You should know that you will never be safe from us".

Many others have had much worse experiences. Those who were handed over to the Americans or to the Afghan government after imprisonment and interrogation by Pakistanis would be as happy as if they had been freed.

I asked many prisoners this question: what is the difference between Pakistani jails and Afghan or American jails? The answer was always the same: Afghan and American prisons were much better than the Pakistani ones.

Men like Sayyed Mohammad Akbar Agha, Doctor Yasar, Mufti Abdul Hakim, and hundreds of other prisoners became disabled due to the beatings and the torture inflicted on them during their imprisonment. Some of them cannot work any more on account of their injuries.

We have tried our best to get human rights organizations and the international community to evaluate the prisons that Americans and Pakistanis made for Afghans on Pakistani territory, in order to try to help the prisoners, but so far even an organization like the International Committee of the Red Cross (ICRC) is still waiting to obtain permission to visit, to connect prisoners with their families and to inspect these prisons. Even though many human rights organizations have tried to influence America, Pakistan and Afghanistan to respect human rights, nothing has changed yet. Only God knows what will happen.

Why the United States is Failing

Although the United States of America and its NATO allies still claim success, in fact they are pulling the wool over their peoples' eyes and saying that they have achieved a lot in Afghanistan.

They do not mention the words "failure" or "defeat", no matter how many difficulties they face. But the truth is that after eight years in the region, dozens of problems have arisen, blood is being shed, poverty and unemployment are at their peak and the roots of the economy are drying up. Security is limited to the cities and towns. The hatred between the two sides is increasing, to such an extent that now the soldiers of America and NATO cannot even secure themselves—let alone begin to bring security to the Afghan people. Instead of turning their guns and tanks on the so-called enemy, they are pointing them at the oppressed people.

This whole plot of war was decided very soon after 11 September 2001. America's blood had already started to boil before that time; they were just looking for an excuse. America should have used its mind and its logic after 11 September; they should have investigated. Their haste was their hubris.

The war itself was their biggest mistake: attacking Afghanistan was the wrong move after 11 September. The Bonn conference that imposed

American ideas and inflicted certain Afghans on the Afghan people was their second mistake. The alliances they made, cooperating with known warlords and war-criminals and helping the same people back to power who had once before ruined the country and bled its people—all of this was a policy failure. Afghanistan will pay the price for that mistake. An attempt to follow the war effort with a targeted campaign to hunt and kill the *Taliban* has much to do with the conditions right now in the south and east of the country.

Many of the rules and laws that were imposed on Afghanistan interfere with its culture, a mistake that has been made over and over again by foreign invaders and Afghan rulers alike. Disrespect for religious values, and the use of religious symbols to pressure prisoners, both these things were coupled together with a policy of hate and bias toward religious *madrassas* which has alienated much of the rural population. Putting a price on the head of prominent Muslims, as well as interfering in the election process and the *Loya Jirga* directly robbed the new government of its legitimacy. And finally the prisons, the decision to violate all human rights, to place Afghans outside any law, the silence and complicity of America and the international community has lost the respect and trust of the Afghan people. Without trust there will be no peace. Still people believe that they can find a military solution to a political problem, ignoring all lessons from history.

* * *

The decision to invade Afghanistan and wage war against its people was a mistake, because it drove America and Afghanistan into a quagmire. The door was wide open for talks and negotiations; there was a way that would have spared many lives. But America was sure that it would win the war easily. The Afghan puppets had assured them that Afghans would welcome the Americans and that people were unhappy with some of the laws of the *Taliban*. The leaders of the Northern Alliance had also given the green light. In essence, the sanctions of the United Nations and the lack of recognition for our government had sabotaged our economy and robbed us of the time we would have needed to progress. But America rushed into a vengeful and hasty decision to wage war, invading the defenseless territory of Afghanistan. It was a mistake. They should have sought a way towards peace and negotiation instead.

The Bonn Conference, through which America imposed its will by bringing together a small group of Afghans, often hailed as a ground-breaking moment, was a bigger violation of Afghanistan's independence than the American invasion. Fundamentally there were two problems with the Bonn Conference; America gave power to the Northern Alliance in order to strengthen its own position, and suppressed Pashtuns while calling them *"Taliban"*. But an important point was overlooked—there were no real representatives of Afghanistan at Bonn, or at least they were not given the opportunity to make decisions about what Afghans really wanted. The decisions made were illegal in any sense.

On account of the American invasion and the toxic decisions of Bonn, certain people—those whose cruel swords had grown blunt from overuse on the Afghan people—were welcomed into power. The criminals from the Communist regimes and those selfish looters who called themselves *"mujahedeen"* are responsible for much of the destruction and tragedies of the past. They wanted to take power once again to trade in people's lives, and to bring back their terror and looting. They overshadowed even the crimes of the Soviets. They drew America into a quagmire and spawned many problems. These groups are the enemies of the real *mujahedeen* and of the *Taliban*.

America has been quite successful in bribing people in Afghanistan. They started handing out sacks of dollars to the Northern Alliance—beginning in Panjshir—to get them to use their ground forces against the *Taliban*. After the American forces descended during the collapse of the *Taliban*, they accelerated the bribing process and they continue it to this day. But America used its money for other things as well, hiring puppet spies among the Afghans to strengthen its position, and by putting a bounty on the heads of the leaders of the *Taliban* and *Al Qaeda*. They exploited the poverty of Afghans to the utmost. On the say-so of these greedy spies, innocent people were martyred, hatred was spawned, and the gap between the people and the government widened. Afghanistan's independence was entombed. It also blackened America's reputation.

The attack on Afghan culture and its Islamic values has exposed the true face of the Americans to the world. The enmity of America with Islam and Muslims as expressed by this thing they call "terrorism" is clear for all to see. There are many examples: Firstly, when the Americans came to Afghanistan for the first time, they thought there would encounter no resistance. They closed all the religious *madrassa*s with the help of their puppets; even in the mosques, only young boys were allowed. The education of students in the mosques stopped. This plan was implemented mostly in Kandahar, Zabul, Uruzgan and some other provinces. The fact that this plan was not completed is a different issue. Secondly, eliminating the word *"jihad"* from the curriculum of the schools and some other subjects was extremely worrying. *Jihad* is a central concept within Islam, and understanding it is an obligation of every single Muslim. Thirdly, efforts to give men and women equal rights in everything and paving the way for co-education under the name of international law, and allowing women to take off their scarves; this was another such plan. They also started enmity with all Islamic organizations in the world, especially *jihadi* organizations, and tried to eliminate them. There are lots of examples, but we might single out their support for Israel and for the destruction of the elected government of Palestine.

Attacks on Afghan culture by the Americans are now a common occurrence. Now it happens in every corner of the country under one guise or another. For example: when the American invaders target an Afghan they believe to be an enemy according to their puppet spies' reports, first they identify his house in the village. Then in the middle of the night they land with their helicopters. The American soldiers raid the house. Prior to entering the house, they blow up the gate instead of knocking, they strip the person they are targeting in front of his wife and family. They search women and they break open boxes instead of unlocking them. Then they take the person away like wild animals, or they just kill him with bullets or knives in front of his wife and children, in his own house. Let's stay with this example—legally, how many violations have they committed? One: entering people's houses without their permission; two: searching the women; three: stripping the person in front of his family members. It would be easy to fill a book naming all the abuses and crimes they commit.

The Americans have put prices on the heads of many people, have put people on a blacklist, and taken their God-given rights from them. They have provoked people into fighting them out of self-defence. This is not conducive to peace. Why then, when the Afghan administration claims that it is trying to conduct peace talks with Hekmatyar, why is the American administration still promising millions of dollars to whoever finds him?

The American government still holds strong prejudices against Islamic *madrassas*. At times it seems that it sees no difference between terrorist training camps and the religious schools, a position that is damaging its relationship with the Muslim world. Based on the poor understanding of the *madrassas*, America has long set out to pressure Pakistan, Saudi Arabia and other Muslim countries to change their curriculum and has led a campaign against *Ulemaa'* who preach about *jihad*. Rumours that pass through the Islamic world suggest that a number of *Ulemaa'* were assassinated as part of the United States' plan to influence Islamic teaching.

The *Loya Jirga* was a farce: America pressured representatives on issues of hiring and firing of personnel; agendas were prepared in advance; UNAMA pushed people; bribes and back-room deals were the norm; and some representatives were even threatened and were taken to Guantánamo. *Loya Jirga*s and other such institutions are an integral part of Afghanistan's culture, and are the traditional way to find solutions to problems. Using these traditional institutions can solve many of Afghanistan's problems, but attempts to manipulate them will backfire and cause more damage than good, in particular when they are poorly understood to begin with.

America made an irreversible mistake in their choice of friends, ignoring their history with Afghanistan. The Afghan allies they chose were often warlords who had returned to Afghanistan in the wake of battle, using America and damaging the very foundations of the new Afghanistan they planned to create. Another strategic mistake was to allow Great Britain to return to the south, or Afghanistan in general. The British Empire had fought three wars with Afghanistan, and their main battles were with the Pashtun tribes in southern Afghanistan. They were responsible for the split of the tribal lands, establishing the Durand line. Whatever the reality might be, British troops in southern Afghanistan, in particular in Helmand, will be measured not on their current actions but by the history they have, the battles that were fought in past. The local population has not forgotten, and, many believe, neither have the British. Many of the villages that see heavy fighting and casualties today are the same that did so some ninety years ago.

There are even fundamental flaws in the very construction of the Afghan government that show a lack of understanding of Afghanistan and its people. From the very beginning Pashtuns were underrepresented, even though President Karzai is Pashtun; this alone is an inbuilt weakness. Furthermore, the government system and its mechanisms are far too advanced for Afghanistan. There is a lack of control within departments and ministries, with little means of ensuring that subordinate departments and ranks obey the orders of their superiors. Parts of the government appear to be under the control of foreigners and not the President, his ministers or the cabinet. There are government officials and members of the cabinet that are mistrusted by the population. The very structure of the government, the division of the army, the cabinet and the other organs have been decided by foreigners.

Information is key to any conflict. The foreign troops in Afghanistan have poor intelligence, though, and have too often listened to people who provided them with false information, who use the foreigners for their own goals and target their own enemies or competitors. America often admits mistakes, but the public never hears that an informant who provided them with false information that led mistakes is to be punished and held accountable for his action. As long as this is the case, we must assume that America cooperates with them and that military operations, based on false information, are actually planned and executed for other reasons, and are not in fact mistakes after all.

The US and its allies solely rely on force, and even the so-called peace talks are accompanied by threats. It is astonishing that after eight years, with tens of thousands of troops, warplanes and equipment, and a vast national army, facing down some estimated ten thousand insurgents, leaving some two-thirds of the country unstable, that foreign governments still believe that brute force is a solution to the crisis. And still they send more troops. The current conflict is a political conflict and as such cannot be solved by the gun.

The biggest mistake of American policy makers so far might be their profound lack of understanding of their enemy. The US brought an overwhelming force to Afghanistan. They arrived with a superior war machine, trying to swat mosquitoes with sledgehammers, destroying the little that was left of Afghanistan and causing countless casualties on their mission, knocking down many more walls than killing insects. Till this very day it is this lack of understanding and their own prejudices that they still struggle with.

The new Obama administration appears to be making as many mistakes as their predecessors. The decision to bring a special envoy who will diminish the authority of Afghan officials, coupled with the appointment of General McChrystal, a man who was previously responsible for covert operations, are both steps in the wrong direction. The mounting number of civilian casualties together with the ill-made attempts to cover up massacres will doubtless further alienate the Afghan people. America now is at risk of following the same path as the Soviet Union. If America does not wake up from its trance of self-proclaimed omnipotence, Afghanistan will be its demise.

Ever since America invaded Afghanistan, they have come to many junctions in the road and all too often they have made the wrong decisions. They are on unfamiliar territory, and they know little about Afghanistan. Today the situation in my birthplace of Kandahar looks like an unhealthy amalgam of the worst of the Russian times and the civil war that followed. Once again Afghans are fighting each other, and President Obama, who had the option to choose a new path, seems to have made his mind up. And once again foreign troops will arrive in great numbers trying to solve a problem they are part of. How much longer will foreigners who fail to understand Afghanistan and its culture make decisions for the Afghan nation? How much longer will the Afghan people wait and endure? Only God knows. Once again I pray for peace. Once again I pray for Afghanistan, my home.

Mullah Abdul Salam Zaeef
Kabul, June 2009

NOTES

KANDAHAR: PORTRAIT OF A CITY

1. The final number killed in the attack will never be known, but it likely reached at least 110 (based on the testimony of witnesses, policemen and the staff of the ICRC-supported Mirwais Hospital).
2. Van Dyk, J. (1983) *Inside Afghanistan* (New York: Author's Choice Press).
3. Dupree, N. (1977) *An Historical Guide To Afghanistan* (Kabul: Afghan Tourist Organisation).
4. According to Afghan government statistics as of the 2008–9 reporting period, the district then known as Panjwayi (no longer the same size following district boundary reforms post-2001) currently has around 157,000 inhabitants.
5. Maley (2002): 21.
6. Mohammad Taher Aziz Kamnam wrote *De Kandahar Atalaan* (1986), for example, as well as the famous collection of stories, *De Kandahar Cherikaan* (1986).
7. William Maley (ed.), *Fundamentalism Reborn? Afghanistan and the Taliban*, London, Hurst & Co., 1998.

FOREWORD

1. Ahmad Shah Baba (1722–1772) was born in Herat and went on to rule a huge empire stretching from India to eastern Persia. A Durrani Pashtun from Kandahar, he remains an important figure in the popular imagination.
2. Mirwais Khan (of the Hotaki Ghilzai tribe) was the founder of the Hotaki dynasty and led the tribal revolt which eventually resulted in the foundation of something akin to the modern Afghan state. His tribe were then superseded by the Durranis.
3. Spin Boldak is located on the border with Pakistan. The road is the main route for passengers travelling by car to Pakistan.
4. Gul Agha Sherzai is originally from Kandahar province and is the son of one of Kandahar's most famous 1980s *mujahedeen* commanders, *Hajji* Latif, the so-called 'lion of Kandahar'. He served as the governor of Kan-

245

dahar in the early 1990s following the fall of the Najibullah regime in Kabul, as well as from 2001–2003 after the fall of the *Taliban*.

5. Asadullah Khaled is originally from Ghazni province and served as governor of that province from 2001–2005 and as governor of Kandahar from 2005 to August 2008.
6. These are all districts of Kandahar province.
7. Afghans—and all Muslims—have two main religious days of celebration called *Eid*, more or less equivalent to the Christian Christmas. The days of *Eid* are characterised by special prayers and sermons, as well as by an emphasis on family, friends, and the giving of gifts. They are known as *eid al-Adha* and *eid al-Fitr*.
8. 'International Security Assistance Force'; this is the NATO-led mission mandated by the United Nations Security Council in a resolution passed on 20 December 2001.
9. Note that ISAF and the Afghan government have restricted access to the airport. Passengers travelling on domestic and international flights from Kandahar must either take an official bus (there is only one) from the city to the airport, or they must have a contact within the airport who can get them inside.
10. Woollen (or, nowadays, increasingly synthetic) shawl worn by many Afghans as part of their traditional dress. During the winter the material will often be thick and warm, whereas the summer variant of the *patu* will be thinner. The *patu* is not just used to keep warm, though; Afghans sit on it when outdoors, and often perform their daily prayers on the same *patu* that they wear.

1. DEATH AT HOME

1. The second-largest village in Panjwayi district (this includes Zheray district which was only recently split away from Panjwayi, and as such people still think of the old district borders). There are many grape orchards irrigated by the river that flows through the village. Zangiabad is situated in a particularly fertile area of Panjwayi district, in between two branches of the main river in Kandahar province. Well-known figures from Zangiabad include Khan Mal (Alikozai), a tribal elder, Toran Abdul Hai (Noorzai), *Hajji* Shabozai (Achekzai) and Gulan.
2. Zahir Shah was the King of Afghanistan from 1933 to 1973, when his cousin seized power while he was in Italy for medical treatment. Born in 1914 and the only surviving son of Nadir Shah, he was crowned King when his father was assassinated. His reign is now remembered nostalgically as a time of peace and stability; he died of old age in Kabul in July 2007.
3. Panjwayi district is one of the greenest areas of Kandahar province. With mountains to the west and to the east, there is a central, highly-fertile area where pomegranates and grapes are cultivated.

4. Small village near Qalat in Zabul province. Very few people lived there during the time of Zahir Shah; those who did were mainly from the Tokhi, Taraki Ghilzai, or Alikozai tribes. Watermelons were cultivated there at that time, as well as nuts, although by and large the area was desert.

5. Zabul province didn't exist until March 1964. It was previously part of Kandahar until the reforms of 1964 created several new provinces. In the south Zabul province is mainly referred to by the name of its provincial capital, Qalat. Pashtun tribes with significant populations in Zabul include the Noorzai, Tokhi, Andar, Suleimankhel and Jamalkhel.

6. Each tribe is further sub-divided: *Mullah* Zaeef's tribe, and that of his family, is Akhundkhel Suleimankhel, part of the larger Hotaki Ghilzai grouping.

7. Note also that there are large Pashtun minorities elsewhere, especially in central and northern Afghanistan.

8. The holy *Qur'an* is the religious book of Muslims around the world, literally translated as "recitation", as Muslims believe it is the result of direct revelation of God to the Prophet Muhammad (PBUH) starting in 610 A.D.

9. The established custom or precedent established and based on the example of the Prophet Muhammad. It offers a separate set of principles of conduct and traditions which were recorded by the Prophet's companions. These customs complement the divinely revealed message of the *Qur'an*. A whole field of jurisprudence has grown up alongside the study of the *Sunna*. The *Sunna* is recorded in the *ahadith* (pl. of *hadith*). The *Sunna* represents the prophetic "norm".

10. Religious school common in southern Afghanistan and Pakistan as the first choice for education (especially for the rural poor). Schools are by and large for boys only, although girls are educated in some, and the syllabus mainly constitutes a full outline of the religious sciences, often including the expectation that graduates will learn various holy books off by heart (notably, the *Qur'an* itself).

11. Mushan finds itself between two branches of the River Arghandab which passes through Panjwayi district. At the time there were just ten to twelve prominent families living in the village, each with somewhere between five and ten members. There were perhaps 250 houses in the area, and Sayyeds and Eshaqzai were the main tribes. The local tribal strongman—the *malik* of the area—had endowed a mosque which went by his name, Sayyed Hanif Agha. *Hajji* Noor Mohammad Khan (Eshaqzai by tribe) was a *mujahed* tribal leader who came from Mushan. Other prominent commanders from Mushan include: Alauddin Agha (Sayyed by tribe; fought with Gailani's *Mahaz-e Milli*); Baluch Juma Gul (Baluch), and *Mullah* Ghaffar (Eshaqzai by tribe).

12. Pashmol is also located in Panjwayi district, and saw much of the heavy fighting of the Soviet war. It continues to be the site of clashes between the *Taliban* and ISAF and NATO forces in Kandahar province. Some 2000-

3000 families lived there at the time. The main tribes were the Kakar, Alikozai and Achekzai. Local farmers cultivated grapes, wheat and the area is dotted with many *kishmishkhana*s, long wooden houses used to dry raisins. *Mullah* Mohammad Rabbani (Kakar by tribe), the *Taliban* deputy head, was from Pashmol, as was *Hajji* Hashem Khan (Khogiani) and *Hajji* Samad Khan (Kakar), both of whom are still alive.

13. Religious functionary or cleric extremely prevalent outside the cities in Afghanistan. They will usually be the single religious authority (having attended a *madrassa* during childhood, or maybe because they can read some Arabic and thus the language of the *Qur'an*) in a particular village. As such their authority is usually limited to religious matters.

14. Michael Barry reports that one official at the Ministry of Agriculture remarked at the time: "If the peasants eat grass, it's hardly grave. They're beasts. They're used to it" (Barry, 1974: 182).

15. Another title, indicating religious understanding, the *Imam* of any location is the person who leads the congregation in the five daily prayers.

16. Rangrezan is a small village of approximately 230 houses in Maiwand district of Kandahar province. Tribally it was predominantly Mohammad-zai, as was the whole area. Faiz Mohammad Agha (Sayyed/Noorzai by tribe) was a well-known figure who was born in Rangrezan; he fought with Sayyaf's *Ittehad-e Islami* during the 1980s *jihad*.

17. Basic and primary initial textbook used by religious students. It offers a basic introduction to the Arabic alphabet, some Islamic phrases, and some very elementary arithmetic. It was later translated into Pashtu, but at the time Zaeef was studying it was available only in Arabic. There should be no confusion over the name of the book; at the time, the group we now refer to as *Al Qaeda* didn't exist, and as such the textbook bore no relation to Osama bin Laden's group, which was founded in August 1988 (Bergen, 2006: 49, 73–6, 82–86, 94–95).

18. One of the two main official languages of Afghanistan, Pashtu is spoken by most ethnic Pashtuns in Afghanistan and across the border in Pakistan. There are different dialects from region to region, even to the extent that a man from Kandahar in the south might find it difficult to follow a conversation in Khost in the south-east.

19. A *sura* is literally a "chapter" of the *Qur'an*. Divided into 114 separate such *sura*s, the *Qur'an*'s chapters are ordered by descending length rather than their chronological appearance or date of revelation.

20. Small amulets or pieces of paper, often including verses from the *Qur'an* that are believed to cure illness and protect against misfortune; a popular alternative to medicine in the rural south, especially in the absence of qualified doctors; also known as *tsasht* or *dam*.

21. One of the five "pillars" of Islam, the practice of almsgiving or *zakat* is widespread and encouraged in southern Afghanistan. It is also—to a certain extent—systematised in such a way that it is in many instances a highly formalised type of charitable donation, whereby those with finan-

cial means must donate 2.5 per cent of their annual earnings and liquid assets for the needy. Apart from a nominal sum given to them by the government, the religious clergy—particularly in rural areas of the south— often have to rely on *zakat* and other donations from their fellow villagers. In Afghanistan this exists alongside the tradition of Ushr, whereby 10 per cent of profits are shared out to fellow villagers.

22. One of a series of extra prayers that people can perform in addition to the five obligatory prayers, *eshraq* is performed early in the morning when the sun has just started to rise.

23. One of the *sura*s or chapters of the *Qur'an*; it is commonly recited just before death.

24. "Verily We shall give life to the dead, and We record that which they send before and that which they leave behind, and of all things have We taken account in a clear Book (of evidence)" (*Qur'an* 36:12, Yousuf Ali translation).

25. In traditional Afghan culture, older close friends of the family are often referred to as "aunt" or "uncle".

26. In traditional village culture, many of the people living there are related to each other, so it is possible for both men and women to mix socially. Otherwise, just the elders (men and women) are able to move between segregated parts of the house.

27. Charshakha is a small village of some 25–30 houses in Panjwayi district of Kandahar province. It is not a famous place, and is inhabited mainly by Mohammadzai tribesmen. The whole area around the village is owned by just a handful of families. Well-known figures (Mohammadzai by tribe, and still alive) who came from Charshakha include Hakim Mir Hamid Khan (the father of Mahmoud Haqiqat), Sardar Abdullah Jan (the father of *Hajji* Ghafour) and *Hajji* Ghafour Aka (a tribal elder).

28. Zaeef stayed with his cousins Habibullah, Obaidullah, Mohammad Aslam and Mohammad Akram in Charshakha.

29. Sangisar is located on the main highway from Herat to Kandahar and has many gardens and orchards. Some two-thirds of the land around Sangisar consists of vineyards and one-third is reserved for wheat cultivation. Well-known figures from Sangisar include *Hajji* Ghousuddin (Achekzai by tribe); the tribal elder Malem Mir Walay (Baluch by tribe); *Hajji* Sardar Mohammad (Barakzai by tribe, who fought with Sayyaf's *Ittehad-e Islami*) who was killed in 2006 in Zheray in the fighting there; and *Hajji* Lala (Achekzai by tribe, who fought with Mujadidi's party) who was killed in 1992.

30. *Mawlawi* is a title used by graduates of *madrassas* who have also received further religious education. It is the equivalent of postgraduate study for scholars of Islam. A *mawlawi* is a member of the *Ulema'*, the Islamic clergy.

31. *Mawlawi* Niaz Mohammad (Hamidzai Achekzai by tribe) was a religious cleric living in Sangisar, Panjwayi district; he supported the Communists. His family was originally from Uruzgan.

32. Noor Mohammad Taraki (1917–1979), born in Ghazni to a Ghilzai nomadic family, was the leader of the party, the People's Democratic Party of Afghanistan (PDPA), which took power in the Communist coup in April 1978. Head of the party's *Khalq* faction, Taraki ruled until intra-party disputes resulted in his execution in October 1979.

33. Literally translated as "people" or "masses", the *Khalq* was a faction of the PDPA (People's Democratic Party of Afghanistan) headed by Noor Mohammad Taraki and Hafizullah Amin, and was opposed to the *Parcham* faction headed by Babrak Karmal.

34. The PDPA or People's Democratic Party of Afghanistan was an Afghan Marxist party founded in 1965. Intra-party disputes led to an internal schism, and by 1967 the *Khalq* and *Parcham* factions were operating separately. The PDPA seized power in the "Saur" coup of April 1978.

35. The *Mehdi* is a religious figure commonly portrayed in messianic and eschatological tones. Although not mentioned in the *Qur'an*, the idea is that the *Mehdi* will deliver the world from corruption and bring justice. The *Mehdi* is, however, mentioned in the *hadith* record.

36. *Saheb* is a term of respect used after someone's title in southern Afghanistan. It is used for one's elders, the educated, those with high government positions and so on.

37. *Firman* or "edict" no. 8 of 2 December 1978 set out the framework of the land reform. The idea was that small "peasant" farmers would be more inclined to support the regime, coupled with the more general centrality of land reform to the Communist ideal. The edict defined seven different categories of land (separated by distinctions of quality). Any one family could henceforth not own more than six hectares of land of the highest category. Redistribution would be carried out primarily in favour of day labourers. Agrarian reform was abolished by Karmal in March 1981 in the hope of winning over ordinary Afghans. Other policies enacted included "the establishment of an official clergy, the policy of nationalities, the recruitment of notables and the establishment of militias" (Dorronsoro, 2005: 179).

38. One *jerib* is a unit of land equivalent to 2000 m^2 or 0.2 hectares.

39. *Sayyed*s are descendents of the Prophet Muhammad (PBUH) who live in Afghanistan. They are seen as a tribe unto their own by Pashtuns. In Afghanistan, the term is sometimes also used for healers and holy men in general. *Sayyed*s are highly respected by the rural people.

40. *Khan*s are tribal chiefs and/or heads of communities. It is an honorific title often also used to describe those who own large portions of land. The title is usually added as a suffix to an individual's name.

41. *Malik*s are more localised versions of *khan*s. The title is used to denote the local strongman at the district or sub-district level, and this often also means that that person is somehow employed by the government to give some outreach for micro-management of particular issues.

42. Hafizullah Amin (1929–1979), born in Paghman to Kharoti Ghilzai Pashtuns, was appointed Minister of Foreign Affairs following the Saur coup. He ousted Noor Mohammad Taraki in September 1979, but was himself assassinated in December that year after falling foul of his Soviet sponsors. He was replaced by Babrak Karmal of the *Parcham* faction.

43. *Mawlawi* Mir Hatem was a religious cleric (Noorzai by tribe) living in Nadi village, near Sobat, Maiwand district, who supported the Communists. He was killed on the first night of the Karmal regime (27 December 1979).

44. The Communists were frequently spoken of as *kufr*. The verbal noun form of this word literally translates from the Arabic meaning "disbelief". The openly anti-religious policies of the PDPA were swiftly written off as being those coming from *kufr*.

45. *Mujahedeen* is the plural version of *mujahed*, which literally translates from the Arabic as "one who engages in *jihad*" or "one who struggles". Often translated as "holy warrior", the term does not necessarily have a connection with the practice of war, but rather can be used to refer to spiritual inner struggle (to be a better person and so on).

46. Located just a few kilometres away from the city centre, Sanzari is near Bagh-e Pul to the west of Kandahar City. It is a large village, inhabited at the time by approximately 3000 to 5000 people. Famous residents of Sanzari include Habibullah Jan, the Alizai tribal strongman who was assassinated in July 2008. During the *jihad* era, Sanzari was crammed full of people (even to the extent that two or three families would share a house). The leaders of the area had struck a deal with the Soviets which stated that the latter wouldn't attack provided the *mujahedeen* did not do so either. The people of Sanzari even helped the Russians to look for landmines on occasion. The village is predominantly Alizai by tribe.

2. THE CAMPS

1. *Haram* is a religious term used to denote that which is not permitted by Islam. It is the opposite of *halal*, which literally translates as "that which is permitted".

2. By the beginning of the 1990s, over six million Afghan refugees were living outside the country.

3. Chaman is a city very similar to Kandahar itself, located in Baluchistan province of Pakistan. At the time, Chaman had over 100,000 inhabitants. Tribally, approximately 70 per cent of the city is Achekzai and the remaining 30 per cent is Noorzai. Chronic water supply problems (even today) mean that there are few gardens in the city. It is a moderately mountainous area, much like Kandahar, surrounded by many villages scattered around the city's outskirts. People refer to an "old" Chaman and a "new" Chaman. "Old" Chaman dated from the nineteenth century and perhaps only two thousand families still live there now.

4. *Ziarat*s are holy places where certain deceased "saints" and other such holy people are buried. In the conception of Islam practised by many people in southern Afghanistan, worshippers visit these tombs in order to pray that the holy men will intercede on their behalf. Certain *ziarat*s, for example, are popular among women hoping to become conceive. Southern Afghanistan and the border areas of Pakistan have many of these shrines.

5. Panjpayi camp was its name before the Afghan refugees came. The five main camps in the area were: Surkhab, Saranan, Jangal, Panjpayi and Girdi Jangal.

6. Ablutions or *wudu* are obligatory cleansing rituals for Muslims to be performed before prayer. It consists of washing the hands, mouth, face, arms up to the elbows, and feet. In the absence of water, clay or sand may be used.

7. A *jama'at* may literally be translated from the Arabic as "group", but here it denotes a session of communal prayer of one of the five daily prayers.

8. Afghans—and all Muslims—have two main religious days of celebration called *Eid*, more or less equivalent to the Christian Christmas. The days of *Eid* are characterised by special prayers and sermons, as well as by an emphasis on family, friends, and the giving of gifts. They are known as *eid al-Fitr* and *eid al-Adha*.

9. Sher Mohammad Khan (Eshaqzai by tribe and originally from Taloqan village) was a *Hizb-e Islami* commander who later joined Gailani's *Mahaz-e Islami* when they received extra weapons for distribution. Still alive, he was a candidate for the Afghan parliamentary elections in 2005. During the *mujahedeen* regime he was the head of the Education Ministry for Kandahar province.

10. Front lines were where the conflict took place. The battlefield in "greater" Kandahar was extremely fluid and these "fronts" were the main organizational principle that distinguished the different small groups of fighters.

11. *Mujahedeen* would go to the fronts for specific time and then return to recuperate, see their family and so on in Pakistan, before going back to Afghanistan. The same system is more or less in place nowadays and used by the groups opposed to the Karzai government. This is not to state that the current problem has its roots in Pakistan.

12. *Jihad*, a notoriously difficult word to translate, is derived from an Arabic root meaning "to struggle", "to exert oneself", or "to strive". As such, the word *jihad* can mean different things depending on the context: sometimes a struggle against evil inclinations, or at other times a reference to legally-sanctioned (by the Islamic legal code) war. See Bedawi and Bonney (2005) and Bonner (2006) for more.

13. Famous commander (Baluch) from Nelgham who fought with Hekmatyar's *Hizb-e Islami*. He was very well known at the time, and had a good reputation. Previously in Zangiabad, his front was in Mahalajat, although he also fought in the area from Charshakha to Sanzari. He is still alive.

14. Abd ul-Rabb al-Rasul Sayyaf (1946–), a Kharoti Ghilzai Pashtun from Paghman, is an Islamic scholar educated in Al-Azhar (Egypt) who founded his own political party, the *Ittehad-e Islami baraye Azadi-ye Afghanistan* ("Islamic Union for the Freedom of Afghanistan") in Peshawar in 1981. He speaks fluent Arabic and his party was very closely aligned with Arab donors during the 1980s. As a consequence his party received a large proportion of the funding, prompting many commanders in the south to switch from whatever party they were affiliated with to Sayyaf's *Ittehad* in order to receive more supplies. Sayyaf continues to play a role in Afghan politics.
15. *Mullah* Shahzada (Taraki by tribe) was the son of *Hajji* Mohammad Gul Aka. He was a very young *Talib*, and had a big, dark beard. Originally from Mira Khor (Maiwand district) he was a friend of *Mullah* Zaeef's father before the war, and they met at his house. He was killed in Nelgham in the middle of the war. He was educated in Pakistan at a *madrassa*.
16. *Qari* Shahzada was Achekzai by tribe and had a reputation for being a courageous fighter that still endures in Kandahar today.
17. *Mullah* Mohammad Sadiq Akhund (Achekzai by tribe) initially fought with *Harakat* but switched to Sayyaf's *Ittehad-e Islami* when they received large quantities of weapons. He had roughly a hundred *mujahedeen* fighting with him. Initially from Tirin Kot (Uruzgan province), he was a friend of *Mullah* Zaeef's father. Following the fall of the *Taliban* in 2001, with whom he was fighting, *Mullah* Mohammad Sadiq Akhund was captured and taken to Guantánamo Bay prison. He was there at the same time as *Mullah* Zaeef but was later released and is still alive.
18. 100 Pakistani rupees could buy 100 kilos of flour or 10 kilos of cooking oil at that time.

3. THE *JIHAD*

1. These were Russian Spetssnaz (Special Forces).
2. Commander Abdul Raziq (Alikozai by tribe) was around thirty years old at the time, initially fighting with *Harakat* but later transferring (like many) to Sayyaf's *Ittehad-e Islami*. He had approximately fifty men fighting with him, and was well-respected among *mujahedeen* of the time.
3. Nelgham was a small village that cultivated mostly grapes. Alizai, Sayyeds and Kakar were the big tribes of the area. Aside the Arghandab river and between the big centres of Sangisar and Taloqan, there were many *mujahedeen* operating in the Nelgham area on account of its location. Well-known figures from Nelgham include: *Hajji* Hamid Agha (Sayyed by tribe, who fought with Gailani's *Mahaz-e Milli*), a *jihadi* commander; *Mullah* Abdul Hakim Akhund (Noorzai by tribe); and Shah Wali Khan (Alizai by tribe, who fought with Rabbani's *Jamiat*), a well-known tribal elder of the area at that time.

4. *Mawlawi* Nazar Mohammad (Noorzai by tribe) was originally from Sia Chuy, and was the first *Taliban* judge in Kandahar at the beginning of the *jihad* period. He was replaced by *Mawlawi* Pasanai *Saheb*. Known as "Titi *Mawlawi Saheb*" (literally "small" *Mawlawi Saheb*) on account of his short stature and hunchback, he was uneducated and sentenced many to death. He had grey hair, and was killed in early fighting in Pashmol.

5. *Mawlawi* Pasanai *Saheb* (Ismaelkhel by tribe) was the senior *Talib* judge following the death of *Mawlawi* Nazar Mohammad. Originally from Shah Juy (in Zabul province), he died after the 2001 invasion, probably in 2002 of old age. He was well-known in Kandahar for having rejected (and continuing to reject) reports of Massoud's assassination in September 2001. He was the most famous of the older generation of *Taliban* judges.

6. *Hajji* is a title technically given only to those who have been on the *Hajj*, the Islamic pilgrimage to Mecca which is one of the five pillars of the Muslim faith, but which in Afghanistan (and elsewhere in the Muslim world) is sometimes used merely as a term of respect for the middle-aged and elderly.

7. *Hajji* Mohammad Gul Aka (Taraki by tribe) was the father of *Mullah* Shahzada and active as a tribal elder. He fought primarily in Nelgham during the *jihad* but is originally from Mira Khor in Maiwand district of Kandahar. He is still alive.

8. The Balazan and Jaghuri weapons were old single-shot rifles that sometimes dated back to the previous century. The Balazan was a German weapon, and the Jaghuri was American. They were able to shoot over a long distance.

9. Weapons used by the *mujahedeen* weren't necessarily originals. Many were copies made in Pakistan or coming from China. Copied weapons were often of an inferior quality.

10. *Mullah* Khawas Akhund (Eshaqzai by tribe) was an illustrious commander in Pashmol. Originally from Baghran (Helmand province), he fought alongside *Mullah* Nek Mohammad Akhund but was killed by Russian bombers in the late 1980s.

11. The Soviet invasion force consisted of a mixture of Airborne and Motorised Infantry personnel, amounting to approximately 85,000 troops. It was labelled the "40th Army". Official Soviet sources referred to it as a "limited contingent" (*ogranichennyi contingent*).

12. There were numerous medical training courses on offer in Quetta at the time. *Mullah* Zaeef took his at *al-Jihad* hospital, attending a basic seminar after returning from Afghanistan for the second time. They were taught basic healthcare, how to stop bleeding and other basic preventative measures to keep the wounded alive in order to bring them to Pakistan for proper medical care. The hospital was run by a non-governmental organization (NGO), and attendance at the training courses was obligatory for each *mujahed*. According to one estimate, some 256 NGOs were involved

in aid to the Afghans, of which fifty operated in Afghanistan (Baitenmann, 1990).

13. Zheray is the name of a desert to the north of Panjwayi district. It was separated and became a district of its own in 2005. During the Soviet time, Zheray desert was a large army base from which they used to attack Pashmol and Panjwayi. They had many tanks there, as well as missiles, which they would launch at the surrounding villages at all times of the day.

14. The *Atan* is a traditional Pashtun dance. Participants move in a circle while clapping their hands to the rhythm and spinning around. One person in the circle will be the leader and other will follow his moves. It is often performed at celebrations and weddings.

15. This bookish tendency has leant to the popular conception of the *Taliban* as not having been very good fighters during the *jihad*.

16. *Mullah* Burjan (Achekzai by tribe) was a resident of Deh Merasey and had been wounded during fighting in Panjwayi by a tank shell. He was approximately thirty years old at the time, a strong man with a thick black beard. He was the brother of *Hajji* Bahauddin.

17. *Mullah* Mehrab is the name of an area near to the Registan desert south of Kandahar City. It is named after a *Mullah* who is buried there, and although there is a *ziarat* or shrine to his name it is unclear when this *Mullah* Mehrab lived.

18. The RPG or Rocket Propelled Grenade, along with the AK-47 Kalashnikov rifle, is one of the weapons most strongly identified with the Afghan *mujahedeen*. At the beginning of the *jihad*, however, neither weapon was common. Later on, with increased funding coming from abroad, the RPG was used with great effect against tanks and Armoured Personnel Carriers or APCs. Both the AK-47 rifle and the RPG continue to be used against foreign troops as of 2009.

19. Afghanistan's nomadic peoples. The word "Kuchi" derives from the Dari "*kuch kardan*" which means "to be on the move" or "to be moving". Kuchis uproot their homes twice a year with the seasons and are found all over Afghanistan. There used to be many living in the Registan desert, but the 1980s war and the ensuing drought forced many to settle permanently in camps in Pakistan.

4. LESSONS FROM THE ISI

1. *Mawlawi* Abdul Qadir (Barakzai by tribe) was an Afghan *mullah* living in Quetta. He was originally from Maruf district of Kandahar province.

2. Kandahari Mosque in Quetta was a small two-storey mosque connected to the "Kandahar Market" on the street below.

3. *Mullah* Mir Hamza (Achekzai by tribe) was known as *Hajji* Lala and was originally from Tirin Kot (Uruzgan province). He was a *mujahed* during the *jihad* but didn't have a big reputation among other *mujahedeen*.

4. *Hajji* Karam Khan (Achekzai by tribe) was a *mujahed* during the 1980s *jihad* and a tribal elder in the years that followed. He continues to play a role in politics in Kandahar, and is especially active in the Achekzai *shura* that meets every Friday in Kandahar city.

5. The business of *jihad* was divided between two senior figures, the *Amir* or "Leader" and the Commander. The *Amir* would attend to administrative matters, raise funding, and, in some cases, would serve as the public face of a given "front". The Commander would spend most of his time on the "front" itself, fighting and dealing with any problems that would occur on a day-to-day basis inside Afghanistan.

6. ISI, or Inter-Services Intelligence, is the main Pakistani military intelligence wing. Especially prominent in the funding and supplying of weapons to the Afghan *mujahedeen*, ISI has become synonymous with the strong involvement of Pakistan's military in political affairs.

7. According to one Pakistani account written by Brigadier Yousuf after he worked with the ISI during the 1980s, approximately 80,000 *mujahedeen* were trained in Pakistan during the 1980s. At end of 1983 the ISI had two dedicated camps with capacity for two hundred trainees; by mid-1984 they were putting one thousand through the system at a time; and by 1987 they had seven camps operating simultaneously (Yousaf and Adken, 1992).

8. Commander Abdullah was the senior figure in charge of the distribution of weapons for Sayyaf's office for the whole of southern Afghanistan. He was Wardaki by tribe, and highly respected by *mujahedeen* for his work to supply weapons to the fighters. During the post-2001 regime, he took a position as the governor of Lowgar province but was assassinated.

9. *Ittehad-e Islami baraye Azadi-ye Afghanistan* ('Islamic Union for the Freedom of Afghanistan') was founded in Peshawar in 1981 by Abd ul-Rabb al-Rasul Sayyaf. Initially established as an alliance of parties—an attempt to unify the sprawling morass of political groupings in 1980s Peshawar—*Ittehad-e Islami* soon took on characteristics and loyalties of its own.

10. *Harakat-e Enqelab-e Islami* ("Movement of the Islamic Revolution") was one of the earliest *mujahedeen* movements to be formed. During the early 1980s it was one of the largest political groupings. Many of its traditionalist members went on to make up a significant portion of the fledgling "*Taliban* movement" post-1994.

11. *Mawlawi* Nabi Mohammadi (1921–2002) was an *Alim* or Islamic scholar (Ahmadzai Pashtun by tribe and born in Lowgar province) who went on to lead the traditionalist *Harakat-e Enqelab-e Islami* party. He served as Vice-President of Afghanistan in the *mujahedeen* government of the early 1990s, but had good relations with the *Taliban* once they took power.

12. *Mullah* Naqibullah (c.1950–2007) also known as *Mullah* Naqib or *Mullah* Gul Akhund) was born in Charqulba village in Arghandab district of Kandahar province. Head of the Alikozai tribe until his death in October

2007, *Mullah* Naqib was extremely prominent as a *jihadi* commander during the 1980s *jihad*. He fought with his men in his native Arghandab district. He continued to play an instrumental role in the upheavals of the mid-1990s and early-2000s.

13. Sarkateb Atta Mohammad (Ludin by tribe) was the strongest *Hezb-e Islami* commander in southern Afghanistan during the 1980s *jihad*. Originally from the old city in Kandahar, he controlled the area of Western Kandahar from Bagh-e Pul up to Shah Agha Durrayi. He lived in Quetta after the *Taliban* took power in 1994. He is still alive, and runs an auto spare-parts store in Dubai.

14. Lay opinion continues to hold that the decision to ship "Stinger" missiles to the *mujahedeen* was the decisive factor in the Soviets losing the war; the *mujahedeen* obtained roughly one thousand "Stinger" missiles between 1986 and 1990. Mark Urban, however, has estimated that Soviet losses from Stingers amounted to ninety helicopters and planes—less than 20 per cent of the total losses up to the point of Soviet withdrawal (Urban, 1990).

15. Hafizullah Akhundzada (Noorzai by tribe) was originally from Maiwand district of Kandahar province.

16. *Mullah* Wali Mohammad (Taraki by tribe) is from Kandahar City. He first fought for *Harakat* during the *jihad*, but then changed over to Sayyaf's *Ittehad*. He is still alive and runs a shop in Kandahar City.

17. A *kareez* is a water management system used to provide a reliable supply of water to human settlements or for irrigation in hot, arid and semi-arid climates. Also known as *Kariz* or *Qadaat*.

18. *Mullah* Abdul Ghani was originally from Kandahar province and was a well-known commander in Mahalajat. He fought mainly together with Sayyaf's *Ittehad*.

19. The PK is a Soviet 7.62mm machine gun weighing approximately 16 kilograms. It has an effective range of 1000 metres.

20. Nazar Mohammad (Baluch by tribe) was originally from Sangisar. He was very young at the time of the ambush described—his beard had only just started to grow. He was killed in the ambush described in chapter 4.

21. *Roshandaz* are flares used to illuminate the ground at night. Also known as *Roxana* (see chapter 3).

22. *Mullah* Nasrullah (Achekzai by tribe) was originally from Nelgham. He lost both his legs in the *jihad*. He was treated in Germany but died soon after arriving there.

23. An Arabic loan word used in Dari and Pashtu to mean "martyred". It carries religious connotations, fitting into the theology of *jihad*. Martyrs, in Islamic theology, go straight to heaven—they do not have to wait for the day of judgement. It is important to add that it is not only "warriors" who are counted among the *shuhada'* (pl. term in Arabic for "martyrs"); for instance, civilian victims of conflict in the Muslim world are often described as *shuhada'*. Nor is this a modern corruption: classical Arabic sources, for instance, describe the victims of the Franks and the Mongols as martyrs.

5. BITTER PICTURES

1. See Urban, 1990; Maley, 2002.
2. One study of war-related death rates for Afghanistan stated that between 1978 and 1987 unnatural deaths in Afghanistan amounted to 876,825 (Khalidi, 1991). In 1995, the World Health Organisation estimated the physically disabled as totalling "nearly 1.5 million persons" (WHO, 1995).
3. In 1985 the United States gave $250 million to the *mujahedeen*, as much as all previous years of funding since 1980 combined. Between 1980 and 1992, the United States gave $2–3 billion to the *mujahedeen* in total; roughly the same amount came from Arab donors (Coll, 2004: 102).
4. Mahalajat is an area connected to Kandahar City which was contested by the *mujahedeen* throughout the war. The cultivated fields and raisin-drying houses provided excellent terrain for a low-to-medium intensity conflict.
5. An area in the west of Kandahar City, the main prison is also located there.
6. Chilzina literally translates as "forty steps" and is a historical site dating back to the early sixteenth century, when the Mughal Emperor Babur conquered Kandahar. It consists of a rock cut chamber at the top of the forty steps and is inscribed with an account of Babur's empire.
7. *Ashrar* was a term universally used by the Afghan Communists and Soviets to refer to the *mujahedeen*. It literally translates as "people who stir up chaos".
8. Bismillah was well-known for his cruelty at the time, and his reputation endures up to the present day in Kandahar.
9. Jendarma (from the French *gendarmes*) was a police station near to Mirwais Mina (western Kandahar), consisting of just four or five rooms; it was closed when the *Taliban* came to power, but rebuilt by the post-2001 Karzai government.
10. Major Abdul Hai (also known as *Toran* Abdul Hai or *Loy* Toran *Saheb*) was killed in Zangiabad in 1981. Noorzai by tribe, he initially fought with Hekmatyar's *Hizb-e Islami* but later changed to Sayyaf's *Ittehad-e Islami*. He was the brother of Najibullah.
11. *Mawlawi Saheb* Dangar was Noorzai by tribe, and killed before the *jihad* ended. He was responsible for all matters relating to Finance and Logistics and worked together with *Mawlawi* Faizullah Akhundzada.
12. *Mullah* Mazullah Akhund (Noorzai by tribe) was originally from Deh Rawud (Uruzgan). He was later killed along with *Mullah* Pacha Akhund in Shabega by the Russians.
13. Khan Abdul Hakim (Noorzai by tribe) fought together with *Mawlawi* Faizullah Akhundzada. He is still alive.
14. *Mullah* Mohammad Omar (Hotaki Ghilzai by tribe) was born in Uruzgan province in approximately 1962. He fought with *Harakat* during the 1980s *jihad*, and was eventually chosen as leader of the nascent *Taliban*

movement that emerged in 1994. He is widely believed to be alive, probably living either in Pakistan or in Afghanistan.

15. *Mullah* Feda Mohammad (Noorzai by tribe) was originally from Kandahar City. He fought first with *Harakat* and then, like many other *mujahedeen*, went over to Sayyaf's *Ittehad*. He was killed near Heirazi during the 1980s.

16. *Mullah* Obaidullah Akhund (Alikozai by tribe) was originally from Nelgham and was known for being a tough fighter but of a quiet nature. He is believed to have been born in approximately 1968. He acted as Defence Minister during the *Taliban*'s rule. During the 1980s *jihad* he acted as *amir* of the front of *Mullah* Mohammad Sadiq Akhund. When Karam Khan left the front, *Mullah* Obaidullah took his place as commander. He is almost certainly still alive and is one of the senior *Taliban* commanders operating in Pakistan, although there were credible reports that he had been arrested on 26 February 2008 and that he continued to be held in a Pakistani jail.

17. *Mullah* Najibullah (Eshaqzai by tribe) was from Band-i Taimur (Maiwand district of Kandahar province). He was only temporarily deafened in the attack, and is still alive and continues his work as a *mullah* in southern Afghanistan to this day.

18. *Mullah* Marjan (Achekzai by tribe) was originally from Deh Merasay (Panjwayi). Around 32 years old in 1987, he was killed in Mahalajat during the late 1980s. He was known for his good singing voice.

19. The *Ghazal* is a genre of poetry commonly used in both Pashtu and Farsi/Dari verse.

20. For more on the siege of Arghandab and *Mullah* Naqib's involvement, see Anderson, 2003: 151–82.

21. *Mullah* Naqib and his Alikozai tribe remain widely-known for their participation in the *jihad*, particularly in Arghandab district. The Alikozai fighters have a reputation for toughness and bravery, only overshadowed by the parallel but widespread allegations of cruelty and criminality.

22. *Mullah* Nek Mohammad Akhund (Noorzai or Ghilzai by tribe) was originally from Deh Rawud in Uruzgan province.

23. *Mullah* Mohammad Akhund (Achekzai by tribe) was a prominent military commander who also served post-1994 with the *Taliban* but was later killed in Shurab following Ismael Khan's attempt to push back the *Taliban* from Herat towards the south. *Mullah* Mohammad was a close friend of Lala Malang.

24. *Ramazan* (also known as *Ramadan*) is the name of a month in the Islamic calendar during which all Muslims are obliged to fast during the hours of daylight. There are exceptions to this obligation though, for example for the sick and those who are travelling.

25. *Ulemaa'* are literally "those who have knowledge"; it refers to religious scholars (primarily used for the Sunni clergy) who have been educated in the religious "sciences" (the *Qur'an*, the *Sunna* and the *Hadith*s etc).

26. Abdurrashid Dostum is an Uzbek commander notorious for switching sides numerous times during the war in Afghanistan. During the 1980s, he led a mostly-Uzbek militia who fought for the Soviets, only to change sides and be awarded a position in the *mujahedeen* government. His militia was the most well-known and feared of the Afghan armed forces during the 1980s. He continues to play a prominent role in Afghan politics, both in Kabul and in the north.

27. *Mullah* Nooruddin Turabi (Achekzai by tribe) was originally from Tirin Kot (Uruzgan province) and fought with *Harakat*, and then later with Sayyaf's *Ittehad*, during the 1980s *jihad*. He commanded a hundred fighters, and was later appointed Minister of Justice under the *Taliban*. He is still alive.

28. *Mullah* Ahmadullah Akhund (Kakar by tribe) was originally from Gush Khana (in Mahalajat region of Kandahar). He served as assistant to *Mullah* Ghaws, one of the strongest commanders of Commander Abdul Raziq. He was later killed near Kandahar airport.

29. *Mullah* Abdul Ghani Akhund (Taraki by tribe) was a commander originally from Kandahar City. He was renowned for assassinating (or *cherik* in the original Pashtu, which has far fewer of the negative connotations of the word "assassin" in English) Russian military personnel, and was in fact one of the first to do so. He was later *amir* of his own front in Kandahar province and is still alive.

30. *Hajji* Latif (Barakzai by tribe) was one of the key figures of the 1980s *jihad* in Kandahar. He was the father of Gul Agha Sherzai, the current governor of Nangarhar, and was well-known for fighting in Mahalajat area of Kandahar. *Hajji* Latif was poisoned on 8 August 1989. He fought for Gailani's *Mahaz-e Milli* party.

31. *Mullah* Burjan (Kakar by tribe) was originally from Taloqan village of Panjwayi district in Kandahar. A prominent commander, he fought with *Harakat* during the 1980s *jihad* but was killed in 1996 following the *Taliban*'s takeover of Kabul. Many rumours speculate as to the identity of his killers—often claiming ISI involvement.

32. Known as *Hajji* Amar *Saheb*, *Hajji Mullah* Ali Mohammad Akhund (Achekzai by tribe) was commander (with *Harakat*) of a *Taliban* front in Zalakhan during the 1980s *jihad* and a pious person. After the *Taliban* took power in the late 1990s, he served as Consul on the Chaman border crossing. He is still alive.

33. To be called a cinema boy is considered shameful even today in Kandahar. It roughly equates to "gangster", or "tough boy" or even the British term "lout".

34. There was a custom in the *Taliban* front lines to pray *Surat Yasin Sharif* after the dawn prayer, *Surat al-'Amm* after the late afternoon prayer, and the *Surat Tabarak al-Azi* after the late evening prayer. One *Talib* would recite the sura and the others would listen to him.

35. This is a term of respect denoting seniority.

6. WITHDRAWAL

1. Babrak Karmal was the President of Afghanistan between December 1979 and November 1986, when he was deposed by Najibullah. Born in Kabul in 1929, he was brought into Afghanistan by the Soviets when they sent troops into the country. He died in 1996 in Moscow.

2. Najibullah (Ahmadzai by tribe) succeeded Babrak Karmal and was President of Afghanistan from November 1986 to April 1992. Born in 1947 in Kabul, he was a prominent figure in the Communist PDPA and a member of its *Parcham* faction. When the *Taliban* captured Kabul in 1996, they tortured and executed him before publicly displaying his body.

3. KhAD is an abbreviation of *Khedamat-e Ittla'aat-e Dawlati*, or "State Security Service". Its name was changed to WAD by President Najibullah, but it is still commonly used to refer to the internal state security apparatus.

4. "For the period from October 1989 through October 1990, Congress cut its secret allocation for the CIA's covert Afghan program by about 60 per cent, to $280 million" (Coll, 2004: 216).

5. Noor ul-Haq Ulumi (Barakzai by tribe) is originally from Kandahar province and is a former Communist Army General. He was governor of Kandahar during the transition period at the end of the 1980s when a "cash-for-compliance" scheme was launched by the Najibullah government in which Ulumi handed out huge sums of money in exchange for a much less combative *mujahedeen*.

6. A *Hadith* is a report of the words and actions of the Prophet Mohammad (PBUH) as determined and authenticated by a chain of evidence and proof (known as *asnad*). It is an important part of the oral tradition of Islam, and they survive in written form in collections codified by religious scholars.

7. Wire reports from the time suggest that this meeting took place on 14 April 1992.

8. Gul Agha Sherzai became the governor of Kandahar; *Mullah* Naqibullah took the Army base; Amir Lalai took the area of the city up to Eid Gah Gate as well as the textile mill and workshops; *Hajji* Ahmad took the airport; *Ustaz* Abdul Haleem took the KhAD offices, the police headquarters and prison; Sarkateb took the Bagh-e Pul area and the area around the grain silo.

9. The *familee* barracks was inhabited by the families of members of the government or military. Nowadays, it pales in comparison to its new neighbouring complex, Ayno Meena, but some families continue to live there and have purchased the houses and land from the government to continue doing so.

10. *Hajji Mullah* Yar Mohammad Akhund (Popolzai by tribe) was a big commander fighting for Khalis' *Hizb-e Islami* during the 1980s *jihad*. After the *Taliban* took power he was appointed as governor of Herat and then Ghazni, but was killed in Ghazni in 1999 in the middle of a meeting. The

identity of his killer has never been discovered, and the circumstances of his death (witnessed by many) are somewhat mysterious.

11. Sibghatullah Mujaddidi was born in 1925 in Kabul. Educated in Afghanistan as well as at Al Azhar in Cairo, he led one of the main *mujahedeen* political parties from Peshawar during the 1980s, and served as interim president in June 1992. He continues to play a role in Afghan politics in Kabul.

12. Burhanuddin Rabbani was born in 1940 in Faizabad (Badakhshan province in the north-east of Afghanistan). He was educated in Kabul and at Al Azhar in Cairo, before returning to Afghanistan in 1968. He was head of one of the major political parties of the 1980s *jihad*, the *Jamiat-e Islami*. He served as president of Afghanistan between 1992 and 1996, until the *Taliban* took Kabul. He continues to play a role in Afghan politics in Kabul.

13. *Jabha-ye Milli baraye nejat-e Afghanistan* ("National Liberation Front of Afghanistan") was established by Sibghatullah Mujaddidi during the 1980s in Peshawar. It was one of the major political parties of the *jihad*.

14. The *Ka'aba* is located in Mecca (Saudi Arabia). It is the spiritual focus towards which all Muslims face as they perform their daily prayers. Muslims believe that it was built by Abraham/Ibrahim. It plays a role during the *Hajj* rituals as well.

15. Ahmad Shah Massoud, born in Panjshir in 1953, was one of the most famous resistance commanders of the 1980s *jihad* against the Soviets, and played a prominent role in the politics and fighting of the 1990s prior to his assassination just days before the attacks on the World Trade Center in 2001. He served as Minister of Defence in 1992, and led the "Northern Alliance" against the *Taliban* in the late 1990s. He was known as the "Lion of Panjshir".

16. Panjshir is a valley system north of Kabul commonly associated with the resistance commander Ahmad Shah Massoud. The population is largely Tajik, and inhabitants converted to Sunni Islam as late as the sixteenth century. It is located close to the Salang Pass, which made it ideal for fighting against the Soviets, who were themselves never able to take control of the valley.

17. A roundabout in central Kandahar, the centre contains a monument to "martyrs" who died in battle. It was built between 1946 and 1948 (Dupree, 1977: 282).

18. Gulbuddin Hekmatyar, born in Kunduz in 1954, is the leader of the *Hizb-e Islami* political party. He rose to prominence during the 1980s *jihad*, during which he received a disproportionately large share of funding for the *mujahedeen*. He was prominent in Islamist circles in Afghanistan prior to the Soviet invasion, and also served as Prime Minister in Kabul in May 1992. He disappeared in 2002, and is believed to be hiding in the mountains of north-eastern Afghanistan and conducting operations against the Afghan government and foreign military forces.

19. *Ustaz* Abdul Haleem (Noorzai by tribe) was born in approximately 1960 and was one of the most prominent commanders of the 1980s *jihad* in southern Afghanistan. Born in Maiwand district of Kandahar province, he was eventually forced out of his position near Sarpoza prison when the *Taliban* took over control of the city. He continues to play a role in local politics, and was advisor to the former governor of Kandahar, Asadullah Khaled.

20. Abdul Hakim Jan (Alikozai by tribe) was a tribal strongman and *mujahed* from Arghandab district of Kandahar province. One of the only commanders to fight against the *Taliban* down in Kandahar while they were in power, he was the last commander standing in the way of the *Taliban* taking Arghandab. He was well-known in Kandahar for his very particular style and appearance: he only ever wore blue, and used to wear three pairs of the Afghan traditional clothes on top of each other. He was killed on 17 February 2008 along with scores of others in Afghanistan's most deadly suicide bomb attack to date.

21. *Ghazi* literally translates as "Islamic warrior" and is a loosely approximate alternative for the term *mujahed*.

22. As a literal translation, this may not make sense. In Pashtu, though, the reference to the father-son relationship indicates respect.

23. Amir Lalai (Popolzai by tribe) is originally from Wayan (Shah Wali Kot district). He is the son of *Hajji* Mir Ahmad and participated in the 1980s *jihad* in Wayan. He is currently serving as an MP in Kabul.

24. *Moalem* Feda Mohammad (Alikozai by tribe) is originally from Panjwayi district centre and was a big *mujahedeen* commander fighting with Khalis' *Hizb-e Islami* during the 1980s *jihad*. He fought with the *Taliban* in Mazar-e Sharif, where he was captured and sent to Guantánamo prison. He was released back to Afghanistan, but now is fighting foreign military forces from Pakistan. He is still alive.

7. TAKING ACTION

1. *Hajji* Ahmad (Achekzai by tribe) was the son of *Hajji* Maghash. He fought with Mujaddidi's *Jabha-ye Milli* during the 1980s *jihad* and was one of the main commanders in southern Afghanistan during the early 1990s. He and his men took Kandahar's airport in the division of the province that occurred after the fall of the Najibullah government.

2. Baru (Popolzai by tribe) was a *mujahedeen* commander who fought with Sayyaf's *Ittehad-e Islami* but who retains an extremely bad reputation in Kandahar nowadays. He was known for marrying girls for one month, taking a dowry from their fathers for her, then divorcing the girl and refusing to return her dowry. The *Taliban* hanged him in the first days after they swept through Kandahar province.

3. A Chaman hat is the multi-coloured open-fronted cap that many Pashtuns of the south wear. At the time it was extremely common, particularly in Kandahar province.

4. LM Cigarettes were one of the most popular brands of the time (alongside Kent and Winston). Important figures and senior commanders would often only smoke the LM brand (produced in America).

5. A famous Soviet-era Pashtun female singer from Kandahar, formerly married to the other big Pashtun singer of the era, Mangal, from Laghman. Naghma started her career in the Schools' Choir of the Soviets, and later sang with Mangal. She then went to Pakistan and recorded most of her work there. Along with Nazia Iqbal she is perhaps the Pashtun singer most popular with taxi-drivers in Afghanistan and around Quetta etc.

6. Kandahar society is infamous for the practice of homosexual relations with minors, although the exact numbers involved are no doubt small. This started before the *jihad* period, but became more common during and throughout the civil war.

7. It is instructive that many of those living in southern Afghanistan in 2009 use the same term when referring to the police forces working in their villages and districts.

8. Shah Baran (Achekzai by tribe) was originally a *mujahed* fighting with Sayyaf's *Ittehad-e Islami* but who changed to the side of the Afghan government when Esmat Muslim defected in the first half of 1985. He had a checkpoint manned by thieves from Zangal camp, and everyone was afraid of him.

9. *Chelam* is an Afghan pipe for smoking tobacco and hashish. It was a common habit at the time.

10. This likely means sexual slavery.

11. *Hajji* Khushkiar Aka (Achekzai by tribe) was the tribal elder of a village near Salehan (Kandahar province).

12. Abdul Qudus was originally from Pashmol and was a *mujahed* with *Mullah Hajji* Mohammad Akhund. He was killed at the Shomali plains, north of Kabul, when the *Taliban* were first ambushed there in October 1996.

13. *Mullah* Neda Mohammad (Achekzai by tribe) was from Deh Merasay (Kandahar province) and was killed recently in Salawat (Kandahar) during a night raid on his home by NATO/ISAF Special Forces troops.

14. Saleh (Noorzai by tribe) was from a village called Dwah in Panjwayi district. He killed many civilians at his checkpoint on the Kandahar-Kabul highway and was widely feared as a robber.

15. The *shari'a* is the body of legislative knowledge used by Islamic scholars and lawyers in the various schools of jurisprudence that have emerged since the emergence of Islam. There are five prominent schools of Islamic law that are followed by both Sunnis and Shi'a: Hanafi, Hanbali, Maliki, Shafii and Ja'fari.

16. *Mullah* Abdul Rauf Akhund (Alizai by tribe) was originally from Kajaki district (Helmand province) and was a very important *Taliban* commander. He had a mosque in Pashmol and fought in the 1980s *jihad* together with *Hajji* Mohammad Akhund. He was killed in the early years of the *Taliban*'s rule in 1994 or 1995.

17. *Mawlawi* Abdul Samad (Khunday by tribe) was from Tirin Kot (Uruzgan province) although further back his family was originally from Arghestan district of Kandahar. After the *Taliban* took power he was first District Chief of Spin Boldak district of Kandahar, then head of the Electricity ministry in Kandahar, then head of the Agriculture ministry in Helmand. He is still alive.

18. Abdul Ghaffar Akhundzada (Alizai by tribe) is originally from Zendahor. An extremely big commander (with Mohammadi's *Harakat*) during the 1980s *jihad*, he had approximately 4000–5000 men fighting under him in three separate divisions. After the *Taliban* swept into Helmand province in 1994/5, he was one of the large commanders to resist and they fought for several months before he fled to Pakistan. He was later killed in Pakistan.

19. Chief *Mullah* Abdul Wahed (Alizai by tribe) was a well-known *Hizb-e Islami* commander, later switching to Rabbani's *Jamiat*. He had a prominent position in the *Taliban* government and is still alive.

20. *Mawlawi* Atta Mohammad (Eshaqzai by tribe) was originally from Sangin and fought with *Jamiat* as a *mujahed* during the 1980s *jihad*. He was middle-aged at that time, but was killed (by unidentified attackers) in Quetta during the *Taliban*'s rule.

21. *Mullah* Sattar (Ghilzai by tribe) was a *mujahed* who rose and became a commander during the *Taliban*'s rule. He was killed at Erganak (near the northern Kunduz province) in an American airstrike in 2001.

22. *Hajji* Bashar (Noorzai by tribe) was born in 1964 in southern Afghanistan. During the 1980s he fought against the Soviet Union with Sayyaf's *Ittehad-e Islami* party and allegedly rose to become one of the worlds biggest drug lords, the so-called "Pablo Escobar of Afghanistan". He had strong ties to *Mullah* Mohammad Omar and the *Taliban* during which he increased his involvement in the opium trade. Following the ousting of the *Taliban*, *Hajji* Bashar tried to align himself to the US. In an attempt to prove his loyalty to them, *Hajji* Bashar travelled to New York where he spent several days in a hotel in Lower Manhattan answering questions from US government agents. He cooperated with them and hoped to prove that he would be a vital asset to the American and Afghan governments. He was, however, subsequently arrested on the basis of a sealed indictment against him. After a short trial in late September 2009 he was found guilty of an "international drug trafficking conspiracy". On May 1st 2009 he was sentenced to life in jail.

23. *Mullah* Sher Mohammad Malang (Popolzai by tribe) was one of *Mullah* Malang's commanders during the *jihad* period. After the *Taliban* took control in the south in the mid-1990s, *Mullah* Sher Mohammad served on the Kandahar *shura* at the beginning. He was appointed as governor of Nimruz and then later served with the military. He is still alive, although he was arrested and held at the American base at the former house of *Mullah* Mohammad Omar for a long time.

24. The people of southern Afghanistan commonly drink a sour-milk drink with their meals called *shlumbay*. It is made from yoghurt, water and salt, sometimes with small diced chunks of cucumber.
25. *Mullah* Masoom (Eshaqzai by tribe) was originally from Taloqan in Panjwayi district of Kandahar. He was a *mujahed* with *Mullah Hajji* Mohammad Akhund. He is still alive.
26. BBC Pashtu used to be one of the most respected sources of information for the people of southern Afghanistan. During the 1980s and early 1990s, the BBC was often the only radio station broadcasting in the area, and its reports were treated as absolute truth. Nowadays the popularity of the station has decreased in the southern provinces, in part because of the large number of alternative stations that have sprung up since 2001.

8. THE BEGINNING

1. Equivalent to roughly 300 kilos of wheat at the time—or lunch for 10–15 people with healthy appetites in one of Kandahar's better restaurants.
2. A *Mura* is the word used to denote the wife of a *Mullah*.
3. Daru Khan (Popolzai by tribe) was from Kulk (near Pashmol in Panjwayi). He originally fought as a *mujahed* with *Harakat* but then switched to Sayyaf's *Ittehad-e Islami*. He is still alive.
4. Yaqut was from Kolk (Kandahar province) and was not known in Kandahar for anything aside from having a checkpoint.
5. Bismillah (Alikozai by tribe) was originally from Pashmol and led a small group during the 1980s *jihad* but was not a prominent figure in Kandahar.
6. Pir Mohammad was originally from Pashmol and led a small group during the 1980s *jihad* but was not a prominent figure in Kandahar.
7. Qayyum Khan was originally from Pashmol and led a very small group during the 1980s *jihad* but was not a prominent figure in Kandahar.
8. Abdul Wasi (tribe unknown) was originally from Panjwayi district. He was the son of Ghulam Dastgir.
9. The *Jamiat* party was one of the best known and well-funded parties during the 1980s *jihad*. Many of the most significant commanders in southern Afghanistan were affiliated to *Jamiat*, including *Mullah* Naqibullah, Commander Abdul Razzaq (both Alikozai) and Habibullah Jan (Alizai).
10. Long hair was the style at the time, and the shaving of one's head was thus a potent symbol of submission and allegiance.
11. *Mullah* Mohammad Rabbani Akhund (Kakar by tribe) was a *Hizb-e Islami* (Khalis) commander during the 1980s *jihad*. He commanded a half-dozen groups totalling about 120 fighters.
12. Azizullah Wasefi (Alikozai by tribe) was a tribal elder who supported the return of the former king, Zahir Shah. He went to America during the early 1990s, but was in Pakistan after the *Taliban* took power.
13. Hamid Karzai (Popolzai by tribe) is originally from Karz (Dand district, Kandahar province) and was born there in 1957. His father was the leader

of his tribe and a well-known figure (also serving as an MP during Zahir Shah's reign). Hamid was studying in India at the time of the Soviet invasion. During the 1980s he worked in Pakistan as a liaison for the *mujahedeen*. He considered joining the *Taliban* government in 1994, but ended up trying to mobilise opposition to them. He worked for a brief period as a consultant with the oil company Unocal, but following the fall of the *Taliban* in 2001 he eventually came to be selected as president in 2002 and elected again in 2004. As of March 2009 he is still serving as Afghan president.

14. Nadir Jan (Alikozai by tribe) was originally from Arghandab district of Kandahar province and was the brother-in-law of the Alikozai tribal elder and commander, *Mullah* Naqibullah. They were known for having bad relations among each other. Nadir Jan was killed in Keshkinakhud in 1995 along with two of his friends.

15. *Mawlawi* Abdul Razaq (Noorzai by tribe), originally from Spin Boldak district of Kandahar province was a big *Harakat* commander during the 1980s *jihad* who later went on to be the Secretary in charge of Finance for *Herat* province during the *Taliban*'s rule. He is still alive.

16. *Mullah* Akhtar Jan (Noorzai by tribe) fought with *Hizb-e Islami* during the 1980s *jihad*. He was the District Chief of Spin Boldak during the Rabbani government. He is still alive.

17. Mohammad Nabi (Noorzai by tribe) fought during the 1980s *jihad* but was not officially affiliated to any of the "*mujahedeen* parties" in Pakistan. Many civilians were allegedly killed at his checkpoints and he fled to Pakistan after the *Taliban* took power.

18. Mansur (Achekzai by tribe) was one of Esmat Muslim's commanders. He ran a checkpoint on the highway, but he was killed in Registan resisting the *Taliban* on 30 October 1994 and was one of the first of the militia commanders to be hanged by the *Taliban*; his body was displayed prominently beside the highway for many days.

19. The *Dashaka* or DShK heavy machine gun was Soviet-manufactured and can fire up to 600 rounds per minute with a maximum range of 1500 metres against ground targets.

20. Soft silk-like cloth used for turbans.

21. Jabbar "*Qahraman*" (literally Jabbar "the hero", one of the titles the Soviets sometimes bestowed on Afghan fighters) is Noorzai by tribe and operated a very successful militia in southern Afghanistan during the late 1980s and early 1990s. Originally from Kardanay (in Spin Boldak district), he has a bad reputation in Kandahar province nowadays dating back to the time of his militia. He currently lives in Moscow.

22. These six *Taliban* fronts were run by: *Mullah* Burjan, *Mawlawi* Abdul Samad, *Mullah* Obaidullah, *Hajji Mullah* Mohammad, *Mullah* Abdul Sattar, and *Mullah* Abbas. The commanders of these fronts were: *Mullah* Mohammad Sadiq, *Mullah Hajji* Mohammad, *Malem* Feda Mohammad, Hafizullah Akhundzada, Lala Malang (also known as Akbar Agha), and *Shahid* Rahmatullah Jan.

23. *Mullah Hajji* Mohammad Omar was a famous commander in the Pashmol area, who fought together with *Mullah* Burjan and *Mullah* Mohammad Hassan. He is not to be confused with the *Taliban* leader, *Mullah* Mohammad Omar (minus the title "*Hajji*").

24. Herat Gate is located in the centre of Kandahar City, near to the Governor's Palace.

25. Note that commanders weren't always in control of their men at all times.

26. *Hajji* Amir Mohammad Agha (Nasar by tribe) is originally from Jelahor (Arghandab district of Kandahar). He first fought with *Harakat* during the 1980s *jihad* and then shifted to Sayyaf's *Ittehad-e Islami*. He is *Mullah* Mohammad Omar's father-in-law through marriage, and is still alive.

27. *Mullah* Mohammad Hassan (Babur by tribe) fought with *Harakat* during the 1980s *jihad*. He was appointed governor of Kandahar in 1994 after the *Taliban* seized control. There is some confusion relating to the presence of another figure called *Mullah* Mohammad Hassan who was also governor of Kandahar (later on). This later *Mullah* Hassan (who also fought with *Harakat*) can be distinguished by only having one leg, and by being Achekzai by tribe.

28. Akhtar Mohammad Mansur (Eshaqzai by tribe) was originally from Band-i Taimour (Maiwand district of Kandahar province) and fought as a *mujahed* with *Mullah* Faizullah Akhund and *Mawlawi* Obaidullah during the 1980s *jihad*. He is still alive.

29. *Mullah* Abdul Salam was from Chenarto (in Shah Wali Kot district of Kandahar) and was appointed Army chief after the *Taliban* took the city. He fought as a *mujahed* during the 1980s *jihad* together with *Mullah* Shirin in Zelakhan.

30. Kandahar's "Arg" or fortress is said to have been built during the early nineteenth century and at one time was the residence of the governors of Kandahar.

31. The *Welayat* is the Governor's Palace, located in the centre of Kandahar City and near to Herat Gate.

32. Arabic phrase literally translated as "God is the Greatest", although more approximate to "God is Great".

33. "*Allahu Akbar*", a phrase often used as a chant or slogan.

34. A *rak'a* is one act of prostration performed during the ritual of daily prayers. A *rak'a* is one complete cycle within the prayer; a prayer may be two, three or four *rak'at* (pl.) long. The first *rak'a* ends in a prostration (*sujdaah*), but the second and fourth end in a sitting (*jalsa*). The third ends in a sitting if it is the final *rak'a*, otherwise in a prostration. There are extra prayers that you can carry out in the evening etc called *nafal* prayers.

35. The *kalima* is the phrase all Muslims use to affirm their faith, and—if said three times in the presence of two Muslim witnesses—is also used when someone converts to Islam.

36. Kandahar's Mirwais Hospital (also known as the "Chinese hospital" on account of the support and funding it receives from China). The land on

which the hospital was built was originally flower gardens, but a hospital was built there during Amanullah Khan's reign in the early twentieth century.

37. This was not the Obaidullah who went on to be *Taliban* Defence Minister. This *Mawlawi* Obaidullah was a judge and Islamic legal scholar from Loy Wiyala (in Kandahar City). He is still alive.

9. ADMINISTRATIVE RULE

1. Ismael Khan was born in 1946 in Shindand (near Herat). He fought in western Afghanistan against the Soviets and was affiliated with *Jamiat-e Islami*. He continues to play a role in Afghan politics as Minister of Power.

2. Lashkar Gah is the central town in Helmand and had an approximate population of 21,000 in the late 1970s, much less than its current number. Built on the site of an ancient town dating back to Sultan Mahmoud of Ghazni, it was famous for the cotton press operating under the Bost Corporation, and well known for a pleasant landscape with the river, and the forest in Bolan. There was also a stone and carpentry factory which polished the Rukhan stones for which Helmand is famous.

3. Gereshq was a small village during the days of the *Taliban*, not like now, but it was reputed to contain more people than Lashkar Gah at that time. It is located on the road between Kandahar and Herat.

4. *Mullah* Mir Hamza Akhund (Noorzai by tribe) was from Deh Rawud district of Uruzgan province and was district chief of Gereshq at the beginning of the *Taliban*'s rule.

5. This was later renamed by the *Taliban* as *Bagh-e Islami* (Islamic Garden). It was originally built during the reign of the king Zahir Shah and it was first called *Bagh-e Shahi* ("Royal Garden"). Zahir Shah lived there when he came to Herat. Otherwise it was a place for other government officials to meet with other high-ranking officials. After the fall of the Communist regime and the victory of the *mujahedeen*, it was renamed *Bagh-e-Azadi* ("Freedom Garden"). Its name has currently reverted to *Bagh-e Azadi*. Ordinary people are not allowed to enter, and it is usually guarded.

6. *Hajji Mullah* Yar Mohammad was seen by the people of Herat as being more moderate in nature than other *Taliban*. There was once a demonstration by women in the city and the *Taliban* disrupted the demonstrators with water tanks and hoses from the Fire Department. When *Mullah* Yar Mohammad heard about the means used against the demonstrators he denounced the practice, ordered that these actions not be carried out against women again and went to talk to local elders about the issue.

7. *Mullah* Abdul Salam was widely disliked by the residents of Herat. He was also seen as being independent from Kabul or the orders of those above him in the *Taliban* hierarchy. He suffered from a chronic pain problem and in due course became addicted to injections of Pentazocin (an opiate).

8. *Mullah* Serajuddin (Noorzai by tribe) was a powerful *mujahedeen* commander who later headed the border forces under the *Taliban*'s rule regime. Many people in Herat believed him to be one of the most cruel of the *Taliban* in their city.

9. Mohammad Anwar is still alive and living in Herat.

10. See Gannon, 2006.

11. *Mullah* Fazl Akhund (Kakar) was head of the Army Corps under the *Taliban*. Originally from Tirin Kot (Uruzgan province), he fought as a *mujahed* during the 1980s *jihad* but wasn't famous as a commander during that time. He was captured in 2001 after surrendering to General Dostum with 10,000 *Taliban* soldiers, and is still being held in Guantánamo prison.

12. *Mullah* Khan Mohammad Akhund (Alizai by tribe) was originally from Baghran district of Helmand province. He fought during the 1980s as a *mujahed* and was a friend of *Hajji* Rais of Baghran. He was killed in Shekardara district of Kabul in 2000.

13. Mohammad Naeem Akhund was originally from Uruzgan. He was a friend of *Mullah* Gholam Rasul (from Baghran district of Helmand province). Mohammad Naeem Akhund was killed in the final battle in Takhar in 2001.

14. General Malik was Dostum's second-in-command in northern Afghanistan. His brother was killed in June 1996 and he knew his own life was threatened. He made a deal with the *Taliban* to hand over the north to them, but reneged on his agreement, expelling and killing *Taliban* forces (an Amnesty International report estimated the number of dead as being around 2000). From May 1997 he was the de facto senior military commander in northern Afghanistan for a few months until mid-November when he was reported to have fled the country.

15. The Salang Pass and its tunnel were built by Soviet experts and opened for public use in 1964. At an altitude of 11,000 feet, the 1.7 mile long tunnel was an engineering feat at the time. Soviet forces were often ambushed here during the 1980s.

16. Bashir Baghlani was an active *Hizb-e Islami* commander from Baghlan. He also served there as a *Taliban* commander, switching sides after spending a year in a Kandahar jail. Under the Karzai government he served as governor of Badghis and Farah provinces. He died of heart failure in late April 2007.

17. Five million Afghanis was roughly equivalent to 600 or 700 kilos of wheat at the time.

18. *Mullah* Dadullah (Kakar by tribe) was born around 1966 in a village called Munara Kalay in Char Chino district of Uruzgan province to a Kuchi family, but his family moved to Deh Rawud (Uruzgan) soon after. He was active in the 1980s *jihad* and a strong ally of the "*Taliban* movement's" leader *Mullah* Mohammad Omar. He lost his leg fighting in western Afghanistan in 1994 but went on to play significant roles in battles in

central and northern Afghanistan pre-2001. He rose to prominence in 2006 (particularly in the western media) as the "butcher of the south" for videos in which he beheads so-called "spies". He was killed by ISAF forces in May 2007.

19. Mazar-e Sharif is the largest city in northern Afghanistan, 435 km north-west of Kabul. It has a current estimated population of at least 200,000 and is inhabited mainly by Uzbeks and Tajiks. The city became a major commercial center in the 1930s and the 1970s saw the building of a modern-style city. Mazar became a vital base for the USSR's troops and the communist regime in Kabul thanks to its proximity to the border with the USSR. Between the withdrawal of the communists in 1989 and the collapse of the Najibullah government in 1992, Mazar-i Sharif increasingly came under the control of the militias (Rabbani's *Jamiat-i Islami* and Dostum's *Junbesh-i Milli*).

20. This area (and the road that provided access) was built as a separate pathway towards Bagram when Dr Najibullah was in power.

21. Commonly-used expression in the Muslim world, literally translated as "if God wills". While often held as evidence for a purported fatalism in Islam, the term is sometimes used to indicate that something will certainly happen (i.e. that God has the power to make it happen, or alternatively that God doesn't prevent it from happening).

22. Woollen (or, nowadays, increasingly made from synthetic materials) blanket worn by many Afghans as part of their traditional dress.

23. *Mawlawi* Agha Mohammad, originally from Kunduz, was the head of the office of the Ministry of Defence during the *Taliban*'s rule. He was quite young at the time.

24. *Mawlawi* Abdul Hai was originally from Shorabak district of Kandahar province. He had fought as a *mujahed* during the 1980s *jihad*, and was killed in 2006.

25. *Mawlawi* Ataullah (probably from Panjshir province) was a religious scholar. He was Minister of Information and Culture in the initial period following the fall of Kabul in 2001. He is still alive.

26. By September 1997, the conflict between the *Taliban* and Massoud north of Kabul had caused nearly 180,000 civilians to flee and the *Taliban* reportedly poisoned wells and destroyed irrigation channels on the Shomali plains (Rashid, 2002: 62). The extent of this destruction is still heatedly disputed by former and current members of the *Taliban*, however a significant minority of senior *Taliban* were known to have dissaproved of the tactics employed in Shomali at the time.

10. MINES AND INDUSTRIES

1. Matiullah Enaam (Bakhtiar by tribe) was originally from Kandahar province and a *Mullah* by training. He did not fight during the 1980s *jihad*.

2. Ariana Afghan Airlines started operations in July 1955, transporting passengers internationally and domestically. Considerable foreign investment (both from the west and the east) supported the fledgling company and allowed it to grow. By the mid-1990s, however, Ariana had a poor reputation and the UN Security Council passed a resolution banning it from flying internationally. This was lifted in early 2002, but the airline continues to be dogged by complaints about its safety record and other allegations.
3. 400,000 Pakistani Rupees was an extremely large amount of money at the time. You could buy a 3–4 bedroom house with that money at the time, or almost two of the best cars then available.
4. *Mawlawi* Ahmad Jan *Saheb* was originally from Zurmat district of Paktya province. He was close to Nasrullah Mansour, the head of an alternative *"Harakat"* political party.
5. *Mawlawi* Mohammad Azam Elmi (Totakhel by tribe) was from Sayyed Karam district of Paktya province. He was young at the time (and accordingly had not fought during the 1980s *jihad*). He was killed in a car accident in Saudi Arabia in 2006.
6. This factory was a power plant and produced fertilizer.
7. Unocal is a US-owned oil and gas company that operated between 1890 and 2005 (before merging into the Chevron Corporation). Many figures associated with the United States government have worked for Unocal, including Hamid Karzai and Zalmai Khalilzad.
8. Bridas is an Argentinian oil and gas company that has been involved in central Asia since the early 1990s.
9. Noor Sultan Nazarbayev (born in 1940) has served as president of Kazakhstan since 1990. From 1967 he rose to power through a succession of Communist Party posts and was voted as president of independent Kazakhstan in a popular vote in 1991. He has been criticized for holding the reigns of power close and distributing senior posts to family and friends.
10. Ghee is a type of clarified butter used extensively in south-Asian cooking.
11. Rukham marble comes from Helmand and is one of the best-known exports of the area around Lashkar Gah.

11. A MONUMENTAL TASK

1. First set of sanctions imposed by UN Security Council in October 1999, but with no effect. On 19 December 2000, Security Council imposed more sanctions on the *Taliban* (resolution 1333), including an arms embargo and a clause stating that all *Taliban* offices abroad should be shut.
2. Abdul Rahman Zahed was originally from Khorwar in Lowgar province. He fought during the 1980s *jihad* with Mohammadi's *Harakat* in Lowgar.
3. *Mullah* Mutawakil (Kakar by tribe) is originally from Keshkinakhud in Maiwand district of Kandahar. He is not known for being a *mujahed* dur-

ing the 1980s *jihad*, but his father, Abdul Ghaffar Barialai, who was killed during Taraki's rule, was (and remains) an extremely famous Pashtu poet in southern Afghanistan.

4. *Mawlawi* Sayyed Mohammad Haqqani (Achekzai by tribe) was a very strong figure at the time. He was previously living in Quetta and now is sought by Pakistani, Afghan and western governments for involvement in miltary activities in Panjwayi district of Kandahar as well as in Pakistan. He is currently believed to have a good position with the *Taliban*.

5. Rafiq Tarar was president of Pakistan from 1998 to 2001. Born in 1929, he was affiliated with the Muslim League.

6. *Qazi* Habibullah Fawzi was originally from Ghazni and fought in the 1980s *jihad* together with Gailani's *Mahaz-e Milli*. He is still alive.

7. *Mawlawi* Abdul Qadeer *Saheb* is originally from Hesarak district of Nangarhar province. He fought during the 1980s *jihad*.

8. Abdul Sattar was Pakistan's Foreign Minister between 1999 and 2002, having previously served in Austria, India and the Soviet Union.

9. Moinuddin Haider served as Pakistan's Interior Minister between 1999 and 2002. He was previously involved in the Pakistani military and is now a retired lieutenant general of the Army.

10. The Saur Coup was a Marxist seizure of power that took place on 27 April 1978; it ushered in eleven years of Communist rule.

11. By the early 1990s, there were over six million refugees living outside Afghanistan (Maley, 2002: 154).

12. General Mahmud Ahmed was around fifty years old at the time, spoke Urdu and English and had a scar on his face. He served as Director General of ISI until 8 October 2001 when he retired. He is still alive. He was in Washington on 11 September 2001 and worked together with the US government following the attacks in New York and Washington.

13. General Jailani was middle-aged and didn't speak Pashtu.

14. Brigadier Farooq was a Pakistani Pashtun in his mid-forties. He was tall in stature.

15. Colonel Gul was roughly fifty-five years old at the time, Pashtun and with a tall/heavy-set figure. He was involved in the famous convoy that travelled from Pakistan in November 1994 onwards to Turkmenistan.

16. Major Zia was a Pakistani Pashtun in his mid-forties.

12. DIPLOMATIC PRINCIPLES

1. Aziz Khan is a career diplomat, not to be confused with the retired Pakistani general who served in the army between 1966–2004.

2. Abdul Samad Hamid was Deputy Prime Minister during the Zahir Shah monarchy and post-2001 was involved in the early stages of the Rome process but he left that soon after joining. He is still alive, but must be extremely old by now.

3. Literally translated from the Arabic as "ransom" or "redemption from certain obligations by a material donation or a ritual act". It refers to the payment (as per Islamic *shari'a* law) that should be made to preclude revenge.

4. On 6 January 2001 Arif Ayyub, the Pakistani Ambassador to Kabul, submitted notes for a speech due to be given at a Pakistani Foreign Ministry "Envoys Conference" on 18–19 January 2001 in which he estimated that there were five hundred Arabs left over in Afghanistan from the time of the 1980s *jihad*, as well as "500 Chechens, 100 Uighurs, 1000 Uzbeks, 100 Tajiks, 100 Bengalis, 100 Moros, and 5,000 Pakistanis". (Judah, 2002: 74)

5. Saifullah Akhtar was a well-known criminal of Pakistani nationality.

6. *Mawlawi* Mohammad Qasem was Pakistani and head of *Harakat ul-Mujahedeen* (a militant Islamist group operating primarily in Kashmir).

7. These ceremonies are official graduation celebrations for when a student (or *Talib*) graduates from his religious school. A turban is traditionally tied onto the heads of the graduates. This happens all over the Muslim world, although not always with turbans.

8. "Peace Be Upon Him"; a phrase traditionally used after mentioning the Prophet's name.

9. *Pashtunkhwa* is the name often given by Pashtun nationalists to the proposed state that would be created out of parts of Afghanistan and Pakistan. In 2008 it was also proposed as an alternative name for the North-West Frontier Province or NWFP.

10. *Jamiat-e Ulema-ye Islam* is a political party in Pakistan, founded in 1945 in a split from the *Jamiat-e Ulema-ye Hind*. Members are followers of the Deobandi tradition. Two famous and prominent figures currently part of this party are *Mawlana* Sami ul-Haq and *Mawlana* Fazl ur-Rahman.

11. Barelwi Islam is a popular movement of Sunnis (mainly in South Asia) that coalesced around the figure of Ahmad Reza Khan in the nineteenth century. There is historical enmity between Barelwi Muslims and Deobandis and Salafists.

12. *Sipah-e Sahaba Pakistan* is a Sunni sectarian organisation founded in September 1985 following a split from *Jamiat-e Ulema-ye Islam*. They are most active regarding Sunni-Shi'a issues in Pakistan, and are associated with a wide range of violent actions against the Shi'a community.

13. The Pakistan People's Party (PPP) was founded in November 1967 by Zulfikar Ali Bhutto. It is closely associated with the Bhutto family, and to date the party's leader has always been drawn from that family.

14. Mahmud Khan Achekzai (born 1948) is a prominent Pashtun nationalist based in Quetta, Pakistan.

15. The Awami National Party is a secular Pashtun nationalist party in Pakistan, currently led by Asfandyar Wali Khan.

16. Asfandyar Wali Khan (born 1949) is originally from Charsadda (near Peshawar) is the head of the Awami National Party. He is opposed to the

Taliban and has been targeted for assassination several times, most recently in a suicide-bomb attack in October 2008.

17. Chaudhry Shujaat Hussain (born 1946) is a Pakistani politician affiliated with the Muslim League. He served as Prime Minister between June and August 2004. He was also Minister of the Interior between 1990 and 1993.

18. Mohammad Ijaz ul-Haq is the son of Zia-ul-Haq (the former president of Pakistan). Born in 1953, he served as Minister of Islamic Affairs in Pakistan between 2004 and 2007. He is associated with the Muslim League.

19. *Mawlana* Fazal Rahman (born 1953) is the head of a section of the *Jamiat-e Ulema-ye Islam* political party. He has served in Pakistani politics (including in the National Assembly) and also ran against Musharraf for the presidency.

20. *Mawlana* Sami ul-Haq (born 1937) is chancellor of the Haqqania *madrassa* in Pakistan, a post he took on the death of his father in 1988. He is often referred to as the "father of the *Taliban*", a reference to the large volumes of Afghan "*Talibs*" who passed through his *madrassa*. He leads a section of the *Jamiat-e Ulema-ye Islam* party.

21. *Jamaat-e Islami* is a major Pakistani political party. Founded in Lahore in August 1941 by Sayyed Ab'-Ala Mawdudi, the *Jamaat-e Islami* advocates an Islamic state in Pakistan.

22. *Qazi* Hussein Ahmad (born 1938) is the Pakistani head of the *Jamaat-e Islami*. He joined the party in 1970 and was an active member from the start. He was elected to the Pakistani senate in 1986 for six years.

23. *Shah* Ahmad Noorani *Saheb* (1926–2003), also known as Noorani Mian, was a Barelwi Islamic scholar from Pakistan who founded *Jamiat Ulema-e Pakistan* and co-founded *Muttahida Majlis-e Amal*.

24. The Qartaba conference takes place each year in Lahore (near Manserah) and is organized by *Jamaat-e Islami*. Usually lasting three days, religious and political issues are discussed.

25. The conference of Deoband was held in Peshawar 8–11 April 2001. It was attended by a reported half a million delegates and was organized by *Mawlana* Fazl ar-Rahman's *Jamiat-e Ulema-ye Islam*. Resolutions adopted at the conference included expressions of concern about the continued presence of American soldiers in Saudi Arabia. Statements from Colonel Qadhafi, *Mullah* Mohammad Omar and Osama bin Laden were read out to the assembled crowd.

26. *Mawlawi* Abdul Kabir (Safay by tribe) is originally from Zadran (Paktya). He was governor of Jalalabad during the *Taliban*'s rule, and also head of the eastern military zone. The UN "travel ban" list states that he was born between 1958 and 1963. News agencies reported that he had been captured in Pakistan in July 2005, but other sources (including a statement issued by *Mullah* Mohammad Omar) indicated that this wasn't the case and that he is now Eastern Zone (Nangarhar, Laghman, Kunar and Noorustan provinces) commander for the *Taliban*. He allegedly attended

the "*iftaar* meeting" hosted by the Saudi King in Mecca in September 2009 in which negotiations with the *Taliban* were reportedly discussed.

27. Pervez Musharraf (born in Delhi in 1943) was President of Pakistan (2001–2008) following a *coup d'etat* in 1999 displacing Rafiq Tarar.

28. Osama bin Laden spent time in southeast Afghanistan during the 1980s *jihad*, followed by years in Saudi Arabia and Sudan, before returning back to eastern, then southern, Afghanistan from 1996 where he organised and planned several terrorist attacks on US interests culminating in those of 11 September 2001; he is believed still to be alive. The role that Osama bin Laden played in the 11 September attacks is still disputed by former and current *Taliban* members. Specifically, members of the *Taliban* leadership at the time worry that if they are perceived to have known about bin Laden's involvement, then they are somehow culpable as well. This is an opinion shared by *Mullah* Zaeef.

29. For more see Judah, 2002: 5.

30. The Ghauri missile is a medium-range ballistic missile first tested in April 1998.

31. See Musharraf, 2006.

13. GROWING TENSIONS

1. *Tablighi Jamaat* is an association of the religious that has a prominent following in south Asia and the Muslim world. Founded by *Mawlana* Mohammad Ilyas Kandhalawi, a prominent member of the Deobandi movement, *Tablighi Jamaat* members are explicitly apolitical, and see their mission as *da'wa* or conversion/reform. They meet each year in huge gatherings in Afghanistan, Pakistan and elsewhere.

2. Abdul Haq (Ahmadzai by tribe) is originally from Nangarhar province and was born there in around 1958. He fought during the 1980s *jihad* and was affiliated with Khalis' *Hezb-e Islami* party. He was executed on 26 October 2001 while trying to foment resistance against the *Taliban*.

3. *Mullah* Saleh Mohammad Malang (known as *Mullah* Malang) is originally from Badghis although he was educated in Kandahar. He fought as a *mujahedeen* commander with Khalis' *Hezb-e Islami* during the 1980s *jihad* and is now a member of parliament representing Badghis province.

4. *Mawlawi* Abdul Wali was originally from Sia Chuy (Kandahar province) but he did not fight during the 1980s *jihad*. He was killed in summer 2006 in Pashmol fighting Canadian soldiers.

5. *Sarparasti Shura* translates literally as "acting council" and refers to the five *Taliban* leaders who ran the government in Kabul at the time.

6. This refers to a confusion between *Mullah* Mohammad Rabbani and Burhanuddin Rabbani, the leader of *Jamiat* political party.

7. This phrase from the *Qur'an* is taken from *Surat ul-Baqara* (2), verse 156: "To God we belong, and to Him we are returning". It is traditionally spoken by Muslims when a death or some other sorrow has recently occurred.

8. This is a *hadith*. It literally translates as: "There is no obedience to the crea-
ture in his disobedience to the Creator (*Allah*)", which implies that Muslims
ought not to obey (or do not have to obey) a person who is directly diso-
beying God (a bad ruler, for example). The *hadith* dates back to a story
from the time of Harun al-Rashid, the Abbasid caliph most commonly
associated with Baghdad and the tales of the "1001 Nights". It may be
found in at least two major *hadith* collections: the *Musnad* of Ahmad ibn
Hanbal, and the *Mustadrak* of al-Hakim an-Naysaburi.

14. THE OSAMA ISSUE

1. Spanish diplomat (now retired) born in 1940 who was Personal Representative of the Secretary General for Afghanistan and Head of the United
Nations Special Mission to Afghanistan (UNSMA) (2000–1). He also
served as the European Union's Special Representative in Afghanistan,
2002–8.
2. For more see http://www.unwire.org/unwire/19991202/6099_story.asp and
http://www.globalpolicy.org/security/issues/afgnst.htm.
3. A title technically given only to those who have been on the *Hajj*, the
Islamic pilgrimage to Mecca which is one of the five pillars of the Muslim
faith, but which in Afghanistan (and throughout the Muslim world) is
sometimes used merely as a term of respect for the middle-aged and
elderly.
4. William Milam (born in Arizona, USA) was a career diplomat until his
retirement from the US Foreign Service in July 2001. He served as Ambassador to Pakistan between August 1998 until July 2001. He is currently a
Senior Policy Scholar at the Woodrow Wilson Center in Washington DC and
author of *Bangladesh and Pakistan: Flirting with Failure in South Asia*.
5. Kabir Mohabat held dual Afghan and American citizenship. He was Zadran
by tribe and originally from Paktya province. His appointment to the
American embassy was temporary and limited to passing on a specific message in the case of Osama.
6. Zalmai Khalilzad (born in Mazar-e Sharif in 1951) was US Ambassador to
Afghanistan (2003–2005), US Ambassador to Iraq (2005–2007) and US
Ambassador to the United Nations (2007–2009). He remains involved in
Afghan affairs.
7. Note that bin Laden—while not considered as important as he is now—was
on the United States' "Top Ten Wanted" list (following the bombings of the
two African embassies in 1998). President Clinton had launched cruise missile strikes on targets within Afghanistan following these attacks.
8. Christina Rocca was alleged to have worked for the CIA's Operations
Directorate since 1982 and was nominated for appointment as Secretary of
State for South Asia in April 2001. Some sources suggest she was closely
involved with the funding and arming of the anti-Soviet *mujahedeen* during
the 1980s.

9. In this apocryphal tale, during the 1970s a Pakistani fighter jet once crossed into Afghan airspace along the border in the southeast. The Afghan border commander—determined to follow protocol—wrote an urgent letter to Kabul to receive instructions as to how he should act. Six months later—the postal systems were notoriously slow—a reply arrived from Kabul: "Shoot it down".

15. 9/11 AND ITS AFTERMATH

1. Sohail Shahin (Totakhel by tribe) was originally from Sayyed Karam district of Paktya province. He fought as a *mujahed* during the 1980s. He is still alive, but very old now.
2. Tayyeb Agha (Naser/Sayyed by tribe) was one of *Mullah* Mohammad Omar's deputies. He was originally from Jelahor in Arghandab district of Kandahar, and fought with *Harakat* and Khalis' *Hizb-e Islami* during the 1980s *jihad*. He was the brother of the well-known commander Lala Malang.
3. "In the name of God, the merciful, the compassionate"
4. On 7 August 1998, two car bombs were simultaneously detonated in Nairobi (Kenya) and Dar as-Salaam (Tanzania) at the site of the United States embassies in those two cities. Hundreds were killed and bin Laden was subsequently added to the United States' "Ten Most Wanted" list.
5. See Musharraf, 2006.
6. Malik Zarin was a dual Afghan-Pakistani national and tribal elder who fought as a commander primarily in Kunar province.
7. Padshah Khan Zadran (Zadran by tribe) is originally from Paktya province and is known as the "Dostum of the south-east". After 11 September he worked with the Karzai government and served as governor of Paktya in 2001 and 2002. He was elected as a Member of Parliament in 2005.
8. Hamid Agha (Sayyed by tribe) commanded 300–400 men during the Soviet *jihad*, during which he fought for Gailani's *Mahaz-e Milli*. He is originally from Nelgham.
9. Wendy J. Chamberlin (born 1948) was US Ambassador to Pakistan between 13 September 2001 and 28 May 2002. She has worked at UNHCR, USAID and at the United States Department of State and is currently the president of The Middle East Institute, a respected think tank.
10. *Mullah* Akhtar Mohammad Osmani (Eshaqzai by tribe) was originally from Sangin (in Helmand province) but didn't make a name for himself during the 1980s *jihad*. He was the Army commander of Kandahar province while the *Taliban* were in power post-1994.
11. *Mullah* Abdul Ghaffar (Popolzai by tribe) was originally from Sangin district (Helmand province) and was a young man when he was working at the ministry (and so unlikely to have fought in the 1980s *jihad*).
12. Maiwali is located in Pakistan's Punjab.

13. Colonel Imam was a Pakistani national who became well-known (particularly in southern Afghanistan) during the 1980s as the main channel of US-Saudi-ISI funding for the *mujahedeen* down in Quetta. He was responsible for training sessions and the distribution of funds/resources. Most commanders in southern Afghanistan knew him.

16. A HARD REALISATION

1. North West Frontier Province in Pakistan.
2. All-enveloping garment worn by the great majority of women in southern Afghanistan when they are in public. Famously imposed as obligatory dress by the *Taliban* in the 1990s, the *burqa* is most often referred to by Afghans as *chadari*. Sky-blue is its most common colour, but shades of brown, green and even red are to be found.
3. *Ameen* is the direct and literal equivalent version/pronunciation of the word "Amen" used by Christians.
4. 250,000 Pakistani Rupees was equivalent to 30,000 kilos of wheat at the time.
5. Legally authoritative opinion issued by Islamic religious scholars. This term is best known from the *fatwa* issued by Ayatollah Khomeini in Iran in 1989 calling for Salman Rushdie's execution following the publication of *The Satanic Verses*.
6. Literally translated as "blood that is permitted/allowed", it refers to the claim (disputed among legal scholars) that people (including Muslims) can be killed if they are working against Islam (for example), or even cooperating with Americans in Afghanistan.
7. United Nations Office for the Coordination of Humanitarian Affairs.

17. PRISONER 306

1. Mohammad Ali Jinnah (1876–1948) the first post-partition Governor General of Pakistan was a politician, generally regarded as the father of Pakistan. He was also head of the Muslim League.
2. *Mullah* Mohammad Fazl (born approximately 1967 or 1968) was born in Char Chino district of Uruzgan province. He was the Deputy Defense Minister in the final days of the *Taliban*. According to information taken from Combat Status Review Tribunals held at Guantánamo, *Mullah* Fazl commanded "3000 front-line troops in Takhar province in October 2001". As of December 2008, he has not been released from Guantánamo.
3. *Mullah* Noori was the *Taliban* governor of Balkh province. He was originally from Shah Juy district of Zabul province. He is still being held in Guantánamo.
4. *Mullah* Burhan is originally from Kajaki district of Helmand province. He was held in Guantánamo but has since been released.

5. *Mullah* Abdul Haq Wasseeq *Saheb* (born approximately 1971) was originally from Qara Bagh district of Ghazni province. He was the deputy head of the *Taliban*'s security services (NDS/KhAD) in Kabul. He was captured together with *Mullah* Ghulam Rohani on 9 December 2001. He testified at his Combatant Status Review Tribunal that he worked for the *Taliban* governor of the northern Takhar province. Circumstantial evidence suggests he was a close associate of *Mullah* Mohammad Omar. He is still being held in Guantánamo.

6. *Mullah* Ghulam Rohani (born approximately 1976) was originally from Ghazni (district centre) and worked in the intelligence department during the *Taliban*'s rule. One of the first twenty detainees to be transported to Guantánamo on 11 January 2002. He was transferred from Guantánamo to Kabul's *Pul-e Charkhi* jail on 12 December 2007.

7. This is a reference to all the Afghans who were detained, went missing or were murdered during the initial purges of the Communist regime.

8. The waterless ablution for prayers one performs when one is ill, is at risk of falling ill through contact with cold water, or if there is no water. Instead, you wipe yourself with the dust of unsullied pieces of clay. The intention is thus symbolic.

9. Arabic phrase literally translated as "praise be to God". This phrase is used frequently by Muslims in ordinary conversation.

10. The International Committee of the Red Cross (ICRC) was founded in 1863 and is mandated to implement the 1949 Geneva Conventions. With a focus on areas of conflict, the ICRC has been active in Afghanistan since the Soviet invasion. They remain one of the few organizations that Afghans respect, in part due to their mediation on behalf of detainees as described by *Mullah* Zaeef.

11. Throughout this account *Mullah* Zaeef mentions names of people he met while at Guantánamo, Bagram and so on. These names are the actual names (as far as he could remember) which may be distinguished from some of the official (false) names given by the detainees themselves to American authorities. The editors have tried, where possible, to identify detainees in footnotes and have matched up the names.

12. Adil Mabrouk bin Hamida (born in 1970) was originally from Tunis, the capital city of Tunisia. Evidence given at his Combatant Status Tribunal Review stated that he was living in Italy, but travelled to Afghanistan in early 2001. As of 5 March 2009, he has been incarcerated in Guantánamo for seven years and one month. He remains there.

13. Mohammad Nawab was originally from Mecca, Saudi Arabia.

14. One of the four main Islamic schools of legal thought, it is predominant in Afghanistan (and also is the largest in terms of adherents globally). Named after the legal scholar Abu Hanifa (d. 767), it advocates a more liberal approach to the Islamic law or *shari'a*.

18. GUANTÁNAMO BAY

1. Abdul Rauf Aliza was born in 1981 in Afghanistan (according to the US Department of Defence) and is originally from Helmand province. He confessed during his Combatant Status Review Tribunal that he was Alizai by tribe and that he lost his leg during the 1980s *jihad* against the Soviets. He was repatriated to Afghanistan (to *Pul-e Charkhi* prison) on 12 December 2007.
2. Suleiman (also known as Mohammad Alim) is Mehsud by tribe and originally from Waziristan. The name that he took after his release was Abdullah Massoud, and he was killed in Zhob by the Pakistani government in 2008.
3. Born in Jalalabad, Afghanistan, Badr (born approximately 1970) has a Masters degree in English literature. At the time of his transfer to Guantánamo he had already been imprisoned in Afghanistan for writing satirical articles about the US and the *Taliban*. He was released from Guantánamo before the Combatant Status Review Tribunals began. He wrote a highly critical book with his brother (now back in Guantánamo) about Guantánamo which was published in 2006 in Afghanistan.
4. General Miller (born 1949) was the senior military commander of Guantánamo prison from 2002, and many link his counsel to "soften up" prisoners in Iraq to the Abu Ghraib prison scandal of March 2004. He retired in 2006 having served in the US Army for thirty-four years.
5. Camp Echo is one of seven separate camps that make up Guantánamo Bay detention facility. It is used to hold prisoners in solitary confinement. So-called 'high-value' prisoners are often held here in special restricted-access cells.
6. Ahmed (al-)Rashidi (born approximately 1966) is a Moroccan citizen. He was captured in Pakistan in 2002, but transferred from Guantánamo to Morocco in April 2007. Rashidi spent seventeen years in London, working as a chef in a number of restaurants before travelling to Afghanistan in October 2001. Prison authorities nicknamed him "the General", apparently on account of his "influence and sense of self-importance" (Golden, 2006). Rashidi was subject to a practice known as the "frequent flyer programme", in which prisoners would be arbitrarily moved around to different cells at all times of day and night, and would be subjected to six-hour interrogations, all to deprive them of sleep. An investigator working with *Reprieve* found evidence that Rashidi had in fact been working in London at the time when he was claimed to be "receiving training at the Al Farooq training camp in July 2001" as Combatant Status Review Boards alleged.
7. Ayman Sa'id Abdullah Batarfi (born approximately 1967) is a Yemeni national who was born in Cairo, Egypt. He claimed that he was working as a doctor at the battle of Tora Bora in 2001 when captured. The journalist Sami al-Hajj, released from Guantánamo on 1 May 2008, claimed that Yemeni detainees (like Batarfi) had been driven insane through the admin-

istration of hallucinogenic drugs in Guantánamo. He has not been released as of December 2008.

8. Tariq Abdul Rahman was from Helmand and has since been released back to Afghanistan.

9. Camp Delta was a detention facility in Guantánamo Bay that started operations in April 2002. It is made up of at least seven detention camps (camps 1–6 and Echo).

10. Camp 5 differs from other camps at Camp Delta in that it is a two-story maximum-security multi-winged complex made of concrete and steel. It cost $31 million to build (although another source referred to the facility as being a $16 million one), is designed to hold 100 detainees and was completed in May 2004. Those that are considered the most dangerous and those deemed to have the most valuable intelligence are housed there. One source claimed that roughly 16 per cent of all detainees were held in Camp 5.

11. Abu Haris was from Kuwait, and was born in approximately 1972 or 1973.

19. GRAVEYARD OF THE LIVING

1. Mashaal Awad Sayyaf al-Harbi (born appoximately 1980) was born in Saudi Arabia. He was captured in Mazar-e Sharif in Afghanistan in 2001, and released from Guantánamo and transferred back to Saudi Arabia on 19 July 2005.

2. Mukhtar Yahya Naji al-Warafi (born approximately 1976) is a Yemeni citizen. He was accused of assisting the *Taliban* in 2001 by helping maintain a "special [medical] clinic for the Arabs". As of December 2008 he remains in Guantánamo.

3. Yousuf Nabiev (born approximately 1964) was born in Isfara, Tajikistan. He was released from Guantánamo prior to the start of Combatant Status Review Tribunals in July 2004.

4. Qala-ye Jangi was a fortress in which "*Taliban* and *Al Qaeda* prisoners" were being held. Prisoners staged an uprising between 25 November and 1 December 2001. Of the approximately 300 prisoners being held there, only 86 survived the ensuing battle, during which air strikes were called in by foreign Special Forces operatives.

5. Adjectival use of Yousuf's nationality. *Tajiki* literally translates as "from Tajikistan".

6. Jawzjan province is located in the north of Afghanistan and is a stronghold of support for Dostum. There are over 400,000 people living there, in an area slightly smaller than Massachusetts state in the USA. It shares a border with Turkmenistan and Uzbekistan.

7. Abdul Ghani was born in approximately 1984. Evidence listed against him in the Combatant Status Review Boards stated that he had "participated in

a BM 12 missile attack against a U.S.A.F. transport aircraft while it was departing Kandahar Airfield [in November 2002]". As of December 2008 he remains in Guantánamo.

8. Allah Noor (Barakzai by tribe) is from Farah province and fought with the Communist government during the 1980s *jihad*. He was working as a security commander in Kandahar airport at the time of Abdul Ghani's capture.

9. The *USS Cole* was attacked on 12 October 2000 by a speedboat suicide bombing while it was anchored in the Yemeni port of Aden. Seventeen American soldiers were killed (as well as the two attackers).

10. These Enemy Combatant Status Tribunal Review Boards began hearings in July 2004. These sessions were one-time legal proceedings that sought to determine whether the designation as "enemy combatant" was appropriate for each prisoner being held in Guantánamo. 574 tribunals were held, but only 37 of these were observed and open to members of the press. Detainees were not obliged to attend their Tribunal Review Boards, and many did not attend, choosing instead to submit a written statement to the Board.

11. The Administrative Review Board is a United States military body that conducts an annual review of suspects being held in Guantánamo. These hearings were criticized by human rights advocates because detainees were not entitled to legal counsel, could not learn what allegations that had to defend themselves against, and suspects had no presumption of innocence. The first set of hearings took place between 14 December 2004 and 23 December 2005.

12. For more on these events see Golden, 2006.

13. Colonel Michael Bumgarner (born 1959) was the commander in charge of Guantánamo for a substantial part of *Mullah* Zaeef's detention there. See Golden, 2006, for a full discussion of his involvement in negotiations with the prisoners.

14. Shakir Abdur Rahim Mohammad Ami was born in 1968 in Medina, Saudi Arabia. He was captured in Afghanistan in December 2001. Shakir claimed to have been working for a Saudi charity in Afghanistan, al-Haramein Foundation, at the time of his detention. In Guantánamo he participated in (and eventually helped end) hunger strikes in 2005, 2006 and 2008. In September 2006, Shakir's attorneys filed a motion arguing for his removal from isolation in Guantánamo, where he had been held for 360 days at the time of filing. Their motion was denied. He remains in Guantánamo as of February 2009.

15. Sheikh Abdul Rahman (also known as Abd al-Fattah al-Gazzar) was born in Cairo, Egypt, in 1965. He was captured in Pakistan in December 2001. His leg was injured in the US bombing campaign, and reportedly was amputated in November 2005. As of 6 March 2009, he has been held at Guantánamo for seven years and two months. He remains there.

16. Ghassan Abdullah al Sharbi was born in Jeddah, Saudi Arabia, in 1974. He went to school in the United States, studying electrical engineering at university in Arizona. He was captured in Pakistan in March 2002. Evidence given in his Combatant Status Review alleged that fellow Guantánamo inmates called him the "electronic builder" and "Abu Zubaydah's right hand man". He was reportedly subject to the "frequent flyer programme". As of 3 March 2009, he has been held in Guantánamo for six years and nine months, where he still remains.

17. Sabir Mahfouz Lahmar was born in Constantine, Algeria, in May 1969. He is a Bosnian citizen and was captured there in October 2001, charged with conspiring to attack the US Embassy in Sarajevo, Bosnia-Hercegovina. On 20 November 2008 a US federal judge ruled that Mr Lahmar was not being lawfully held and ordered his release. As of 5 March 2009, he has been held at Guantánamo for seven years and two months. He remains there.

18. Sheikh Abu Ali (also known as Ala Mohammad Salim and Sheikh Ala) is an Egyptian citizen. He filed a request with American authorities while in Guantánamo not to be repatriated to Egypt because he had been imprisoned and tortured there. He remains in Guantánamo as of March 2009.

20. GETTING OUT

1. Literally "in peace" (from the Arabic).
2. Prostration with forehead, palms of the hands, knees and feet touching the ground. It is part of the ritual of Islam's five daily prayers.
3. All Guantánamo returnees are officially handled by Mujaddidi's Peace and Reconciliation Commission. As of February 2009, 63 detainees have been returned to Afghanistan from Guantánamo. At its peak, Guantánamo contained 110 Afghans. There are only 27 currently remaining. 8 ex-detainees were re-captured for various reasons, including 3 who were subsequently re-released (figures from the Peace and Reconciliation Commission office in Kabul).

21. NO WAR TO WIN

1. Mani al-Utaybi and Yasser Talal al-Zahrani, both Saudis, and Ali Abdullah Ahmed from Yemen.
2. Approximately, "hello" or "greetings", this is a shortened version of *as-salamu aleikum* ("Peace be upon you").

BIBLIOGRAPHY

Anderson, Jon L. (2003) *The Lion's Grave: Dispatches from Afghanistan.* (New York: Grove Press).

Baitenmann, Helga (1990) "NGOs and the Afghan War: The Politicisation of Humanitarian Aid", *Third World Quarterly*, vol. 12, no. 1, pp. 62–85.

Barry, Michael (1974) *Afghanistan.* (Paris: Éditions du Seuil).

Bedawi, Zaki and Bonney, Richard (2005) *Jihad: From Qur'an to Bin Laden.* (New York: Palgrave Macmillan).

Bergen, Peter (2006) *The Osama bin Laden I Know: An Oral History of al Qaeda's Leader* (New York: Free Press).

Bonner, Michael D. (2006) *Jihad in Islamic History: Doctrines and Practice.* (Princeton: Princeton University Press).

Coll, Steve (2004) *Ghost Wars: the Secret History of the CIA, Afghanistan, and bin Laden, from the Soviet Invasion to September 10, 2001.* (London: Penguin Books).

Dorronsoro, Gilles (2005) *Revolution Unending.* (London: Hurst).

Dupree, Nancy Hatch (1977) *An Historical Guide to Afghanistan.* (Kabul: Afghan Tourist Organization).

Dyk, Jere van (1983) *In Afghanistan: An American Odyssey.* (Lincoln: Authors Choice Press).

Gannon, Kathy (2006) *I is for Infidel: from Holy War to Holy Terror in Afghanistan.* (New York: Public Affairs).

Golden, T. (2006) "The Battle for Guantánamo", *The New York Times*, 17 September.

Judah, Tim (2002) "The Taliban Papers", *Survival*, vol. 44, no. 1, pp. 69–80.

Kaplan, Robert D. (1990) *Soldiers of God: With Islamic Warriors in Afghanistan and Pakistan.* (New York: Vintage).

Khalidi, Noor A. (1991) "Afghanistan: Demographic Consequences of War, 1978–1987", *Central Asian Survey*, vol. 10, no. 3, pp. 101–26.

Maley, William, ed. (1998) *Fundamentalism Reborn? Afghanistan and the Taliban.* (London: Hurst).

Maley, William. (2002) *The Afghanistan Wars.* (London: Palgrave Macmillan).

Musharraf, Pervez (2006) *In the Line of Fire.* (London: Simon & Schuster).

Rashid, Ahmed (2002) *Taliban.* (London: I.B. Tauris).

BIBLIOGRAPHY

Urban, Mark (1990) *War in Afghanistan* (London: Macmillan Press).

WHO (World Health Organisation) (1995) *Brief Note on Health Sector of Afghanistan: From Emergency to Recovery and Building from Below* (Stockholm: Donors' Meeting on Assistance for Afghanistan's Long-Term Rehabilitation and its Relationship with Humanitarian Programmes, 1–2 June).

Yousaf, Muhammad and Adken, Mark (1992) *The Bear Trap: Afghanistan's Untold Story*. (London: Leo Cooper).

CHRONOLOGY

Year	Age	Historical context
1915	−53	Zaeef's father born (approx)
1962	−6	Zaeef's uncle (*Mullah* Nezam) killed in Zheray desert—approx
1968	0	Zaeef born in Zangiabad (Panjwayi, Kandahar); mother dies (7 months)
1969	1	Moves to Mushan (Maiwand district)
1970	2	Living in Mushan
1971	3	Zaeef's younger sister dies
1972	4	Moves to Rangrezan (Maiwand district)
1973	5	Living in Rangrezan
1974	6	Living in Rangrezan
1975	7	Zaeef's father dies; Moves to uncle's house in Charshakha
1976	8	Living in Charshakha
1977	9	Move to Sanzari (near Nagehan) once fighting begins
1978	10	Moves to Sanzari (near Nagehan) once fighting begins; Flees to Pakistan (Nushki, then Panjpai camp) with uncle and sister on smuggling route
1979	11	Living in Panjpai camp

AD date	Age	Historical context
1915	−53	
1962	−6	
1968	0	
1969	1	
1970	2	
1971	3	Famine in central and northern Afghanistan
1972	4	Famine in central and northern Afghanistan
1973	5	Coup by Daud (July); Zahir Shah exiled in Italy
1974	6	
1975	7	
1976	8	
1977	9	
1978	10	Communist coup brings Taraki and Amin to power (Daud killed); uprisings in countryside (Kunar esp)
1979	11	Guerilla attacks in Kandahar begin (February); Uprising in Herat (March); Soviet Union forces (approx 85,000 troops) invade Afghanistan (December)

1980	12	Living in Panjpai camp
1981	13	Living in Panjpai camp
1982	14	Living in Panjpai camp
1983	15	Zaeef goes to fight in Afghanistan (Pashmol, then Nelgham)
1984	16	Zaeef moves back to Quetta to continue his studies
1985	17	Weapons training with ISI in Pakistan; then back to fight in Kandahar
1986	18	Wounded in wrist in Afghanistan; returns to Pakistan for treatment, then back to Kandahar to fight
1987	19	Zaeef in Kandahar to fight
1988	20	Participates in battle of Khushab and defends against the final Russian offensives in Kandahar (including the siege of Arghandab)
1989	21	Finishes war against the Soviets; returns home
1990	22	Zaeef becomes a father
1991	23	Civil war causes Zaeef to flee to Pakistan (again)

1980	12	Countrywide demonstrations (February); US boycott Moscow Olympic Games (July)
1981	13 .	Five *mujahedeen* groups create an alliance (August); Fierce fighting in Kandahar City
1982	14	Soviet offensive in Panjshir (June); *Mujahedeen* storm Kandahar jail (August)
1983	15	Soviets adopt new counter-insurgency tactics down south; "Peace talks" begin in Geneva (June); Soviet reinforcements arrive in Kandahar (June)
1984	16	US approves $50 million covert aid to the *mujahedeen* (July); Soviet offensive in Pashmol (September)
1985	17	Soviets try to seal off Iran/Pakistan border (February); Esmat Muslim defects to the Afghan government side (May); "Proximity" talks in Geneva (June and August)
1986	18	US agrees to provide Stinger missiles to *mujahedeen* (April); Siege of Kandahar City (April); Heavy fighting in Kandahar for most of the year
1987	19	10th round of talks in Geneva (February); *Mujahedeen* target air assets in southern Afghanistan (Spring/Summer)
1988	20	Geneva Accords signed (April); *Al Qaeda* "founded" during meeting in Peshawar (August); Soviets leave southern Afghanistan (August); Heavy air bombardment of southern Afghanistan (Autumn)
1989	21	Russians leave Afghanistan (January); *Hajji* Latif poisoned in Kandahar (August)
1990	22	Demonstration in Quetta in support of the return of former King Zahir Shah to Afghanistan (February); Tanai attempts coup against Najibullah (March)
1991	23	Massive earthquake in Kandahar (February)

1992	24	Starts work as Imam of mosque in Kandahar
1993	25	Living in *Hajji* Khushkiar Qala (Kandahar)
1994	26	Intial discussions of the "*Taliban* movement"; takes Kandahar; starts work in judiciary with *Mawlawi* Pasanai Saheb
1995	27	Goes to Dilaram (Farah) to fight Ismael Khan; then returns to Pasanai following injury; then visists Herat; Zaeef put in charge of Herat's banks
1996	28	In Herat working with the banks; leaves job and returns to Kandahar; one month at home "reflecting" before *Mullah* Mohammad Omar calls for him
1997	29	Appointed Administrative Director of Defence ministry (Kabul)
1998	30	Acting defence minister for a period of nine months (Kabul); Transfers to Ministry of Mines, Industry and Natural Resources
1999	31	Working at the Ministry of Mines, Industry and Natural Resources
2000	32	Working at the Transport Administration Commission; Appointed ambassador to Pakistan (Islamabad)
2001	33	Zaeef arrested (either late December 2001 or January 2002)
2002	34	Zaeef handed to US by Pakistan (from Islamabad); goes to Kandahar, a military ship, Bagram, and then Guantánamo
2003	35	Detained in Guantánamo
2004	36	Detained in Guantánamo

1992	24	Najibullah regime falls (April); Kandahar divided among *mujahedeen* commanders (April); civil war
1993	25	Fighting amongst commanders in Kandahar City (April and August)
1994	26	*Taliban* movement takes Kandahar; starts work in judiciary with *Mawlawi* Pasanai Saheb
1995	27	*Taliban* take Herat (September)
1996	28	*Taliban* take Kabul (September)
1997	29	Bin Laden moves to Jalalabad from Sudan (May)
1998	30	*Taliban* take Mazar, then lose it; US cruise missile attacks on Afghanistan
1999	31	Uprising against *Taliban* in Herat (May); Abdul Ahad Karzai assassinated (July); Military coup in Pakistan brings Musharraf to power (October)
2000	32	Ismael Khan escapes *Taliban* jail (March); *Mullah* Mohammad Omar bans poppy cultivation (August)
2001	33	11 September attacks in NYC/Washington; fall of *Taliban* (November/December)
2002	34	Return of former King Zahir Shah (April); *Loya Jirga* in Kabul (June);
2003	35	NATO takes over ISAF (August)
2004	36	*Loya Jirga* in Kabul makes Karzai official president (January); Combatant Status Review Tribunals start in Guantánamo (July); Presidential elections (October/November)

2005	37	Zaeef released from Guantánamo (September)
2006	38	Zaeef publishes "Picture of Guantánamo" in Pashtu in Afghanistan and Pakistan
2007	39	Living in Kabul
2008	40	Travels to Kandahar (February); house arrest for making media comments; travels to Saudi for *Hajj*
2009	41	Gives repeated media statements on the necessity of ending the war through talks and dialogue; living in Kabul

2005	37	Massive prisoner hunger strike in Guantánamo; Parliamentary and provincial elections held (September)
2006	38	Anti-US protests in Kabul (May); NATO takes over command of troops in southern Afghanistan (July)
2007	39	*Mullah* Dadullah killed (May); Clashes across Afghan-Pakistani border (May); former King Zahir Shah dies (July)
2008	40	*Taliban* free hundreds of prisoners from Kandahar Jail (June); Suicide bomb attack on Indian embassy kills over fifty (July)
2009	41	United States increase troop numbers in Afghanistan (especially in the south); Afghan tribal militias suggested as a solution, as are negotiations with the *Taliban* leadership

GLOSSARY

Alhamdulillah Arabic phrase literally translated as "praise be to God". This phrase is used frequently by Muslims in ordinary conversation.

Allahu Akbar Arabic phrase literally translated as "God is the Greatest", although more approximate to "God is Great". See *takbir*.

Ashrar A term derived from the Arabic (the plural term, meaning "evildoers") universally used by the Afghan Communists and Soviets to refer to the *mujahedeen*. It literally translates as "people who stir up chaos".

Atan Traditional Pashtun dance. Participants move in a circle while clapping their hands to the rhythm and spinning around. One person leads the circle while the others follow his moves. It is often performed at celebrations and weddings.

Azzan Islamic "call to prayer", traditionally called out by a *mu'azzin* from the top of a minaret; but nowadays often pre-recorded. It is the name of the recitation that mosques broadcast to announce each of the five daily prayer times. Also known as *adhan*.

Baaja Pashtu word used to denote the husband of the sister of someone's wife.

Burqa All-enveloping garment worn by the great majority of women in southern Afghanistan when they are in public. Famously imposed as obligatory dress by the *Taliban* in the 1990s, the *burqa* is most often referred to by Afghans as *chadari*. Sky-blue is its most common colour, but shades of brown, green and even red are to be found.

Chelam	The Afghan equivalent of the western "bong", for smoking tobacco and hashish. It was a common way of ingesting drugs during the 1980s and 1990s.
Dam	Small amulets or pieces of paper, often including verses from the *Qur'an* that are believed to cure illness and protect against misfortune; a popular alternative to medicine in the rural south, especially in the absence of qualified doctors. See *tawiiz* and *tsasht*.
Dashaka	The Dashaka or DShK heavy machine gun was Soviet-manufactured and can fire up to six hundred rounds per minute with a maximum range of 1500 metres against ground targets.
Eid	Afghans–and all Muslims–have two main religious days of celebration called *Eid*, more or less equivalent to the Christian Christmas. The days of *Eid* are characterised by special prayers and sermons, as well as by an emphasis on family, friends, and the giving of gifts. They are known as *eid al-Fitr* and *eid al-Adha*
Eshraq prayer	One of a series of extra prayers that people can perform in addition to the five obligatory prayers, *eshraq* is performed early in the morning when the sun's disc has just risen above the horizon (but not while part of it is still below the horizon). The canonical prayer at this time isn't allowed.
Fidya	Literally translated from the Arabic as "ransom" or "redemption from certain obligations by a material donation or a ritual act". It refers to the payment (as per Islamic *shari'a* law) that should be made to preclude revenge.
Fatwa	Legally authoritative opinion issued by Islamic religious scholars. This term is best known from the *fatwa* issued by Ayatollah Khomeini in Iran in 1989 calling for Salman Rushdie's execution following the publication of *The Satanic Verses*.
Ghazi	Literally translates from the Arabic (but is used throughout the Muslim world) as 'Islamic warrior' and is a loosely approximate alternative for the term *mujahed*. See *mujahed* and *jihad*.

Hadith	A report of the words and actions of the Prophet Mohammad (PBUH) as determined and authenticated by a chain of evidence and proof (known as *asnad*). It is an important part of the oral tradition of Islam, and they survive in written form in collections codified by religious scholars.
Hajji	A title technically given only to those who have been on the *Hajj*, the Islamic pilgrimage to Mecca which is one of the five pillars of the Muslim faith, but which in Afghanistan (and throughout the Muslim world) is sometimes used merely as a term of respect for the middle-aged and elderly.
Halal	A religious term used to denote that which is (legally) permitted by Islam. It is the opposite of *haram*, which literally translates as "that which is not permitted".
Hanafi	One of the four main Islamic schools of legal thought, it is predominant in Afghanistan (and also is the largest in terms of adherents globally). Named after the legal scholar Abu Hanifa (d. 767), it advocates a more liberal approach to the Islamic law or *shari'a*. See *shari'a*.
Haram	A religious term used to denote that which is not permitted by Islam. It is the opposite of *halal*, which literally translates as "that which is permitted".
ICRC	The International Committee for the Red Cross, founded in 1863 and working to aid victims of war around the world, has had a long and committed relationship to Afghanistan for over twenty-five years.
Imam	Title and term of respect used to refer to the person who leads a congregation in the five daily prayers. In the Sunni world it can also refer to a distinguished religious scholar or leader, e.g. *al-imam abu hanifa*. For Shiites it refers, in addition, to "the twelve Imams" of *Shi'a* belief.
Imam-e Mehdi	A religious figure commonly portrayed in messianic and eschatological tones. For Shi'a Muslims, the *Imam-e Mehdi* is identified with the "twelfth Imam", who is believed to have gone into

a state of hiding or occultation (*ghayba*) in the 9th Century. The *mahdi*, therefore, is alive right now, and will emerge toward the end-times to rid the world of oppression and injustice. He is not mentioned in the *Qur'an*.

Insha'allah
Commonly-used expression in the Muslim world, literally translated as "if God wills". While often held as evidence for a purported fatalism in Islam, the term is sometimes used to indicate that something will certainly happen (i.e. that God has the power to make it happen).

ISI
"Inter-Services Intelligence" is the main Pakistani military intelligence wing. Especially prominent in the funding and supplying of weapons to the Afghan *mujahedeen*, ISI has become synonymous with the strong involvement of Pakistan's military in political affairs.

Jama'at
May literally be translated from the Arabic as "group", but in Afghanistan it is used to denote a session of communal prayer of one of the five daily prayers.

Jerib
One *jerib* is a unit of land equivalent to 2000 m² or 0.2 hectares.

Jihad
A notoriously difficult word to translate, *jihad* is derived from an Arabic root meaning "to struggle", "to exert oneself", or "to strive". As such, the word can mean different things depending on the context: sometimes a struggle against evil inclinations, or at other times a reference to legally-sanctioned (by the Islamic legal code) war. See Bedawi and Bonney (2005) and Bonner (2006) for more. Also see *mujahed* and *mujahedeen*.

Ka'aba
Located in Mecca (Saudi Arabia), it is the spiritual focus towards which all Muslims face as they perform their daily prayers. Muslims believe that it was built by Abraham/Ibrahim. It plays a role during the *Hajj* rituals as well.

Kalima
The phrase all Muslims use to affirm their faith, and–if said three times in the presence of at least two witnesses–is also used when someone converts to Islam. Literally meaning 'word' in Arabic,

	it is short for *kalimatu al-shahada*, or "the word (i.e. phrase) of witnessing".
Kareez	A water management system used to provide a reliable supply of water to human settlements or for irrigation in hot, arid and semi-arid climates. Also known as *Kariz* or *Qadaat*.
KhAD	an abbreviation of *Khedamat-e Ittla'aat-e Dawlati*, or "State Security Service". President Najibullah changed its name to WAD, but it is still commonly used to refer to the internal state security apparatus.
Khalq	Literally translated as "people" or "masses", the *Khalq* were a faction of the PDPA (People's Democratic Party of Afghanistan) headed by Noor Mohammad Taraki and Hafizullah Amin, and was opposed to the *Parcham* faction headed by Babrak Karmal. See *Parcham*.
Khan	A tribal chief and/or head of a community. It is an honorific title often also used to describe those who own large portions of land. The title is usually placed after the name of a person. See *malik*.
Kuchi	Afghanistan's nomadic peoples. The word *Kuchi* derives from the Dari "*kuch kardan*" which means "to be on the move" or "to be moving". *Kuchi*s uproot their homes twice a year with the seasons and are found all over Afghanistan. In Kandahar, there used to be many living in the Registan desert, but the 1980s war and the ensuing drought forced many to settle permanently in camps in Pakistan.
Kufr	The verbal noun form of this word literally translates from the Arabic to mean "unbelief". In Afghanistan, the Communist regime was frequently spoken of as embodying *kufr*. The openly anti-religious policies of the PDPA were swiftly written off as being those coming from a state of *kufr*.
Madrassa	Religious school common in southern Afghanistan and Pakistan as the first choice for education (especially for the rural poor). Schools are by and large for boys only, although girls are

educated in some, and the syllabus mainly constitutes a full outline of the religious sciences,
often including the expectation that graduates
will learn various holy books off by heart (notably, the *Qur'an* itself).

Malik
Localised versions of *khan*s. The title is used to
denote the local strongman on the district or sub-
district level, and this often also means that that
person is somehow employed by the government
to give some outreach for micro-management of
particular issues. See *khan*.

Mawlawi
A title used by graduates of *madrassa*s who have
received further religious education as well. It is
the equivalent of postgraduate study for scholars
of Islam. A *mawlawi* is a member of the *Ulema'*,
the Islamic clergy.

Mujahed
See *mujahedeen* and *jihad*.

Mujahedeen
The plural version of *mujahed*, which literally
translates from the Arabic as "one who engages
in *jihad*" or "one who struggles". Often translated as "holy warrior", the term does not necessarily have a connection with the practice of war,
but rather can be used to refer to spiritual inner
struggle (to be a better person and so on). See
mujahed and *jihad*.

Mullah
Religious functionary or cleric extremely prevalent outside the cities in Afghanistan. They will
usually be the single religious authority (having
attended a *madrassa* during childhood, or maybe
because they can read some Arabic and thus the
language of the *Qur'an*) in a particular village.
As such their authority is usually limited to religious matters.

Mustabahu d-dam
Literally translated as "blood that is permitted/
allowed", it refers to the claim (disputed among
legal scholars) that people (including Muslims)
can be killed if they are working against Islam
(for example), or even cooperating with Americans in Afghanistan.

NWFP
North-West Frontier Province, the smallest of
Pakistan's four provinces.

Pahj	Soft silk-like cloth used for turbans.
Parcham	Literally translated as "flag", the Parcham were a faction of the PDPA (People's Democratic Party of Afghanistan) headed by Babrak Karmal, and was opposed to the *Khalq* faction lead by Noor Mohammad Taraki and Hafizullah Amin.
Patu	Woolen (or, nowadays, increasingly made from synthetic materials) blanket worn by many Afghans as part of their traditional dress. During the winter the material will often be thick and woolen, whereas the summer variant of the *patu* will be thinner. The *patu* is not just used to keep warm, though; Afghans use it to sit on when outdoors, and often perform their daily prayers on the very *patu* that they wear.
PDPA	"People's Democratic Party of Afghanistan", an Afghan Marxist party founded in 1965. Intra-party disputes lead to a split developing, and by 1967 the *Khalq* and *Parcham* factions were operating separately. The PDPA seized power in the "Saur" coup of April 1978.
Qari	Title used before people's names in Afghanistan. It refers to the practice/skill of being a *Qari'* (Arabic loan-word) which literally means someone who is able to recite the *Qur'an*.
Qazi	A judge. The word comes from the Arabic, and is used to denote the person who adjudicates, usually having studied in a *madrassa* or theological seminary.
Qur'an	The holy *Qur'an* is the religious book of Muslims around the world, literally translated as "recitation" as Muslims believe it is the result of direct revelation of God to the Prophet Muhammad (PBUH) starting in 610 A.D.
Ramazan	Also known as *Ramadan*, this is the name of a month in the Islamic calendar during which all Muslims are obliged to fast during the hours of daylight. There are exceptions to this obligation though, for example for the sick and those who are travelling.
Rak'a	One act of prostration performed during the ritual of daily prayers. A *rak'a* is one complete cycle

within the prayer; a prayer may be two, three or four *rak'at* (pl.) long. The first *rak'a* ends in a prostration (*sujdaah*), but the second and fourth end in a sitting (*jalsa*). The third ends in a sitting if it is the final *rak'a*, otherwise in a prostration.

Roshandaz	Flares used to illuminate the ground at night. See *Roxana*.
Roxana	Flares used to illuminate the ground at night. See *Roshandaz*.
RPG	Rocket Propelled Grenade; along with the AK-47 Kalashnikov rifle, the RPG is one of the weapons most strongly identified with the Afghan *mujahedeen*. At the beginning of the *jihad*, however, neither weapon was common. Later on, with increased funding coming from abroad, the RPG was used with great effect against tanks and Armoured Personnel Carriers or APCs. Both the AK-47 rifle and the RPG continue to be used against foreign troops as of 2009.
Saheb	A term of respect used after someone's title in southern Afghanistan. It is used for one's elders, the educated, those with high government positions and so on. Also known as *sahib*.
Salaam	approximately, "hello" or "greetings", this is a shortened version of *as-salamu aleikum* ("Peace be upon you").
Sayyed	*Sayyed*s are descendents of the Prophet Muhammad (PBUH) who live in Afghanistan. They are seen as a tribe unto their own by Pashtuns. In Afghanistan, the term is sometimes also used for healers and holy men in general. *Sayyed*s are highly respected by the rural people.
Shahid	An Arabic loan word used in Dari and Pashtu to mean "martyred". It carries religious connotations, fitting into the theology of *jihad*. Martyrs, in Islamic theology, go straight to heaven—they do not have to wait for the day of judgement. It is important to add that it is not only "warriors" who are counted among the *shuhada'* (pl. term in Arabic for "martyrs"); for instance, civilian victims of conflict in the Muslim world are often

described as *shuhada'*. Nor is this a modern corruption: classical Arabic sources, for instance, describe the victims of the Franks and the Mongols as martyrs, too.

Shari'a The body of legislative knowledge used by Islamic scholars and lawyers in the various schools of jurisprudence that have emerged since the emergence of Islam. There are five prominent schools of Islamic law: Hanafi, Hanbali, Maliki, Shafii and Ja'fari.

Sujdaah Prostration with forehead, palms of the hands, knees and feet touching the ground. It is part of the ritual of Islam's five daily prayers.

Sunna The established custom or precedent established and based on the example of the Prophet Muhammad. It offers a separate set of principles of conduct and traditions which were recorded by the Prophet's companions. These customs complement the divinely revealed message of the *Qur'an*. A whole field of jurisprudence has grown up alongside the study of the *Sunna*. The *Sunna* is recorded in the *ahadith* (pl. of *hadith*). The *Sunna* represents the prophetic "norm". See *hadith*.

Sura literally a "chapter" of the *Qur'an*. Divided into 114 separate such *sura*s, the *Qur'an*'s chapters are ordered by descending length rather than their chronological appearance or date of revelation.

Tablighi A member of the *Tablighi Jamaat*, an Indian reform movement founded in 1927 that emphasises religious elements of Islam over the political, and that advocates the mission of *da'wa* or conversion.

Tayammum The waterless ablution for prayers one performs when one is ill, is at risk of falling ill through contact with cold water, or if there is no water to speak of. Instead, you wipe yourself with the dust of unsullied pieces of clay. The intention is thus symbolic.

Takbir "*Allahu al-Akbar*", a phrase often used as a chant or slogan. See *Allahu al-Akbar*.

Talib	Singular version of *Taliban*. See *Taliban*.
Taliban	Plural version of *Talib*. Used to refer to religious students, mainly those who are graduates of *madrassa*s. The term gained notoriety in the mid-1990s on account of the movement that took the word as its name on account of the large number of *madrassa* student supporters. See *madrassa* and *Talib*.
Tawiiz	Small amulets or pieces of paper, often including verses from the *Qur'an* that are believed to cure illness and protect against misfortune; a popular alternative to medicine in the rural south, especially in the absence of qualified doctors. See *dam and tsasht*.
Tsasht	Small amulets or pieces of paper, often including verses from the *Qur'an* that are believed to cure illness and protect against misfortune; a popular alternative to medicine in the rural south, especially in the absence of qualified doctors. See *tawiiz and dam*.
UAE	United Arab Emirates.
Ulema'	Plural version of *'Alim*. Literally "those who have knowledge"; it refers to religious scholars (primarily used for the *Sunni* clergy) who have been educated in the religious "sciences" (the *Qur'an*, the *Sunna* and the *Hadith*s etc). See *Hadith*, *Qur'an* and *Sunna*.
UNOCHA	United Nations Office for the Coordination of Humanitarian Affairs.
Zakat	One of the five "pillars" of Islam, the practice of almsgiving or *zakat* is widespread and encouraged in southern Afghanistan. It is also–to a certain extent–systematised in such a way that it is in many instances a highly formalised type of charitable donation, whereby those with financial means must donate 2.5 per cent of their annual earnings and liquid assets for the needy. Apart from a nominal sum given to them by the government, the religious clergy–particularly in deeply rural areas of the south–often have to rely on *zakat* and other donations by their fellow villagers.

Ziarat

A holy place where a certain deceased "saint" or other such holy person is buried. In the conception of Islam practiced by many in southern Afghanistan, people visit these tombs in order to pray that the holy men will intercede on their behalf. Certain *ziarat*s, for example, are popular among women wanting to become pregnant. Southern Afghanistan and the border areas of Pakistan have many of these shrines.

SUGGESTIONS FOR FURTHER READING

Islam

Armstrong, Karen (1995) *Muhammad: A Biography of the Prophet.* (London: Gollancz).

Bonney, Richard (2004) *Jihad: From Qur'an to bin Laden.* (London: Palgrave Macmillan).

Haroon, Sana (2007) *Frontier of Faith: Islam in the Indo-Afghan Borderland.* (London: Hurst & Co Publishers Ltd).

Hodgson, Marshall G. S. (1977) *The Venture of Islam* (3 vols). (Chicago: University of Chicago Press).

Lings, Martin (1987) *Muhammad: His Life Based on the Earliest Sources.* (Vermont: Inner Traditions Press).

Nasr, Vali (2006) *The Shia Revival: How Conflicts within Islam Will Shape the Future.* (New York: W.W. Norton & Company).

Rodinson, Maxime (2002) *Muhammad.* (London: I.B. Tauris).

Political Islam and Radicalism

Gerges, Fawaz A. (2005) *The Far Enemy: Why Jihad Went Global.* (Cambridge: Cambridge University Press).

Kepel, Gilles (2003) *Jihad: The Trail of Political Islam.* (London: I.B. Tauris).

Mandaville, Peter (2007) *Global Political Islam.* (London: Routledge).

Nasiri, Omar (2006) *Inside the Jihad: My Life with Al Qaeda.* (London: Hurst & Co. Publishers Ltd.).

Olesen, Asta (1995) *Islam and Politics in Afghanistan.* (London: Routledge).

Roy, Olivier (1990) *Islam and Resistance in Afghanistan.* (Cambridge: Cambridge University Press).

———, (1994) *The Failure of Political Islam.* (London: I.B. Tauris).
Wright, Lawrence (2006) *The Looming Tower: Al-Qaeda and the Road to 9/11.* (New York: Knopf Publishing Group).

Afghan General History

Coll, Steve (2004) *Ghost Wars: the secret history of the CIA, Afghanistan, and bin Laden, from the Soviet invasion to September 10, 2001.* (London: Penguin Books).
Dorronsoro, Gilles (2005) *Revolution Unending. Afghanistan: 1979 to the Present.* (London: Hurst & Co Publishers Ltd).
Dupree, Louis (1980) *Afghanistan.* (Princeton: Princeton University Press).
Edwards, David (1996) *Heroes of the Age: Moral Fault Lines on the Afghan Frontier.* (Berkeley: University of California Press).
Ewans, Martin (2002) *Afghanistan: a new history.* (London: Routledge).
Noelle, Christine (1997) *State and Tribe in Nineteenth-Century Afghanistan.* (London: Curzon).

Pashtuns and Tribes

Barth, Fredrik (1965) *Political Leadership Among Swat Pathans.* (London: Athlone Press).
Caroe, Olaf (1958) *The Pathans.* (Oxford: Oxford University Press).
Johnson, Thomas H. and Mason, Chris (2007) "Understanding the Taliban and Insurgency in Afghanistan", *Orbis*, vol. 51, no. 1.
Qudoos, Syed Abdul (1987) *The Pathans.* (Lahore: Freozsons).

Southern Afghanistan

Chayes, Sarah (2006) *The Punishment of Virtue: Inside Afghanistan After the Taliban.* (New York: Penguin Press).
Smith, Graeme (2011) *Blood and Dust* (working title) (Toronto: Knopf).

The Soviet Invasion

Alexievich, Svetlana (1992) *Zinky Boys: Soviet Voices from the Afghan War.* (New York: W.W. Norton & Company).

Borovik, Artyom (1990) *The Hidden War: A Russian Journalist's Account of the Soviet War in Afghanistan*. (New York: Grove Press).

Dyk, Jere van (1983) *In Afghanistan: An American Odyssey*. (Lincoln: Authors Choice Press).

Edwards, David (2002) *Before Taliban: Genealogies of the Afghan Jihad*. (Berkeley: University of California Press).

Feifer, Gregory (2009) *The Great Gamble: The Soviet War in Afghanistan*. (New York: Harper).

Grau, Lester W. and Gress, Michael A. (2002) *The Soviet-Afghan War: How A Superpower Fought And Lost*. (Kansas: University Press of Kansas).

Guibert, Emmanuel (2009) *The Photographer*. (New York: First Second Books).

Kaplan, Robert D. (1990) *Soldiers of God: With Islamic Warriors in Afghanistan and Pakistan*. (New York: Vintage).

Maley, William (2002) *The Afghanistan Wars*. (London: Palgrave Macmillan).

Yousaf, Muhammad and Adken, Mark (1992) *The Bear Trap: Afghanistan's Untold Story*. (London: Leo Cooper).

Taliban

Giustozzi, Antonio (2007) *Koran, Kalashnikov and Laptop: The Neo-Taliban Insurgency in Afghanistan 2002–2007*. (London: Hurst & Co. Publishers Ltd).

———, (ed.) (2009) *Decoding the New Taliban: Insights from the Afghan Field*. (London: Hurst & Co. Publishers Ltd).

Griffin, Michael (2003) *Reaping the Whirlwind: Afghanistan, Al Qa'ida and the Holy War*. (London: Pluto Press). Revised edition.

Maley, William (ed.) (1998) *Fundamentalism Reborn? Afghanistan and the Taliban*. (London: Hurst & Co. Publishers Ltd).

Marsden, Peter (2002) *The Taliban: War and Religion in Afghanistan*. (London: Zed Books).

Rubin, Elizabeth (2006) "In the land of the Taliban", *The New York Times*, 22 October.

Smith, Graeme (2008) *Talking to the Taliban*, www.theglobeandmail.com/talkingtothetaliban/.

Zaeef, Mullah Abdul Salam (forthcoming) *Taliban: A History*. (London: Hurst & Co. Publishers Ltd).

Post-9–11 Afghanistan

Anderson, Jon L. (2003) *The Lion's Grave: Dispatches from Afghanistan*. (New York: Grove Press).

Fisk, Robert (2005) *The Great War for Civilization: The Conquest of the Middle East* (London: Fourth Estate).

Johnson, Chris and Leslie, Jolyon (2004) *Afghanistan: the Mirage of Peace*. (London: Zed Books).

Rashid, Ahmed (2008) *Descent into Chaos: How the War Against Islamic Extremism is Being Lost in Pakistan, Afghanistan and Central Asia*. (London: Allen Lane).

Fiction, Travel Literature and Films

Afghan, 1989. [Documentary film] Directed by Jeff Harmon. USA: Duce Films.

Chaffetz, David (1981) *A journey through Afghanistan*. (Chicago: University of Chicago Press).

Elliot, Jason (2000) *An Unexpected Light: Travels in Afghanistan*. (London: Picador).

Jihad, 1986. [Documentary film] Directed by Jeff Harmon. USA: Duce Films.

Osama, 2003. [Film] Directed by Siddiq Barmak. Afghanistan: Barmak Film.

Shah, Saira (2004) *The Storyteller's Daughter: Return to a Lost Homeland*. (London: Penguin Books).

ABOUT THE AUTHOR

Mullah Abdul Salam Zaeef was the Taliban's ambassador to Pakistan in 2001 and one of the most well-known faces of the movement following the 9–11 attacks. Born in southern Afghanistan in 1968, he played a role in many of the historical events of his lifetime: as mujahed in the 1980s war against the Soviets, to administrative positions within the Taliban movement, to imprisonment in Guantanamo jail, to a role of public advocacy and criticism of the US-backed Karzai government following his release in 2005. He lives in Kabul.

About the Editors

A graduate of the School of Oriental and African Studies (BA Arabic and Persian), *Alex Strick van Linschoten* first came to Afghanistan six years ago as a tourist. In 2006, he founded AfghanWire.com together with Felix Kuehn. He is currently working on a book and PhD at the War Studies Department of King's College London on the interactions between Sufi groups and militant jihadi organisations in Iraq, Afghanistan, Chechnya and Somalia, as well as on a history of southern Afghanistan 1970–2001. He has worked as a freelance journalist from Afghanistan, Syria, Lebanon and Somalia, writing for Foreign Policy, International Affairs, ABC Nyheter, The Sunday Times (UK), The Globe and Mail (Canada) and The Tablet (UK). He speaks Arabic, Farsi, Pashtu and German and can get by in French and Dutch. He lives in Kandahar, Afghanistan.

Felix Kuehn travelled to Afghanistan first some five years ago, having spent several years in the Middle East including just short of a year in Yemen, where he first learnt Arabic in 2002. In 2006, he founded AfghanWire.com together with Alex Strick van Linschoten. He is currently working on a history of southern Afghanistan 1970–2001. He speaks Arabic, English and German and can get by in French and Spanish. Felix holds a degree from the School of Oriental and African Studies (BA Arabic and Development Studies), and lives in Kandahar, Afghanistan.

INDEX